POUR L'AVENIR DU
BÉLUGA
FOR THE FUTURE OF THE BELUGA

POUR L'AVENIR DU
BÉLUGA

FOR THE FUTURE OF THE BELUGA

Compte rendu du
Forum international
pour l'avenir
du béluga

●

Proceedings of the
International Forum
for the Future
of the Beluga

Sous la direction de
Jacques PRESCOTT et Michel GAUQUELIN

1990
Presses de l'Université du Québec
Case postale 250, Sillery, Québec G1T 2R1

ISBN 2-7605-0550-2

Dépôt légal – 2e trimestre 1990
Bibliothèque nationale du Québec
Bibliothèque nationale du Canada
Imprimé au Canada

TABLE DES MATIÈRES

LE COMITÉ D'ORGANISATION

Président

Jacques Prescott
Fondation pour la sauvegarde des espèces menacées

Membres

Jean Désy
Conseil régional de l'environnement
du Saguenay-Lac-Saint-Jean-Chibougamau

Johann Ellefsen
Alcan

Léopold Gaudreau
Ministère de l'Environnement du Québec

Linda Ghanimé
Fondation pour la sauvegarde des espèces menacées

Bruce McKay
Greenpeace

Agathe Savard (Fernand Therrien)
Société linnéenne du Québec

Yvan Vigneault
Ministère des Pêches et des Océans du Canada

Jacqueline Vincent
Ministère de l'Environnement du Canada

Secrétariat général

Le Groupe Média Science inc.

LES COMMANDITAIRES

Alcan
Fondation de la faune du Québec
Habitat faunique du Canada
Hydro-Québec
Ministère de l'Environnement du Canada
Ministère de l'Environnement du Québec
Ministère des Pêches et des Océans du Canada
Ministère des Transports du Canada
Ministère du Loisir, de la Chasse et de la Pêche du Québec
Ministère du Tourisme du Québec
Office de planification et de développement du Québec (OPDQ)
Ultramar Canada inc.

LE MOT DU PRÉSIDENT

BIENVENUE À TADOUSSAC

Au nom du Comité d'organisation du Forum international pour l'avenir du béluga, bienvenue à Tadoussac.

Réunis à l'endroit même où vivent les bélugas du Saint-Laurent, à la confluence du fleuve et du Saguenay, nous avons tous à cœur un objectif commun : mieux connaître les raisons des problèmes que rencontrent nos bélugas, trouver les moyens d'actions pour garantir leur survie et nous assurer que ces moyens seront effectivement mis en œuvre.

Espèce menacée de disparition, le béluga du Saint-Laurent mérite toute notre attention, que nous soyons scientifiques, membres de groupe environnemental ou socio-économique, représentants d'entreprise privée ou de ministère et organisme gouvernemental.

La qualité de nos conférences, de nos exposés, de nos discussions, de nos questions et des réponses que nous apporterons sera, je n'en doute pas, à la hauteur des attentes que nous avons tous. Des attentes que partage toute une population, gens d'ici ou gens d'ailleurs, attachée à ses bélugas.

Jacques Prescott
Président du Comité d'organisation
et président de FOSEM

UN FORUM POUR LES BÉLUGAS

Le 29 septembre 1988, plus de 300 personnes envahissaient l'hôtel Tadoussac. Parmi ces participants se trouvaient quelque 30 chercheurs invités à faire le point sur l'état de la population de bélugas du Saint-Laurent, sa distribution dans l'estuaire, l'état de son habitat naturel et les impacts de la pollution de l'eau sur la santé de ces mammifères marins.

Les chercheurs ont présenté de nombreuses suggestions sur les avenues de recherche future. Ils ont mis en évidence la nécessité de réaliser d'autres inventaires de la population de bélugas pour en déterminer la structure et l'évolution et identifier les habitats qu'elle fréquente. On a aussi exprimé le besoin de mieux connaître la pollution du Saint-Laurent et ses effets sur les diverses composantes de l'écosystème et on a conclu de façon unanime sur la nécessité de mieux coordonner les efforts de recherche et de suivi de la population de bélugas.

En deuxième partie du Forum, 23 représentants du milieu socio-économique, du monde environnemental et de l'industrie, des scientifiques et des représentants des agences gouvernementales, ont discuté du plan d'action pour favoriser la survie du béluga. Pour la plupart d'entre eux, le Forum constituait l'occasion longtemps attendue d'exprimer leurs préoccupations et leurs recommandations concernant le béluga. Quelques groupes ont profité du Forum pour annoncer leur contribution à la sauvegarde de l'espèce. Les participants ont supporté à l'unisson la création d'un parc marin à l'embouchure du Saguenay. Tous ont souligné la nécessité d'une discussion ouverte et d'une franche coopération entre la communauté locale, les organismes non gouvernementaux et les autorités gouvernementales dans la planification et la gestion du futur parc. On a suggéré fortement d'agrandir les limites du parc afin d'y inclure une plus grande partie de l'habitat du béluga. Le béluga fut également proposé comme emblème officiel du parc.

La plupart des groupes ont considéré comme prioritaire de tenir le public informé sur la situation et les progrès des bélugas. Le ministère des Pêches et des Océans du Canada a annoncé son intention de publier un bulletin d'information sur le béluga sur une base régulière. L'Institut national d'écotoxicologie du Saint-Laurent a profité du Forum pour lancer une campagne d'adoption de bélugas dans le but de financer son programme de recherche. Le Fonds mondial pour la nature et Alcan ont annoncé une importante contribution financière au profit de l'Institut. Les compagnies d'excursions ont affirmé leur intention de poursuivre leurs programmes d'éducation populaire. La Société linnéenne a annoncé de son côté la création du Prix Vadim D. Vladykov, qui sera décerné chaque année pour couronner une contribution remarquable à la cause du béluga.

Conscients que le trafic maritime peut déranger les cétacés, les participants se sont opposés à tout relâchement de la réglementation régissant les activités d'observation des baleines. Un participant a même proposé de restreindre le nombre de permis d'excursions.

Comme on pouvait s'y attendre, la contamination du Saint-Laurent fut au cœur des débats. Rappelant qu'une bonne part des polluants affectant les bélugas proviennent des Grands Lacs, Greenpeace et la Société pour vaincre la pollution (SVP) ont souligné l'importance d'accentuer les négociations canado-américaines sur le contrôle des émissions de HAP et de BPC dans la zone frontalière entre le Québec et l'état de New York. On a insisté également sur l'intérêt de permettre à Québec de participer à ces négociations. Plusieurs groupes ont demandé au Gouvernement fédéral d'appliquer avec plus de rigueur la loi canadienne sur la protection de l'environnement et de faire appel plus souvent à l'article 33 de la loi fédérale des pêcheries pour décourager toute action pouvant entraîner la dégradation de l'habitat des poissons et des cétacés. On a invité les industries de pâtes et papier à cesser toute émission de dioxines et d'organochlorés dans l'eau.

L'UQCN a mis en évidence la nécessité d'implanter une stratégie globale de conservation du Saint-Laurent et a annoncé sa propre contribution à ce chapitre. Le ministre de l'Environnement du Québec, M. Clifford Lincoln, a réitéré sa ferme intention de mettre en place un programme de dépollution industrielle et de s'opposer à tout délai possible à la fermeture des cuves Soderberg de Jonquière (importantes sources de HAP) après l'inauguration de la nouvelle usine d'Alcan à Laterrière. Toutes ces considérations ont contribué à mettre en place le Plan d'action Saint-Laurent du gouvernement du Canada qui impliquera un investissement de plus de 110 millions de dollars au cours des cinq prochaines années.

Les suites du Forum

Suivant les vœux de l'assemblée, le comité d'organisation du Forum se transformera en comité de suivi ayant pour mandat de publier le compte rendu du Forum, de faire connaître les suggestions des participants et d'en assurer le suivi et de contribuer à la préparation d'une version améliorée du plan de survie du béluga.

Bien entendu, le Forum international pour l'avenir du béluga n'a pu régler en un seul week-end les problèmes des bélugas. Mais cet événement a catalysé les efforts des agences gouvernementales impliquées dans le dossier et incité les associations et les organismes non gouvernementaux à poursuivre leurs actions. Le Forum a également contribué à intégrer les efforts de chacun. Il a permis le développement de collaborations nouvelles et suscité l'implication de nouveaux acteurs. Mais plus que tout cela, le Forum a permis à une communauté de s'informer et de s'impliquer dans la conservation d'une espèce menacée constituant un élément vital de son propre environnement.

Jacques Prescott
Président
Fondation pour la sauvegarde des espèces menacées

L'impact du Forum

Alors qu'environ 200 invitations avaient été lancées pour le premier Forum international pour l'avenir du béluga, ce sont finalement 308 personnes qui ont été présentes : scientifiques, représentants d'organismes environnementaux, socio-économiques, gouvernementaux et d'entreprises, étudiants.

Au-delà des conférences scientifiques, et de la journée Forum qui a permis aux organismes du milieu d'apporter leur contribution, le Forum a aussi accueilli les kiosques d'information de plusieurs organismes et diverses activités. Ce sont, par exemple, les dîners-conférences du ministre des Pêches et des Océans du Canada, M. Thomas E. Siddon et du ministre de l'Environnement du Québec, M. Clifford Lincoln, l'annonce de la stratégie québécoise de la conservation et du développement des ressources du Conseil de la conservation et de l'environnement, celle de la campagne « Adoptons un béluga » de l'Institut national d'écotoxicologie du Saint-Laurent, les soirées en hommage à Vadim D. Vladykov de la Société linnéenne du Québec, etc. Conférences de presse et déclarations publiques spontanées de participants ont également rythmé ces trois journées intenses, contribuant ainsi à la dynamique du Forum.

Sans une présence massive de la presse, le Forum n'aurait pas atteint un de ses buts, c'est-à-dire sensibiliser la population à la situation critique des bélugas du Saint-Laurent. Près de 70 représentants de médias sont venus à Tadoussac pour couvrir le Forum. La plupart étaient journalistes, les autres photographes, caméramen, techniciens divers, les médias électroniques représentant la moitié de la presse accréditée. Télévisions, radios, journaux quotidiens et publications périodiques ont parlé abondamment du Forum contribuant ainsi à déclencher un grand intérêt non seulement pour le béluga mais aussi, indirectement, pour les questions d'environnement reliées au Saint-Laurent.

Michel Gauquelin
Vice-président
Le Groupe Média Science inc.

LA SYNTHÈSE DES DISCUSSIONS

INTRODUCTION

Ce document se veut une synthèse des discussions ayant eu lieu au cours du Forum international pour l'avenir du béluga, du 29 septembre au 2 octobre 1988 à Tadoussac. Étant donné que le Plan d'action interministériel pour favoriser la survie du béluga des ministères des Pêches et des Océans et de l'Environnement du Canada a servi de base aux discussions du Forum, la structure de ce document découle du Plan.

Les cinq premiers chapitres portent sur les grands thèmes du Forum : parc marin, contrôle des substances toxiques, participation des citoyens, acquisition des connaissances et contrôle du dérangement. Ces chapitres comprennent les propositions, les points de consensus et les points de divergence qui ont émergé lors du Forum. Aucune distinction n'a été faite entre les propositions formulées par les scientifiques, par les organismes environnementaux ou socio-économiques, lors de la table ronde ou lors des annonces publiques. Dans chaque chapitre, les propositions ont été regroupées selon le sujet et certaines propositions sont générales tandis que d'autres sont plus précises. Afin de refléter le plus fidèlement possible l'esprit du congrès, les points de consensus et de divergence ont été inclus. Les premiers comprennent les questions où l'accord entre les participants était unanime tandis que les deuxièmes regroupent les points litigieux, où les opinions étaient partagées.

Le sixième chapitre est une description du comité de suivi, formé à l'issue du Forum, ainsi que de ses mandats. Sont inclus en annexe : le texte d'une pétition ayant circulé lors du congrès ; un résumé du Plan d'action Saint-Laurent (ministère de l'Environnement du Canada) ; un résumé de la Stratégie de dépollution industrielle (ministère de l'Environnement du Québec).

1. PARC MARIN

1.1 Propositions

PROPOSITION	MOYEN	RESPONSABLE *ÉCHÉANCE*
Appui à la création et à la mise en place d'un Parc marin Saint-Laurent-Saguenay		*Les plus brefs délais*
Coopération fédérale-provinciale essentielle à la réalisation du Parc	Pressions publiques auprès des gouvernements	
Participation des intervenants locaux et régionaux à toutes les étapes de création du Parc et à sa gestion	Groupe « multipartite »	
Définition des limites du Parc et des modalités de sa cogestion	Consultation auprès de la population	
Extension des limites du Parc afin d'inclure une section du Saint-Laurent et une plus grande portion du Saguenay		
Inclusion des habitats de toutes les espèces menacées et délimitation d'une zone de conservation plus vaste que le Parc marin	Approche globale de conservation à l'échelle régionale	
Développement des activités et des équipements d'observation et d'éducation sur les rives	Soutien financier prévu dans le budget du Parc	

1.2 Points de consensus

Les membres locaux, régionaux et gouvernementaux doivent se consulter et s'impliquer conjointement, autant dans la planification du parc marin que dans sa gestion.

1.3 Points de divergence

Les négociations doivent être entreprises rapidement. Pétition.

Le Parc est-il le moyen essentiel de sauvegarde du béluga, le principal problème étant la pollution par les substances toxiques ?

Les limites spatiales du Parc, telles que proposées, sont-elles adéquates ? Est-ce que le Parc ne devrait pas englober une plus grande partie du fleuve et du Saguenay ? Compte tenu de la possibilité que le Parc ne serait pas le secteur où se trouve la plus grande proportion de jeunes, ne faudrait-il pas songer à protéger les habitats critiques du béluga situés à l'extérieur du Parc, à l'aide de zones de conservation ?

2. CONTRÔLE DES SUBSTANCES TOXIQUES

2.1 Propositions

PROPOSITION	MOYEN	RESPONSABLE *ÉCHÉANCE*
Approche coercitive de la dépollution industrielle	Contrôles de pollution plus sévères	
	Application plus rigoureuse des lois et règlements existants sur les pêcheries, l'environnement et la conservation de la faune	Les gouvernements
	Amendes lourdes imposées aux pollueurs	
Contrôle absolu des polluants	Nouvelle réglementation	*Niveau de déversement « 0 » d'ici 1993*
Réduction à la source	Politiques gouvernementale et industrielle	
Réduction obligatoire des HAP	Règlement national de réduction par les alumineries et autres industries	Environnement Canada
Fermeture des cuves Soderberg d'Alcan à Jonquière	Autorisation d'ouverture de nouvelles cuves conditionnelle à la fermeture des anciennes	Environnement Québec
Présence québécoise sur les organismes de protection et de gestion des Grands-Lacs	Représentation au niveau international	
Développement de nouvelles techniques de destruction des déchets toxiques	Recherche	

Contrôle du développement industriel sur les berges du fleuve	Planification à long terme	Les gouvernements

2.2 Points de consensus

L'évaluation des contaminants provenant des Grands-Lacs et du Haut-Saint-Laurent est nécessaire.

3. PARTICIPATION DES CITOYENS

3.1 Propositions

PROPOSITION	MOYEN	RESPONSABLE *ÉCHÉANCE*
Choix concerté des priorités environnementales	Représentations directes des citoyens auprès des gouvernements	
Gestion participative des ressources et du milieu	Organisation souple et représentative	
Sensibilisation des entreprises et des individus	Programme d'adoption	Institut d'écotoxicologie
	Liste « rouge » des menaces	
Sensibilisation des visiteurs, des intervenants socio-économiques, des navigateurs et des plaisanciers	Programmes éducatifs, promotionnels et d'interprétation	
	Création d'un Centre international d'interprétation du béluga du Saint-Laurent	
	Choix du béluga comme emblème officiel du Parc marin	
Informations vulgarisées sur le béluga	Bulletin périodique	MPO
	Contributions de l'extérieur	Comité de rédaction du milieu
	Monographie	

Faire la distinction, dans l'esprit du grand public, entre les bélugas et les croisières aux baleines		

4. ACQUISITION DES CONNAISSANCES

4.1 Propositions

PROPOSITION	MOYEN	RESPONSABLE *ÉCHÉANCE*
Recherches écologiques fondamentales	Budgets gouvernementaux répartis en fonction des priorités sociales	MPO
Détermination de la notion de population viable animale	Analyses de viabilité	
Détermination de la tendance dans l'évolution de la population	Indice proportionnel des animaux gris	Institut d'écotoxicologie
Suivi et évolution de populations témoins		
Recherches sur la fréquence et les causes de mortalité	Programme de dissection des carcasses (WWF, Alcan, MPO) 200 000 $	Institut d'écotoxicologie
Quantification de la pollution transfrontalière	Échantillonage des eaux à la frontière Québec-New York	
Liste des secteurs prioritaires à protéger	Étude de distribution et photo-identification	Institut d'écotoxicologie
Connaissance des habitats essentiels au béluga	Cartographie	
Connaissance des lieux et des périodes à protéger	Études sur l'alimentation	

Tenir compte de la notion de compétition pour la nourriture dans les recherches		
Échanges génétiques entre populations	Technologies de reproduction assistée	
Coordination des approches et des équipes de recherche	Atelier national de concertation	MPO
Programmes de recherche orientés vers la survie du béluga	Nouveaux fonds	Alcan, WWF, FQF, etc.
Rapport annuel de la situation	Groupe de rédaction d'experts et de citoyens	

4.2 Points de divergence

Opposition à la réhabilitation de la population par introduction d'individus de l'Arctique.

La recherche en génétique des populations devrait-elle être prioritaire ? Est-il nécessaire de développer une expertise en ce domaine, à l'heure actuelle ?

5. CONTRÔLE DU DÉRANGEMENT

5.1 Propositions

PROPOSITION	MOYEN	RESPONSABLE *ÉCHÉANCE*
Diminution du dérangement pendant l'alimentation et la mise bas, entre autres	Surveillance des plaisanciers, doublée d'éducation et formation	
	Autorégulation de l'industrie et choix d'horaires adéquats	
	Rationalisation de l'émission des permis d'excursions, d'observation (limite du nombre, des zones, des périodes, etc.)	

	Moratoire de toute nouvelle entreprise d'excursion et fixation éventuelle des quotas
	Séparation des trajectoires des bélugas et des bateaux dans le Saguenay
Reconnaissance des habitats critiques	Regroupement des départs à Tadoussac et protection de la baie Sainte-Catherine
	Interdiction de circulation près des habitats sensibles
Extension spatiale du Parc marin du Saguenay	Représentations aux gouvernements

5.2 Points de consensus

Opposition au relâchement des normes de sécurité concernant la navigation sur le fleuve.

5.3 Divergence

Même si elles sont un outil de sensibilisation important, est-ce que les excursions devraient être poursuivies ?

6. SUIVI DU FORUM

Afin que la portée des discusssions entre les congressistes déborde le cadre temporel du Forum, il a été proposé que le comité organisateur du Forum devienne le comité de suivi, sous la direction de la Fondation pour la sauvegarde des espèces menacées.

Les mandats du comité de suivi sont les suivants :

1. Publication des actes du colloque (conférences et contributions).
2. Acheminement des propositions du Forum.
3. Organisation d'un atelier pour l'élaboration d'une deuxième version du Plan de survie, en collaboration avec le ministère des Pêches et des Océans du Canada et le ministère de l'Environnement du Canada.
4. Établissement d'une stratégie commune entre le Forum et le ministère des Pêches et des Océans du Canada.

ANNEXE I

Tadoussac, le 1er octobre 1988

À: Monsieur le premier ministre du Canada
Monsieur le premier ministre du Québec

Les organismes participants à la table ronde du Forum international pour l'avenir du béluga concluent à l'unanimité que la création d'un parc marin incluant des portions substantielles du Saint-Laurent constitue, à court terme, le principal moyen pour assurer la conservation du troupeau de bélugas.

Les participants vous demandent de prendre des mesures énergiques et immédiates pour en arriver, d'ici un mois, à une entente finale entre vos deux gouvernements concernant ce projet de parc marin.

Nous tenons à vous rappeler que les groupes régionaux devront participer à la définition des frontières de ce parc et avoir une voix dans sa gestion.

ANNEXE II

Les gouvernements fédéral et provincial ont chacun mis de l'avant un programme. Ces programmes sont distincts du Plan de survie du béluga mais ils auront un impact sur le milieu de vie de ce mammifère marin. Les grandes lignes de ces deux programmes, le Plan d'action Saint-Laurent et le Programme de réduction des rejets industriels, sont présentées dans ce document à titre d'aide-mémoire.

Plan d'action Saint-Laurent

Ce programme, du ministère de l'Environnement du Canada, vise la réduction d'émission de polluants dans le fleuve pour les 5 prochaines années.

Le montant total du programme, 110 millions de dollars, est réparti comme suit :

Protection contre les sources polluantes	14 millions
Développement et application de technologies environnementales	50 millions
Conservation des habitats et espèces	25 millions
Restauration des sites	21 millions

Le béluga bénéficiera de ce programme, car son milieu de vie sera amélioré par la réduction de l'émission de substances toxiques dans le Saint-Laurent. De plus, le montant attribué pour la conservation des habitats et des espèces inclut 7,5 millions pour les démarches menant à la création d'un parc marin et 3 millions pour la protection des espèces menacées, dont le béluga.

Dans le cadre du Forum international pour l'avenir du béluga, il a été proposé qu'un conseil d'administration composé de membres du milieu soit mis sur pied pour la révision périodique du plan de travail.

ANNEXE III

Programme de réduction de rejets industriels

D'ici 10 ans, ce programme du ministère de l'Environnement du Québec vise la réduction de 75% de l'ensemble des rejets industriels, qu'ils soient relâchés dans l'eau, dans l'air, dans ou sur le sol. La cible prioritaire du programme comprend 632 entreprises qui sont responsables de 80% des rejets industriels. Les industries polluantes et le délai des actions envisagées se répartissent comme suit :

Secteurs industriels	Nombre d'établissements	
	Action à court terme (1990-1993)	Action à moyen terme (1992-1996)
Pâtes et papiers	57	—
Mines	48	50
Métallurgie	28	43
Chimie	63	99
Pétrole	—	3
Revêtement de surface	—	241
	196	436

Les substances toxiques sont particulièrement visées.

Selon ce programme, les normes des rejets seraient fixées selon les meilleures technologies disponibles économiquement réalisables. De plus, les entreprises devraient obtenir une attestation d'assainissement d'ici 1990. Cette attestation serait valide pour une période de 5 ans et rassemblerait les exigences environnementales auxquelles les entreprises auraient à se soumettre.

Enfin, le Ministère mise largement sur les technologies propres pour réduire les rejets industriels, spécialement les polluants toxiques. Ces technologies sont basées sur l'optimisation des procédés, l'utilisation de matières premières exemptes de toxiques, la réduction à la source des adjuvants et catalyseurs toxiques, la récupération et le recyclage des sous-produits réutilisables. La compagnie qui opte pour les technologies propres sera pendant longtemps bien plus compétitive que celle qui se sera contentée du traitement minimal de ses déchets ; elle n'aura pas à traiter des déchets qu'elle n'aura pas produits. Vaut mieux prévenir que guérir.

Les conférences scientifiques

Ailing Whales, Water and Marine Management Systems An Urgency for Fresh, New Approaches

Leone Pippard
Canadian Ecology Advocates

INTRODUCTION

There was a time, not so long ago, when the waters within viewing distance of this hotel literally boiled with belugas, seals and walruses. When Cartier arrived at the mouth of the Saguenay in September 1535, he was surprised to find large numbers of white whales; "a king of fish", he called them, "which no man had ever seen before or heard of". He said they were "as large as porpoises, and had no sword. They were shaped like grey-hounds as to the head and body, and they were as white as snow, and without a spot."

Another change of scene... in the 1930s. From book "Saguenay... River of Deep Waters" by Blowdyn Davies:

> You may sit around Baie de Tadoussac and watch the white whales play and realize the spirit that seems to animate them. You love their lazy grace, as they twist and turn, playing about in the pure joy of existence and you don't wonder at all why they come to Tadoussac. They have little fear of all the summer visitors for they plunge and roll far inside the Bay even when the ship is docking at the quay. And sometimes while you watch the white whales at play, you see some sleek black heads popping up here and there, in two and threes and fours, for the seals, too, love Tadoussac.

Now in 1988, on any given summer day, you look out on a bay as busy as a beehive, with the comings and goings of pleasure boats and whale-watching vessels.

I personally remember Baie de Tadoussac in 1973 as being rather a sleepy place. But when I was here on a film shoot recently with the Fifth Estate, I was bowled over just watching the whale-watching industry at work. The first boat that loads up in the morning with its 100-odd passengers is Lachance III, followed by the Marie Clarisse, and while the Marie Clarisse is boarding, deep in the bay you can see René Digard's tourist troops, dressed in yellow survival suits, filing their way down the sand slope across the beach to board his zodiacs for a Cousteau-style whale-watching adventure. And this set of excursion events happens three times a day, every day of the week!

It is all very animated and colourful, but very different from before, when the bay was quieter, and seal and beluga were therein...

Belugas, being toothed whales, like dolphins, are members of the whale sub-group called Odontocetes. The oldest known forebears of the Odontocetes date from 30 million years ago, while the beluga whale itself has been evolving for some 3 million years.

Journalists often ask me, "What's special about a beluga whale? Describe it for us". I always feel rather mischievous when I point out the obvious, "Well, it's all white!" *Delphinapterus leucas*, or the "white dolphin without a wing", is this unique white whale which lacks a dorsal fin. This dolphin, however, has some other rather special characteristics.

As Dr. Paul Brodie said in an article he wrote on beluga, "When you study marine animals, whether fish or whales, you become comfortable in the certainty that the front end is always quite rigid, but such complacency is quickly shattered when a beluga turns its head at an abrupt angle and stares back!"

The beluga is, in fact, the most agile whale of its size. But this is hardly surprising when you consider its diverse habitat. It is a surface-breather in an environment where winter can force a solid sheet of ice over its head or shift large areas of pack ice about. In summer it navigates in shallow estuaries and up deep water fjords, where it moves amongst boulders and tidal, temperature, and salinity extremes. In fact the beluga is as much like a seal as a whale, poking its head up between ice pans, and nosing into small rivers. But also it has the impressive capability to dive to a considerable depth. The belugas in the St. Lawrence could easily go to the bottom of the Saguenay River and Laurentian Channel, which are a mere trifling 250 and 350 metres deep respectively. But we know the beluga is capable of going twice that deep... it has been demonstrated they can dive to 640 metres. How does the animal manage to do this and not get the bends? Thirty million years of overall evolution might help.

Having observed the beluga swimming underwater, I can attest not only to their agility but to the fluidity and grace of their movements plus to their precision. You think Canada's flying aces, the Snowbirds, are spectacular in their aerial acrobatics? I can tell you belugas would give them a run for their money. Fifteen belugas in a group can be spaced perfectly equi-distantly apart in the same sort of 'V' squadron formation you see when you watch the Snowbirds. But not only can they roll over in that formation, they can all turn around on a dime without breaking rank, and swim upside down and even back up! How do they coordinate those movements so that they don't ram into one another? You guessed it... some millions of years of fine-tuning the machine... and probably a few hundred years of swimming practice. I know when you see the film Imageries is now making on the beluga, it will be the wonder of the belugas' movements plus their great curiosity that will impress you.

And, if you just have an image of a beluga whale as this rolling white back against a backdrop of blue, then try sometime putting your head beneath the surface or just near the surface and listening. Even without sophisticated hydrophone equipment you can hear the clamour of beluga vocalizations and click trains reach your ear. With a hydrophone in place you will, of course, be even more overwhelmed with the variety of noises these whales make. Besides being great squeakers, these whales can also sing melodically like canaries, grunt like pigs and bark like dogs.

Then there are their echolocation sounds. They can emit three frequency modes of click trains at the same time to echolocate an object, plus they can adapt their echolocation frequency level to adjust to higher or lower ambient noise conditions in their environment.

In Russia, where belugas also dwell along the coast, a noisy neighbour is said to be "screaming like a beluga". In fact, the belugas have one of the most varied vocal repertoires of any whale, and in talkativeness alone they compare to such "chatterboxes" as monkeys and humans. What is all this chattering about? Are they swapping stories and saying where the fish are plentiful today, or reporting that Joe Whale has gone to scout out the Gaspé... once again, for suitable habitat? What all this diverse noise is about, in fact, is still anyone's guess, but the amount of it suggests it goes well beyond just emitting sounds to navigate and to detect objects.

But if we are fortunate enough to have this chatterbox around long enough to discover some more of its secrets, considering that it is we, of all the things the beluga has ever had to contend with in its long evolution, who may end its prospects for future development.

We have not only hunted this whale, but bombed it! We have shot at it for target practice and we have killed it unnecessarily for the collection of bounties, plus we have managed to pollute it to an unbelievable degree so that its dead body is now classed as a hazardous waste site. And on top of all that, we are altering its overall environment as well as the genes of some of the animals themselves.

Don't you think that the degree of disrespect we have shown all of nature throughout the industrial evolution is just about perfectly portrayed in the story of the St. Lawrence beluga whale?

Which may be what explains why this whale has become such a symbol, not only here in Quebec and Canada, but all over the world,... people in faraway places now know about the St. Lawrence beluga whales... in France, in Germany, in the Philippines, in the United States,... they know about them because they are portraying a situation and a human way of being that must assuredly change if we are to hope to have in the future, large, well-evolved mammals such as beluga whales.

I titled my text "Ailing Whales, Water and Marine Management Systems. An Urgency for Fresh, New Approaches", but actually it could have been called, "Ailing Whales, Water and Human Systems", because I believe what is required to help save the beluga whales and to help all of nature survive is to look at how we have chosen to deal with one another.

I would like to talk about some problem areas in our attitudes and approaches that I believe are causing our environment, ourselves, and the beluga whales difficulty today. While I may be a bit esoteric in the beginning, I shall bring this text down to sea level momentarily.

PROBLEM AREA 1: THE PROBLEM OF LOSING SIGHT OF THE WHOLE

In North America we have a society that is exceedingly well structured... both tasks and power are well defined and compartmentalized and the whole thrust is aimed at maintaining existing individual and institutionalized power plus, where possible, adding to it. In the process of structuring society this way, however, it appears we have lost sight of how to bring all this specialized knowledge, which each compartment has acquired diligently, together to effect common good.

Perhaps now, more than ever before, we are beginning to see the folly of this compartmentalized approach with depleted fisheries, pollution, lost fish habitats, an ocean that has turned into a chemical soup and an atmosphere that is in a very threatened way. We have been moving progressively away from a truly interactive evolutionary approach towards an isolating extractive de-evolutionary approach that revolves around mainly managing our own backyards while letting the shared commons fall to pieces.

We know things are not working well in the environment. Yet knowing that, how are we dealing with our approach to the environment? I still see very much in evidence the continuance of the compartmentalized approach where ecology, for example, is dealt with separately from the economy and where governments still separate themselves from the public. We seem to be having a problem with getting at the problem... which brings me to the problem of entrenchment.

PROBLEM AREA 2 : THE PROBLEM OF ENTRENCHMENT

Whether we work in government or in public or private interest groups, companies or institutions, we are spending far too much valuable time and resources defending our positions against all comers rather than coming at our society's collective problems with the intent of finding solutions together. The end result is we are not getting the calibre of projects and solutions we need anymore to get us out of our societal messes, the biggest of all now being the environmental one. Our actions instead are years in the making, and frequently are pale imitations of what was hoped for, and indeed what is required.

A good example of the problem of entrenchment is the development of the proposed Saguenay national marine park. It seemed to take forever for this country to develop a national marine parks policy, but now that we have one we have managed to propose a national marine park for the Saguenay River and the area around its mouth. The problem is, the park is only a fraction of what was originally hoped for by those who have worked for years to see it happen. The proposal has the look in fact of a national marine "parkette" rather than a national marine park. Further, the proposal even fails to meet public expectation of what the park should be encompassing, in terms of its size.

Why has the most minimal proposal of five possible park scenarios got the most government favour ? It is simply the result of isolated and entrenched departmental thinking... that being Environment Canada's Parks Service longtime desire to establish a national land park along the sides of the Saguenay fjord. When the sides became a provincial park instead, Canadian Parks Service just could not shift its focus to looking as well at the St. Lawrence estuary proper. As such, the agency has seriously undermined the chances of achieving adequate conservation in what is a truly magnificient marine area in Canada.

Further, now due to the depth of Environment Canada is Parks Service entrenchment, the public has an uphill battle ahead of it to reverse their thinking. But reverse it we should, because we are desperately in need of setting aside as large a protected area as we can to help conserve the world's wild species plus their pools of genetic diversity, which are worth untold millions.

This is the problem of entrenchment, which leads to the problem of governing.

PROBLEM AREA 3 : THE PROBLEM OF GOVERNING

I strongly feel opportunities for public discussion and debate of matters of relevance to us all mostly threaten our Canadian civil servants who now see it as their right to govern for us. After all is this not what we have government for ? That it governs for us, in place of us. Actually, our governements need to seriously consider getting back to the old Greek idea of governing with the people because that's simply the best way to have the public be aware there are problems that we all should be thinking about and working to resolve. For example, the public needs to work with government in such collaborative projects as the development of parks and protected areas and in formulating regional conservation strategies, just as the public now works with government in the preparation of regional development strategies, and the two items should then form part of a regional forum on conservation and development so that proper balances between the two are struck. This is presume Jean Désy is planning for Saguenay-Lac Saint-Jean in November 1988. I am not saying there are not attempts being made in this regard by government. The government is consulting more with the public than it used to, but government public interaction is still in infant form. It is in the stage of mere consultation with the public, not in the form of full collaboration.

To show you the difference, when Canadian Parks Service came to this region in January of 1986 to explain its national marine parks policy to the public, that was consultation. Parks Service presented its policy and invited your comments and got them. But the agency has chosen to ignore that while the public said what it wanted, which was to actively work with the department in the formation of the project.

The word for all this, of course, is participatory democracy ; the aim of it is to achieve what is now so lost in our compartmentalized approaches... the advancement of common good, and societal purpose... which is the way we need to look after the whole.

PROBLEM AREA 4 : THE PROBLEM OF STRUCTURE

This is in a sense a problem of when we have finally decided to come together, as we have today, to make some changes, and then we diminish our effort by the structure we have chosen to go about our task.

The forum was conceived with a very worthwhile goal in mind and that was to have a public meeting where what everyone knows about beluga could be presented in order to pool efforts and develop some concerted action as to how to save them. But how likely is it that we shall agree on what we should do, let alone how we should do it?

What is a true forum? Public forums come to us from classic Greece. A forum is simply the opportunity for open discussion : one topic or several are addressed by a select group with each participant given sufficient time to express their views. Then the topic is debated by all present and finally after a series of exchanges and analyses, the participants try to arrive at some consensus. Think of our Prime Ministers' conferences today... these are true forums, which have resulted in agreements on our constitution.

However, is this conference a true public forum? Over the next two and a half days we are going to be inundated with all sorts of information by one speaker right after the other, with only an exceedingly brief period following each presentation to discuss publicly the content of what each individual has had to say. Further, when it comes to the Ministers who are invited to this gathering, there will be virtually no opportunity to exchange viewpoints with these leaders, as when they are speaking we are all going to be feeding our faces.

But finally, after considerable ingesting and digesting, we will have the opportunity to discuss collectively all that has gone before in the hope of arriving at some consensus. The trouble is out of the 32 working hours we will be spending in Tadoussac at this gathering, only 2 of those 32 working hours will be spent in an active round-table discussion of the issues at hand.

What is taking place here then is largely a Canadian scientific conference of information exchange, in the guise of a public forum.

PROBLEM 5 : THE PROBLEM OF PUBLIC PRIORITIES

In talking to a journalist the other day he volunteered that the pollution of the St. Lawrence River was a crime against humanity... and that instead of having an Expo '67, we should have used that money to start cleaning up the St. Lawrence River. It's questionable even today, however, that if given the choice, the public would stop our governments from building another Expo in order to deal with the very more pressing problems of our environment, simply because glamorous development is still seen as an investment and pollution cleanup as an expense.

I know, however, that the people of Charlevoix, Manicouagan and Saguenay-Lac Saint-Jean are feeling less and less that way. They thought they were living in a pristine God's country until the problem of the St. Lawrence beluga whale came along. Here the idea of a healthy clean environment is the backbone of the thriving tourist industry. If the whales and water are one day dead and the leaves hang brown on the trees, then the multimillion-dollar tourist industry will simply be dead too. So we are talking about a question of societal priorities... but I hope not just in the context of development versus maintenance, but rather in terms of short-term economic returns versus long-term economic returns, and what of these is likely to be the winning approach that sees us into the future.

Here is where I believe the public must truly start expressing loudly what it wants our government to see as its long-term priorities. You wonder why the beluga are so polluted? Well, there are numerous reasons, but two related to public priorities are we have not paid enough attention to the fact that our environmental agencies have been operating on inadequate budgets. Government environment agencies are just not a major government portfolio. Clifford Lincoln mentioned what the other priority problem is on the program “A Power of One”, the balance is changing, but the government is still pro-development.

When are we, the people, going to let Prime Minister Bourassa know that having a clean healthy environment is the best short- and long-term investment policy this province could have. The Bourassa government thinks it's dealing with the winning long term when it proposes James Bay development schemes... in fact it's dealing with the losing short term.

The point I am making is Mr. Lincoln and Mr. McMillan could use all the support you could possibly give them in strengthening the government's environmental coffers.

Take, for example, if you believe as I do, and many others, that the government's planned expenditure of eight billion dollars on nuclear submarines is a misplaced spending priority, then rather than just complaining about it to your neighbour or best friend, I think it is paramount that you drop the government a line and say you object.

Weigh the priorities we are faced with.

Dr. Béland had a good idea in this respect. He thought of designing a poster that showed a nuclear submarine on one side and a blue whale on the other. The text below each read something like this : “This nuclear submarine will cost you one billion dollars... this blue whale costs you nothing. This nuclear submarine will be obsolete in ten years... this blue whale will not be. This submarine will destroy our environment... this blue whale enhances our environment. Finally the bottom line of the poster, ‘Which would you rather have ?’ ”

The eight billion dollars we are planning to spend on those submarines, ladies and gentlemen, will probably escalate into twenty billion before the task is complete. Twenty billion dollars would do a great deal to restore our environment or a great deal to pay off our national debt on which we are throwing to the wind an extraordinary amount of money just to pay its interest each year. When are we going to get our priorities straight? When we wish someday that we would have? The whole notion of security as traditionally understood in terms of political and military threats to national sovereignty must be expanded to include growing impacts of environmental stress. Remember, there are no military solutions to "environmental insecurity".

I am suggesting that we need to hold national referendums on such expensive matters as this... that the sway of one department desirous of having its nuclear toys must be put to the test of whether or not the nation as a whole thinks this is the best way to secure our future.

PROBLEM 6: THE PROBLEM OF ADEQUATE RESEARCH REVIEW AND DEBATE

A scientist, I find, is very good at justifying what he is doing as very relevant but what the next scientist is doing as not so important. Just look at the CAFSAC report we have all been provided on the present status of the St. Lawrence beluga population and you will get an idea of what I am talking about.

This report is typical of how, in order to justify a new theory, we first proceed to quash the old ones as being unsupportable. Now the view is that it is not possible to link the building of the hydro-dams on the Manicouagan and Outardes rivers with the virtual disappearance of belugas from that area. Nor can geographic isolation yet be supported, nor is there any proof that contaminants are affecting the immune system or reproductive success of these whales. Now, the stage is set for the new theory to be put forward and that is the population is probably just dying out naturally, because it has not been able to adapt to the Saguenay and St. Lawrence rivers which are not typical Arctic environments.

While it also sounds very plausible that the greenhouse effect could warm the St. Lawrence waters sufficiently that the beluga likely might not stand a chance to survive, let's not fail to consider before we adopt these latest theories, that this whale has already been adapting to a changing St. Lawrence system over thousands of years and that belugas in various experiments involving their environment have been shown to be a highly adaptive whale.

Perhaps it would be worthwhile to consider in this argument what light aquarium-kept beluga could shed on this hypothesis.

While I have no trouble in listening to new theories of why the beluga in the St. Lawrence might not be faring so well, I do have trouble when previous theories are dismissed without adequate investigation or review, and I have even bigger problems when relevant facts are overlooked in the presentation or are not sought for inclusion, or when scientific papers are published and government positions are taken, not based on supportable evidence. We have had previously, and we have still got, all these problems when it comes to evaluating the research that has been done on the St. Lawrence beluga... with the result that management decisions are being taken on either nonexistent or flimsy or biased evidence. The point is, by allowing this to happen, we are not helping clarify the beluga's situation... we are just muddying the waters with contradictory opinions.

A perfect example of how we are also continually reinventing the wheel in St. Lawrence beluga research is in regard to aerial surveys of beluga to determine the stock's actual present size. Pierre Béland's team has been conducting numerous aerial surveys on the beluga over the last two years. But when Fisheries and Oceans decided recently to conduct its own survey, was there any attempt to collaborate with Dr. Béland... to learn from his mistakes and his knowledge ? Not at all.

Why, when financial resources are so hard to find, are we reinventing the wheel, every time a new researcher steps into the field ? Why are not we coordinating our approach to see where we have come from and where, based on this, we should go ? Again this gets back to three previously mentioned problems. We need opportunities to present what we know or could present, plus to discuss and debate the validity of methodologies and proposed research priorities in light of current knowledge. We also should not be afraid to have some outside experts monitor our exchanges and give us their opinion.

I would like to know if Fisheries and Oceans might think it should perhaps organize a workshop so that we could discuss in depth our knowledge of the St. Lawrence beluga and its environment. I would personally welcome this opportunity just to put some of that missing evidence on the table that has been sitting in my file cabinets for ten years.

By the way, it is 6 $ million we have to help save the St. Lawrence beluga whale, isn't it ? Why are we hearing that only 3 $ million is being allowed for this purpose in meetings with consultants ? Would Fisheries and Oceans care to clarify what is the real amount being spent on helping ensure the survival of this animal and as I requested of Minister Siddon right after his June 1988 press conference, I would personally like to see a breakdown of exactly where the money is going.

PROBLEM 7 : THE PROBLEM OF LOSING SIGHT OF THE WHALE

I find it rather remarkable that a whale which has animated the St. Lawrence River for centuries, that its real nature is hardly any better known today than the nature of the smallest links in the St. Lawrence system... the zooplankton... and yet I believe knowing its nature and habits is important to helping it survive.

What research, however, other than my own done ten years ago and that of Robert Michaud today, has been accumulated by Fisheries and Oceans on the natural lives and habits of the St. Lawrence beluga whales ? What degree of consideration is being given by Fisheries and Oceans to basic long-term ecology research on the St. Lawrence beluga ?

It is, in fact, because our government had no interest in performing behavioural research on these animals that led Heather Malcolm and myself in 1975 and 1977 to conduct our own private study on the natural behaviour of the St. Lawrence beluga whales. Isn't it interesting that a concrete result of this initiative was we were the first to sound the alarm that the St. Lawrence beluga appeared to be in trouble ? Isn't it interesting that this same ecology research is useful when it comes to needed evidence to halt the development of any proposed marina for Baie-Sainte-Catherine ? Isn't it interesting that this research has also been used in advancing the creation of a marine park in this area to help protect some of the beluga's habitat ?

Yet look over the 1988 Beluga Survival Plan. Basic ecology research on this animal has once again been given short-shrift, yet is the very nuts and bolts information required if you want to know what are the number of calves being born, what are the habitat preferences of females with young, etc. But when it comes to cetacean ecology research, compared to other countries, Canada is in the dark ages, and is apparently choosing to stay there.

PROBLEM AREA 8 : THE PROBLEM OF POLLUTION

I said once to a journalist that some days I wish it would start raining red... that pollution would take on colour so we could see it falling out of the sky, and running red down the sides of our houses, across our driveways and into the streets.

However, we do have warning signs usually of pollution affecting something or other, such as birds, or fish or cows, but usually we try to ignore these signs and wait until the things start to really get out of hand before we do something. In fact, usually the environmental costs of economic activity are not encountered exceeded. Beyond that point, the costs can no longer be avoided. They will be paid. The question is how and by whom and not whether.

This area where we are all in attendance today has a serious polyaromatic hydrocarbon or PAH pollution problem... everyone should now know it's serious, that the substance in question is a carcinogen and that it's raining down on every living thing in this area. But it isn't the only thing that is raining down here or being transported here. It is just one thing on a long frightening list that is in Fisheries and Ocean's, "Statement of Problems of the St. Lawrence Belugas".

If you saw bombs falling out of the sky what would be your reaction ? To stand there and watch them hit or to run for cover ? One would hope you would have the sense to do the latter. But we have people who are prepared to tell us today that yes, while it is true there are many bombs falling there, you really cannot say with certainty that they are going to go off when they hit the ground. These people need to see the bombs hit the ground before it becomes a reality for them. By then, don't you think it is a bit late judging cause and effect ?

Yet who wants to live in a world that is just not quite fatal ? The bombs are falling. We just cannot see them yet.

I once said to my mother when I was a little girl, "People are too smart for their own good". The famous historian E. B. White perhaps said it better. He said, "I am pessimistic about the human race because it is too ingenious for its own good".

We are too ingenious... because we are now using the burden of proof against ourselves. We somehow delight in saying : "You can't prove it... you can't prove pollution is affecting these animals... you can't tell me our resource town is any worse off than any other... you cannot attribute the higher incidence of illness in this area to our pollution... you know people also drink a lot here, and smoke a lot, and they have bad nutrition... all those things could be making them ill."

Tell me, does the St. Lawrence beluga drink too much alcohol and does the St. Lawrence beluga smoke too much and does the St. Lawrence beluga have a bad diet... is that why the beluga whales are ill ?

Let me think what the logical, too-ingenious answer is going to be to this one... I have got it... "Well, we've been told here that the beluga could just be dying out because it is no longer adapted to its environment." Perfect answer. Who's to blame for that ?... "People are too smart for their own good."

I can understand the worker who says, "Look, I know we are working in a polluted place and that it is probably affecting me but what can I do ? I need a job and this one pays real well". I can understand the union which doesn't want the new plant to be built too quickly because that is going to toss some of its members out of work. I can understand that a community that derives sizeable benefits from a polluting company doesn't want to lose those benefits. I can even understand that a company must be competitive and make a profit if it is to stay afloat and support all its employees and the community in which it is in. What I cannot understand, however, is why we think all these things have priority over the survival of life on planet earth ? Have we no capacity to realize we are progressively destroying the life support systems on our planet ?

Perhaps the fatal flaw of the most intelligent, ingenious creature on earth is that we somehow have it imbedded in our survival makeup that while someone else may get hit by those falling bombs... we are probably immune. There have been others who thought that before us... can you think of a recent example ?

I know the people that live and work in Chicoutimi are not going to raise a big fuss about the pollution that is raining down on them because they have got too much at stake. But what about you people down here around the mouth of the Saguenay ? Do you think you are escaping these falling bombs ? Do you think you are somehow immune and that it is only the beluga whale that is being affected ? Anyone done a health study on you lately ? Have you any idea of the state of your community health ?

What do I recommend ? I recommend the public should have the right to receive an annual report on the state of their environment both nationally and regionally, not prepared by the government but by a commission of experts... so that the reporting will not be just putting the best foot forward...we need the real foot put forward.

Why ? Because while the Canadian and Nova Scotian governments are now spending 40 million dollars to get PAHs out of the environment in Sydney, Nova Scotia, here PAHs are being allowed to rain down on you in the tonnes. PAHs are right now listed by the Toxics Working Committee of the Canadian Environmental Protection Act as the number one chemical that must be brought under regulation as soon as possible. Currently PAHs are not regulated, which is why everyone's hands are tied in trying to stop it from being put into the environment. Would you like some more information ? Would you like to see some faster action ?

I remember in the movie "Network" years ago, a scene where Peter Finch as the newsman becomes so inflamed with society that on his nightly national newscast he decides to expound to his listening audience : "I am as mad as hell and I am not going to take it anymore". In the next scene we see people all over the nation leaning out their windows yelling the same, "I'm as mad as hell and I'm not going to take it anymore". The scene was very funny but it had a very serious side.

I am not suggesting you get as mad as hell, but I am suggesting you get involved in helping restore our commons in one way or another, which will in turn help save the St. Lawrence beluga whales.

CONCLUSION

Over the course of this century, the relationship between the human world and the planet that sustains it has undergone a profound change. When the century began, neither human numbers nor technology had the power to radically alter planetary systems. As the century closes, not only do vastly increased human numbers and their activities have that power, but major unintended changes are occurring in the atmosphere, in soils, in waters, among plants and animals and in the relationships among all of these.

The animal that we are here today to try to help is a very good example of one of the outcomes of this rapid rate of change where we have had insufficient time to assess and advise... so that here we are perhaps its eleventh hour trying to play catchup for years of neglect, and worse, trying to go forward with outmoded approaches very much in evidence. This situation now deeply worries many people while many others are still not very anxious about it.

But the world commissioners who wrote the report "Our Common Future" were unanimous in their conviction that we needed to start right now making these significant changes in our attitudes and approaches to human development if we wished the planet to survive. They further indicated that we needed to start making these changes by means of vast campaigns of education, public participation and debate.

Here then, in this forum, is a place where we just might begin this discussion of change in earnest. It will, however, take all our will to come to some commonly shared conclusions. Further, I believe it will require in the next three days that we set aside our personal egos and ambitions to think of the whole.

Take in the charm of Tadoussac and view the whales in their home... and then when you are talking or listening, keep thinking of the beauty and life you have around you, and what our world would be like without this. If we can keep these images as our focus, then perhaps, ladies and gentlemen, we just might begin here the process of accomplishing something rather wonderful.

In closing, I would like to cite you a paragraph from Henry Beston's book, *The St. Lawrence* on the St. Lawrence beluga.

"What dweller by the river, watching either from a ship's deck or the height of some great cape can ever forget that bone-white turning in the blue world of the stream? Like a wheel turning in the water, the white appears, turns, and sinks in the vast plain of ripples and coiling eddies spread below. In my experience, I have never seen the whale by itself and alone. The sight of a first is soon followed by the discovery of a second; presently some five or six or a company will be found wheeling and plunging by, coming like gods with the tide and like gods playing in the waves as if it were still the morning of the world."

What the white whale or beluga brings to the St. Lawrence and Saguenay rivers, is the gift of the presence of life. May it always be so. Think of the whole... think of the whale.

IUCN'S Species Survival Program

Ulysses Seal
International Union for the Conservation of Nature

I think it is probably appropriate that, in contrast to Leone Pippard, who came up in the dawn — hopefully — of a new day, I came in the depths of night and arrived at a time of movement of the vampires and the wee-willies. Because, in a very real sense, that's what much of the function of the people I work with is. It is to try to pick up the pieces and the strands that are left all over this planet as the result of the multiple effects that human beings are having on the planet.

If you have the opportunity, either by physical movement and transport, or, like myself, by video, to view this planet from space, you will see a swirl of clouds and colors. This swirl reflects the appearance and the results of the presence of life on this planet. The history of life on this planet traces back at least 3,6 billion years. The pushing of the presence, incidentally, of life on the planet back to two billion years and earlier just occurred in Canada, in some of the upthrust ancient rocks here.

Looking at those videos provides a dramatic emphasis on the fact that for us this planet is both unique and singular. I seriously doubt if very many of us will get very far off the surface beyond that of an occasional airplane flight. As I say, life originated perhaps 3,6 billion years ago. In the ensuing 3,6 billion years, the seas, the surface, the skin, the atmosphere, now contain upwards of 30 million different species of life form. In the course of the blink of an eye, a matter of a few thousand years. Today, there are more than five billion of us on the surface of the planet. That is an increase from 1,6 billion in 1900. We are projecting by the year 2050, we the demographers and bing counters in general, that there will be more than eight billion people on the planet. There is a very real possibility that we will increase briefly to as many as ten billion, and then perhaps lapse backwards a bit, through catastrophe.

We really only respond to catastrophe — the first talk made that abundantly clear. In fact, I anticipate that in your intensity of interest, you represent a peak or a pinnacle of interest of the five billion humans on the planet or those like you, interested enough to come to meetings like this — but it is not nearly extensive enough — not enough of us are dying — not enough of us are sterile, not enough of us are getting cancer fast enough, not enough of us are feeling directly the effects of what we are doing on a micro-scale on this planet — to respond to crisis.

I really didn't deeply appreciate this until I started this process of species survival planning. We are currently doing it in over 40 countries on the planet, and we are limited only because the number of us are limited — although we are trying very hard to expand the cadre of people coming in, in a sense as ecological, not even ecological, positions — we are species positions — tempting to prevent simply the transition to the funerals. Most of the time the intensity of the interest in doing something is greatest when the numbers of a given species have achieved "zero" in the wild. There are many examples of this.

The basic macro-scale events that are providing the background of changes in the ecosystems on this planet — I will just briefly enumerate them because then we're going to go quickly down to the local and the micro-scale, which is really part of where we are at now — relate fundamentally and basically to the increasing human population on the planet and the fact that we are competing for, and using, an increasingly large fraction of the net primary productivity. This is reflected fundamentally and simply and easily in the rapid increase in the use of wood both for fuel and food, directly and indirectly.

There are also the changes caused overall in climate by the increase of gases, notoriously known as "the greenhouse effect". In Florida now, our species survival planning for the whole southern half of Florida is taking as part of its springboard the projection that over the next 40 years, we will see as much as a four-foot rise in water levels. A number of our parks will become marinas.

So the sea rise level, whatever the reason for it, appears to be occurring at least in some of our coastal regions, and will ultimately challenge us to spend billions of dollars to support trillions of dollars of investments.

The ultraviolet flux increases as a result of ozone depletion — all of these are things we can do something about but we do nothing about. That is, in our local immediate action in terms of the beluga, for example, there are things that are more acutely a crisis than these macro-scale planetary changes.

Widespread air pollution, which was referred to, from multiple sources and of multiple kinds. Acid rain is one of great concerns in Canada. Of particularly great concern in the United States has been lead pollution from leaded fuels and old paints. It has been recognized for a long time that these leads are a major source of toxicity in inter-city environments. Our pollution agency became acutely concerned, however, when it became evident that it probably was a contributory event for cardiovascular disease in middle-aged white males — and guess who runs our pollution agencies. So we have finally got very intense regulations and policies changing our use of lead in fuels.

Then, of course, the widespread use of pesticides, fertilizers and finally the trauma that's going to be with us for the next 50 years, that probably will lead to some increase in regulatory events affecting human populations, are the conflicts in economic policy between nations and regions.

Commonly when we talk about the events, we talk first about habitat destruction, the cutting of forests, this is driven, of course, by both the need for fuel and for products and with that comes monoculture and the great reduction in biodiversity. The reasons for it are us; they're inescapable and we have not dealt with the problem of ourselves.

Tropical forests, 80% of the biodiversity of this planet is concentrated in those regions, on the terrestrial biodiversity. And they are the regions being subjected to far and away the greatest devastation at present. However, our interest in the temperate regions is equally great because the proportional decrease in biodiversity is at least as great as it is in the tropics. What's happening to the species? It is very simple — habitat is being competed for and reduced.

Another event is unsustainable exploitation, note I do not say illegal, unsustainable — and it is an enormous range of things. It is something you have been acutely aware of in whaling or the cetaceans because of the tremendous concern and interest in international whaling. But this is only one of many forms of unsustainable exploitation. It can range from poaching to utilization for acute local needs that are difficult to contend against.

Again, the result is loss of living space, loss of creatures and crowding of our charismatic mega-vertebrates into smaller and smaller habitats and coming with that the dawning realization that there is not, on the surface of this planet, a single park large enough to sustain, on an indefinite basis as an evolving species, many of the species contained within those parks. The combinations of size in relation to needs for long-term evolution is simply not being met by current park philosophies.

The few large ones that might have had an opportunity are being thoroughly devastated by poaching in Africa.

We currently project that over the next 50 years, 1 500 types of mammals, birds, reptiles and amphibians (or herps) will go extinct in the wild without direct, intensive management and it is our impression, on the basis of current experience, that most of those are going to require short-term management or a respite in captivity simply because we will not move rapidly enough to achieve their survival in the wild.

As a part of the process that has developed internationally in conservation, you heard mention the International Union for the Conservation of Nature (IUCN) in Minneapolis. Well, the IUCN is not in Minneapolis: I am, and one or two other people are. The International Union for the Conservation of Nature is actually a worldwide organization encompassing 114 countries, 124 governmental agencies and, now, over 100 non-governmental organizations. It is the premier in the sense of the largest, most extensive and perhaps most influential international conservation organization. It has been in existence about 40 years.

Its primary objective is conservation of biodiversity on the planet and then, with that, a series of strategies for doing this. A world conservation strategy has been devised but has been remarkably ineffective. It has been useful as a device for organizing thought, for recognizing that it is a non-trivial task, and has really led to a series of other actions concentrated in regional and country areas and conservation strategies that are beginning to be far more effective.

The IUCN is composed of a series of commissions, one of which on the bottom — species survival, my parent commission — now includes more than 110 specialist groups made up of over 300 specialists of various sorts — scientific experts and others from over the world. All are volunteers. All are experts in one way or another in the species or regions which they represent in their specialist group.

There is no funding to speak of, of course, that is why we are volunteers and all of us that are effective generate our own money. But one of the other contributions of the IUCN and the species survival commission has been the generation of the annual list now, this so-called red data book, or red list, for identifying endangered and threatened animals.

This book, as a reporting system, has really served as a major reporting system to the planet, calling attention to some of its diversity that is being seriously challenged or that has gone extinct.

The specialist groups themselves are engaged in developing action plans, that is, reporting on the status of the groups of interest to them in their parts of the world, trying to put that down on paper, suggesting projects and ways and means of preventing extinction, or providing for the long-term conservation of the ecosystem and the species within it.

In the case of primates, the primates specialist group, in its review of over 100 taxa has already identified 14 for which they have turned to us, the captive breeding specialist group of which I am chairman, and asked us to bring them into captivity because they don't think they're going to make it on their own in the wild through any actions that can be taken at present.

An action plan has been generated by the cetacean specialist group but this is an effort to encompass the world's cetaceans. It is a thin volume but it doesn't begin to represent the amount of work and effort that has been made in generating support systems for cetaceans internationally.

The group which I head, the captive breeding specialist group, as I said, has come into play particularly because of the inability of the other 109 specialist groups to cope with the continued conservation of some of the species or systems in their care. So, many of those groups turn to us and seek information or assistance in providing species survival plans that can be enacted to provide at least a temporary respite for some of the species that may play a key area in the ecosystems of interest.

In the context, members of our group not only have expertise in how to manage animals in captivity, but, far more importantly, in small population biology, population viability analysis and developing interactive plans for management of fragmented species both in the wild and in captivity.

As you might guess, we are experts on fragmented species when you consider that in our data base reporting system we have over 285 zoos — I happen to be managing tigers over much of the work in captivity and jointly with some of the countries — and the tigers that I manage are spread out over 150 zoos and that is real fragmentation. It also involves substantial working together, meeting together, forum activity, to arrive at management plans oriented to the management of these animals as biological populations rather than as simple exhibit animals to be replaced at will.

What has happened is that fewer and fewer animals are carrying a larger and larger genetic burden, for continuing the representation of their species. You have heard this with belugas with reductions in numbers from many thousands to the hundreds. In fact, then, the heritage of thousands and millions of years of evolution where each of these species has been concentrated in fewer and fewer representatives, with the net result that management of those species is going to have to be intense in the wild as well as in captivity. This increases the burden both on the species and on ourselves.

We could hope for a technological fix, many people have, simply tuck them away in a freezer and cryo-preserve them — whether it is embryos or semen — or as mammoths, freeze them whole if you have the resources, or the quagga, recently bits of skin and muscle located in a museum specimen doing DNA sequencing and, who knows, perhaps eventually a cloning and regenerating of one of those creatures, or at least pieces of it here and there.

So, we have come full circle in a few thousand years and, incidentally, the people that wrote about Noah and Noah's Ark, the legend, were better animal husbandry people than many of those that have since translated the legend. If you remember they said "two by two". Actually Noah said "six by six" in the original legend if you choose to read some parts of the Bible to check out my sources. In any case, they were much closer to reality in the larger numbers.

With all of that, what I want to do now, with this general, broad, introductory material, is to zing you a little bit. I don't think that to do what we have to do for the beluga or any other species we can do simply by repetition of things that all of us know well. I have said nothing that most of you haven't heard many times before. I anticipate I will say some things that many of you may not have "seen" before. First, conservation strategy, what will it be based on? Viable populations. Tricky, tricky term, "viable". There are 400 recovery plans in North America, the United States, that include the statement "viable populations". The first two to provide a definition for the word "viable" were written in the past year. There are 398 of them that didn't provide any definition, and that definition has ranged from 50 animals to 1 million depending on the particular inclination of the writers of the particular plan. In no instance was it based upon small population biology analysis — until two that were written in the past year.

Fundamentally, the objective is to preserve species as a component of their originating ecosystems. We didn't do it with the California condor; it is extinct in the wild. We didn't do it with the black-footed ferret; it is extinct in the wild — it lives in captivity. I understand that you are close on some populations of the beluga whale. I don't think we are going to do the beluga whale in captivity very satisfactorily. Of all the whales, it is one that is managed in captivity but I would shudder to think of trying to maintain a viable population, in any kind of meaningful sense, of this species in captivity, even as a backup system. The belugas have a definite role to play in captivity, in terms of education and research and learning more about the species.

Un plan d'action pour la survie des bélugas du Saint-Laurent

Mimi Breton
Ministère des Pêches et des Océans du Canada

INTRODUCTION

Le 21 juin 1988, lorsque l'Honorable Tom Siddon, ministre des Pêches et des Océans du Canada, avait annoncé en son nom et au nom de l'Honorable Tom McMillan, ministre de l'Environnement du Canada, le Plan d'action interministériel pour favoriser la survie du béluga du Saint-Laurent, il avait spécifié que « ce plan servira de base aux discussions du prochain Forum international sur l'avenir des bélugas du Saint-Laurent ».

C'est donc cette étape que nous abordons ensemble aujourd'hui. Pour qu'elle soit le plus profitable possible, et pour qu'elle permette à chacun de connaître les démarches déjà entreprises pour la conservation des bélugas, je résumerai, dans un premier temps, la problématique des bélugas du Saint-Laurent et de leur conservation. Cet exercice permettra de faire comprendre globalement la base sur laquelle reposent actuellement les éléments du plan d'action. Les prochains exposés du Forum vous permettront ensuite de faire un bilan personnel des connaissances internationales sur la question.

Dans un second temps, j'introduirai les éléments du plan d'action proposés par le ministère des Pêches et des Océans du Canada et le ministère de l'Environnement du Canada et discuterai, de façon plus spécifique, les actions concernant la gestion des ressources.

Ici même, à l'hôtel Tadoussac, en 1983, il y a donc 5 ans, le ministère des Pêches et des Océans du Canada organisait une première réunion afin d'informer les gens de la région de la situation des bélugas (et d'autres cétacés) et de solliciter leur coopération pour la mise en œuvre d'actions visant la conservation des bélugas. Près de 70 personnes s'y étaient présentées et la rencontre avait permis de jeter les bases d'un plan pour contrôler le dérangement des cétacés et en particulier des bélugas. Depuis, un Comité consultatif a été créé et ce Comité aide à revoir annuellement la situation relative au dérangement et à identifier les mesures correctrices. Le Ministère souhaite sincèrement que le présent Forum international mènera à des résultats tout aussi positifs.

1. PROBLÉMATIQUE DES BÉLUGAS DU SAINT-LAURENT ET DE LEUR CONSERVATION

Il était une fois, il y a de ça bien des années,...

Le béluga est une espèce qui habite les eaux arctiques et sa présence dans le Saint-Laurent remonte à la fin des dernières grandes glaciations (voir figure 1).

Il est logique de supposer que la distribution a déjà été continue et qu'il pouvait y avoir échange entre les groupes (Fortin, 1930; Packard, 1891; Hantzsch, 1909; Lorn, 1897 dans Vladykov, 1944).

Les études des populations de l'Arctique nous ont appris que le béluga effectue, au printemps et à l'automne (dans le contexte arctique), des migrations, souvent sur de longues distances (par exemple sur plus de 1 000 milles entre la mer de Beaufort et celle de Béring dans l'ouest de l'Arctique canadien) pour retrouver certains estuaires en été et des zones libres de glace en hiver. Ces zones libres de glace (comme au détroit d'Hudson) reçoivent les groupes de bélugas d'origine diverse, ce qui, par ailleurs, rend difficile la distinction entre les populations.

Maintenant, si on examine la situation géographique de la population actuelle de bélugas du Saint-Laurent, on peut constater qu'elle constitue une population distincte, isolée dans un habitat restreint, dans lequel les animaux doivent trouver une nourriture suffisante, les zones appropriées pour toutes les activités que peut pratiquer une espèce à caractère social (comme le soin des jeunes, la ségrégation périodique des sexes, etc.) ainsi que les conditions permettant la survie en hiver.

La température très froide des eaux de l'estuaire du Saint-Laurent et du Saguenay et les secteurs de forte productivité liés à la présence de phénomènes océanographiques favorables, dont la rencontre de masses d'eau de température et de salinité différentes et riches en éléments nutritifs et la présence d'eau libre de glace en hiver, constituent les

FIGURE 1

Transgressions marines et distribution des bélugas

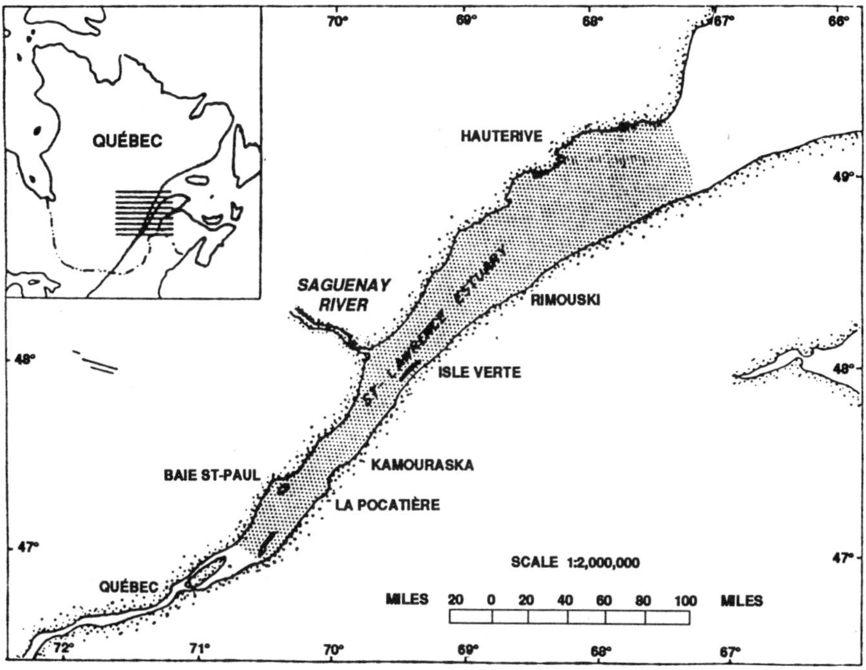

facteurs primaires essentiels, leur ayant permis de survivre dans cette limite méridionale de leur aire de distribution.

Outre les notes retrouvées dans les carnets des explorateurs et les souvenirs des ancêtres de la région laissant croire à la présence d'un très grand nombre de bélugas occupant une aire de distribution plus vaste, sans toutefois apporter de précision sur les nombres, les premières données scientifiques sur les bélugas du Saint-Laurent sont celles associées à la chasse (Vladykov, 1944). L'exploitation de cette population a débuté au 18e siècle mais la chasse la plus intense a eu lieu de 1860 à 1945.

Les estimations des captures, basées sur les statistiques de la quantité d'huile et du nombre de peaux obtenues, portent à croire que des captures annuelles de plus de 200 baleines ont eu lieu au cours de trois périodes, soit 1886-1890, 1915-1921 et 1932-1938. Les années de pointe ont été 1889 (850 individus), 1915 (900 individus) et 1935 (692 individus) et finalement 1942 (403 individus) (voir figure 2).

Le nombre élevé des captures révèle que la population était beaucoup plus importante par le passé, au moins au début de chaque période d'exploitation. On a estimé à 5 000 le niveau de la population « initiale » à

FIGURE 2

Courbe des prises ajustées à l'aide d'une moyenne mobile quinquennale (M. Hammil, 1988)

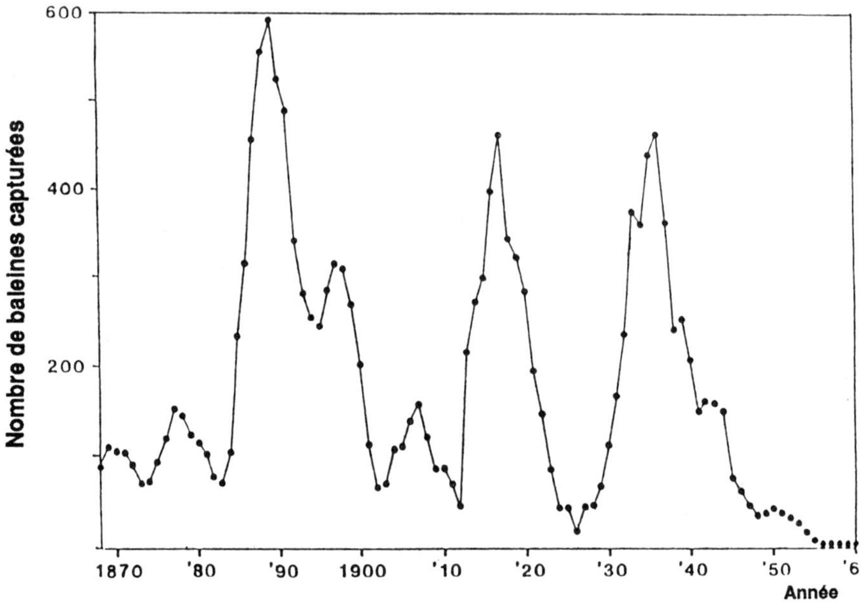

l'aide de diverses hypothèses, lesquelles sont toutefois difficilement vérifiables.

De plus, il est possible que la population du golfe du Saint-Laurent ait été en contact avec des populations plus septentrionales. Par conséquent, les effectifs réels représentaient probablement un certain niveau de migration entre le golfe et les eaux plus au nord ainsi que des apports locaux par reproduction et des pertes entraînées par l'exploitation.

On a tenté, à plusieurs reprises, d'évaluer le nombre de bélugas toujours présents dans la population du Saint-Laurent à partir de bateaux ou d'aéronefs. Les conférenciers invités discuteront en détail, durant le Forum, le degré de précision de ces méthodes, l'évolution récente de la population ainsi que sa dynamique. Je me contenterai donc de mentionner que les effectifs actuels sont généralement évalués à environ 500 bélugas.

Ce niveau ne constitue qu'un faible pourcentage du nombre de bélugas qui fréquentaient le Saint-Laurent au 19e siècle, même si l'estimé de population initiale ne constitue évidemment qu'un ordre de grandeur et ne peut être pris comme un estimé absolu.

Comme on l'a vu précédemment, cette baisse importante dans la population est reliée principalement à un effort de chasse considérable jusqu'au début des années 1950 avec, par la suite, des captures occasionnelles jusqu'à l'interdiction de toute chasse par la loi fédérale sur les pêcheries en 1979.

Puisque la population semble avoir été capable de récupérer à deux reprises d'une chasse intensive (par reproduction locale ou immigration), pourquoi est-elle demeurée à un bas niveau en dépit de l'arrêt de toute forme de chasse et pourquoi se retrouve-t-elle maintenant (depuis 1983) classée parmi la liste des populations menacées du Comité sur la faune menacée d'extinction au Canada?

Plusieurs facteurs peuvent contribuer à empêcher la récupération ou l'accroissement de la population. Les diverses hypothèses formulées se classent en deux groupes, soit celui des facteurs naturels, sur lesquels nous n'avons pas de contrôle et celui des facteurs résultant de l'activité humaine dont le contrôle est possible et déjà amorcé dans plusieurs cas (voir tableau 1).

TABLEAU 1

Facteurs pouvant contribuer à maintenir la population de bélugas du Saint-Laurent au niveau actuel

Facteurs naturels	Facteurs résultant de l'activité humaine	
	Dérangement	Contamination
• Variation environnementales	• Modification d'estuaires	• Contaminants chimiques organiques (BPC, DDT, MIREX, HAP, Pesticides)
• Détérioration du bagage génétique	• Aménagement côtier	• Métaux lourds (mercure, etc.)
• Compétition avec d'autres mammifères marins	• Activités de construction	
• Arrêt de l'immigration	• Circulation maritime et aérienne	
	• Pêche commerciale	
	• Recherche	

L'analyse de ces facteurs comprend deux facettes ; d'une part, il faut déterminer leur effet et leur niveau d'impact sur la population de bélugas et d'autre part, on doit dresser un bilan de la situation relativement aux possibilités de contrôle.

Certains de ces facteurs font déjà l'objet des projets de recherche comme par exemple l'analyse du taux de contamination par diverses substances chimiques toxiques des tissus de bélugas trouvés échoués.

Toutefois, il n'existe encore que très peu de données permettant de comprendre comment ces facteurs agissent sur les individus de tout âge et sexe de la population (santé, reproduction, survie) et, conséquemment, sur le nombre total de bélugas dans la population, sur sa dynamique et finalement sur son évolution.

Notons que ces bélugas peuvent vivre près de 30 ans et que leur état physiologique peut résulter d'événements passés, surtout au niveau des substances non dégradables accumulées dans leurs tissus.

Les exposés qui vont suivre vous feront connaître les données disponibles présentement et vous permettront de comprendre, par ailleurs, les problèmes reliés à l'étude de ces animaux. C'est donc de cette base d'information qu'est parti le Comité interministériel fédéral et provincial chargé d'élaborer la problématique de la survie des bélugas du Saint-Laurent.

Au cours de l'élaboration de la problématique, le groupe n'a pas pu, en général, dépasser le stade de l'hypothèse pour la détermination de l'effet et du niveau d'impact. Les tableaux 2 et 3 résument les conclusions avancées.

2. PLAN D'ACTION POUR LA SURVIE DES BÉLUGAS DU SAINT-LAURENT

Les connaissances actuelles sur les bélugas du Saint-Laurent ne permettent pas de prévoir leurs chances de survie ni de quantifier l'impact des facteurs nocifs.

L'identification d'actions de sauvegarde n'est donc pas simple. Bien sûr, on pourrait avancer qu'en agissant de front sur tous les facteurs identifiés, on finira par avoir un impact positif sur la qualité de l'écosystème du Saint- Laurent et, conséquemment, sur la survie des bélugas.

Cette approche néglige toutefois plusieurs considérations d'ordre biologique et socio-économique avec lesquelles nous devons composer.

— D'abord, d'autres facteurs d'ordre naturel peuvent agir négativement sur la population de bélugas.

— Ensuite, plusieurs contaminants toxiques ne sont plus produits ou ont une utilisation restreinte mais, à cause de leur très

TABLEAU 2
Agents de dérangement sur la population de bélugas du Saint-Laurent

FACTEURS	AGENT/CAUSE	EFFET					NIVEAU D'IMPACT POTENTIEL		
		déplacement	écho-location	habitat	alimentation	pollution chimique	faible	moyen	élevé
Dérangement	Navigation de plaisance et motorisée	•	•						•
	Tourisme commercial en mer	•	•						•
	Construction: dragage dynamitage modification aux milieux riverains		 •	• • •			•	 •	 • •
	Recherche en mer: Comportement baleines autres types de recherche		 •				 •	 •	 •
	Pêche			•	•		•		
	Circulation aérienne	•					•		
	Traversiers		•				•		
	Transport commercial	•					•		

TABLEAU 3

Impacts, actualisation et source des contaminants organiques retrouvés dans la population de bélugas du Saint-Laurent

COMPOSÉS	NIVEAU D'IMPACT ESTIMÉ		ACTUALISATION		SECTEURS	
	Faible	Élevé	Présente	Passée	Industriel	Agricole
HAP (BaP)		●	●	●	●	
BPC		●		●	●	
MIREX		●		●	●	
DDT		●		●		●
LINDANE	●		●			●
HEPTACHLORE	●			●		●
ALDRIN	●		●			●
CHLORDANE	●		●			●
DIELDRIN	●		●			●
ENDRIN	●		●			●
HCB	●		●		●	●

grande stabilité, demeurent accumulés dans l'environnement. On a pu mesurer dernièrement l'ampleur du problème relié à l'élimination des déchets dangereux (*i.e.* : accident de Saint-Basile-le-Grand).

— La lutte contre les contaminants toxiques relève à la base d'un choix social et économique ; certains pesticides, par exemple, continuent d'être utilisés pour des cas spécifiques et ce qu'on épand sur les cultures, jardins et pelouses retourne éventuellement à la mer (fleuve). Les hydrocarbures aromatiques polycycliques (HAP) sont non seulement des produits de certains procédés industriels mais aussi des sous-produits de la combustion de la matière organique et peuvent être libérés dans l'atmosphère par les feux de forêts, une cheminée résidentielle, un barbecue et le gaz d'échappement d'une automobile.

— Finalement, les coûts impliqués pour le « Grand nettoyage » sont très élevés.

L'alternative est de tenter de concentrer les interventions sur les facteurs, ou la combinaison de facteurs, dont l'élimination présente la plus forte probabilité d'entraîner un impact positif sur la population de bélugas. Cette alternative constitue l'approche privilégiée par le Comité interministériel. De façon empirique, les facteurs les plus susceptibles d'avoir un niveau d'impact élevé ont donc été identifiés (tableaux 2 et 3) et sont devenus la cible du plan d'action.

Le plan d'action interministériel repose sur trois considérations principales :

1. Les actions doivent être orientées vers les facteurs associés aux interventions humaines, puisque ce sont les seuls sur lesquels on peut agir.
2. Les actions doivent aussi comprendre une part de recherche scientifique afin d'améliorer nos connaissances sur la biologie et l'environnement des bélugas du Saint-Laurent, ce qui permettra de raffiner les interventions pour leur sauvegarde et aussi éventuellement, nous l'espérons, de pouvoir mesurer les améliorations de leur santé et, déterminer à long terme, si possible, les tendances de leur évolution.
3. Finalement, les actions doivent engager tous les acteurs dont elles dépendent. En effet, les facteurs de dérangement ou de pollution impliquent chacun de nous, du citoyen au politicien.

Dans ce sens, la participation de chacun à ce Forum international et sa contribution positive à la finalisation d'un plan de survie assureront au processus les meilleures chances possibles de succès.

Les actions du plan interministériel proposé par les ministères des Pêches et des Océans et de l'Environnement du Canada, en juin 1988, viennent s'ajouter à celles que le ministère des Pêches et des Océans du Canada fait déjà au niveau du contrôle du dérangement par la navigation de plaisance et par l'industrie d'observation des baleines dans l'estuaire ainsi qu'à la surveillance des travaux pouvant modifier les habitats.

Ces actions se répartissent en trois étapes :

À court terme : À être entreprises dans l'immédiat si elles n'ont pas encore été mises en œuvre et pouvant se poursuivre sur plusieurs années.

À moyen terme : Sur une base de cinq ans avec une évaluation en 1992.

À long terme : Actions à être redéfinies selon les connaissances acquises.

TABLEAU 4

Échéancier du plan d'actions proposées

Court terme:	En cours ou amorcées dès la première année du plan.
	Se poursuivent durant plusieurs années.
Moyen terme:	Programme de cinq ans.
	Évaluation en 1992.
Long terme:	Plan à être redéfini en fonction des connaissances acquises.

Chaque étape comprend un groupe d'actions pour :

— le contrôle du dérangement,
— l'accroissement des connaissances,
— le contrôle des substances chimiques.

TABLEAU 5

Groupe d'actions identifiées

1. Accroissement des connaissances
2. Contrôle du dérangement
3. Contrôle des substances toxiques

Le Dr Boulva, directeur de l'institut Maurice-Lamontagne, exposera et discutera le groupe d'actions relatives à la recherche scientifique.

Nous examinerons donc les actions proposées ou en vigueur pour le contrôle du dérangement ainsi que celles pour le contrôle des substances chimiques (voir les tableaux 6, 7 et 8).

TABLEAU 6

Actions pour le contrôle du dérangement

Court terme		Moyen / Long terme
• Plan annuel de directives	————>	
• Avis pour évaluation impact	————>	
• Émission permis recherche	————>	
• Promotion parc marin	————>	• Implantation d'un parc
• Élaboration système permis pour croisières d'observation et ajustements à la réglementation	————>	• Application et évaluation des règlements et de l'information diffusée
	————>	• Acroissement de la surveillance dans certaines aires fréquentées par les bélugas

TABLEAU 7

Actions pour le contrôle des substances chimiques toxiques

Court terme		Moyen / long terme
• Adoption de la loi canadienne pour la protection de l'environnement	————>	• Évaluation de la toxicité environnementale de certaines substances toxiques présentes dans les tissus de bélugas
• Dépollution industrielle	————>	
• Suivi et contrôle des sources de polluants des Grands Lacs, du Saint-Laurent et de ses ses tributaires	————>	
		• Mesure de flux des contaminants dans la chaîne alimentaire du béluga
		• Amélioration des installations portuaires
		• Caractérisation des sites fédéraux pouvant contenir des déchets contaminés le long du Saint-Laurent

TABLEAU 8

Accroissement des connaissances

Court terme		Moyen / long terme
• Conseils scientifiques sur l'état de la population et les priorités de recherche		
• Monographie sur la biologie du béluga		
• Forum international pour l'avenir du béluga		• Évaluation des impacts du stress causé à la population
• Évaluation de la population et délimitation de la répartition	——————>	• Recherches sur la dynamique des populations
	——————>	• Évaluation des pertes d'habitats et identification des habitats essentiels
• Évaluation du degré de consanguinité et des conséquences	——————>	• Évaluation des caractères génétiques
• Identification et mesure des contaminants dans les bélugas et étude de leurs effets	——┐	
• Étude du cheminement des substances chimiques toxiques dans la chaîne alimentaire	——┴——>	• Développement d'objectifs et de normes de qualité pour la protection de la vie aquatique
• Monitoring des concentrations de contaminants dans l'habitat du béluga	——————>	
• Examen de la possibilité scientifique d'introduire des individus de l'arctique		

Finalement, j'aimerais présenter les acteurs qui ont et auront un rôle à jouer dans la mise en œuvre du plan d'action pour la survie des bélugas du Saint-Laurent (voir tableau 9).

TABLEAU 9

Intervenants dans le cadre du plan d'action pour la survie des bélugas du Saint-Laurent

Organismes gouvernementaux	Organismes non gouvernementaux
FÉDÉRAL	
• Ministère des Pêches et des Océans du Canada	• Greenpeace
• Ministère de l'Environnement du Canada	• Fondation pour la sauvegarde des espèces menacées
• Ministère de la Défense nationale	• World Wildlife Fund
• Ministère du Transport Canada	• Société pour vaincre la pollution
	• Union québécoise pour la conservation de la nature
PROVINCIAL	• Société linnéenne
• Ministère de l'Environnement du Québec	
• Ministère du Loisir, de la Chasse et de la Pêche	
• Ministère de l'Agriculture, des Pêcheries et de l'Alimentation	

CONCLUSION

Vous avez sans aucun doute réalisé la complexité que présente la conservation de la population de bélugas du Saint-Laurent, tant par la nature et le nombre des facteurs pouvant l'affecter que par la diversité des intervenants concernés et la limite des connaissances sur les processus impliqués.

Je vous ai présenté le plan d'action interministériel qui contient les démarches prévues à court et à moyen terme pour contrôler les facteurs jugés néfastes tout en acquérant les connaissances qui permettront de raffiner nos interventions à moyen et long terme.

Je vous invite à lire attentivement les présentations suivantes car elles constituent une occasion unique de faire le point sur les connaissances scientifiques. Ces connaissances permettront peut-être en conclusion du Forum, grâce à vos suggestions, d'ajouter de nouvelles actions au plan de survie ou de l'améliorer par des modifications spécifiques aux actions proposées.

Le Forum international pour la sauvegarde des bélugas aura alors atteint ses objectifs : même si on ne peut garantir que la population survivra au 20e siècle, nous pourrons être assurés de la volonté de chacun d'y arriver et d'y contribuer.

Il nous reste maintenant à faire le souhait suivant en guise de conclusion :

...« Et ils vivront nombreux jusqu'à la fin des temps »...

Le béluga du Saint-Laurent. Proposition pour un plan de recherche

Jean Boulva
Directeur régional des Sciences
Ministère des Pêches et des Océans du Canada

1. INTRODUCTION

Ce document résume le plan de recherche sur le béluga du Saint-Laurent que le ministère des Pêches et des Océans du Canada (MPO), responsable de la gestion de cette espèce, compte réaliser de 1988 à 1993.

2. CONTEXTE

La présentation par Madame Breton a décrit de façon détaillée le cheminement qui a mené à l'élaboration d'« Un plan d'action pour la survie des bélugas du Saint-Laurent ». Le plan de recherche proposé se veut une réponse directe aux interrogations soulevées dans le plan d'action. Le présent document ne décrit donc pas l'évolution de la population ni ne liste les incertitudes à propos des paramètres vitaux de la population. Il résume plutôt des raisons qui motivent les recherches proposées, les moyens qui seront utilisés et les résultats qui sont attendus.

Il est toutefois important de rappeler que la présence de cette population de béluga (*Delphinapterus leucas*), une espèce arctique, dans le fjord du Saguenay et l'estuaire du Saint-Laurent constitue un reliquat des dernières glaciations. Il est probable que la répartition de l'espèce était continue durant la dernière glaciation et que la fin de celle-ci a laissé cette population emprisonnée dans ces eaux méridionales.

3. ACTIVITÉS DE RECHERCHE PROPOSÉES

Les recherches proposées permettront de réduire l'intervalle de confiance des estimés de population, d'identifier les aires de répartition à chaque saison ainsi que les habitats préférés, d'obtenir une meilleure connaissance de la pathologie et des facteurs de mortalité, de caractériser la population d'un point de vue génétique, d'étudier le cheminement et les effets des contaminants et de quantifier les modifications d'habitat qui sont survenues depuis les années quarante.

Cette information permettra d'accroître les connaissances sur le béluga du Saint-Laurent et de formuler les perspectives d'avenir du troupeau selon différents scénarios d'intervention. Il est évident, cependant, que la réalisation d'un programme de recherche important et la mise en vigueur de strictes mesures de contrôle ne peuvent garantir la survie d'une population. La pollution peut être éliminée, le dérangement contrôlé et l'habitat restauré, mais on ne peut éliminer la possibilité que d'autres facteurs, à l'échelle planétaire, constituent la principale menace pour la survie de cette population.

Les projets présentés ici constituent le volet Sciences du MPO du plan de survie du béluga et représentent une partie importante de la contribution du MPO au plan d'action du Saint-Laurent. Les autres parties de la contribution du MPO au plan d'action du Saint-Laurent sur l'évaluation des écosystèmes et la restauration des habitats sont également pertinents à la problématique du béluga mais elles se situent dans un contexte plus large et ne feront pas l'objet de présentations à ce Forum.

Les besoins de recherche sur cette population ont été revus récemment par le Comité scientifique consultatif des pêches canadiennes dans l'Atlantique (CSCPCA) du MPO (document consultatif 88/16 du CSCPCA) et cette révision a servi de base aux projets décrits plus bas.

3.1 Évaluation des populations

À l'exception de la répartition estivale du béluga dans le fleuve même, on connait peu de choses des déplacements saisonniers des bélugas et de leur répartition dans l'estuaire et le golfe durant le reste de l'année.

Dans le cadre de ce projet, des relevés aériens visuels seront réalisés mensuellement entre Pointe-des- Monts et Québec au printemps et à l'été. Ces relevés seront prolongés à l'est jusqu'à la rivière Romaine à l'automne et en hiver. Des relevés par photographie aérienne seront effectués durant l'été pour évaluer les effectifs et la structure de taille de la population. L'information sur la répartition spatiale ainsi recueillie sera comparée aux données environnementales pour tenter d'identifier lesquelles influencent la répartition des bélugas.

Ces travaux permettront d'améliorer la précision des estimés de population et également de mettre au point une méthode standardisée qui permette de suivre l'évolution de la population.

3.2 Statut génétique et niveau de contamination des bélugas vivants

Le faible nombre d'individus que compte cette population permet de soupçonner que la consanguinité pourrait être un facteur qui diminue les chances d'accroissement du troupeau.

La méthodologie et le protocole d'échantillonnage pour ce projet seront mis au point sur des populations nordiques de bélugas. Si une méthode entraînant peu de risques pour le béluga peut être mise au point, elle sera appliquée au béluga du Saint-Laurent pour recueillir des échantillons de peau et de graisse. Les échantillons de peau seront utilisés pour déterminer le sexe de l'animal et la lignée parentale selon la technique « d'empreinte digitale d'ADN ». Les échantillons de graisse permettront d'évaluer la concentration en contaminants chez les animaux vivants.

La détermination du statut génétique de cette population de bélugas, particulièrement le coefficient de consanguinité, permettra d'évaluer les chances de survie à long terme de la population et d'identifier si l'immigration a été un facteur d'accroissement dans le passé. La possibilité d'identifier les animaux individuellement et d'en prélever des échantillons sans les affecter permet de suivre les concentrations de contaminants dans la population, au fil des ans et d'en étudier les effets.

3.3 Cheminement et effet des contaminants

Peu de travaux expérimentaux ont été effectués pour évaluer l'effet des contaminants chez les populations de mammifères marins. Bien que les preuves circonstancielles et épidémiologiques existent, peu de preuves directes de l'effet des contaminants sur la physiologie et la reproduction des mammifères marins sont disponibles.

Compte tenu de la petite taille de la population de bélugas du Saint-Laurent, il n'est pas possible d'étudier la dynamique des contaminants directement sur cette population. Toutefois, d'autres espèces plus abondantes comme le phoque commun, le phoque gris, le phoque du

Groenland et le pourcil offrent des possibilités d'étudier les interrelations entre l'âge, le poids, le sexe et la diète. Ces espèces peuvent également être gardées en captivité afin de déterminer les niveaux critiques de contaminants pour les systèmes immunologique, endocrinologique et reproductif.

Des programmes de cueillette de données seront établis dans l'estuaire pour identifier les aires d'alimentation et les niveaux de contamination des populations cibles. Le programme d'échantillonnage des échouages continuera dans le cadre de ce projet.

Ce projet permettra de monter une importante banque de données sur les niveaux de contamination des mammifères marins dans l'estuaire du Saint-Laurent ainsi que les proies qui constituent les principales sources de contamination. Il sera également possible de comparer le niveau de contamination des animaux échoués avec les animaux vivants ainsi que d'évaluer les niveaux critiques de contaminants dans les organismes vivants.

3.4 Modification d'habitat

L'habitat du béluga du Saint-Laurent a été modifié de façon prononcée durant le 20e siècle. Parmi ces modifications, notons l'augmentation de la circulation maritime, la construction de ports pour petites embarcations, le harnachement des rivières à des fins hydroélectriques et l'augmentation de la présence humaine. Il est impossible d'établir un niveau cible pour l'accroissement de la population tant que ces modifications d'habitat n'auront pas été quantifiées.

Le projet permettra d'identifier la capacité de support de l'estuaire du Saint-Laurent et de déterminer s'il est possible que la population atteigne de nouveau les niveaux antérieurs.

4. CONCLUSION

Le ministère des Pêches et des Océans du Canada est confiant que la réalisation de ce plan quinquennal de recherche sur le béluga du Saint-Laurent permettra d'apporter les réponses scientifiques qui contribueront à choisir des mesures de conservation appropriées en vue d'augmenter les chances de survie du béluga.

Le programme scientifique proposé répond directement aux questions soulevées dans la problématique du béluga du Saint-Laurent, dans le plan de survie du béluga du Saint-Laurent et aux recommandations de recherches formulées par le Comité scientifique consultatif sur les pêches canadiennes dans l'Atlantique. Tous les chercheurs impliqués souhaitent la survie du béluga et leur contribution se traduira par la poursuite de l'excellence dans la réalisation de ce plan de recherche. Nous comptons sur vos commentaires constructifs pour bonifier notre plan de recherche.

N.B. Les personnes ou groupes intéressés par l'avenir du béluga du Saint-Laurent peuvent faire parvenir leurs commentaires à :

Dr Jean Boulva
Directeur régional, Sciences
Institut Maurice-Lamontagne
Ministère des Pêches et des Océans du Canada
C.P. 1000
Mont-Joli (Québec) G5H 3Z4

Une copie du plan de recherche final sera envoyée aux personnes ou groupes qui en feront la demande.

An Overview of the Distribution, Exploitation and Conservation Status of Belugas, Worldwide

Randall R. Reeves
Okapi Wildlife Associates

INTRODUCTION

The white whale or beluga, *Delphinapterus leucas*, has a nearly circumpolar distribution in high latitudes of the northern hemisphere. Nowhere does it occur normally south of 45° N. In this paper, I outline the species' world distribution, mention briefly the nature and levels of current exploitation, review published estimates of current and past population sizes, and discuss some ways in which the population in the St. Lawrence River differs from other beluga populations. My main objective is to give participants in the conference some perspective on the relative importance of the St. Lawrence belugas, by placing them in the context of the world population of the species.

I. The concept of stocks

Before describing the beluga's world distribution, it is necessary to mention briefly how the various populations or stocks are defined. Ideally, a stock is a group of animals which freely interbreeds but which experiences no immigration or emigration. This ideal is seldom realized with whales, since they are capable of moving long distances and face few insurmountable physical barriers. The boundaries separating whale stocks may be environmental, such as water-temperature differences, current patterns, or ice coverage; behavioral, involving conservative tendencies of animals to follow traditional migration routes or to remain year- round in familiar areas ; or historical, caused by overhunting or habitat modification by humans.

In the case of belugas specifically, there is considerable uncertainty about where stock boundaries should be drawn. Since on a worldwide scale the species' effective distribution is restricted to marine and estuarine waters between about 50° N and 80° N, the relevant zoogeographic boundaries would be primarily those blocking east-west movements by the animals. The North American and Asian land masses are obvious barriers, as is Greenland to a lesser degree. As will be seen shortly, the Alaskan and Kamchatkan peninsulas function as barriers between beluga stocks in the North Pacific-Bering Sea region. Extensive areas of permanent ice cover can block the movements of belugas, but their ability to survive in heavy ice conditions makes them less restricted in this way than are most other cetaceans.

Because many belugas make annual migrations covering 1 000s of kilometers, and some belugas wander far outside their population's "normal" range (see below), it would be unwise to assume that stock boundaries are inviolate. To my knowledge, there is, as yet, no published evidence of genetic differences among putative beluga stocks. The study by Sergeant and Brodie (1969) of body size differences among belugas from various areas provided a preliminary framework for distinguishing among stocks on morphological grounds. Mitchell and Reeves (1981) and Reeves and Mitchell (1987b) considered the fact that beluga populations in certain areas have declined after intensive exploitation, while populations in areas with less intensive exploitation have not, as indirect evidence of stock separation. Finley *et al.* (1982) argued that groups of belugas which traditionally summer in different estuaries or estuarine complexes are essentially isolated, at least seasonally.

In the absence of permanent, impenetrable barriers for dividing stocks, questions about stock separation in belugas can be debated endlessly. However, for practical purposes, managers responsible for conserving or protecting beluga stocks need to consider management units which make sense biogeographically and politically. They must take account of central tendencies in the whales' behavior and at the same time consider patterns of human predation on the whales and possible impacts of various human activities other than whaling. While gross distinctions, such as those between the Bering Sea and Eastern Canadian stocks, or the Hudson Bay and Svalbard stocks, may be easy to make, the finer-scale distinctions, such as those between stocks within the Bering Sea or within Hudson Bay and Hudson Strait, can be extremely difficult. In the following discussion, my references to beluga "stocks" should not be taken to imply that such groups are genetically isolated or that there is no mixing among them. Rather, they should be understood to be provisional or proposed stocks, recognized primarily for management purposes.

II. Centers of abundance

On Figure 1, I have attempted to show the effective world distribution of the species. It is important to recognize that much of the indicated range, particularly in areas well away from coasts, is inferred rather than documented. For example, in an area like Hudson Bay, the belugas appear to migrate mainly along coasts, aggregating in summer mainly in estuaries. There is no evidence of their presence in large numbers throughout the main body of the bay, away from the coasts. In the Sea of

FIGURE 1

Approximate World Distribution of Belugas

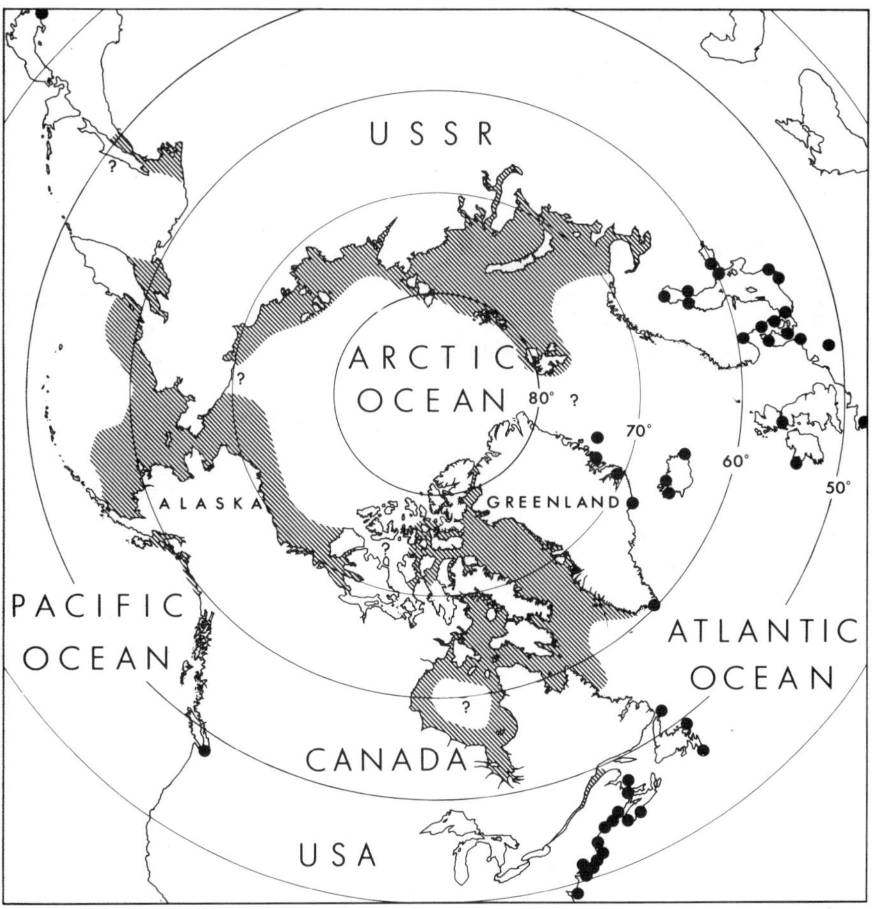

Notes: Hatching indicates effective range; dots represent extralimital records; question marks mean there is uncertainty about their occurrence. Map prepared by Randall R. Reeves.

Okhotsk, on the other hand, the indicated range probably underrepresents the actual range, as in winter belugas there may occupy much of the continental shelf region (Ivashin 1986).

Kleinenberg *et al.* (1969) concluded that the beluga's distribution is truly circumpolar and not amphiboreal. The hiatuses indicated on Figure 1 in the East Siberian Sea, near Victoria Island in the Central High Arctic of North America, and off the north and east coasts of Greenland should be viewed only as areas of low population density and (or) sporadic occurrence of belugas rather than as places where absolute barriers to their movements exist.

Largely because they gather near shore and have traditionally been exploited in summer, beluga stocks are usually defined on the basis of their summer distribution. Alaskan investigators have identified four provisional management stocks of belugas that occur in or pass through Alaskan waters. The Bristol Bay stock of 1 000-1 500 animals, the Norton Sound/Yukon Delta stock of 1 000-2 000, the eastern Chukchi Sea stock of 2 500-3 000, and the eastern Beaufort Sea stock of more than 11 500 (Lowry *et al.* in press). The eastern Beaufort Sea stock is of particular interest to Canada, as several hundred animals are taken from this stock each year by Native people in the Mackenzie Delta region. A fifth Alaskan stock is centered in Cook Inlet, with at least occasional movement by animals into other coastal areas of the northern Gulf of Alaska.

In the Sea of Okhotsk there are two main areas where belugas congregate in summer : one in the central western portion around the Shantar Islands and the Amur River estuary ; the other in the northern portion. Although whales from these two areas may mix in winter, there is little doubt that together they are largely isolated from the stocks in the Bering Sea.

The belugas distributed along the northern coast of the Union of Soviet Socialist Republics (USSR) certainly congregate in particular embayments and estuaries during summer. Some or most of those summering in the White and Kara seas apparently move into the Barents Sea for the winter. However, some overwintering also occurs in both the White and Kara seas (Kleinenberg *et al.* 1969). I was unable to find a satisfactory description of stock relationships among these whales, although Soviet catch data have been reported separately for the various seas and in some cases for specific regions within the seas (*e.g.* Gulf of Ob, Yenisey and Pyasina bays).

In Canada, a minimum of six stocks is generally recognized. The High Arctic population which summers primarily in the eastern Canadian Arctic, especially Prince Regent Inlet, Barrow Strait, and Peel Sound, and probably winters mainly off West Greenland, has been estimated at 6 300-18 600 animals (Smith *et al.* 1985). The Cumberland Sound stock, which summers primarily at the head of Cumberland Sound but probably disperses into Frobisher Bay, Davis Strait, and eastern Hudson Strait at other seasons, is estimated at 400-600 animals (Richard and Orr 1986). The Ungava Bay stock, which is nearly extirpated, formerly occupied large estuaries in southern Ungava Bay during summer (Reeves and Mitchell 1987b; Smith and Hammill 1986). Belugas are very widely distributed in Hudson Bay, James Bay, and Foxe Basin. Populations summering on the east and west sides of Hudson Bay have generally been regarded as separate stocks, the eastern stock containing well over 1 000 (Smith and Hammill 1986) and the western stock at least 12 000 animals (Finley *et al.* 1982; P. Richard, personal communication). The St. Lawrence stock of a few hundred whales is generally confined in summer to areas upstream of Anticosti Island (Sergeant 1988). The sixth Canadian stock is the one centered in the Mackenzie Delta region of the eastern Beaufort Sea, which is shared with Alaska (see above).

III. Limits of distribution

On Figure 1 some "extralimital" records of belugas are plotted. I consider these to be outside the effective, or normal, range of the species, and they are shown simply to illustrate the tendency of belugas to wander, or stray, over considerable distances.

In the western North Atlantic belugas have occurred occasionally along the coasts of southeastern Canada and the northeastern United States, usually alone or in small groups (Reeves and Katona 1980). They are generally assumed to be strays from the St. Lawrence stock, although there is no direct evidence to support such an assumption. The southern limit for extralimital records is Cape May, New Jersey (*ca* 39° N).

In the eastern North Atlantic belugas have been recorded in many western European countries (see, for example, Aguayo L. 1978 for a review of records from the Baltic Sea; Jensen *et al.* 1987 for a review of records in Danish waters; Slijper 1967 for a review of records in Dutch waters; Fraser 1974 for a review of records in the British Isles). According to Fraser (1974, p. 22), the "southernmost known limit of the White Whale's range in Europe" is at *ca* 47° N on the Atlantic coast of France. The animals reaching European coasts probably belong to one or more stocks centered for at least part of the year in the Barents Sea.

Between Europe and North America, belugas occasionally appear in northern Iceland (Saemundsson 1939) and around the southern tip of Greenland, at *ca* 60-61° N (Kapel 1977: table 1). (On August 11, 1988, I observed a beluga in Søndre Sermilik Fjord near Cape Farewell). Belugas occur sporadically off East Greenland (Dietz *et al.* 1985).

In the eastern North Pacific there is an unconfirmed record of a sighting near Tacoma, Washington, in 1940, and a group of 21 belugas was seen more recently in Yakutat Bay, Gulf of Alaska. Thus, belugas, most likely those belonging to the Cook Inlet stock, might sometimes wander as far south as *ca* 47° N on the American west coast; there are at least sporadic movements by belugas outside Cook Inlet and into the Gulf of Alaska (Harrison and Hall 1978).

In the western North Pacific belugas generally do not occur farther south than Lapérouse Strait, at the southern tip of Sakhalin Island (*ca* 46° N) (Nishiwaki 1966). However, one was taken recently in a set net in the southern Sea of Japan at *ca* 35° N (Kasuya *et al.* 1984).

IV. Levels of exploitation

Belugas have been hunted, trapped, or netted in most areas where they occur (or occurred) in numbers large enough to make commercial operations profitable. They have also been taken for subsistence in areas where they appear inside the hunting radius of Native communities. Except possibly in the Soviet Union, there is no longer any commercial exploitation of belugas (a few are live-captured in western Hudson Bay for exhibit and research). The completeness and accuracy of catch data vary greatly, although over the past 10-20 years the documentation of catches has improved dramatically, particularly in North America and Greenland.

After the recent sparse summary by Ivashin and Mineev (1981), the reporting situation in the USSR remains somewhat unclear. Although the commercial fisheries for belugas in the Sea of Okhotsk and Soviet Bering Sea ended by the late 1960s (Berzin 1981; Berzin *et al.* 1986), commercial whaling, regulated by catch quotas, apparently has continued in the Barents, White, and Kara seas, particularly by collective farms near Barkhanovo and Singeiskiy (Ivashin and Mineev 1981). Substantial catches have continued to be made in the Soviet Arctic, totaling well over 5 000 whales since 1969 (Ivashin and Mineev 1981; USSR Progress Reports to the International Whaling Commission [IWC]). The large catch of 506 reported for the Bering Sea in 1985 was the result of a winter ice entrapment of 2 500-3 000 in the Bering Strait region (Ivashin and Shevlyagin 1987). If that exceptional catch is not included, the entire Soviet catch reported for the five years 1981-1985 averaged about 225 belugas.

In Alaska, the annual secured catch from 1980 to 1986 averaged about 240 whales, with the total kill about 345 (Lowry *et al.* in press). The estimated annual catch and kill in the western Canadian Arctic in recent years were 135 and 225, respectively (Lowry *et al.* in press). In eastern Canada, the total reported catch averaged about 620 belugas from 1982 to 1985 (P. Richard, pers. comm.). In West Greenland, an average of close to 800 belugas have been taken annually during the 1980s (Denmark Progress Reports to the IWC).

Many factors contribute to the difficulty of obtaining complete and accurate statistics on the human-caused mortality of belugas. Among these are the vast and often remote distances over which the hunting and netting take place; the manner in which the products (meat and muktuk) are removed from the carcasses and consumed locally; and the unpredictable, sometimes opportunistic, nature of the hunt.

The problem of accounting for whales killed or seriously wounded but not secured by the hunters must always be borne in mind in evaluating catch statistics for belugas. Hunting equipment and methods, hunter skill, water depth and clarity at the hunting site, and weather and ice conditions are among the factors affecting the loss rate. Although most compilers of such data recognize that the secured catch underrepresents the actual kill, only a few authors (for example, Fraker 1980; Seaman and Burns 1981; Lowry *et al.* in press) have been able to address this problem rigorously.

V. Status of the stocks

The current world population of belugas is probably greater than 50 000. The total population in North America alone, which I take to include the animals which seasonally migrate between Alaskan and Soviet waters of the Bering and Chukchi seas and those which move seasonally along the Greenland side of Baffin Bay and Davis Strait, can be estimated as more than 40 000.

"Initial", or pre-commercial exploitation, population sizes have been estimated for only a few areas, and in most cases the estimates are very crude, conservative first approximations. They are nevertheless sufficient to demonstrate that some beluga stocks have been severely reduced from historic levels. The stocks of greatest immediate concern in Canada are:

1) Ungava Bay stock, reduced from more than 1 000 to several hundred or much less (Finley *et al.* 1982; Smith and Hammill 1986; Reeves and Mitchell 1987b).
2) Cumberland Sound stock, reduced from more than 5 000 to 400-600 (Mitchell and Reeves 1981, 1987c; Richard and Orr 1986).
3) St. Lawrence stock, reduced from more than 5 000 to 350-500 (Reeves and Mitchell 1984).

The small Cook Inlet stock in Alaska apparently is comparable in size to the St. Lawrence stock and is similarly isolated from larger populations to the north. Although still exploited to some extent (Hazard 1988), the Cook Inlet stock is generally regarded as stable. I am unaware of any estimate of its initial size.

Two other Canadian stocks, one summering in eastern Hudson Bay and the other in the eastern High Arctic, deserve close attention. The eastern Hudson Bay population has been reduced from historic levels, although the extent of its depletion as well as its relationship to other Hudson Bay and Hudson Strait populations remain unclear (Smith and Hammill 1986; Reeves and Mitchell 1987a). The large High Arctic stock is not heavily exploited in Canada but is heavily exploited off West Greenland (Reeves and Mitchell 1987c).

The beluga stocks inhabiting the Bering, Chukchi, and Beaufort seas are generally large, and their current exploitation rates are considered sustainable, with the possible exception of the Norton Sound-Yukon Delta stock (Lowry *et al.* in press). Taking the aggregate Alaskan stocks together with those summering in the Soviet Far East, there may be more than 25 000 whales in this region.

It is difficult, on the basis of information presently available, to evaluate the status of stocks in the Sea of Okhotsk and in the Barents, White, Kara, and Laptev seas. Berzin *et al.* (1986) stated that the beluga fishery in the Sea of Okhotsk declined during the 1950s "due to a decrease in numbers [of whales]", and the fishery was closed in the late 1960s. These authors also noted that the number of belugas in Udskaya Guba (west Sea of Okhotsk) is "considerably lower than when fishing was conducted there". One recent published estimate for the entire Sea of Okhotsk is 6 000-10 000 belugas (International Whaling Commission 1980, p. 120). More recent aerial surveys have confirmed that there are at least several thousand belugas in this sea (Berzin *et al.* 1986). There is no estimate of initial population for the Sea of Okhotsk, but more than 12 000 whales were caught there in the ten-year period 1927-1936 (Kleinenberg *et al.* 1969, p. 317).

Beluga populations in the Barents, White, Kara, and Laptev seas apparently have not been censused in the way those of the Okhotsk Sea have. A recent estimate of the total beluga population along the northern Eurasian coast is 1 500-3 000 (International Whaling Commission 1980, p. 120). Combining the Soviet catches reported for the Barents, White, and Kara seas, a total of more than 14 000 was taken in the 10 years 1957-1966 (Kleinenberg *et al.* 1969; Ivashin and Mineev 1981). In addition, Norwegian commercial whalers took 3 407 belugas in Svalbard waters during 1945-1960 (Lønø and Øynes 1961). Thus, the aggregate initial population in these seas may have been well over 15 000. The International Whaling Commission's Subcommittee on Small Cetaceans has expressed concern about the status of these stocks, noting that either recent catch levels are well above even the gross annual production or the current population estimates are too low (International Whaling Commission 1980, 1981).

VI. Special importance of the St. Lawrence population

The St. Lawrence beluga stock, when viewed in the context of the aggregate world beluga population, is numerically insignificant, representing less than 1 percent of the total. However, there are aspects of this small, relict population which make it special, if not unique:

a) Few other stocks of belugas are isolated to the same degree as the St. Lawrence stock. Although the possibility that some movement of whales into and out of the St. Lawrence through the Strait of Belle Isle occurred in the recent past, or even still occurs, cannot be discounted, there is no evidence for it. Some emigration from the St. Lawrence apparently occurs through Cabot Strait, but this very likely results in a net loss to the population as there is no evidence of immigration through Cabot Strait.

b) No human residents along the shores of this stock's range claim a historic or current need for exploiting these whales. Most other beluga stocks are hunted, at least seasonally, by Native people for subsistence. Since these people generally are viewed as having historic or traditional hunting rights, any attempt to limit or reduce the hunting mortality must take account of human needs as well as the health of the whale population. Of all beluga populations, that in the St. Lawrence should be one of the easiest to protect from direct exploitation.

c) The accessibility of belugas in the St. Lawrence for research and tourism is unmatched anywhere. It is not surprising that the important acoustic work of Schevill and Lawrence (1949) was accomplished in the lower Saguenay River, where in the late 1940s they found belugas "remarkably numerous".

d) As a relict population of an arctic and subarctic species living in a cold temperate environment, the St. Lawrence belugas would appear to be living "out of context". In most areas where they occur in large numbers, belugas are in close proximity to only one mysticete, the bowhead, *Balaena mysticetus*, and only one other odontocete, the narwhal, *Monodon monoceros*. In the St. Lawrence, they are part of a more diverse cetacean fauna which includes neither the bowhead nor the narwhal but which does include various mysticetes (fin, *Balaenoptera physalus*, blue, *B. musculus*, minke, *B. acutorostrata*, and humpback whales, *Megaptera novaeangliae*) and odontocetes (harbor porpoises, *Phocoena phocoena*, and Atlantic white-sided dolphins, *Lagenorhynchus acutus*, mainly). This feature of the St. Lawrence belugas makes them scientifically and aesthetically all the more interesting.

VII. Literature cited

AGUAYO L., A. *Smaller, Cetaceans in the Baltic Sea*, Report of the International Whaling Commission, n° of cat. 28 : 131-146, 1978.

BERZIN, A. A. *A Note on the Recent Distribution and Numbers of the White Whale in the Soviet Far East*, Report of the International Whaling Commission, n° of cat. 31 : 527-529, 1981.

BERZIN, A. A., VLADIMIROV, V. L. and DOROSHENKO, N. V. *Cetaceans in the Coastal Waters of the Okhotsk Sea : Results from Aerial Surveys*, Report of the International Whaling Commission, n° of cat. 36 : 395-398, 1986.

DIETZ, R., HEIDE-JØRGENSEN, M.-P. and BORN, E. W. *Havpattedyr i Østgrønland : en litteraturundersøgelse*, Report for Råstofforvaltningen for Grønland og Grønlands Fiskeri — og Miljøundersøgelser, by Danbiu ApS. (Biologiske Konsulenter), Henningsens Allé 58, DK-2900 Hellerup, 1985.

FINLEY, K.J., DAVIS, R.A. and SILVERMAN, H.B. *Aspects of the Narwhal Hunt in the Eastern Canadian Arctic*, Report of the International Whaling Commission, n° of cat. 30 : 459-464, 1980.

FINLEY, K. J., MILLER, G. W., ALLARD, M., DAVIS, R. A. and EVANS, C. R. *The Belugas (*Delphinapterus leucas*) of Northern Québec : Distribution, Abundance, Stock Identity, Catch History and Management*, Canadian Technical Report of Fisheries and Aquatic Sciences, n° 1123, 1982.

FRAKER, M. A. *Status and Harvest of the Mackenzie Stock of White Whales (*Delphinapterus leucas*)*, Report of the International Whaling Commission, n° of cat. 30 : 451-458, 1980.

FRASER, F. C. *Report on Cetacea Stranded on the British Coasts from 1948 to 1966*, British Museum (Natural History), n° 14, 1974.

HARRISON, C. S. and HALL, J. D. *Alaskan Distribution of the Beluga Whale*, Delphinapterus leucas, Canadian Field-Naturalist, n° of cat. 92(3) : 235-241, 1978.

HAZARD, K. "Beluga Whale *Delphinapterus leucas*", in *Selected Marine Mammals of Alaska, Species Accounts with Research and Management Recommendations*, Lentfer, J. W. (ed.), Washington, D. C. Marine Mammal Commission, pp. 195-235, 1988.

INTERNATIONAL WHALING COMMISSION. *Report of the Sub-committee on Small Cetaceans*, Report of the International Whaling Commission, n° of cat. 30 : 111-128, 1980.

INTERNATIONAL WHALING COMMISSION. *Report of the Sub-Committee on Small Cetaceans*, Report of the International Whaling Commission, n° of cat. 31 : 140-153, 1981.

IVASHIN, M. V. *USSR. Progress Report on Cetacean Research, June 1984 to May 1985*, Report of the International Whaling Commission, n° of cat. 36 : 179-182, 1986.

IVASHIN, M. V. and MINEEV, V. M. *Notes on the Distribution and Whaling for White Whales (*Delphinapterus leucas Pallas, *1776)*, Report of the International Whaling Commission, n° of cat. 31 : 589-590, 1981.

IVASHIN, M. V. and SHEVLYAGIN, K. V. *The White Whale (*Delphinapterus leucas Pallas, *1776) : Entrapment and Escape in the Ice of Senjavin Strait,*

USSR, Report of the International Whaling Commission, n° of cat. 37 : 357-359, 1987.

JENSEN, B., KINZE, C. Chr. and SØRENSEN, T. B. *Observations of White Whale (*Delphinapterus leucas*) in Danish Waters during 1983 and 1984*, Natura Jutlandica, n° of cat. 22(4) : 85-88, 1987.

KASUYA, T., TOBAYAMA, T. and MATSUI, S. *Review of the Live-Capture of Small Cetaceans in Japan*, Report of the International Whaling Commission, n° of cat. 34 : 597-602, 1984.

KLEINENBERG, S. E., YABLOKOV, A. V., BEL'KOVICH, B. M. and TARASEVICH, M. N. *Beluga (*Delphinapterus leucas*) Investigation of the Species*, translated from Russian, originally published 1964, Jerusalem, Israel Program for Scientific Translations, 1969.

LØNØ, O. and ØYNES, P. *White Whale Fishery at Spitzbergen*, Norsk Hvalfangst-tidende, n° of cat. 50(7) : 267-287, 1961.

LOWRY, L. F., BURNS, J. J and FROST, K. J. *Recent Harvests of Belukha Whales in Western and Northern Alaska and Their Potential Impact on Provisional Management Stocks*, Report of the International Whaling Commission, n° 39, in press.

MITCHELL, E. and REEVES, R. R. *Catch History and Cumulative Catch Estimates of Initial Population Size of Cetaceans in the Eastern Canadian Arctic*, Report of the International Whaling Commission, n° of cat. 31 : 645-682, 1981.

NISHIWAKI, M. *Distribution and Migration of Marine Mammals in the North Pacific Area*, 11th Pacific Science Congress, Symposium n° 4, 1966, 49 p.

REEVES, R. R. and KATONA, S. K. *Extralimital Records of White Whales (*Delphinapterus leucas*) in Eastern North American Waters*, Canadian Field-Naturalist, n° of cat. 94(3) : 239-247, 1980.

REEVES, R. R. and MITCHELL, E. *Catch History and Initial Population of White Whales (*Delphinapterus leucas*) in the River and Gulf of St. Lawrence*, Naturaliste canadien, n° of cat. 111 : 63-121, 1984.

REEVES, R. R. and MITCHELL, E. *History of White Whale (*Delphinapterus leucas*) Exploitation in Eastern Hudson Bay and James Bay*, Canadian Special Publication of Fisheries and Aquatic Sciences, n° 95, 1987a.

REEVES, R. R. and MITCHELL, E. *Catch History, Former Abundance, and Distribution of White Whales in Hudson Strait and Ungava Bay*, Naturaliste canadien, n° of cat. 114 : 1-65, 1987b.

REEVES, R. R. and MITCHELL, E. *Distribution and Migration, Exploitation, and Former Abundance of White Whales (*Delphinapterus leucas*) in Baffin Bay and Adjacent Waters*, Canadian Special Publication of Fisheries and Aquatic Sciences, n° 99, 1987c.

RICHARD, P. R. and ORR, J. R. *A Review of the Status and Harvest of White Whales (*Delphinapterus leucas*) in the Cumberland Sound Area, Baffin Island*, Canadian Technical Report of Fisheries and Aquatic Sciences, n° 1447, 1986.

SAEMUNDSSON, B. *Mammalia*, Zoology of Iceland, n° IV(76), 1939.

SCHEVILL, W. E. and LAWRENCE, B. *Underwater Listening to the White Porpoise (*Delphinapterus leucas*)*, Science, n° of cat. 109 : 143-144, 1949.

SEAMAN, G. A. and BURNS, J. J. *Preliminary Results of Recent Studies of Belukhas in Alaskan Waters*, Report of the International Whaling Commission, n° of cat. 31 : 567-574, 1981.

SERGEANT, D. E. *An Update of the Status of White Whales (*Delphinapterus leucas*) in the St. Lawrence Estuary, Canada*, Biological Conservation, n° of cat. 45 : 287-302, 1988.

SERGEANT, D. E. and BRODIE, P. F. *Body Size in White Whales (*Delphinapterus leucas*)* Journal of the Fisheries Research Board of Canada, n° of cat. 26 : 2561-2580, 1969.

SLIJPER, E. J. *White Whales in Netherlands Waters*, Sonderdruck aus Z. f. Saugetierkunde, n° of cat. 32(2) : 86-89, 1967.

SMITH, T. G. and HAMMILL, M. O. *Population Estimates of White Whales,* Delphinapterus leucas, *in James Bay, Eastern Hudson Bay, and Ungava Bay*, Canadian Journal of Fisheries and Aquatic Sciences, n° of cat. 43(10) : 1982-1987, 1986.

SMITH, T. G., HAMMILL, M. O., BURRAGE, D. J. and SLENO, G. A. *Distribution and Abundance of Belugas,* Delphinapterus leucas, *and Narwhals,* Monodon monoceros, *in the Canadian High Arctic*, Canadian Journal of Fisheries and Aquatic Sciences, n° of cat. 42(4) : 676-684, 1985.

An Update of the Status of White Whales *Delphinapterus leucas* in the St. Lawrence Estuary, Canada

D. E. Sergeant and W. Hoek
Department of Fisheries and Oceans Canada

INTRODUCTION

A population of white whales *Delphinapterus leucas* Pallas lives isolated geographically from other more northern populations in the middle estuary of the St. Lawrence River (Vladykov, 1944). Its present distribution from May to November lies between about 47° 30′ to 48° 20′N, and 69° 15′ to 70°W with a seaward extension in winter to the outer Gaspé coast (Figure 1). This population is very accessible to observers on both sides of the estuary, a region of small towns, villages and summer homes. It tolerates ship traffic of c.1 passage h^{-1} along the St. Lawrence Seaway in all months, together with passage of small craft including motor boats and sailboats in summer. In the last decade, tourist viewing of cetaceans has developed in the most upstream section of the Laurentian Channel by small craft working mainly out of Tadoussac (Figure 1), and this activity impinges on the seaward part of the present range of the white whale population. Since this population is known to have declined greatly from historic levels (Laurin, 1982a; Reeves and Mitchell, 1984), it was important when intensive research began in 1982 to assess its present level and trend in numbers and its reproductive and mortality rates. An earlier paper on the biology (Sergeant, 1986) included these topics. This paper includes two new surveys (one of total population and one of reproductive rate) and reassesses an older (1973) survey. It therefore amplifies and updates the older paper, and also summarizes conservation measures achieved and remaining problems perceived at time of writing.

FIGURE 1

Map of middle St. Lawrence estuary with place names and (inset) the lower Great Lakes-St. Lawrence system

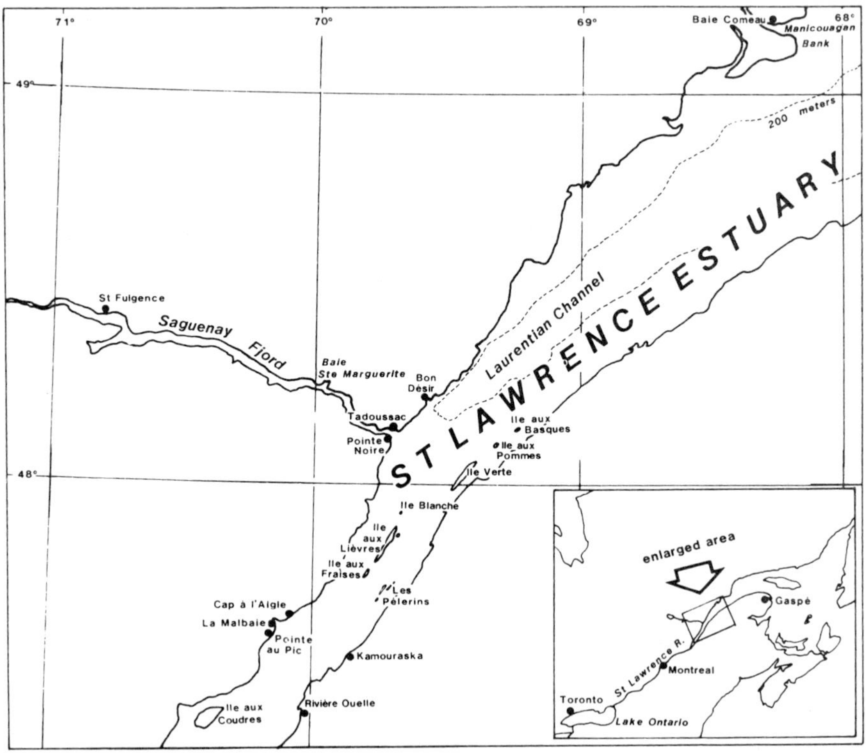

HISTORY OF EXPLOITATION

Commercial trapping of white whales occurred in shallow water in the upstream area of the former distribution, at Île aux Coudres on the north shore and Rivière-Ouelle on the south, until the animals were extirpated from this region in about the late 1920s (Reeves and Mitchell, 1984). At the population's seaward limit on the north shore, around the Manicouagan Peninsula, again in shallow water, commercial hunting was intensive during the 1930s, and a sample of 161 animals coming mainly from this region was examined by Vladykov (1944) in 1938 and 1939. The part of the population that inhabited this area in summer was apparently extirpated by about 1964, according to Laurin (1982b) obtained information that at least one scarred animal returned annually in summer to Manicouagan Bank. In the area presently inhabited by white whales in summer the water is relatively deep, and it is probable that the success rate of hunting was not as high as hunting or trapping in shallow water, as Andrew's observations (1916) at Île aux Pommes in June 1909 suggest. Catch statistics (Figure 2) from Laurin (1982a), show a sharp reduction in catches through the late 1930s, 1940s and 1950s with catches ceasing about 1960. Although this evidence does not necessarily imply a reduction in numbers, impressions of numbers and density at various dates imply that the population shrank in parallel with the catches. Thus Howell (1935), describing a single day's boat trip between Saint-Siméon and Tadoussac and return in 1934, estimated the numbers seen as at least 800 with many more beyond his field of vision, and "the number of whales such that one was reminded of whitecaps, particularly well defined [under calm conditions] and somewhat less numerous than whitecaps would ordinarily appear". The same metaphor was used by two informants, Mrs. M. Elliott and Mrs. H. D. Morrison (personal communication), who lived in summer homes in the 1930s on the coast near La Malbaie. Since 1960, when we first started observing white whales in the St. Lawrence, one could not gain such impressions of widespread density of animals. During the 1970s, sport hunting of white whales continued in the region of Tadoussac (Pippard & Malcolm, 1978; Figure 3) but was becoming socially unacceptable by the end of the decade. With increasing summer tourism and interest in the white whales and other cetaceans through the 1970s and 1980s, former hunters could become tourist guides in the Tadoussac to Escoumins area.

FIGURE 2

Catch history of the St. Lawrence white whales, from Laurin (1982)

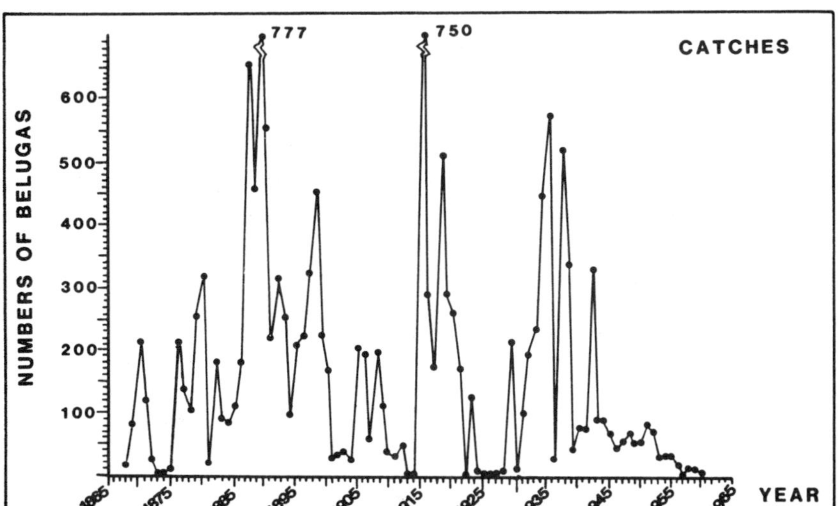

FIGURE 3

Two adult male white whales landed by sport hunters at Tadoussac in summer, 1962. (From colour slide, courtesy Mr and Mrs H. D. Morrison.)

DISTRIBUTION

The present distribution of white whales in spring to autumn is restricted to about a 100-km length of the St. Lawrence estuary with occasional excursions upstream and downstream. In winter it extends downstream to the corner of the Gaspé peninsula (Sergeant, 1986), which may provide the needed foraging area during a period of partial ice cover. Since the St. Lawrence River current on the south shore, combined with intense water mixing in the estuary, provides the east- and south-setting Gaspé current, animals so displaced are ready candidates for transport southward, which Sergeant and Brodie (1969) and Sergeant (1986) showed to take place mainly in spring and early summer. White whales occur south to the Bay of Fundy and even to New Jersey (Reeves and Katona, 1980), and apparently do not return north. Most probably come from the St. Lawrence, since animals were reported at the intermediate sites of Prince Edward Island and Nova Scotia. This emigration cannot be quantified but might involve some one to three animals a year, judging from the frequency of extralimital records. Within the smaller summering region the population is heterogeneously distributed (Sergeant, 1986). Our aerial surveys as well as shore-based observations from Pointe-Noire, Baie-Sainte-Marguerite and southwest Île aux Lièvres (Figure 1) have shown that calves occur in the main St. Lawrence around Île aux Lièvres over about three-quarters of the summering range (Figure 4). In the northeast sector of this range over the deep water of the Laurentian Channel calves are absent and a compact herd of 100-200 animals is repeatedly seen, largely made up of white adults. These include the largest animals, which must be males because of the known sexual dimorphism of the species. This readily identifiable herd undergoes only small displacements (Figure 4). In between, groups of white and grey animals with very few (1%) young calves move in and out of the Saguenay fjord for residence times of hours, days, or weeks. Two young calves were identifiable in a photograph of a group of 30 animals in Baie-Sainte-Marguerite on August 3, 1984; a group of this size was present here on most days in July 1985. Less is known about a group reported to occur at times in summer at Saint-Fulgence at the head of the northeast arm of the Saguenay (Figure 1). Here the freshwater discharge from the Saguenay River, as well as the shallow coast, provides conditions similar to those observed at Baie-Sainte-Marguerite which may attract the animals.

FIGURE 4

Distribution of animals with calves and adult herd in the St. Lawrence estuary from survey data 1982-86

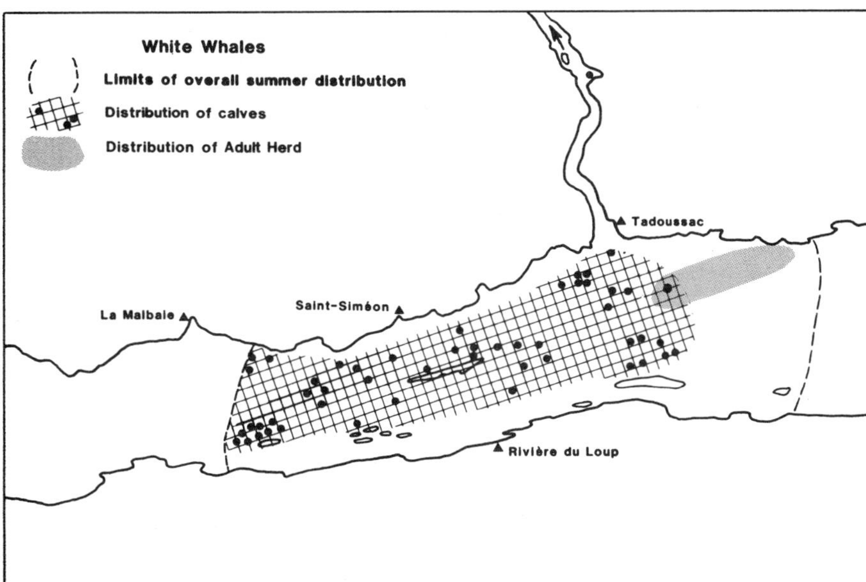

CONSERVATION

In 1979 the Canadian government prohibited hunting of this population "Beluga Protection Regulations under the Fisheries Act", PC 1980-2939, in *Canada Gazette II*, 114 (21), p. 3445 SDR/80-835, 12 November 1980. The now well-developed whale-watching industry in the St. Lawrence estuary is centred at Tadoussac and the two nearest downstream settlements of Grandes Bergeronnes and Les Escoumins. Most visitors wish to see the large cetaceans (finback, minke and blue whales) which inhabit the water over the Laurentian Channel (Figure 1), in which lives the adult herd of white whales (Figure 4) ; therefore, little disturbance is provided to the upstream, reproductive animals. Nevertheless, regulations by the Department of Fisheries and Oceans now prohibit even approach to white whales. (Other species may be approached at low speed).

By 1986, all island groups in the middle estuary were under the control of conservation organizations, either governmental or private (in one case a sympathetic family ownership), which has prevented developments which might have increased small craft traffic.

CURRENT ESTIMATE OF ABUNDANCE AND REPRODUCTIVE RATE

Materials and methods

Census details

In 1973, three reconnaissances of white whale distribution in the St. Lawrence estuary were run from fixed-wing aircraft, in May, July and September. A fourth, in February 1974, was unsuccessful due to "frost smoke" caused by intense cold. In the first survey only fifty 20 cm × 20 cm black and white photographs were taken at a scale of 1 : 6 000 in the area of distribution, and this area was surveyed (Figure 5A), allowing an approximate estimate of numbers by multiplication of area and mean density (Table 2).

In 1982, two observers conducted a stratified survey from a helicopter at 305 m (Sergeant, 1986). Randomly arranged transects, each 0.8 km wide, running perpendicular to the long axis of the estuary, were spaced between 1.6 and 14.5 km apart in the central stratum (Figure 5B) ; no animals were seen in either the upstream or downstream strata which were surveyed in the same way at less frequent intervals. In this survey no allowance could be made for whales which were diving sufficiently deep to be invisible. However, each observer looking forward could view animals for about one minute before they passed under him and were lost to view, allowing him to obtain the highest estimate within a group.

Observers on both sides of the aircraft obtained comparable counts, thus no correction was made for the fact that the second observer was in the back seat with an, apparently, less favourable field or view.

In 1984, an aerial photographic survey was run over the known area of white whale distribution using a two-engined, fixed-wing aircraft equipped with a Wild RC-8 camera (Figure 5C). The film used was Kodak double-X aerographic 2405 (estarbase), yielding rolls of positive transparencies, which were viewed over a light table equipped with rollers to feed the film back and forth. In this survey, 7 transect lines were run spaced evenly apart along the axis of the estuary at a scale of 1 : 6 000. These lines covered some 0.367 of the area of the estuary inhabited by white whales. The lines were repeated at a scale of 1 : 2 000 (and therefore covered only one-ninth of the previously surveyed area) in order to attempt to measure the ratio of calves to total animals.

In 1985, a similar survey, stratified on the basis of previous surveys, was made at a scale of 1 : 6 000 (Figure 5D). Lines in the dense stratum covered c.0.66 of the total surveyed area at a calculated coverage of 0.88.

FIGURE 5

Detail of surveys of white whales in the estuary of the St. Lawrence in A, 1973; B, 1982; C, 1984; D, 1985

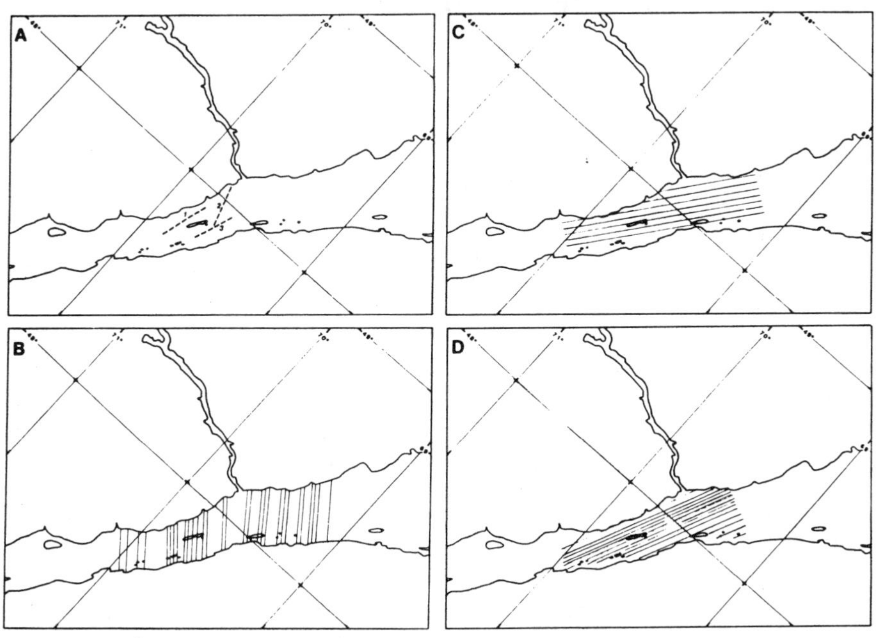

However, the desired precision of navigation was not achieved, probably owing to local anomalies in the Loran-C velocities over land in the vicinity of the estuary (Anon., 1986). This error is potentially serious since it could have led to duplication of counting of animals (once, two neighbouring lines showing many animals converged slightly) and thus could have led to overestimates of density. Lack of seaward landmarks for repositioning the lines in question did not allow correction of this error, but comparison of estimates of the ratio of the adult herd to total estimated numbers of animals in 1984 and 1985 (see below) suggested that the error was not large. These navigational problems limit the use of intensive aerial survey for population estimates of this herd.

The lower altitude survey of 1984 at a scale of 1 : 2 000 produced only 30 animals in 598 photos, so that the low population density of the animals limits the use of this type of survey for calculating the number of calves, or typing the animals by size.

In 1982 the lower part, and in 1984 the whole, of the Saguenay (with the exception of the extreme northwest arm) were surveyed; 30 animals were observed in Baie-Sainte-Marguerite in 1984. In 1985 the Saguenay was not surveyed but independent, shore- or water-based estimates near date of survey suggested an addition of only about 10 animals.

Correction factor for invisible animals

In a photographic survey, with exposure time of 1/250 s, correction was needed for diving animals. The depth to invisibility varied greatly, from very turbid water in the south channel of the St. Lawrence, and peat-stained water in the Saguenay outflow at low tide, to relatively clear, intensively mixing oceanic water in the northeast zone of the surveys.

Estimates of diving times of groups of whales, measured from a boat in early August 1984, averaged about 1.5 min, and 0.5 of observed time. However, these estimates not only had high variances but bore no necessary relation to the visibility of animals as seen from an aircraft. An empirical correction was developed using the overlap of adjacent photos, which varied from about 0.15 to 0.25 of photographed area in 1984 and 1985 surveys. In some photos, single whales or groups occurred in the overlapping area. Numbers of whales were summed for such overlapping pairs, and the mean number compared with the greater of the two numbers. (If unique animals were seen in the smaller of the two counts, they were added to the greater.) The ratio gives a minimal correction for diving animals, minimal because some animals may still have been invisible in both photographs. Since photo pairs occurred randomly with respect to water clarity, the correction is an average for the whole

TABLE 1

Correction of Photographic Population Estimates for Diving, Invisible Whales using Overlapping Photos

Year	Number of photos	Number of animals				Ratio
		Lesser	Greater	Mean	Adjusted greater[a]	Adj. greater / Mean
1984	2 x 7	22	25	23.5	27	$\frac{27}{23.5} = 1.15$
1985	2 x 11	21	32	26.5	32	$\frac{32}{26.5} = 1.21$
Mean						1.18

[a] Adding individuals seen only in lower count.

survey. Estimated numbers were multiplied by this ratio which had a mean value of 1.18 for 1984 and 1985 combined (Table 1).

Calculation of estimates of abundance

After addition of calculated, invisible animals, the estimated area of coverage was calculated and, planimetrically, the whole area covered by the survey. Error estimates were calculated by the methods of Smith *et al.* (1985).

Estimates of calf ratio

The peak period of births of white whales in the St. Lawrence is June and July and about 95% of births probably take place between May and August inclusive (Sergeant, 1986). Calf counts were made in August or September. Since high-altitude (1: 6000) photos did not reliably show all calves, which frequently keep very close to the mother, and since low-altitude (1 : 2000) photos taken on a systematic basis did not give a large enough sample size, it was necessary to make a selective survey of groups of whales using a helicopter. This was done from an altitude of 255 m in August 1983 visually; but a visual estimate of numbers of calves lacked precision and a permanent record. In September 1986, 70-mm colour transparencies (Kodak Ektachrome, 64 ASA) were taken at 305 m (scale 1: 1800) at about 1/500 s from a Bell 206-C helicopter. Whale numbers and those of calves were tallied from the transparencies using a microfiche reader (Minolta RP 407A).

Disturbance by the helicopter at 305 m caused some animals to dive, which might have been avoided by photography at 457 m since imagery was good. This disturbance was more of a bias against females and calves since they were in small groups which could submerge completely and be missed, while larger groups (usually not containing calves) left some individuals at the surface and therefore still gave a result.

This method has one other potential bias. Photography of reproductive and nonreproductive groups should be in proportion to abundance but this sampling can only be achieved in a subjective way. We were only able to check the accuracy of results by one independent method. This was to use ground-level counts of the ratio of calves to total animals made at Ile aux Lièvres in July 1984, as representative of the reproductive component of the population and then to multiply this figure by the ratio of reproductive component to total population, as determined from the high-level photographic counts of 1984 and 1985, in order to correct for the known heterogeneity of the population with its large, practically nonreproducing, adult herd. (Animals moving up and down

TABLE 2

Results of Aerial Surveys of White Whales, 1973 to 1985

Year	Method	No. of animals observed	Proportion of selected area surveyed	Corrected estimate	95 % Confidence limit	Area inhabited (km^2)
1973	Photo (sample)	43	0.083	443[b]	229-658	1007.4
1982	Visual	143	0.279	512[c]	360-715	1275
1984	Photo	135	0.39	431[b]	187-773	1919.3
1985	Photo	379	(0.852)[a] (0.385)	530[b]	285-775	1696.8
Mean						488

[a] Two strata
[b] Corrected for diving
[c] Uncorrected

the Saguenay were classified as nonreproducing, but were not usually seen in systematic surveys.)

RESULTS

Total numbers

Results of all four surveys in 1973, 1982, 1984 and 1985 are given in Table 2 and show a population of about 500 animals.

Corrections for diving were applied for all surveys except the visual survey of 1982. Confidence limits were narrowest for the 1982 estimate with its frequent random, transverse lines. (The abandonment of this system in 1984 and 1985 was due to its inconvenience for photography, when the approach to each line must be carefully made, and is time-consuming.)

The means of the estimates do not suggest any detectable change in abundance of animals in the thirteenth year period, and this conclusion is reinforced by the similarity in the inhabited area throughout. This parameter, however, is very imprecise, since a few animals at its periphery may greatly enlarge its value. For this reason it was probably underestimated in the rather superficial survey of 1973.

Calves

On August 4, 1983, a visual estimate of calves was 14/169 or 0.083 but confusion certainly occurred between 0- and 1-year animals. On September 15-17, 1986, a photographic estimate gave 12/216 or 0.055 calves.

In July 1983, the percentage of calves at southwest Île aux Lièvres was 0.09. In August 1984, the adult herd (without calves) represented 0.433 of the total and in September 1985, 0.467, with some risk of duplication. Using the lower figure, the reproductive portion of the population is 0.567, giving 0.051 calves, which is close to the direct estimate.

Dynamics of the population

The reproductive rate measured is half or less than that estimated for Arctic animals using similar direct counts (generally 0.10-0.16, Sergeant, 1986). Stability of the population would be achieved if reproduction plus immigration equalled deaths plus emigration. The number of annual births can be calculated as 0.051-0.055 × 500 = 25-27. Immigration cannot accurately be estimated, since the coasts north of the

St. Lawrence are not heavily peopled, but may be very low since the next northern population of white whales, that occurring in Ungava Bay, is now heavily depleted (Smith and Hammill, 1986). Deaths were chronicled over a period of three years of intensive study in 1983-85 by Drs. Daniel Martineau and Pierre Béland (personal communication) using a network of observers, and varied from 8 to 15 per annum with a mean of about 12. This figure excluded the winter months of December to March when shores were ice-bound. Sergeant (1986) showed that, as observations of dead animals became more intensive, a former summer peak tended to disappear, suggesting that it was not real but due to greater frequency of summer observations. Therefore one may assume equal probability of deaths in all months, which would give a year-long estimate of 12/0.8 or about 15 per annum. If losses due to emigration are about 2 per year, we have 17 animals lost as compared with 25 gained. Thus, either unobserved deaths are about 8 in number (c 0.33 of total) or if fewer, the population is slowly increasing.

ROLE OF ORGANOCHLORINES

Organochlorine pollutants are highly suspect as the source of the abnormally low reproductive rate of this population. An alternative possible effect, a high level of neonatal deaths, has not been observed among dead animals (Sergeant, 1986). Evidence is as follows: 1) very high levels of both DDTs and PCBs have been observed among dead animals collected (Sergeant, 1980; Martineau *et al.*, 1987). Highest levels were found in an approximately six-month-old calf, of body length 188 cm, found floating dead at Bon-Désir in late January 1971; this proved to show 827 ppm of EDDT in wet weight of blubber, 800 ppm of PCBs. Highest levels could, however, be expected in a suckling calf. Although PCB and DDT levels increased with age in both sexes, levels were lower in adult females than adult males, doubtless due to its transfer from the mother to the calf in the milk (Martineau *et al.*, 1987). 2) An experiment feeding diets with higher and lower levels of PCBs, but without differences in other contaminants, to harbour seals (Phoca vitulina) was reported by Reijnders (1986); reproduction was inhibited in the experimental group but was normal in the control group. In mink (Mustela vison), fish diets high in PCBs were shown to inhibit implantation of the embryo (Aulerich *et al.*, 1973). Ovulation rates in adult female white whales from the St. Lawrence were found to be normal (Sergeant, 1986) but nothing further is yet known of reproductive rates from this sample, since numbers of adult females found dead are not yet enough for an estimate to be made of pregnancy rate, and many dead animals are in any case old, which could bias the pregnancy rate downward (Sergeant, 1986). However, the most likely interpretation of events is that PCBs, or a component of them, have reduced implantation success or have proved toxic to the fœtus at some stage.

Massé *et al.* (1986) note the presence of polycyclic aromatic hydrocarbons (PAHs) in the Saguenay as a possible additional source of contamination to the white whales. These substances apparently occur also in the St. Lawrence River, and PCBs in the Saguenay (M. Gilbertson, personal communication).

As to the time curve of PCB pollution in the Great Lakes-St. Lawrence system, Norstrom *et al.* (1985) found high levels (c. 150 ppm) of PCBs in the eggs of herring gulls (*Larus argentatus*) in 1971-72, declining to about 75 ppm by 1977 but showing no further decline to 1982. Durham and Oliver (1983), using sediments dated by 210Pb and taken from Lake Ontario just below the outfall of the Niagara River (a known source of PCBs), found that PCBs increased rapidly in 1960-1962 and declined steadily through the late 1960s, reaching a plateau (at about one-third peak values) through the 1970s. Nicholson (1986) reports PCB values in lake trout (*Salvelinus namaycush*) from Lake Ontario to have increased from 1981 to 1983, though such increases were not seen in a small forage fish, smelt (*Osmerus mordax*).

Many uncertainties remain, such as physiological effects of PCBs and other contaminants in white whales, and relative inputs of pollutants from the Great Lakes, the St. Lawrence River, the Saguenay and the estuary itself (where a spillage of PCBs was recorded in 1984 from the Baie-Comeau area). Decreases of PCBs in the 1970s have not been maintained and further stringent efforts at cleanup are required.

The metabolic route of inputs to the white whales could be by such food species as herring (*Clupea harengus*), which supports a commercial fishery at L'Île-Verte within the predator's range. Khalil *et al.* (1985) reported levels of DDT of the order 100-1 000 ug kg -1 in lipid, 10-100 ug kg -l in fresh tissue, from muscle of these adult herring. PCBs were not reported on, but M. F. Khalil (personal communication) gives 20-200 ug kg -1 PCB in wet weight of muscle, increasing from the lower to the higher level with age of fish.

Time lags in the uptake and transfer of pollutants in the physical system and food chain include time for downstream transport (≤ 1 year), and growth rate of biological components (*e.g.* 3 years to maturity in a herring; about six years in a white whale (Sergeant, 1973 ; Goren *et al.*, 1987)). Thus the lag from peak of pollution in Lake Ontario to peak effect on reproduction of white whales is, in all, about ten years.

A recent advance in reduction of pollutants from the Great Lakes-St. Lawrence system (press release February 1987) is an agreement by Canada, the USA, Ontario and New York to reduce levels of pollutants in the Niagara River and to remove dumps of toxic materials near its banks.

ACKNOWLEDGEMENTS

We acknowledge gratefully Didier Marchessaux, Michel Verburg, Marie-Thérèse Voutsinos, Johanne Ouellet, Selma Low and Monica Borobia who helped in collection and analysis of data; and Jean Laurin, Leone Pippard, Pierre Béland and Daniel Martineau, who may not necessarily agree with our conclusions but whose discussions and publications greatly aided this synthesis. Jean Boulva and Arthur Mansfield helped realization of the work program. Jean Bédard, William Doidge, Michael Gilbertson, Keith Hay, Austin Reed, Randall Reeves, and Thomas Smith provided additional data, advice or review.

REFERENCES

ANDREWS, R. C. *Whale Hunting with Gun and Camera*, London, D. Appleton and Co. New York, 1916.

ANON. *Canadian Coast Guard Radio Aids to Marine Navigation (Atlantic and Great Lakes)*, 1 April, 1986, TP 146E, vol. 31, n° 1EE.

AULERICH, R. J., RINGER, R. K. and IWAMOTO, S. *Reproductive Failure and Mortality in Mink Fed on Great Lakes Fish*. J. Reprod. Fert., suppl. 19, n° of cat. 365-76, 1973.

DURHAM, R. W. and OLIVER, B. G. *History of Lake Ontario Contamination from the Niagara River by Sediment Radiodating, and Chlorinated Hydrocarbon Analysis*, J. Great Lakes Res., n° of cat. 9: 160-8, 1983.

GOREN, A. D., BRODIE, P. F., SPOTTE, S., RAY, G. C., KAUFMAN, H., GWINNET, A., SCIUBBA, J. and BUCK, J. D. *Growth Layer Groups in the Teeth of an Adult belukha Whale Delphinapterus leucas of Known Age*, Evidence for two annual layers, Mar. Mamm. Sci., n° of cat. 3: 14-21, 1987.

HOWELL, A. B. *Observations on the White Whale*, J. Mammal., n° of cat. 16: 155-6, 1935.

KHALIL, M. F., LABBÉ, J., HORTH, A. C. and ARNAC, M. *Chlorinated Hydrocarbons: Pollutants or Indicators of Fish Stock Structure*, Int. J. Environ. Anal. Chem., n° of cat. 21: 105-14, 1985.

LAURIN, J. *La chasse au béluga Delphinapterus leucas du Saint-Laurent et statut actuel de la population*, Québec, Société de zoologie, Carnets de zoologie, n° of cat. 42: 23-27, 1982a.

MARTINEAU, D., BÉLAND, P., DESJARDINS, C. and LAGACÉ, A. *Levels of Organochlorine Chemicals in Tissues of Beluga Whales Delphinapterus leucas from the St. Lawrence Estuary, Québec, Canada*, Arch. environ. Contam. Toxicol., n° of cat. 16: 137-47, 1987.

MASSÉ, R., MARTINEAU, D., TREMBLAY, L. and BÉLAND, P. *Concentrations and Chromatographic Profile of DDT Metabolites and Polychlorobiphenyl (PCB) Residues in Stranded Beluga Whales Delphinapterus leucas from the St. Lawrence Estuary, Canada*, Arch. environ. Contam. Toxicol., n° of cat. 15: 567-79, 1986.

NICHOLSON, H. F. (ed.). *Progress Report of the Great Lakes Fisheries Research Branch for 1983*, Canadian Technical Report of Fisheries and Aquatic Sciences, n° 1495, 1986.

NORSTROM, R. J., CLARK, T. P. and WESELOH, D. "Great Lakes Monitoring Using Herring Gulls", *in Hazardous Contaminants in Ontario: Urban and Environmental Effects*, Hutchinson T. C. (ed.) and Evans, S. M., Toronto, Institute of Environmental Studies, University of Toronto, 1985, pp. 86-93.

PIPPARD, L. and MALCOLM, H. *White Whales Delphinapterus leucas, Observations on Their Distribution, Population and Critical Habitats in the St. Lawrence and Saguenay Rivers*, Department of Indian and Northern Affairs, Canadian Parks Services, Project C1632, Contract 76-190, 1978, (mimeographed).

REEVES, R. R. and KATONA, S. K. *Extralimital Records of White Whales Delphinapterus leucas in Eastern North American Waters*, Canadian Field Naturalist, n° of cat. 94 : 239-47, 1980.

REEVES, R. R. and MITCHELL, E. *Catch History and Initial Population of White Whales Delphinapterus leucas in the River and Gulf of St. Lawrence, Eastern Canada*, Naturaliste Canadien (Rev. Ecol. Syst.), n° of cat. 111 : 63-121, 1984.

REIJNDERS, P. J. H. *Reproductive Failure in Common Seals Feeding on Fish from Polluted Coastal Waters*, London Nature, n° of cat. 324 : 456-57, 1986.

SERGEANT, D. E. *Biology of White Whales Delphinapterus leucas in Western Hudson Bay*, Journal of Fisheries Research Board of Canada, n° of cat. 30 : 1065-90, 1973.

SERGEANT, D. E. *Levels of Mercury and Organochlorine Residues in Tissues of Sea Mammals from the St. Lawrence Estuary*, Int. Council Explor. Sea, Marine Env. Quality Committee, CM 1980/E55, 1980, (mimeographed).

SERGEANT, D. E. *Present Status of White Whales Delphinapterus leucas in the St. Lawrence Estuary*, Naturaliste Canadien (Rev. Ecol. Syst.), n° of cat. 113 : 61-81, 1986.

SERGEANT, D. E. and BRODIE, P. F. *Body Size in White Whales, Delphinapterus leucas, Journal of Fisheries*, Research Board of Canada, n° of cat. 26 : 2561-80, 1969.

SMITH, T. G. and HAMMILL, M. O. *Population Estimates of White Whale, Delphinapterus leucas in James Bay, Eastern Hudson Bay and Ungava Bay*, Canadian Journal of Fisheries and Aquatic Sciences, n° of cat. 43 : 1982-7, 1986.

SMITH, T. G., HAMMILL, M. O., BURRAGE, D. J. and SLENO, G. A. *Distribution and Abundance of Belugas, Delphinapterus leucas, and Narwhals, Monodon monoceros, in the Canadian High Arctic*, Canadian Journal of Fisheries and Aquatic Sciences, n° of cat. 42 : 676-84, 1985.

VLADYKOV, V. D. *Chasse, biologie et valeur économique du marsouin blanc ou béluga Delphinapterus leucas du fleuve et du golfe Saint-Laurent*, Québec, Département des Pêcheries, 1944.

Counting Whales

Michael C. S. Kingsley
Fisheries and Oceans Canada

Population estimation is a central occupation of natural resource managers. It is at once the measure of the success of previous policies and the source of future decisions. It is a branch of natural resource science in which the mathematical techniques are carefully scrutinized and hotly disputed. Resource managers may say there are fewer, while resource users contend there are more, while ecology advocates insist that the population, or the entire species, is disappearing fast.

Whales offer a difficult problem to the survey scientist, as they inhabit remote and widespread areas and are mobile in three dimensions. Three methods have been found most useful: they are area survey, mark-recapture, and migration counts. This last method has been used for populations such as the western Arctic bowhead, which travels a well-defined migration route every year and passes by a headland, in this case Point Barrow, from which it can be conveniently counted.

Surveys by area are not population-directed; they are instead directed to the estimation of the density of animals in a given area. If they are sample surveys, the sample is not taken from a population of animals, but from a "population" of square miles. This given, area surveys are most useful in three circumstances: where there is a firm association between a population of interest and an area surveyed, so that the density of the species in the area is a measure of population size; where the area itself, and the use made of it by one species or another, is of prime interest, as in impact assessment studies; and where the species studied is widespread and sedentary, so that there is no true population, but the numbers of animals must be expressed as densities.

Area search methods require that the individual must be detectable, at least under certain definable conditions, if it is within a survey unit. Strip or quadrat methods assume that the probability of detection is the same for all individuals within a survey unit, and tend therefore to be mathematically simple. Line transect methods do not make this assumption, but suppose that the probability of detection depends on where in the survey unit the individual is. This makes them mathematically complex, and they are useful in cases where individuals are so sparsely distributed that all observations must be used.

Some of the practical problems of area survey for whales are caused by the size and remoteness of the areas to be surveyed; others are associated with the requirement that an individual should be detected if it is present, and refinement of survey technique has centred on this problem.

Persistent searching of survey units has been recommended for moose and other ungulates, but is inappropriate for surveys for whales in open water, where the dictates of transportation, the unmarkability of survey quadrats, and the mobility of the subjects require that survey units be linear.

Photographic surveys are expensive, but have compensating advantages. In all surveys where comparisons have been made, photographic surveys have produced higher counts than visual, and photo counts can be checked and recounted to ensure accuracy. Camera surveys are also robust against widely varying densities of individuals, which can overload visual observers. Studies have shown that visual observers tend to underestimate seriously when densities are high or groups large. If flying photographic surveys, it makes sense to fly with the widest possible film, and good results have been obtained using Wild RC series mapping cameras, which use 9-inch film. Photographed from 3 000 feet with a 6-inch lens, a 3.9-metre beluga produces a 0.62-mm image, which is large enough to be counted under a dissecting microscope. However, a 1.2 metre calf produces only a 0.21 mm image, which is at the limit of recognizability. Kodak Aerographic colour negative film and colour positive film have both been used; the processed roll film is counted on a light table with the aid of a dissecting microscope.

Photographic surveys can provide much additional information beyond simple counts of numbers such as length structure of populations and information on behaviour, movements, and habitat use.

In aerial photographic (strip transect) surveys, detection problems are caused by sun glare, rough water, turbidity, and the diving behaviour of the species. Sun glare and the screening of beluga by rough water can both be controlled by careful selection of the conditions under which surveys are flown : a sea state corresponding to winds of Beaufort force 3 or less is taken as an operational standard by experienced survey practitioners for visual surveys of whales in the western Arctic. A polarizing filter might be used in an attempt to reduce glare, but this has not so far been tried on mapping cameras, and would have its own costs in increasing exposure time and image motion. The effect of glare on counts can be controlled by removing the affected areas from the frames when they are being interpreted. The invisibility of submerged whales is so far an intractable problem. Even on the basis of the simplest model that whales are either on the surface and visible, or deep down and invisible, and spend little time shallowly submerged, and that they dive only to feed, the correction factor for submerged animals is likely to vary with the time of year and the time of day, the state of the tide and the weather, and, probably, with both short-term and long-term changes in the prey base and the whale population. Clifftop and aerial behavioural work on narwhal has indicated that correction factors may not be very large: of the order of 20-30%. Behavioural studies, by both direct observation and radiotagging with sophisticated tags, may provide answers. Information on water clarity is also necessary.

A second class of problem may be due to concerted movement of segments of the population while the survey is in progress. If movement takes place in the direction of progress from transect to transect, numbers will tend to be overestimated, and vice versa. These biases are independent of "double counting", and upward bias due to movement may occur even though no single whale appears on two photo frames. This movement bias is countered by coordinated, quickly flown surveys ; but if survey coverage is reduced to get quick transect progression and minimized movement problems, small sample size may reduce survey precision too far.

The other main method, mark-recapture, is indeed population-directed and not area-directed. Its practical application requires that the population be closed, or nearly so ; mobile and apt to be well mixed ; and either easy to catch, mark, and recatch or else reliably provided with natural marks that are individually unique and easy to see and recognize.

St. Lawrence belugas form a relatively closed population with no immigration or emigration, although there are both birth and death. They should be good subjects for mark-recapture studies. However, they lack natural marks, and attachment sites for artificial marks, and although some have marks of various kinds from injuries, there are not enough to be usable for population estimation purposes.

A recent development is DNA fingerprinting from small tissue samples which can be safely taken from live free swimming whales. Indications now are that DNA fingerprints are unique to the individual and can be reliably separated, although whether they can be reliably reidentified is less clear. A whale from which a biopsy sample has been taken and catalogued is, for mark-recapture purposes, "marked". To use this technique it would be necessary to devise a catalogue in which DNA fingerprints could be stored, retrieved, and compared : similar problems have been solved for human fingerprints and for humpback fluke markings, but have required sophisticated data processing.

Statistical problems in mark-recapture by DNA fingerprinting are in sample size and in ensuring equi probable sampling. The problem of sample size may be illustrated by the following example. If there is a population of 500, and all the conditions of mark-recapture experiments are met independent probabilities of mark and recapture, retained marks, closed population an estimate with an error coefficient of variation of 10%, *i.e.* a confidence interval of ±100, would need a mark sample and a recapture sample of 200 each. The population is not fully mixed, but is probably segregated by age and sex, and it is probably more difficult to approach some animals than others, and this will bias population estimates. Analysis of the numbers of whales bearing multiple marks can show whether there are differences in "catchability", but will not necessarily provide a correction. A single year attempt at a mark-recapture population exercise would require very large sample sizes, and once the study is extended over more than one year, the factors of birth and death have to be brought into the calculations, rendering them both more complex and the resulting population estimates less precise.

Additional information that may be available as a by-product of a mark-recapture study by biopsy sampling may include measures of the genetic variability of the population, and information on the movements of individuals and the segregation of the population. Measures of the pollutant load in live whales would also be available, but sex or age information may be missing.

The estimation of population growth rate from survey data alone is a long-term activity. Not only are population estimates subject to a certain level of uncertainty, but the rate of growth of whale populations is small, and the realized growth of any population from one year to the next is certain to vary. The problem is thus one of measuring the medium-term mean of a small varying quantity by means of the differences between annual measures that are themselves imprecise.

Dynamique de la population de bélugas dans l'estuaire du Saint-Laurent

Pierre Béland

Institut d'écotoxicologie du Saint-Laurent

La question qu'on m'a posée le plus souvent est la suivante : combien de bélugas y a-t-il dans le Saint-Laurent ? À première vue, la réponse semble assez simple à obtenir : il suffit de les compter, en espérant ne pas avoir une marge d'erreur trop grande. Mais en réalité, quand on travaille un tant soit peu sur le Saint-Laurent à compter des bélugas en mouvement, on s'aperçoit que la tâche n'est pas simple. On peut voir quatre animaux, mais il est possible qu'il y en ait d'autres sous l'eau, qu'on n'a pas vus.

Mais au fond, quand les gens posent cette question, ce n'est pas vraiment le nombre de bélugas qui les intéresse. Ils veulent savoir si la population augmente ou diminue, ce qui est une question différente. Comment peut-on répondre à cette question ?

Une première approche consisterait à regarder les données historiques, comme l'a fait Randolph Reeves dans son travail, dont on a parlé aujourd'hui. À l'aide de ces calculs, on estime qu'il y en avait 5 000 au début du siècle comparativement aux quelque 500 d'aujourd'hui. À première vue, donc, il y en aurait dix fois moins. Cependant, le chiffre de 5 000 est une évaluation basée sur le nombre de peaux capturées par année et sur la quantité de litres d'huile par animal. Ces données contiennent elles-mêmes des erreurs. De plus, l'évaluation est basée sur un rétrocalcul qui utilise un taux de croissance donné pour la population : on présume qu'elle s'accroît normalement de tel pourcentage par année. Ainsi pour prélever tant de peaux ou d'huile pendant une certaine période, il fallait qu'il y ait eu Y animaux X années auparavant. Mais si on se trompe sur le taux de croissance, par exemple en présumant 8 % par an alors que ce n'est en réalité que 4 %, on s'aperçoit que ce n'est pas 5 000 bélugas qu'il aurait fallu au début du siècle pour entretenir la chasse, mais 10 000.

Quoi qu'il en soit, ces données historiques nous ramènent loin dans le temps. Or ce qu'on veut savoir, c'est ce qui s'est passé dans les 10 ou 15 dernières années. Comment peut-on répondre à cela ? David Sergeant nous parlait précédemment du pourcentage de veaux comme d'un indice de croissance. Il a comparé le pourcentage de veaux dans l'Arctique et dans le Saint-Laurent pour avoir une idée de la croissance de notre population. Il suggère donc cet indice comme méthode ; j'y reviendrai plus loin, car c'est un point très important.

Une troisième méthode consiste à comparer les structures d'âge qu'on avait à l'époque de Vladykov (dans les années trente) par exemple, et celles qu'on a maintenant. Il y a deux écueils dans cette approche. D'abord, les deux séries de données réflètent l'échantillonnage fait par les scientifiques : chacun utilise une méthode différente pour prélever ses données. Si par exemple vous échantillonnez un même tas de gravier ou de sable avec une pelle ou avec un tamis, vous obtiendrez deux images différentes du même tas. Ainsi, quand on compare les bélugas que les chasseurs tuaient à une certaine époque et ceux qu'on trouve maintenant morts sur les rives, on s'aperçoit que ces deux méthodes différentes d'échantillonnage ne sont pas comparables. Deuxièmement, il faut savoir qu'une population ressemble, d'une certaine façon, à un organisme vivant ; elle répond à ce qui se passe dans son environnement. Or, à l'époque où l'on chassait les bélugas, la population répondait à cette mission d'une façon différente d'aujourd'hui. Prenez deux arbres de la même espèce dont l'un n'est pas exploité, et l'autre est taillé tous les mois : on obtient deux profils distincts. En définition, les comparaisons avec le passé ne sont pas très utiles pour comprendre ce qui se passe aujourd'hui.

Une dernière façon de faire est de réaliser des recensements aériens comme on l'a fait entre 1973 et 1988. Ces données, sur une période d'environ 15 ans, ont toujours rapporté entre 300 et 700 animaux. Cela voudrait dire que les bélugas sont très heureux dans une population stable. Mais il est très possible que cette façon de regarder la population ne nous permette pas de voir, qu'en réalité il a pu se passer bien des choses, parce que son pouvoir de résolution n'est pas assez grand. En voici un exemple : supposons qu'on soit passé de 700 à 528 bélugas, ce qui représente une décroissance de 2 % par année, on n'aurait pu détecter cet événement à partir des recensements parce que la variance sur l'estimé est trop grande pour déceler des petites variations. De même, si une population de 500 augmente de 1 % par année, (j'ai choisi de montrer une population qui augmente pour encourager les gens) même après 20 ans de recensements annuels, elle ne sera rendue qu'à 609 individus. On ne détectera jamais ce changement avec une méthode d'échantillonnage par recensement. C'est seulement si la population variait de 2 ou 3% par année, et après 10 à 20 ans, qu'on pourrait détecter un changement. Quant aux bélugas eux, ils auraient noté une augmentation de 8% du nombre d'avions au cours de ces années!

Alors, qu'est-ce qu'on fait ? Est-ce qu'il existe d'autres méthodes ? Il y a des décisions politiques, sociales et économiques impliquant des milliards de dollars, et qui sont prises chaque année par nos gouvernements, en se basant sur des évaluations de notre propre population. Lorsqu'on prédit que la population du Canada va augmenter entre 1964 et 1999, il doit y avoir des méthodes relativement sûres sur lesquelles baser des décisions onéreuses. Ce qu'on fait, c'est que pour chaque classe d'âge (et on ne considère que les personnes de sexe féminin), on calcule combien chaque femme a de bébés par année en moyenne, et combien de ces femmes meurent à chaque année. On arrive ainsi à prédire que la population du Canada passera (comme cela s'est réalisé) de 9 millions à 15 millions entre 1964 et 1999, c'est-à-dire une augmentation de 1% par année. Évidemment, la méthode est facilement applicable aux humains puisque les naissances et les mortalités sont toutes enregistrées. Peut-on l'utiliser chez les bélugas ?

On peut évaluer l'âge des bélugas retrouvés morts sur les rives du Saint-Laurent à partir des lignes de croissance sur des coupes de leurs dents. Avec ces données, représentant un échantillon de la mortalité depuis 1982, on a pu construire une courbe qui représente pour chaque classe d'âge, de 0-2 ans jusqu'à 30 ans, le nombre de morts retrouvés. Cela constitue une courbe de mortalité similaire à celle qu'on utilise chez les humains pour prédire la population future du Canada. Évidemment cette courbe est sujette à interprétation, comme l'a souligné David Sergeant précédemment. Par exemple, elle est incomplète parce qu'on ne trouve jamais de carcasses entre janvier et avril, à cause des glaces sur la rive. Il est probable qu'un animal qui est pris dans la glace soit démantelé et qu'on ne le retrouve jamais. Même pendant l'été, la mortalité qu'on enregistre peut être incomplète. Heureusement, ces absences ne sont pas entièrement problématiques. Par exemple, s'il y avait eu trois fois plus de morts qu'on en a trouvés, mais qu'ils étaient distribués exactement de la même façon en termes d'âge individuel, il n'y aurait pas de problème. On obtiendrait la même courbe de mortalité et on arriverait aux mêmes prédictions. Ce qui est plus important par contre, c'est une différence dans la distribution des mortalités en termes d'âge individuel.

Une première source d'erreur vient de la détermination de l'âge d'un animal. Chez un vieil animal dont la dent a des signes d'usure, on sous-estime son âge réel. Par conséquent, la courbe de mortalité basée sur le décompte des coupes de dents comporte une petite erreur. Cependant, elle n'est pas vraiment importante puisqu'on réalise sans peine qu'une femelle qui a passé un certain âge contribue très peu aux générations futures, comparée à une femelle très jeune. Autrement dit, s'il meure plus de vieux animaux qu'on n'en trouve, cela ne changera pas grand-chose au calcul.

La deuxième source d'erreur est plus importante : y a-t-il plus de jeunes bélugas qui meurent que ce qu'on retrouve sur la plage ? Si c'était le cas, notre évaluation de la population s'en trouverait modifiée. Effectivement, les jeunes animaux morts semblent moins susceptibles d'être rapportés. Un prédateur peut plus facilement démembrer un petit animal qu'un gros. De plus, les gens qui nous rapportent les cas de mortalité en se promenant sur les plages, ou en avion, ou en bateau, vont plus facilement voir un gros animal blanc qu'un petit animal gris. Or, si on sous-estime la mortalité des jeunes, cela aura beaucoup d'influence sur nos prédictions. Il faudra tenir compte de ce fait en construisant notre modèle de prédiction.

Pour appliquer la méthodologie des démographes humains aux bélugas, il ne nous manque plus que les taux de naissance chez les bélugas. Malheureusement, dans le Saint-Laurent, on ne connaît pas ces taux. On a choisi de prendre, comme point de départ, les données qui proviennent de John Burns et de son équipe en Alaska. Ils ont fait une très belle étude sur leurs bélugas et ont constaté que, comme ailleurs dans l'Arctique, les femelles ont en moyenne un jeune tous les trois ans, bien qu'après l'âge de 20-22 ans, elles en aient moins fréquemment.

Avec ces données, nous pouvons construire un modèle démographique de la population de bélugas du Saint-Laurent. L'avantage de ce type de modèle et de son utilisation sur ordinateur est qu'on peut évaluer la croissance présumée d'une population en faisant varier les valeurs des deux paramètres initiaux. Ainsi, si on estime que les jeunes animaux sont sous-représentés dans notre courbe de mortalité, on peut refaire les calculs en modifiant cet élément de la courbe. De même, si on estime que les taux de naissance sont plus bas ici que dans l'Arctique, par exemple à cause de l'effet des produits toxiques, on peut en évaluer les conséquences. En modélisant ainsi, on obtient un graphique représentant des centaines de populations théoriques qui diffèrent seulement par leurs taux de mortalité chez les jeunes et/ou par leurs taux de naissance. On constate qu'elles se répartissent de part et d'autre d'une ligne centrale représentant toutes les valeurs des paramètres qui produisent des populations stables (croissance zéro). D'un côté, se trouvent les populations qui augmentent à divers rythmes annuels (1%, 2%, 3%, ...) ; de l'autre, celles qui diminuent.

Bien sûr, c'est très intéressant, me direz-vous, mais pour répondre à votre interrogation initiale, il me faut maintenant déterminer où se situe la population du Saint-Laurent dans ce nuage de points. Quel élément pourrait-on mesurer sur la population réelle qui nous aiderait à nous situer sur ce graphique ? La première évidence qui nous apparaît,

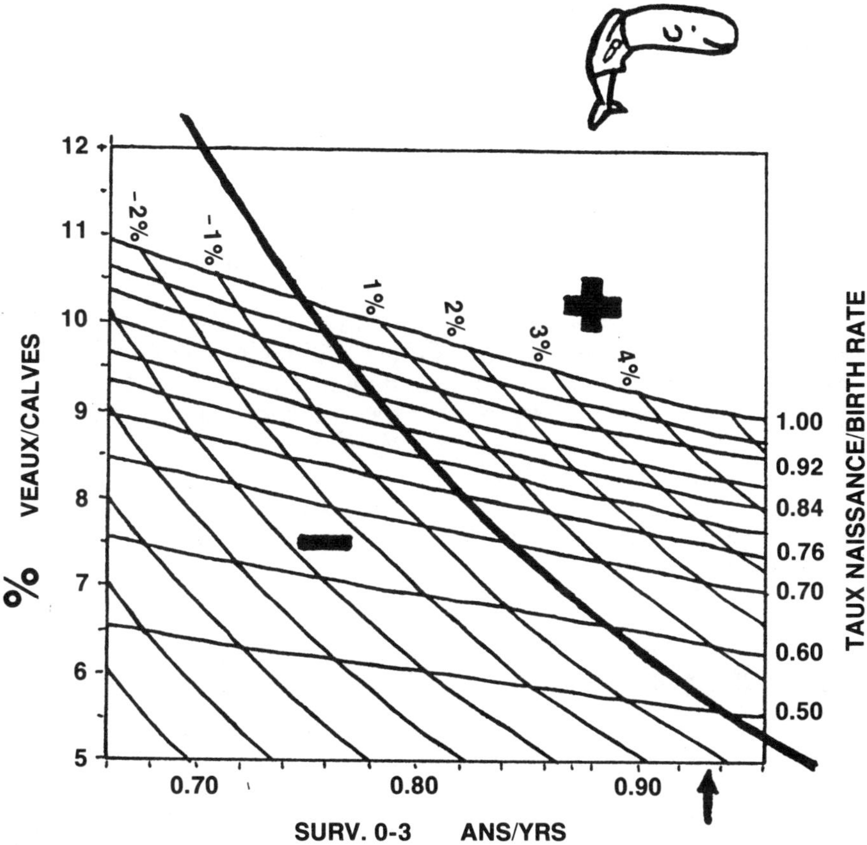

toujours en se basant sur les populations humaines, c'est qu'une population qui a beaucoup de jeunes, qui a une jeune structure d'âge, a plus de potentiel d'accroissement qu'une population vieille. Comparons la situation en Suède où un couple n'a qu'un enfant et au Mexique où le couple a beaucoup d'enfants. On sait très bien que les deux populations n'ont pas le même potentiel d'accroissement. Après x années, on se retrouve avec beaucoup plus de Mexicains, alors qu'en Suède la population est toujours stable. Par conséquent, chez les bélugas, on a pensé tout d'abord déterminer le pourcentage de veaux pour évaluer le taux de croissance de la population. J'ai donc refait mon graphique, mais en représentant toutes les populations possibles en fonction du pourcentage de veaux dans chacun des cas. On constate à nouveau que les points se distribuent de part et d'autre d'une ligne représentant la croissance zéro. Cependant, cette ligne est oblique par rapport à l'axe indiquant la proportion de veaux dans les diverses populations théoriques. Ainsi, si on examine par exemple, toutes les populations qui ont 8 % de veaux, on s'aperçoit qu'il y en a qui diminuent et d'autres qui augmentent. Ce fait indique que, théoriquement, le pourcentage de veaux n'est pas un bon indice de ce que la population est en train de vivre en terme de potentiel de croissance.

Nous avons donc examiné un autre paramètre, soit la proportion de juvéniles dans la population. Il s'agit de tous les animaux qui sont dans les six premières classes d'âge (à l'exception des veaux). Une caractéristique intéressante de ces jeunes, pour fins d'observation sur le terrain, est que leur couleur est grise, comparativement aux adultes qui sont blancs. Encore une fois, l'ordinateur a refait tous les calculs et représenté les diverses populations théoriques, mais cette fois-ci en fonction de la proportion d'animaux gris dans chaque cas. On constate sur ce nouveau graphique que la ligne démarquant les populations en croissance de celle en décroissance est perpendiculaire à l'axe représentant

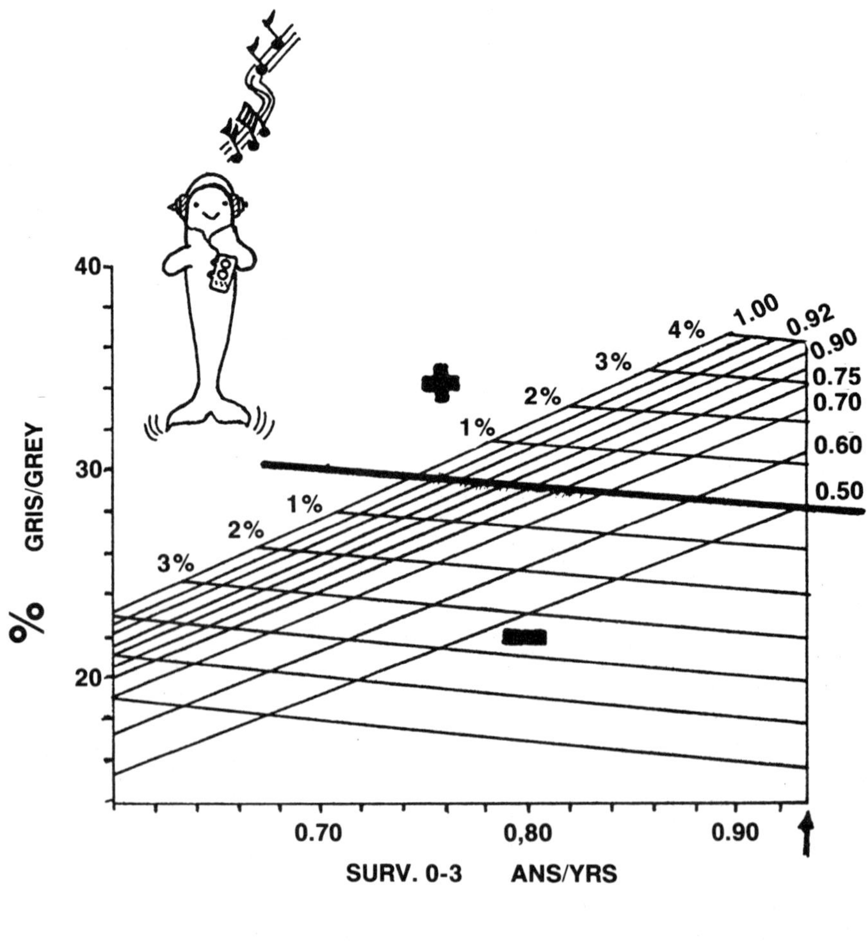

le pourcentage de gris. Par exemple, toutes les populations ayant 34 % d'animaux gris sont au-dessus de cette ligne, donc en croissance ; de même, toutes les populations ayant 20 % d'animaux gris sont sous la ligne, donc en décroissance. Cette ligne se situe aux environs de 30 %. Autrement dit, nous avons là un indice qui, théoriquement, pourrait nous indiquer le taux de croissance de la population du Saint-Laurent.

Pour savoir si la population de bélugas du Saint-Laurent augmente ou diminue, on n'a donc pas besoin de savoir combien de bélugas il y a. On n'a besoin que de connaître les proportions de blancs et de gris. Il faut bien sûr, faire un échantillonnage équivalent dans tous les secteurs que la population habite, ce qui implique qu'on connaisse sa distribution et ses habitudes, pour y compter le nombre d'événements qu'on voit dans une journée : combien d'événements blancs, combien d'événements gris.

Évidemment, même si en théorie ça marche, il reste à évaluer des problèmes d'ordre pratique. Par exemple, deux observateurs vont avoir une opinion différente sur la couleur réelle de tel ou tel animal : gris ou vraiment blanc ? Il y a aussi des erreurs dues à la variance sur l'estimation des proportions de blancs et de gris. Il est possible que la méthode mène à une erreur qui soit de l'ordre de 3 à 4 % de chaque côté de la moyenne. On saura, par exemple, qu'on a entre 26 à 34 % de gris, ce qui n'est peut-être pas nécessairement plus utile qu'un recensement traditionnel.

À tout le moins, la méthode est théoriquement correcte pour évaluer le potentiel de croissance d'une population, par opposition au décompte des veaux qui n'a pas de valeur prédictive. Certainement, le modèle indique des limites au-delà desquelles l'incertitude diminue rapidement. Ainsi, si les observateurs, tout en étant très généreux dans leur façon d'inclure les individus parmi les gris, obtiennent toujours des évaluations au-dessous de 30 %, il y a de fortes chances que la population soit en diminution. Nous avons l'intention de vérifier cette méthode sur le terrain dès la saison prochaine.

Population Analysis of Beluga Whales Based on Vital Rates from Nouveau-Québec

D. W. Doidge
Macdonald College of McGill University

INTRODUCTION

The analysis of the population dynamics of mammals normally depends on large samples of biological specimens to estimate vital rates. The small population of ca 1 500 beluga whales in eastern Hudson Bay limits harvesting and the number of biological specimens available for analysis. Age-specific analyses are further limited because tooth wear in older animals prevents the determination of age which further reduces sample size. Although limited in number, these biological specimens do provide information on life history parameters which is otherwise unobtainable.

Using vital rates from Nouveau-Québec beluga and an alternative stage-specific approach, I model the dynamics of a small population of beluga whales and suggest a technique for the analysis of beluga population dynamics using aerial photography.

POPULATION MODEL

The processes governing a stage-specific beluga population are shown in Figure 1. The model contains four stages and represents beluga life history processes. Although designated by their colour, stages are also classified on the basis of shape and length. Neonates representing young of the year mature into juveniles or darks. The juveniles enter the

FIGURE 1

Processes governing a stage – specific beluga population

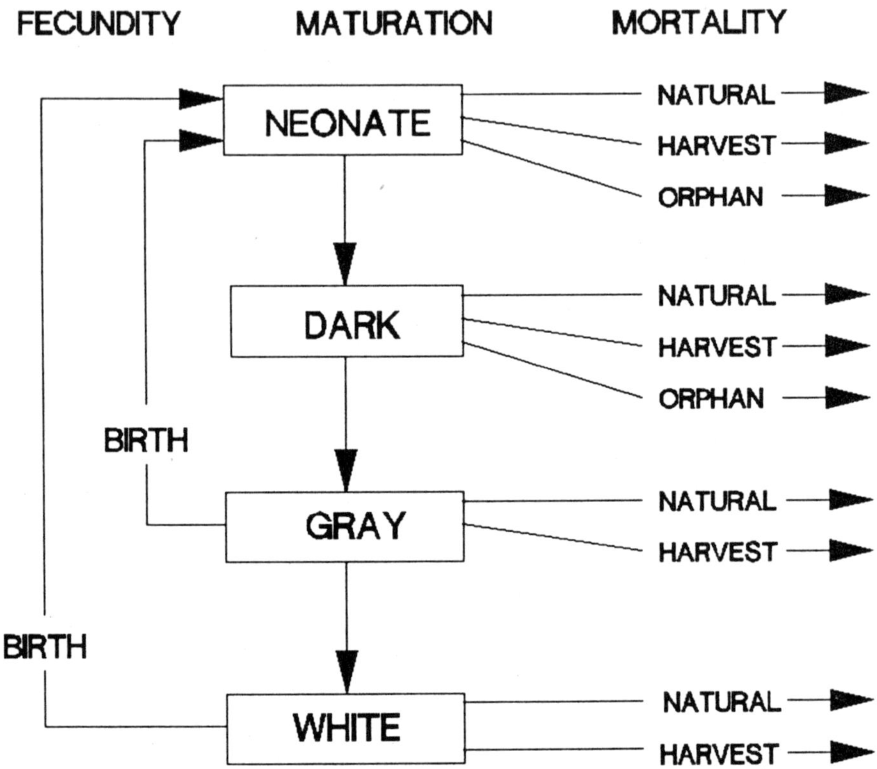

next stage of gray animals which mature into white adults. Both gray and white animals are capable of bearing young. Animals are removed from the population via natural mortality, harvesting and, in the case of the dependent stages of neonates and darks, mortality due to the harvesting of their mothers ("orphans" in Figure 1).

DERIVATION OF VITAL RATES

Before simulations can be made, the vital rates driving the population processes must be known. The length of the breeding cycle is a factor limiting the birth rate. The Nouveau-Québec data indicate a three-year cycle which is based on fetal growth over time and the proportion of females of the various reproductive states in the catch.

After an initial period of nonlinear growth, changes in fetal length with time are linear (Figure 2). From this relation, date of birth can be predicted if birth length is known. In the Nouveau-Québec sample, near-term fetuses are lacking, so I used a birth length of 150 cm from the Soviet North (Kleinenberg *et al.* 1964) which predicts birth to occur in late May. Sergeant (1973) indicates a birth length of 160 cm. The addition of 10 cm to birth length would advance the estimate of birth date to mid June, *i.e.* just before beluga enter estuaries in eastern Hudson Bay. The earlier nonlinear phase of fetal growth is about 8% of the linear phase (Huggett and Widdas 1953). The addition of this portion indicates breeding occurs in early May for Nouveau-Québec beluga. Gestation duration, the interval between these events, is about 13 months, or 14 months if a birth length of 160 cm is used. These estimates are within the 12 to 14.5 month range for gestation found in other beluga populations (Laws 1959, Sergeant 1973, Kleinenberg *et al.* 1964, Brodie 1971). Although birth and breeding occur over a range of dates, only point estimates can be made using this method.

The number of animals either pregnant or lactating in an unbiased catch reflects the duration of those conditions according to the time-

FIGURE 2

Estimation of the duration of gestation based on the fetal growth and an assumed birth length of 150 cm

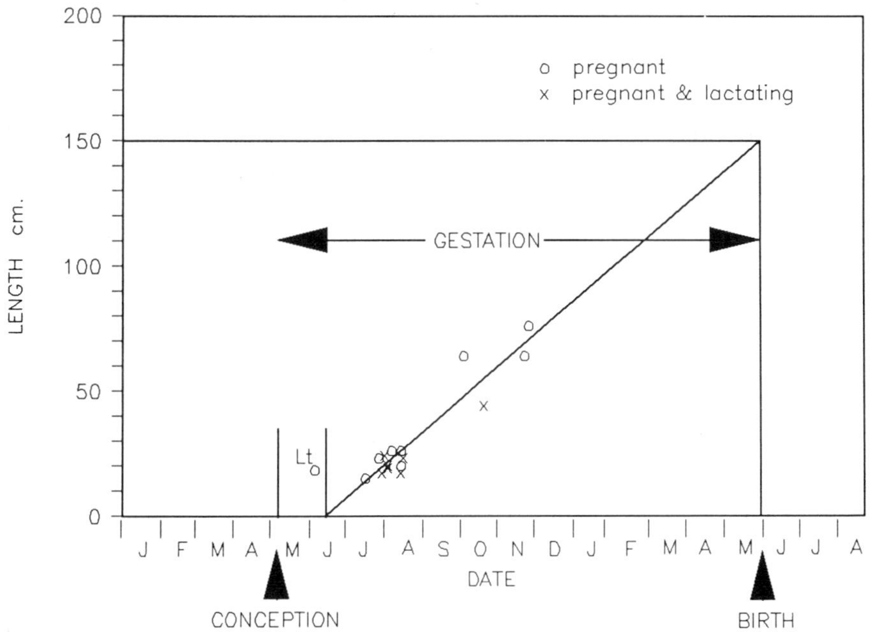

sampling theory (Tyler 1979). Table 1 lists the proportions of lactating, both lactating and pregnant, and pregnant animals from the harvest in Nouveau-Québec and published reports from the Soviet North and West Hudson Bay. Using the Nouveau-Québec example, the ratio of lactating to pregnant animals (51/20) indicates that lactation duration is 2 ½ times that of gestation. For a gestation period of 13 months, lactation should last about 2.8 years. This includes an overlap with pregnancy of ½ year. Thus, the estimated length of the breeding cycle of Nouveau-Québec beluga is about 3.4 years. Any bias in the catch towards lactating animals would increase the estimate of lactation duration. The data in Table 1 generally indicate a three-year breeding cycle for beluga whales. The vital rates used in the population simulations are summarized in Table 2 and discussed below.

Based on a three-year breeding cycle, the maximum annual birth rate would be 0.33 young per adult female if all were sexually mature, bred and carried their fetuses to term. In the Nouveau-Québec sample, the median frequencies of length and age of the gray stage approximate the first occurrence of sexual maturity. I assume ½ the gray stage females are sexually mature and use an annual per capita birth rate of 0.17.

Maturation rate is the inverse of a stage's duration. By definition, the young of the year or neonate stage lasts one year (rate = 1). The three-year breeding cycle indicates that young are calves of the dark stage for a further two years (rate = 0.5). The duration of the gray stage

TABLE 1

Duration of breeding cycle of beluga based on a 13-mounth gestation and reproductive status of the catch

	Harvest statistics			Ratios
Site	Lact + (Lact-Preg)	Preg	L/P	LP/P
Soviet North	17 + (10)	21	1.29	0.48
Soviet Far East	46 + (12)	24	2.42	0.50
W. Hudson Bay	33 + (7)	22	1.82	0.32
Nouveau-Quebec	42 + (9)	20	2.55	0.45

	Estimated duration of breeding cycle (yrs)		
	Lactation	Overlap	Breeding Cycle
Soviet North	1.4	0.5	2.0
Soviet Far East	2.6	0.5	3.2
W. Hudson Bay	2.0	0.3	2.7
Nouveau-Quebec	2.8	0.5	3.4

TABLE 2

Vital rates used in stage - specific population of beluga whales

Process	Rate	Comments	Other sources
BIRTH			
White	0.33	Maximum rate for 3-yr. cycle	0.31 (2)
Gray	0.17	50 % Grays sexually mature	
MATURATION		Inverse of stage duration	
Neonate	1.0	Age Class 0	
Dark	0.5	1-2 yrs. (3-yr. cycle)	
Gray	0.2	Age Class 3-7 (Maturing)	
MORTALITY			
Neonate	0.20		0.33 (1); 0.29 (2)
Dark	0.10		0.11 (2)
Gray	0.05		0.06-0.07 (2)
White	0.05		0.06-0.27 (2)

Sources:
1. Brodie, 1982
2. Burns & Seaman, 1985

is five years based on the age and length data from Nouveau-Québec, which yields a maturation rate of 0.2 animals per year.

Mortality rates are the most difficult to obtain for beluga because of limited sample sizes, tooth wear, catch bias, and the necessity of knowing the population's rate of increase in order to calculate it. Mortality rates are unknown for the Nouveau-Québec stock since the small sample of unworn teeth prevents life table analysis. The rates used here are approximations based on other studies. Rates from a life table analysis of approximately 500 animals of known age from Alaska (Burns and Seaman 1985), and a smaller sample from Cumberland Sound, Baffin Island (Brodie 1982) are given for comparison (Table 2).

SIMULATION RESULTS AND DISCUSSION

Population projections based on these rates give an indication of the expected number and herd composition of a beluga population at a future time, if these rates remain stable. Since the focus of this forum is St. Lawrence beluga, I have modelled an initial population of 500 whales using vital rates from Nouveau-Québec. The simulation uses a stochastic approach which allows birth, death and maturation processes to be governed by chance. Vital rates are normally distributed and allowed to fluctuate within 10% of their mean values to mimic random fluctuations found in nature.

The average herd structure resulting from these simulations is 9% neonates, 13% darks, 21% grays and 57% whites. Assuming one birth every three years, manipulation of mortality rates failed to generate values for the percentage of neonates in the herd in excess of 13%. This is contrary to some field observations which report neonate compositions of 19 to 21% (Caron 1987). This discrepancy may result from group segregation or the incorrect assumption that gray animals do not produce young. Such factors must be taken into account when analyzing herd composition data.

Each line in Figure 3 shows the change in an initial population of 500 belugas over ten years when driven by the vital rates (having a CV of 10%) listed in Table 2. Because of the variance in vital rates, the population's year-to-year growth also varies. For this reason, a fluctuation in population size over a short time span may not reflect the overall population trend.

FIGURE 3

Trajectories of 3 population simulations of 500 belugas over 10 years governed by population processes of figure 1 and vital rates with a CV of 10% (Table 2)

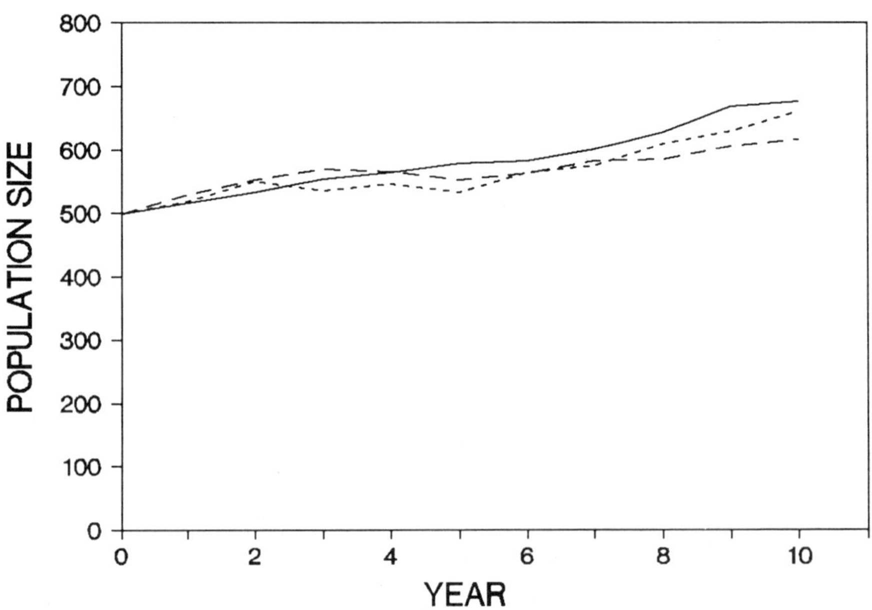

Large numbers of simulations can be used to generate frequency distributions of expected population size for a given set of vital rates. Figure 4 shows results based on 50 simulations, each covering a period of 10 years, for the initial population of 500 animals using the rates given previously. This population grows at about 2% annually. Because of the variance in the vital rates (which is likely to be a closer approximation of nature than the assumption that these rates remain constant over time), the population's size at a future date cannot be predicted with certainty. The frequency distributions of Figure 4 give an indication of the probability of a population being a certain size at a future date, when governed by these particular vital rates.

APPLICATION OF STAGE-SPECIFIC POPULATION ANALYSIS

Population simulations can indicate the expected change over time in a population governed by a particular set of vital rates. The problem remains, though, how to determine these rates for populations such as the St. Lawrence beluga where few or no biological samples are available for analysis.

A stage-specific approach which groups animals from aerial photographs into different classes based on size, shape or color can be used to investigate the dynamics of the population. This method is not dependent on biological samples.

Annual changes in the numbers of each stage reflect the probabilities of those stages becoming the next stage in the subsequent year, or in the case of adults, the probability of producing young. A time series of aerial photos of beluga herds can be analyzed to determine these probabilities. This information on the dynamics of the population can be used to calculate the rate of increase of the population using the technique developed for age-based population analyses (Lefkovitch 1965).

Initial analysis of test data generated by stochastic simulations indicate that the reproductive contribution of the two sexually mature stages of grays and whites cannot be separated when analyzing whale count data. A three-stage model which combines the gray and white animals into one adult class must be adopted.

The use of aerial photographic data is not without bias because of differences between stages in diving ability. Information on time spent diving by each stage must be obtained using telemetric devices. Although dive times are not yet available, time series of aerial photos should be initiated for any beluga stock under investigation. Compared to land- or vessel-based counts which may be subject to considerable error, aerial photographs are a permanent record which provides the least biased

FIGURE 4

Frequency distributions of population simulations shown in figure 3 (n = 50).

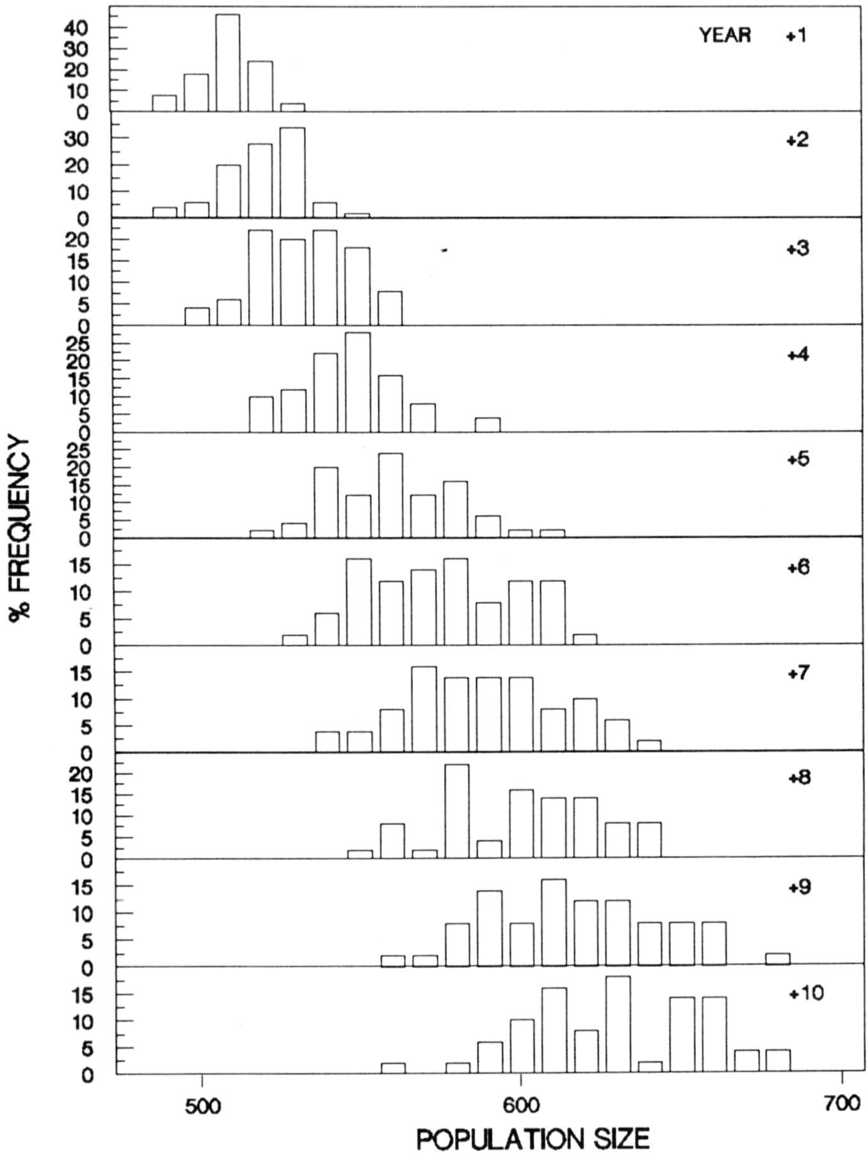

estimate of whale numbers. For this reason, I believe the stage-specific analysis of aerial photos is the best method available for investigating the dynamics of beluga populations, especially those which are small.

ACKNOWLEDGEMENTS

I thank the Department of Fisheries and Oceans Canada, World Wildlife Fund Canada and the Inuit communities of Nouveau-Québec for support of this study of the beluga population ecology between 1983 and 1987. Dr. M. E. Scott, the Institute of Parasitology and McGill University, provided helpful advice concerning stochastic programming techniques.

COMPUTER PROGRAM AVAILABILITY

The stochastic stage-specific population program is available in either compiled or BASIC versions from the author.

REFERENCES

BRODIE, P. F. *A Reconsideration of Aspects of Growth, Reproduction, and Behaviour in the White Whale (Delphinapterus leucas), with Reference to the Cumberland Sound, Baffin Island, Population*, Journal of the Fisheries Research Board of Canada 28: n° of cat. 1309-1318, 1973.

BRODIE, P. F. *The Growth of the White Whale*, Environment Canada, Canadian Wildlife Services and Department of Fisheries and Oceans, 1982, 16 p.

BURNS, J. J. and SEAMAN, G. A. *Investigations of Belukha Whales in Coastal Waters of Western and Northern Alaska II*, Biology and Ecology, Final Report submitted to NOAA, Outer Continental Shelf Environmental Assessment Program, Fairbanks, Alaska, Alaska Dept. of Fish and Game, 1985, 129 p.

CARON, L. M. J. *Status, Site Fidelity, and Behaviour of a Hunted Herd of White Whales (Delphinapterus leucas) in the Nastapoka Estuary, Eastern Hudson Bay*, Montréal, Canada, MSc Thesis, McGill University, 1987, 136 p.

HUGGETT, A. St. G. and WIDDAS, W. F. *The Relationship between Mammalian Fœtal Weight and Conception Age*, J. Physiol, n° of cat. 114:306-317, 1953.

KLEINENBERG, S. E., YABLOKOV, A. V., BEL'KOVICH, B. M. and TARASEVICH, M. N. Beluga: *Investigation of the Species*, Moscow, (Transl. from Russian by Israel Program for Sci. Transl., Jerusalem), 1969, 376 p.

LAWS, R. M. *The Fœtal Growth Rates of Whales with Special Reference to the Fin Whale, Balaenoptera physalus Linn.* Discovery Rep, n° of cat. 29:281-308, 1959.

LEFKOVITCH, P. F. *The Study of Population Growth in Organisms Grouped by Size*, Biometrics, n° of cat. 21 : 1-18, 1965.

SERGEANT, D. E. *Biology of White Whales (Delphinapterus leucas) in Western Hudson Bay*, J. Fish. Res. Bd. Canada, n° of cat. 30 : 1065-1090, 1973.

TYLER, S. *Time-Sampling : A Matter of Convention*, Anim. Behav., n° of cat. 27 : 801-810, 1979.

Options for the Management of Belugas

John J. Burns
Living Resources Inc.

INTRODUCTION

My perspectives about ice-associated marine mammals are based in large part on comparisons of reported studies with my own research experiences in the seas adjacent to Alaska and Siberia. Those adjacent waters include the Gulf of Alaska, the Bering, Chukchi, Beaufort and Okhotsk seas, and the southern margin of the Arctic Ocean north of Alaska. Though much of my work, starting in 1962, was with walruses and phocid seals, belugas have always been a species of great interest. They became a focus of specific research in 1978 and remain a primary involvement. All of my work was ostensibly related to resource management in a region where the harvesting of marine mammals by Native peoples is very significant to local economies. These points are made only to inform the participants of this forum about involvements and geographical reference points that have influenced the evolution of my ideas and concepts about ice-associated marine mammals, particularly belugas.

The Bering-Chukchi region is particularly interesting and comprises extensive, continuous habitat for a variety of ice-associated species including belugas and bowhead whales, walrus, ringed, ribbon, spotted and bearded seals, polar bear and arctic fox. Conceptually, the region can be viewed as having the shape of an hour glass, the constriction being at Bering Strait. The lower or southern part of this hour glass is the region in which those species adapted to subarctic habitats winter and mainly bear their young. The Subarctic Province grades into the cold, northern part of the temperate zone in the southern Bering Sea. The subarctic marine mammals, including belugas, disperse widely after the seasonal maximum extent of late winter ice. Some belugas move into Bering Sea coastal waters, frequenting them during late spring until ice begins to form again in autumn. However, most belugas of the Bering Sea stock migrate far north, some dispersing widely in coastal waters of the eastern and western Chukchi Sea and most being accounted for in waters of the eastern Beaufort Sea and Amundsen Gulf during late June to September. However, little effort has been devoted to investigation of their abundance and distribution in that part of their summer range which is in the Soviet Far East. Presumably, there are similar concentrations in the Long Strait and East Siberian Sea area. All of the belugas that summer north of Bering Strait return to the Bering Sea in late autumn/winter, unless unusually open ice conditions permit some to remain farther north.

The Bering Sea is quite like a cold, northern embayment of the Pacific Ocean, whereas the Chukchi Sea, with a more severe sea ice regime, is like a southern embayment of the Arctic Ocean. The narrow constriction between these two seas, though contributing to regionally different oceanographic characteristics by restricting water flow, permits the extensive seasonal migrations of several marine mammals, including belugas.

From a zoogeographic perspective there are probably no genetically isolated or disjunct stocks or populations of belugas in the Bering-Chukchi region, as there are no barriers to intermingling in the wintering areas and during at least the early part of the breeding season (Burns and Seaman 1985). The seasonal expansion and contraction of range, and the movement of whales through the Bering Strait, no doubt contribute to a high degree of genetic homogeneity. Nonetheless, it is desirable to consider each of the various summer aggregations that occur predictably in coastal waters from Bristol Bay to northwest Canada, as separate management stocks.

Probably there are no other regions within the circumpolar range of belugas that are similar to that occupied by the Bering Sea stock. It seems likely that the complex physiography of Canadian eastern arctic and subarctic waters, for example, tends to foster the existence of stocks that winter in different areas and are isolated during the breeding season.

BACKGROUND

In a general sense, centres of abundance for belugas are in the Subarctic Province. There are stocks (perhaps populations) that occur in the Arctic Province where unique subarctic conditions occur, such as the North Water in Davis Strait. Similarly, there are populations in the Temperate Province, where "cells" of subarctic conditions are maintained by unique physiographic features. Three such low-latitude populations occur; one each in the St. Lawrence (eastern Canada), Cook Inlet/ Shelikof Strait (northern Gulf of Alaska), and waters of the northern Sea of Japan/Gulf of Sakhalin (north and south of the Amur River in the Soviet Far East). The first two of these are now essentially insular. The third, that of the Amur River region, was apparently recently contiguous with other belugas of the western Okhotsk sea (Gurevich 1980), though its current status in this regard is not clear. It is the stocks of the Temperate Province that are currently facing the most insidious and severe threats, mainly resulting from pollution and high human presence. The St. Lawrence population is probably affected to the greatest extent.

It is not difficult to envision major geographic shifts in beluga distribution, northward or southward, associated with episodes of climatic change such as have been documented by Vibe (1967) and Harington (1981). Also, one can envision the mechanisms by which insular populations persist in isolated "refugia" of favorable but discontinuous habitats, during generally warming trends in climate. The Cook Inlet population in south central Alaska is definitely an example of this.

Relationship of the now disjunct St. Lawrence population to others of eastern Canada and Davis Strait seems a more difficult question. Is it now insular because of changed climate, or have its formerly adjacent stocks been so reduced that their traditional ranges no longer overlap, thus greatly reducing opportunity (continuous or irruptive) for ingress and egress? It would seem that both factors are probably operative. A reduction to 10% of their former population size (Reeves and Mitchell 1984, Anonymous 1987), together with a greatly reduced distribution now restricted to the western part of the St. Lawrence estuary, present serious challenges with respect to ensuring survival of this population. As has already been recognized, based on the scope of this forum, the major thrust of a long-range recovery plan involves three major components: 1) maintaining a threshold population size that can sustain current levels of mortality, regardless of cause; 2) habitat improvement, particularly with respect to toxic wastes affecting health of individuals and vigor of the population; and 3) concurrent or subsequent increase of population size based on increased births and survival. Another potential component of a successful recovery plan may well involve management to increase size of adjacent stocks.

DISCUSSION

In a real sense, the plight of belugas in the St. Lawrence is not the problem. Rather, belugas are a signal symptom of an intensifying local and global problem; that of anthropogenic degradation of our air, water and soil. In the St. Lawrence situation, degradation apparently results from increasing human presence in shrinking beluga habitat and, perhaps more importantly, from continuous (and cumulative) large scale pollution from a variety of different sources. Some of the toxic pollutants are apparently causing reduced health and vigor to the whales.

To state that the plight of belugas in the St. Lawrence is merely a symptom of a more serious problem is not meant to imply that focused attention on them is not warranted. It most certainly is. They may well be an important "barometer" or indicator species that reflects the degree of health and integrity of those parts of the St. Lawrence they occupy now and in the future. As long-lived mammals supported by a complex food web, they exhibit, in an integrated way, the effects of man's activities, whether it be expressed in the forms of modified behaviors, changed distributions, pathology or simply as biologically active accumulators of pollutants, the effects of which may not now be clearly understood. Current baseline information derived from belugas and other selected indicator organisms will become a standard against which future change will be measured. On the other hand, a focus on belugas must not be at the expense of programs directed at reducing and hopefully eliminating the real problems of environmental degradation in the St. Lawrence.

The situation with belugas in the St. Lawrence is, in several respects, parallel to that formerly faced by peregrine falcons in many parts of the world. Populations of those raptors were declining precipitously, and they were extirpated from large parts of their range. Environmental contaminants, mainly DDT and its metabolites, were found to be the primary cause of recruitment failures. Actions taken as a result of the presumed and later verified understanding of how DDT was functioning in the environment resulted in eventual successes of two kinds : reductions in worldwide levels of pollution from DDT (hopefully a continuing process), and effective rebuilding of peregrine populations through both increased natural survival and artificial propagation and release of new founders. This awareness and the eventual successes are heartening examples of what may be possible with respect to other living resources in our modern world.

Somewhere in this paper I am supposed to deal with the options for management of belugas. The operative word really is "options". The options must be predicated on the factors influencing or controlling status and trend of the particular stock or population in question, the condition of habitat that supports it, and the goals of a particular management regime. Though there is a long and varied record with respect to managing living resources, including many marine mammals, belugas have generally not been included in conservation programs that involve active, scientifically based management. This is beginning to change. Recent formation of the Alaska and Inuvialuit Beluga Whale

Committee is an effort to increase the tempo of necessary research, and to involve local peoples in the research on and management of the Bering sea population.

In the world that belugas now live, the different stocks exist in the face of vastly different pressures. Some stocks still occupy extensive, relatively unaltered habitats for which the capacity for supporting belugas is unchanged. The primary human pressure on such stocks continues (in some cases for several thousand years) to be direct harvesting for food by Native peoples. Under such circumstances, the primary management procedures involve manipulating take at a level that maintains optimum stock size and recruitment while providing for some agreed level of take. Management procedures in such circumstances are conceptually simple and straightforward, though frequently contentious from social and political perspectives. A conservation regime in such circumstances normally includes individual bag limits and/or area or stock quotas, allowable methods of take and spatial or temporal closures. The management programs attempt to protect animals at critical times or in places where they are especially vulnerable, to fix the maximum (or desirable) allowable level of kill, encourage harvest methods that are humane, effective and efficient, and encourage complete utilization of animals landed.

Though belugas in the St. Lawrence would most certainly have benefited from such regulations in the past, especially since much of the take was for commercial purposes (Vladykov 1944), directed taking is no longer appropriate. Some stocks of belugas that are hunted are also subject to additional kinds of anthropogenic intrusions. These intrusions are quite variable, including such factors as incidental take in fishing gear, direct competition with man for food, purposeful (as for instance with whale-scaring devices for short-term exclusion) or inadvertent displacement, harassment by scientists and whale-watchers and a host of other activities for which impacts are unknown.

For other marine mammals in these circumstances, usually those activities resulting in observable mortality are regulated. The regulatory regime for hunting remains in place, but additional restrictions affecting fishing activities are also implemented, usually involving some level of allowable incidental take.

Belugas in the St. Lawrence are probably a special case in that the stock is so severely reduced already, and those that remain exist in a relict habitat increasingly impacted by environmental contamination (Gaskin 1982, Anonymous 1987, Béland 1988 and personal communication). There are increasing indications that environmental contaminants are probably causing a reduction in fecundity and survival (Anonymous 1987, Béland 1988).

Survival and eventual recovery of the St. Lawrence beluga will not be accomplished through traditional management programs. Survival of the remnant stock will certainly require continued efforts to protect animals from direct human-caused mortality. Beyond that, increase of the much-reduced population size will require a farsighted and innovative program involving both Canadians and Americans working to eliminate the numerous sources of significant environmental contaminants now going into the St. Lawrence system. The possibility of reducing levels of pollutants already present would likewise require bilateral action. At this point we are probably already faced with crisis management as the result of habitat degradation by numerous small increments, each one of which, in isolation, may have been insignificant.

From my perspective, the most immediate information needs for the region in question fall into three general categories : 1) understanding the unique physical attributes of the remnant habitat (bathymetry, water sources and masses, sediment regimes, currents, temperature regimes and ice dynamics) ; 2) understanding the mechanisms and processes by which contaminants are accumulated in the environment and incorporated in belugas ; and 3) understanding the effects of these contaminants on the whales. These kinds of information serve two important functions. The likelihood of effective correction is increased and the baseline information obtained becomes the new standard against which future change (hopefully positive) will be measured.

Belugas of the St. Lawrence are presently a high-profile example of global probability with respect to environmental pollution. The task is to change that probability to a new global possibility, starting in our coastal waters. No existing management program is capable of doing that in the short term. In this instance, we are well advised to initiate immediate actions to stop further pollution, even though the cause and effect relationships are presently vague or unknown. To do otherwise is to increase the probability that belugas of the St. Lawrence will not survive.

REFERENCES

ANONYMOUS. *Statement of Problems of the St. Lawrence Belugas*, Fisheries and Oceans Canada, 1987, 27 p.

BÉLAND, P. *Witness for the Prosecution*, Nature Canada, n° of cat. 17 (4) : 28-36, 1988.

BURNS, J. J. and SEAMAN G. A. *Investigations of Beluga Whales in Coastal Waters of Western and Northern Alaska II, 1985, Biology and Ecology.* Outer Continental Shelf Environ. Assessment Program 1988 Final Reports, n° of cat. 56 : 221-357.

GASKING, D. E. *The Ecology of Whales and Dolphins*, Heinemann Educational Books Ltd., 1982, 459 p.

GUREVICH, V. S. Worldwide Distribution and Migration Patterns of the White Whale (Beluga), *Delphinapterus leucas*, Reports of the International Whaling Commission, n° of cat. 30 : 465-480, 1980.

HARINGTON, C. R., ed. *Climatic Change in Canada-2*, National Museums of Canada, Syllogeus Ser. n° 33, 1981, 220 p.

REEVES, R. R. and MITCHELL E. Catch History and Initial Population of White Whales (*Delphinapterus leucas*) in the River and Gulf of St. Lawrence, Eastern Canada, Naturaliste Canada, n° of cat. 111 : 63-121, 1984.

VIBE, C. Arctic Animals in Relation to Climatic Fluctuations, Mddr. Groenland, n° of cat. 170 (5), 1967, 227 p.

VLADYKOV, V. D. Chasse, biologie et valeur économique du marsouin blanc ou béluga (*Delphinapterus leucas*) du fleuve et du golfe Saint-Laurent, Études sur les mammifères aquatiques III, Québec, Département des Pêcheries, 1944, 194 p.

Mouvements, comportements et zones fréquentées par le béluga du Saint-Laurent

Robert Michaud
Institut d'écotoxicologie du Saint-Laurent

Le fait que les bélugas du Saint-Laurent soient menacés est évidemment malheureux pour plusieurs raisons. L'une, entre autres, est que cela enlève énormément de charme aux travaux de recherche que l'on fait sur les bélugas du Saint-Laurent. Le fait que les bélugas sont menacés confère un caractère d'urgence à ces travaux. Et s'ils n'étaient pas menacés, les études entreprises seraient évidemment tout aussi intéressantes, même si elles n'avaient pas d'applications directes à court terme; un peu comme pour l'alpiniste qui escalade une montagne simplement parce qu'elle est là. Il peut être intéressant d'étudier les bélugas du Saint-Laurent simplement parce qu'ils sont dans le Saint-Laurent, et que ce sont des animaux très, très beaux, qui ont une organisation sociale qui semble assez développée. On leur connaît une capacité de communiquer qui semble assez complexe, même si, évidemment, on ne comprend pas ce que les bélugas se disent. Ils sont également très curieux, et c'est très agréable de travailler sur l'eau avec ces animaux-là.

Indépendamment de ces considérations, l'état actuel de la population requiert effectivement qu'on déploie des énergies pour comprendre l'état de la population de façon à pouvoir éventuellement entreprendre des actions qui seront significatives, à l'intérieur d'une stratégie de protection des bélugas du Saint-Laurent. Une des données dont on a un très grand besoin, c'est une connaissance assez précise de la distribution des animaux à l'intérieur de l'estuaire. C'est là un besoin ressenti dans tous les champs d'études. Lorsqu'on est un politicien par exemple, on veut savoir où sont ses électeurs pour viser juste dans ses actions ; si on est chasseur de baleines, on va vouloir savoir où sont les baleines et quand elles y sont, pour éviter d'envoyer une flotte de baleinières qui revienne bredouille. Dans le cas des bélugas, c'est également très important de connaître leur distribution, pour répondre à la majorité des questions soulevées depuis le début des travaux sur les bélugas du Saint-Laurent.

Si l'on veut, par exemple, élaborer un inventaire, un recensement aérien pour compter les bélugas du Saint-Laurent, si cela demeure une question intéressante, on veut savoir où ils sont, soit pour couvrir l'ensemble de l'aire de distribution, soit pour connaître quelle proportion de l'aire de distribution on a couvert. Si on veut déterminer le pourcentage d'animaux immatures dans la population — ce dont le docteur Béland nous a parlé — ce qui pourrait être un indice intéressant pour évaluer l'évolution de la population, on doit connaître le mode de dispersion des animaux, à savoir : est-ce que tous les adultes se tiennent dans le même secteur et les groupes familiaux dans un autre secteur ? Ce sont des choses qu'on doit savoir. Si l'on veut protéger les habitats, il faut les connaître ; savoir pour qui, quand et pour quels types d'activités ils sont importants. Enfin, des études détaillées de la distribution pourraient nous donner une réponse à une question intéressante : est-ce que tous les bélugas du Saint-Laurent sont exposés aux mêmes conditions environnementales ? Je m'explique : cet été par exemple, pendant tout le mois de juillet, on a observé très régulièrement des bélugas à Saint-Fulgence. Est-ce qu'une partie des bélugas ont une chance de se retrouver à Saint-Fulgence en été et d'autres à l'Île-aux-Coudres ? Ou bien, est-ce que ce sont toujours les mêmes, qui changent de secteur.

Ce que je vais présenter aujourd'hui, c'est un ensemble de données qu'on a récoltées depuis 1986, pour avoir une image précise de la distribution des bélugas dans le Saint-Laurent. Je commencerai par une présentation, une description générale de la distribution en été. Suivra une description plus détaillée de la distribution, mais cette fois dans la portion amont de l'aire de distribution, où l'on a concentré nos efforts depuis 1986. Les données disponibles avant 1986, celles du docteur Sergeant, celles de Malcom et Pippard, suggéraient qu'une très forte proportion des animaux immatures et des veaux se retrouvaient dans la portion amont. C'est pour cela que nous avons travaillé dans ce secteur-là. Et par la suite, les informations recueillies, les méthodes employées serviront à déterminer le pourcentage d'animaux immatures dans la population et à caractériser les habitats critiques.

DESCRIPTION GÉNÉRALE DE LA DISTRIBUTION EN ÉTÉ

La distribution estivale avait été décrite par Pippard et Sergeant comme étant comprise entre Saint-Siméon et, à peu près, les îles

FIGURE 1

Repérage aérien 1987-1988
Aire d'étude

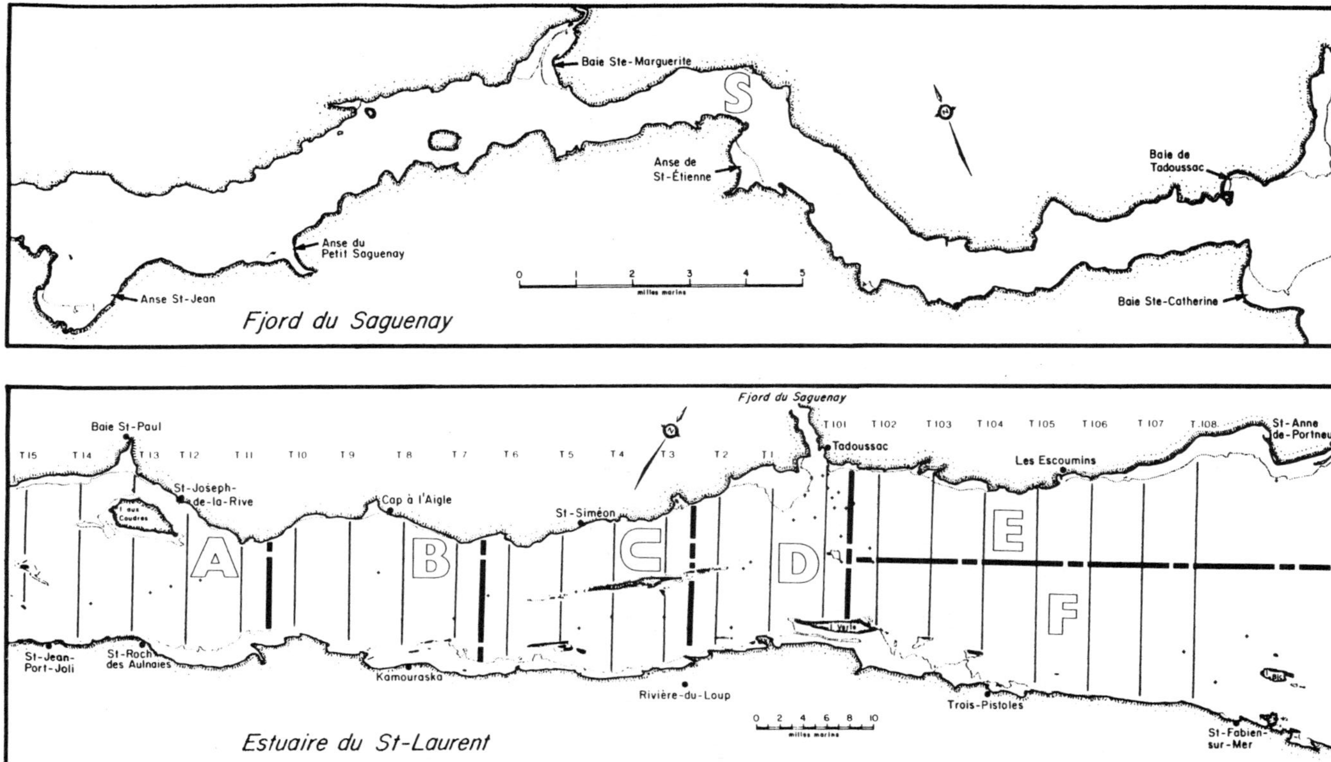

Kamouraska, à l'ouest, jusqu'à Saint-Simon et les Escoumins à l'est, en incluant évidemment la rivière Saguenay, la distribution déterminée ici. Comme on l'a vu hier, les inventaires aériens ont couvert ce secteur, des inventaires qui datent d'avant 1986. En 1987 et 1988, dans le cadre d'un contrat fait pour Hydro-Québec, pour déterminer l'importance ou la fréquentation des bélugas dans ce secteur, une série d'inventaires aériens systématiques ont été effectués. Ils consistaient à faire un survol avec deux avions : un avion qui partait de la rivière Saguenay, pour redescendre rejoindre un deuxième avion, à l'embouchure du Saguenay. Les deux avions se séparaient pour couvrir simultanément le secteur amont et le secteur aval, à une heure dans le cycle de marée qui permettait aux deux avions de couvrir le secteur contre le sens du courant. Ces lignes sont séparées de 4 milles marins — pour vous donner une idée de l'étendue de l'aire de distribution qui était survolée à faible vitesse et à une altitude de 3 000 pieds. Lorsqu'un groupe était repéré, il était encerclé par l'avion, toujours à 3 000 pieds, pour permettre aux observateurs de faire un bon décompte. Pour vous donner une idée de ce qu'on a aperçu lors de ces quatre survols, une distribution qui semble d'un premier coup d'œil assez homogène, de la Batture-aux-Loups-marins, où on a observé des gros groupes de près de 70 animaux, jusqu'à Saint-Simon, où on a pu voir encore de gros troupeaux. Pour l'ensemble des quatre survols, cela a donné une moyenne de 458 bélugas observés. Il faut bien s'entendre, il ne s'agit pas ici d'un estimé de la population. Ce n'était pas l'objectif de ces survols. Le but était de fournir une bonne image de la distribution des bélugas. On utilise donc ce chiffre, 458, et un chiffre qui est intéressant, le coefficient de variation de 6 %. Il donne une idée de l'ampleur des variations d'un survol à l'autre. Les chiffres ont varié très peu d'un survol à l'autre, et on utilisera ce nombre moyen de bélugas pour comparer l'importance des secteurs. Cette apparente homogénéité dans le nombre de bélugas à l'intérieur de l'aire de distribution ne reflète pas une homogénéité dans la distribution proprement dite. Si l'on prend deux survols, on constate deux distributions très différentes. Au mois de septembre 1988, près des trois quarts des animaux observés lors des survols l'ont été près de l'embouchure du Saguenay, tandis qu'au mois de juillet, le très gros groupe était observé loin en aval et loin en amont.

Pour résumer ces quatre survols, qui ont couvert l'ensemble du territoire, je présente ici un histogramme qui donne l'importance relative de chacun des secteurs qu'on retrouve ici : « le S » étant la rivière Saguenay. Les secteurs les plus importants sont D et E et il y a une petite information très intéressante. Si l'on se rappelle du coefficient de variations sur le nombre moyen global, qui était de 6,6 %, ces coefficients de variations vont ici, pour les différents secteurs, de 60 à 142, ce qui montre des variations énormes dans la distribution à l'intérieur de chacun des secteurs, mais pas à l'intérieur de l'aire de distribution. Alors, pour bien comprendre la distribution, il faut savoir que les chiffres varient beaucoup à l'intérieur des différents secteurs. On doit utiliser

FIGURE 2

Distribution des observations de bélugas à l'intérieur des sept secteurs de l'aire d'étude

Les coefficients de variation pour chacune des moyennes sont indiqués au-dessus des barres.

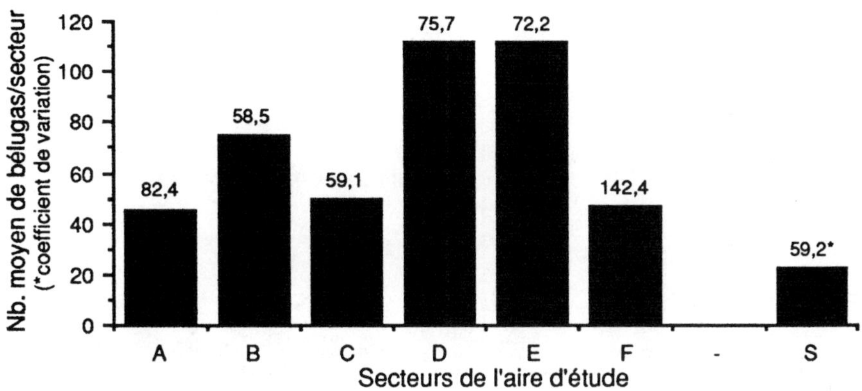

des repérages systématiques et très nombreux pour pouvoir identifier les zones importantes.

En 1987 et 1988, une dizaine de survols aériens ont été faits dans le secteur des îles de Kamouraska jusqu'à la Batture-aux-Loups-marins (secteur A + B), toujours pour le compte d'Hydro Québec et avec le soutien d'organismes comme la Société zoologique de Montréal et Greenpeace. Et à ces dix survols, qui ont couvert exclusivement ce secteur, s'ajoutent les quatre autres survols de l'aire totale. En moyenne, cela a donné 133 bélugas observés dans ce secteur. Le nombre est peu intéressant, mais tout simplement, la proportion entre ce 133 et la moyenne totale 458, nous donne à peu près 26% de la population qui utilise ce secteur. Les zones foncées sont les zones d'utilisation les plus intensives. Le secteur de l'île de Kamouraska ressort comme étant le secteur le plus utilisé. Des bélugas ont été vus là à toutes les occasions et jusqu'à 10% de la population en moyenne fréquente ce secteur. Les autres zones importantes sont la traverse Saint-Roch, Cap-aux-Oies, Rivière-Ouelle.

Le même type d'information a été recueillie pour la distribution en amont, dans un autre secteur, cette fois-ci avec un bateau, utilisant des transects systématiques. L'aire d'étude était comprise entre l'embouchure du Saguenay et les îles de Kamouraska. Elle était séparée en huit parcelles parcourues par des lignes centrales. Plusieurs informations ont été recueillies par bateau. Je présenterai ici seulement les informations qui nous donneront un indice de l'abondance relative des différents secteurs. Pour le faire, on voulait vérifier quelle était notre capacité à compter les animaux en fonction de la distance, en perpendiculaire avec

FIGURE 3

Distribution de la fréquence des observations en fonction de la distance perpendiculaire de la ligne de transect

On remarque une chute de près de 50 % entre 600 m et 700 m. La bande de 600 m de part et d'autre de la ligne de transect a été retenue pour établir les indices d'abondance relative.

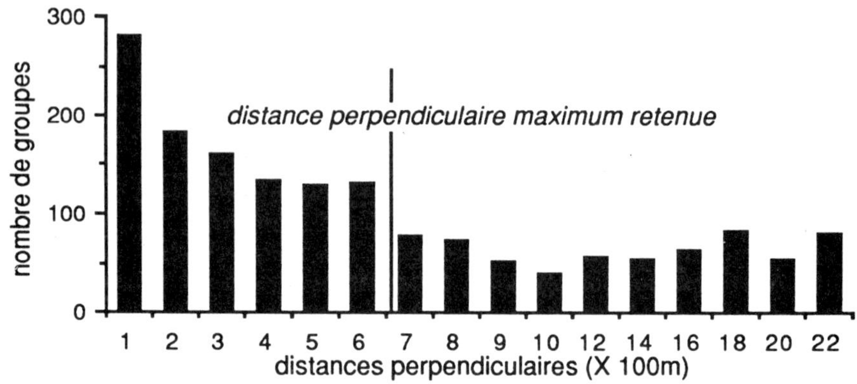

notre bateau. Sur la figure 3, on voit le nombre de groupes observés en fonction des bandes de distance, qui sont 100, 200, 300 mètres. On s'aperçoit qu'après 600 mètres, il y a une chute assez importante, de près de la moitié. C'est donc la bande de 1 à 600 mètres qu'on a conservée pour établir les indices d'abondance. Les résultats obtenus sont présentés à la figure 4 : encore une fois, les zones foncées sont les zones d'abondance relative assez élevée, les secteurs A, C, G et J sont fortement utilisés ; les secteurs D et K, faibles intermédiaires ; et H et B, de faible utilisation.

Toutes ces données recueillies sur la distribution devraient nous permettre plusieurs choses : entre autres, estimer le pourcentage des gris, la proportion d'animaux immatures dans l'ensemble de la population. On a testé cette méthode à l'intérieur des transects en bateau, en 1986. Alors, comme pour les nombres observés, on veut vérifier notre capacité à détecter le pourcentage de gris en fonction de la distance. Et on s'aperçoit que, à l'intérieur d'une bande de 400 mètres, notre capacité à détecter des gris est homogène. Après 400 mètres, il y a une chute assez importante. On a donc conservé les observations faites à l'intérieur des 400 mètres, de part et d'autre du bateau, sur l'ensemble des 105 transects. En tout, l'estimation de proportion de gris a été faite sur un total de 1 248 bélugas. L'image que cela donne, dans l'ensemble de la couverture, c'est un pourcentage de gris moyen estimé à 44 ou 45 %. Si c'était le pourcentage de gris dans l'ensemble de la population, ce serait une très bonne nouvelle. Mais on s'attendait à un chiffre élevé dans ce secteur-là,

FIGURE 4

Distribution des observations de bélugas le long de 8 transects systématiques (A à K) parcourus en bateau en 1986

Pour chacun des transects, le nombre moyen de bélugas par quadrat (2,2 km²) évalué pour l'ensemble du quadrat, ainsi que le nombre de réplicats, sont indiqués entre parenthèses.

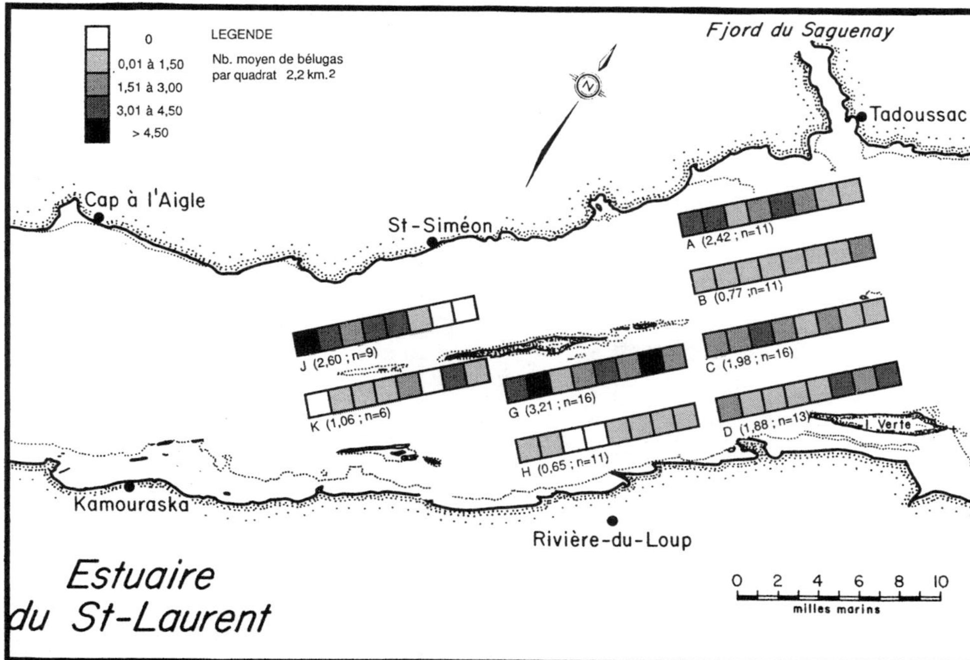

parce qu'il s'agit d'un secteur où on prévoyait rencontrer le plus grand nombre d'animaux immatures. Ce qui est intéressant aussi, c'est la distribution illustrée : les carrés blancs sont les carrés pour lesquels on n'a pas de pourcentage, parce qu'on n'a pas vu suffisamment d'animaux. Autrement pour tous les autres carrés, on voit que la distribution est à peu près homogène, et elle l'est effectivement, passant de 48 à 42, 41, 46, 40, 41, 51. Il n'y a pas de différences significatives entre ces pourcentages de gris.

Toutes ces informations sur la distribution et l'utilisation de cette méthode pourraient nous permettre d'établir le pourcentage de gris dans l'ensemble de la population, ainsi que plusieurs détails sur les habitats critiques. J'ai fait un résumé graphique (figure 5) de toutes ces observations. On reconnaît les secteurs qu'on avait tout à l'heure. Les chiffres en gras représentent le pourcentage d'animaux qu'on a observés dans ces secteurs, pour l'ensemble des quatre survols, c'est-à-dire que, lors des quatre survols, on a vu 24 % des animaux, dans le secteur de l'île Rouge et l'île Blanche, l'île Verte, battures aux Alouettes et les zones hachurées sont les secteurs de fréquentation plus élevée. Ainsi, pour déterminer, par exemple, le pourcentage de gris dans l'ensemble de la population, au lieu d'aller prélever des échantillons au hasard un peu partout, on dispose maintenant d'une information assez fiable pour aller échantillonner de façon proportionnelle dans chacun de ces endroits, et pour déterminer ensuite un pourcentage global des gris dans l'ensemble de la population. C'est la même chose pour l'étude des habitats critiques. On a identifié certains secteurs et, en mettant sur pied les programmes de transects, comme on l'a fait pour cette aire de distribution, en appliquant cette méthode à l'ensemble du territoire, en déployant un effort proportionnel au pourcentage comparatif de l'importance de chacun des secteurs, on pourrait recueillir beaucoup d'informations pour caractériser les habitats critiques. Pour qui sont-ils critiques, quand et pour quels types d'activités ? Pour déterminer ce genre de choses, il faut passer énormément de temps sur l'eau, regarder les animaux, voir quels comportements ils ont, combien de temps ils restent dans chacun des secteurs, et peut-être aussi qui est dans ces secteurs-là. Pour déterminer tout cela, il existe une technique bien simple, qui s'appelle la photo-identification. Elle est utilisable pour à peu près tous les animaux de la planète. Ils ont tous des patrons distincts. Quand c'est dans la pigmentation, comme chez les zèbres, c'est beaucoup plus facile. Chez les bélugas on peut utiliser autre chose : les cicatrices qui sont assez nombreuses chez ces animaux. Et ce dont on s'est aperçu depuis 1985, et en étudiant les banques de données de Leone Pippard et de Andrew McFarlane, c'est que certaines marques restent très longtemps et pourront être très utiles pour étudier la population. Par exemple, on a des photos montrant un animal, Alpha, dont une grosse cicatrice sur la crête dorsale est restée intacte depuis 1980 et deux petites bandes noires sur le côté de l'animal sont aussi restées entre 1980 et 1986-1987. On n'a

FIGURE 5

Sommaire des observations aériennes de bélugas lors des survols de 1987 et 1988
Les pourcentages d'animaux observés dans chacune des zones, pour l'ensemble des quatre survols, sont inscrits en caractères gras. Les zones hachurées indiquent les secteurs de plus fortes concentrations.

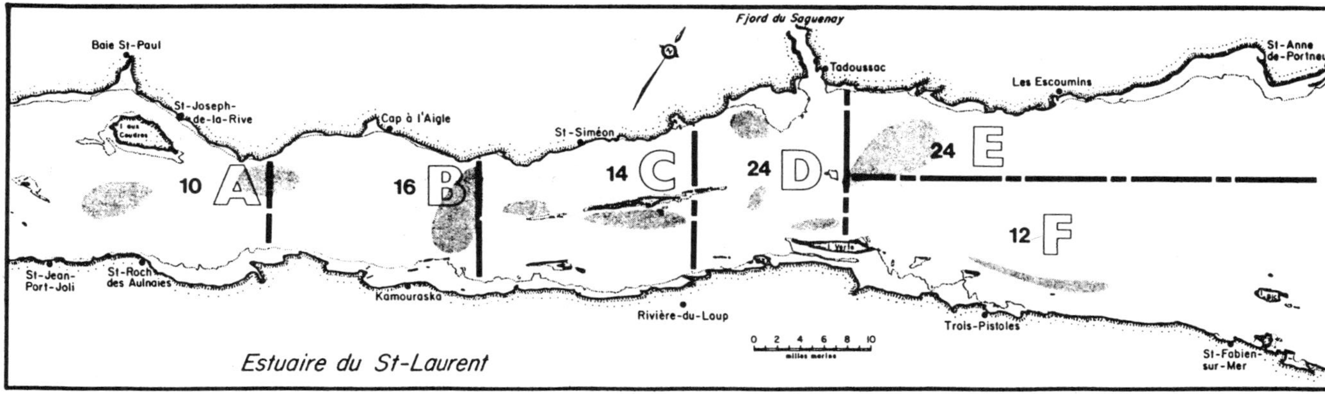

malheureusement pas de photo de Alpha du côté droit pour 1988. Pour Christa, c'est la même chose depuis 1980. On apprend aussi les associations de ces animaux. On sait ainsi que Christa est vue régulièrement avec Walter depuis 1985. On apprend, avec ces programmes de photo-identification, l'histoire individuelle de certains animaux, comme Kilt, observé la première fois en 1986, puis en 1987 et deux fois cette année en 1988. On voit que sa cicatrice, très particulière, a bien évolué. On sait que Kilt est un mâle. Quand les animaux viennent proche du bateau, on peut parvenir à prendre des photos en mettant les mains dans l'eau. Parfois, cela donne des belles photos, des photos intéressantes. On a ainsi photographié Clearasil, qui est le copain de Kilt, dont on voit que c'est un mâle, avec son anus et ses glandes mammaires situés derrière la glande génitale.

Je vous ai fait une présentation très rapide, ce matin, de l'ensemble des données dont on dispose depuis 1986 sur la distribution. Je vous ai aussi montré comment ces données pourront être utilisées pour deux choses bien importantes ; peut-être pour déterminer la proportion des gris dans l'ensemble de la population, qui semble être un indice très prometteur pour évaluer l'évolution, la stabilité ou la décroissance de la population des bélugas du Saint-Laurent ; et aussi pour caractériser les habitats importants pour les bélugas dans le Saint-Laurent, ce qui nous permettrait, par exemple, d'établir une liste des secteurs prioritaires à protéger pour un sanctuaire, une réserve ou un parc marin. Est-ce que l'embouchure du Saguenay est véritablement l'endroit le plus propice ou le plus important pour faire une zone protégée pour les bélugas ? Est-ce que c'est en protégeant ce secteur-là qu'on va avoir le meilleur impact sur la protection des bélugas ? Il faudrait regarder toutes les données pour les autres secteurs. Il y a peut-être d'autres secteurs où il y a plus de veaux, plus d'autres types d'activités.

Variation annuelle des déplacements et de la composition des groupes de bélugas à l'embouchure du Saguenay

Louise M. J. Caron
Ketos

INTRODUCTION

L'embouchure de la rivière Saguenay est au centre de la distribution estivale actuelle du béluga du Saint-Laurent. C'est le point de confluence des bélugas provenant, entre autres, des troupeaux d'adultes souvent observés au large des Escoumins et de ceux composés d'adultes et de jeunes fréquentant les abords de l'Île aux Lièvres et la partie de l'estuaire du Saint-Laurent située en amont de l'embouchure du Saguenay (Pippard 1985 ; Sergeant 1986). Les raisons de l'utilisation de la rivière Saguenay par les bélugas sont encore mal connues. Certains font référence à plusieurs sites présumés d'alimentation situés en amont de l'embouchure (Laurin 1982; Pippard et Malcolm 1978). Les eaux de surface plus chaudes dans le Saguenay (Drainville 1968) ont également été suggérées comme attrait pour les femelles accompagnées de leurs jeunes (Pippard et Malcolm 1978; Sergeant 1986). Quelle que soit la raison, le Saguenay est une importante zone de fréquentation par le béluga et ce, même en présence de perturbations importantes du milieu par l'homme, notamment le trafic maritime.

La Pointe-Noire est située sur la rive sud-ouest de l'embouchure du Saguenay, à l'opposé de la ville de Tadoussac (Figure 1). Ce site est reconnu depuis plusieurs années comme un site privilégié d'observation de bélugas à partir de la terre. La plupart des recherches sur les déplacements et la composition des groupes de bélugas à cet endroit ont eu lieu pendant les mois d'été. Depuis 1973, une série de chercheurs se

FIGURE 1

Site d'observations de bélugas de Pointe-Noire

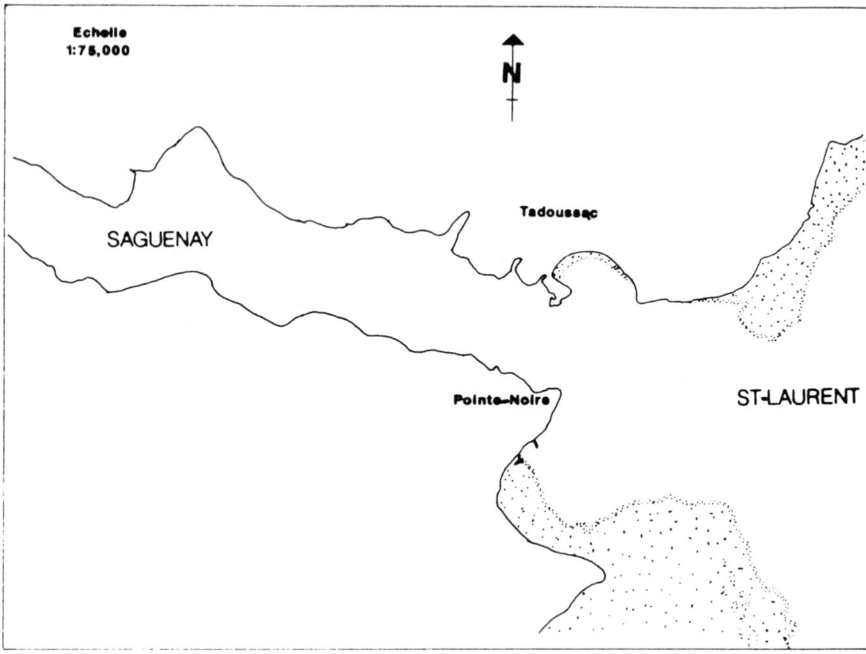

sont succédés à Pointe-Noire : Laurin (1982) entre 1973 et 1975, Pippard et Malcolm (1978) en 1975 et 1977, Sergeant (1986) entre 1982 et 1984, et les naturalistes du groupe Ketos de 1986 jusqu'à tout récemment en septembre 1988. Il existe donc par ce fait une série temporelle d'information relativement longue sur les nombres et les types de groupes qui se déplacent à cet endroit. Il est à noter que les résultats présentés ici correspondent aux sources mentionnées plus haut.

RÉSULTATS ET DISCUSSION

La majorité des observateurs ont utilisé des méthodes d'observation identiques, ou tout au moins comparables entre elles. Celles-ci consistaient à dénombrer les groupes de bélugas en déplacement dans l'embouchure, ainsi que leur composition en classe d'âge (adulte, blanchon, bleuvet et veau). L'horaire d'observation consistait à passer le plus grand nombre possible d'heures à surveiller l'embouchure du Saguenay à l'aide de jumelles ou de lunettes d'approche.

La répartition des heures d'observation de chacune des années d'observation (Figure 2) s'est révélée normale (statistique de Shapiro-Wilk, W > 0,938 : Shapiro and Wilk 1965) et leurs moyennes, variant de 11 heures 52 minutes à 13 heures 12 minutes, n'étaient pas significativement différentes les unes des autres (test T modifié pour variance inégale, p > 0,05 : Sokal and Rohlf 1981). Il serait donc permis ici de comparer l'information contenue dans ces années d'observations.

FIGURE 2

Répartition des heures d'observations à partir de Pointe-Noire de 1975 à 1987

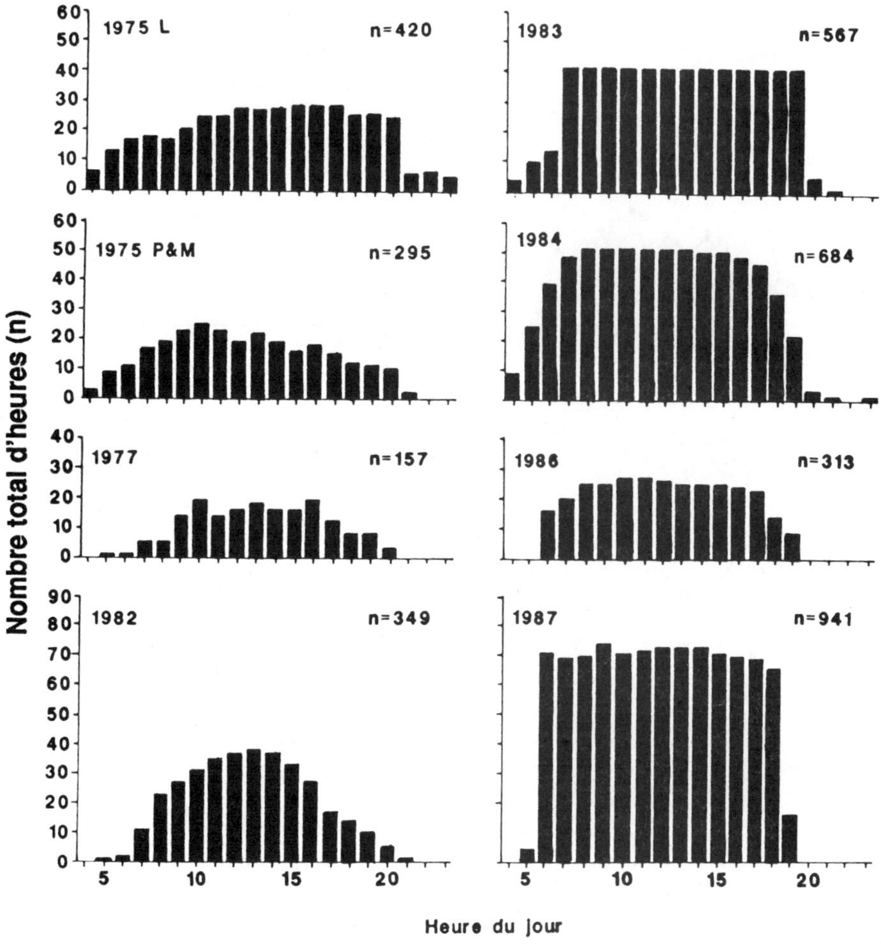

La distribution journalière des passages amont ou aval des bélugas de 1982 à 1987 (Figure 3), exprimée en taux horaire (nb bélugas/nb tranches d'heure), ne montre pas de tendance claire quant à l'heure du jour des déplacements, sauf peut-être en 1987 où il semble y avoir une légère tendance à la baisse vers la fin de la journée. Les lignes pointillées verticales sur ces graphiques délimitent les heures d'observations journalières les plus abondantes. En dehors de ces limites, l'échantillonnage

FIGURE 3

Distribution des taux de passages de bélugas dans l'embouchure du Saguenay selon l'heure de la journée de 1982 à 1987

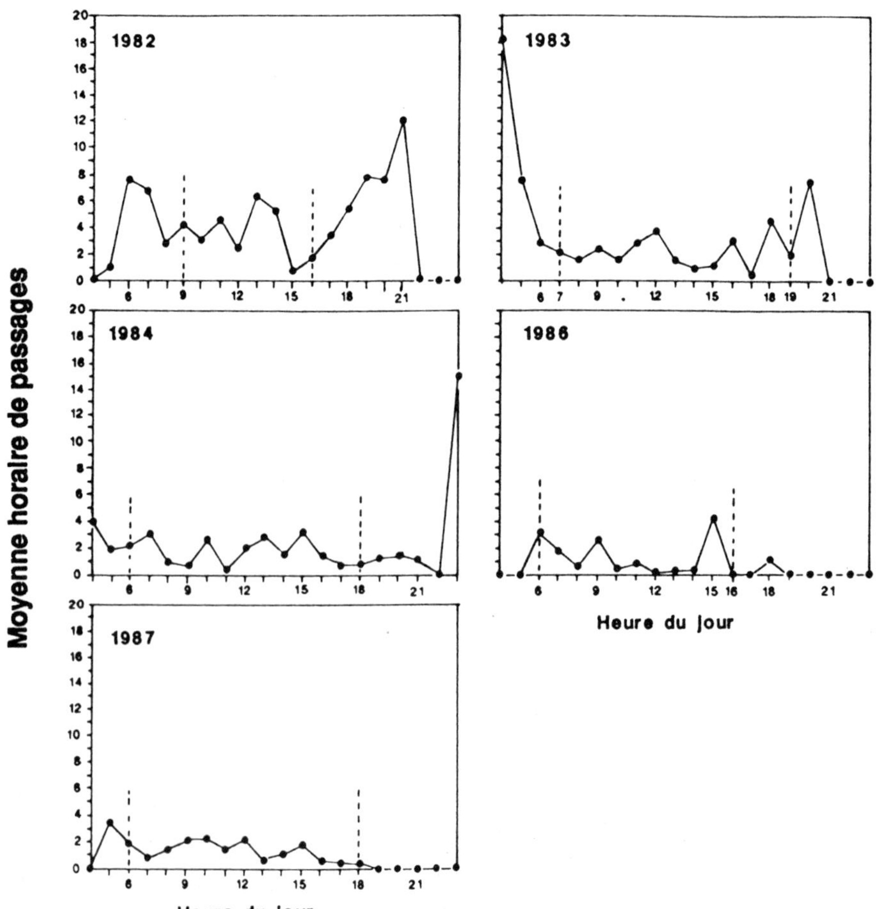

a été plus rare et rend donc la valeur de la moyenne des passages de bélugas moins représentative de ces tranches d'heures. D'autres chercheurs avaient également noté une plus grande abondance de mouvements en avant-midi (Laurin 1982 ; Pippard 1985). On remarque cependant plusieurs pics de passages durant la journée qui nécessiteront de plus amples analyses. Il est intéressant de noter, qu'en 1987, il y a eu une légère prédominance de passages vers l'aval, plus de 58 % des passages observés. Les données de Pippard (1985) pour les années 1975 et 1977 montrent également une légère disparité dans la direction des mouvements, soit environ 56 % de passages vers l'aval.

Les passages horaires de bélugas cumulés mensuellement pour les années 1975 à 1987 (Figure 4) ne montrent pas non plus de tendance ou de patron consistant d'une année à l'autre (Caron et Sergeant 1989, sous presse). Les plus nombreux passages ont eu lieu indifféremment en juin, juillet ou en août. Afin de pouvoir comparer les années entre elles, il semble donc plus adéquat de cumuler les passages de bélugas pour toutes les heures d'observation en sélectionnant les mois consécutifs les plus échantillonnés pour chaque année. Dans le cas présent, les mois de juin, juillet et août ont été retenus.

FIGURE 4

Taux mensuels de passages de bélugas dans l'embouchure du Saguenay de 1975 à 1987

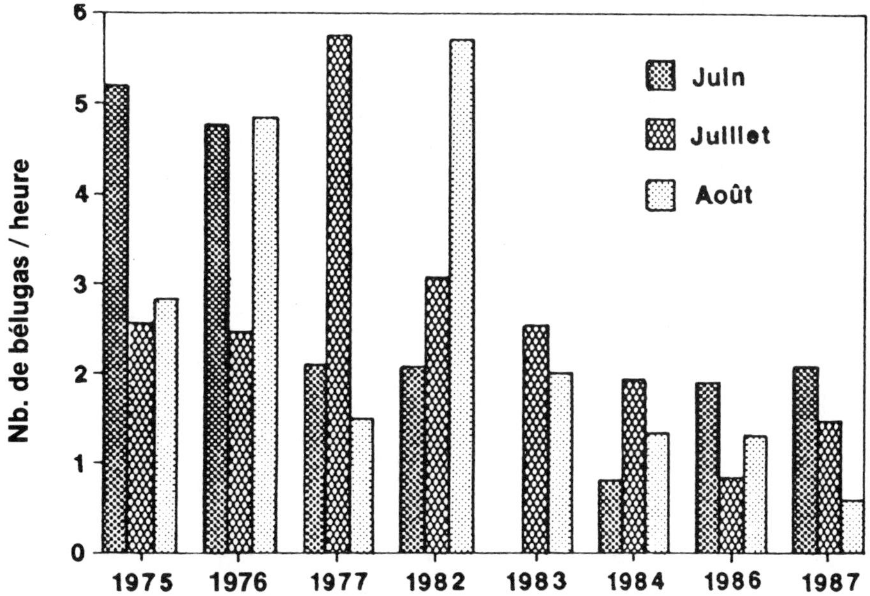

De 1975 à 1988, le taux horaire de passage de bélugas à l'embouchure du Saguenay a passé de près de 4 bélugas à l'heure à environ 1 béluga à l'heure (Figure 5). Cette chute s'est effectuée principalement au début des années 80, soit entre 1982 et 1986, et semble s'être stabilisée à ce taux en 1987 (Caron et Sergeant 1989, sous presse) et en 1988 (0,9 bélugas/heure, données de Ketos non publiées). Il est à noter que pour les années 1982 à 1988, les données contiennent un certain pourcentage d'individus qui n'ont été présents que dans la Baie-Sainte-Catherine, celui-ci étant cependant faible. Or, les taux de passage de bélugas calculés sont, en effet, une légère sur-estimation du taux réel de passage par rapport au taux de passage pour les années antérieures.

Une telle réduction de la fréquence de passage des bélugas dans le Saguenay n'est pas expliquée par une réduction correspondante dans l'effectif de la population du Saint-Laurent. En effet, il semble y avoir un commun accord entre les chercheurs pour dire que la population de bélugas du Saint-Laurent est de 500 individus (Sergeant 1986; Sergeant and Hoek 1988). S'il y a eu un déclin dans la population, il n'est pas de l'ordre du déclin observé à Pointe-Noire. Les causes possibles de la diminution du taux de passage de bélugas seront discutées plus loin.

La grande majorité des passages de bélugas en 1987, soit plus de 80%, ont suivi une trajectoire qui longeait la côte ouest de la rivière Saguenay, à moins de 100 mètres de Pointe-Noire (Figure 6). L'abondante

FIGURE 5

Passages horaires totaux de bélugas à Pointe-Noire de 1975 à 1987

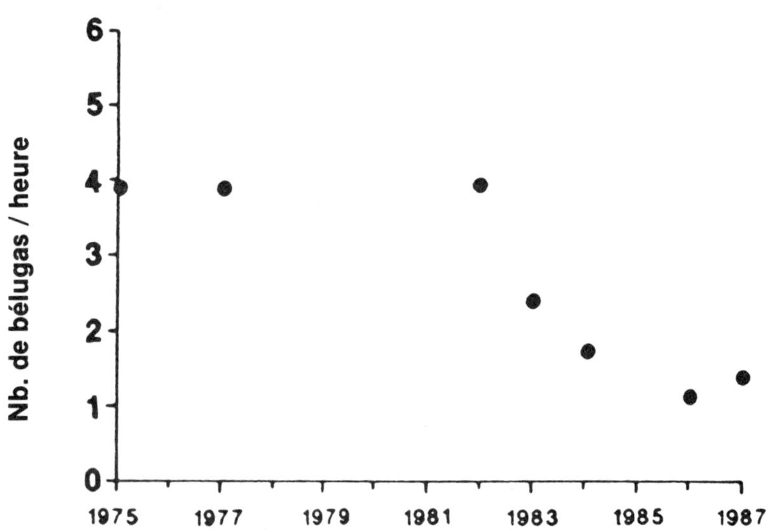

FIGURE 6

Trajectoires empruntées par les bélugas au cours de leurs déplacements dans l'embouchure du Saguenay en 1987

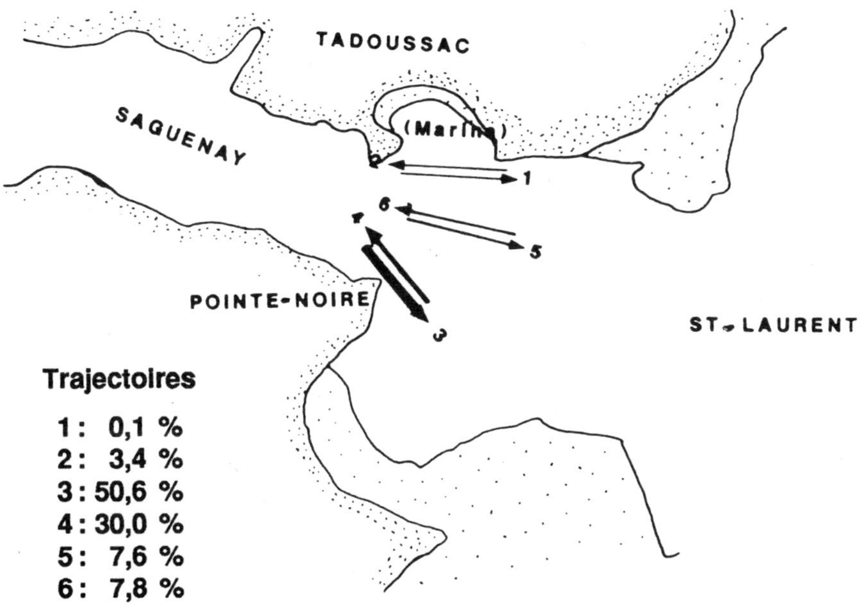

utilisation de cette trajectoire a également été notée par d'autres chercheurs (Pippard et Malcolm 1978 ; Pippard 1985), et est certainement la cause du choix historique de Pointe-Noire comme site d'observation de bélugas. Les autres trajectoires empruntées sont, en ordre décroissant, le chenal central et le long de la rive nord près de Tadoussac, soit 15,4 % et 3,5 % respectivement.

Des groupes, ou unités sociales, peuvent également être identifiés. La définition d'un groupe est certainement un point de litige pour ce genre d'étude, mais les observateurs ont, en général, considéré les groupes comme tout nombre d'individus évoluant relativement près les uns des autres dans la même direction et trajectoire.

Le nombre total de groupes pour les années 1982 à 1988 était de 120, 89, 96, 88, 155, et 185 respectivement (1985 n'ayant pas été échantillonné). La distribution de la fréquence des différentes tailles de groupes (variant de 1 à un peu plus de 100 individus) montre qu'il y a eu, durant cette période, une décroissance de la fréquence des groupes dépassant la vingtaine d'individus et une augmentation des groupes de moins de 10 individus (Figure 7 : tiré d'un article en préparation). Les

FIGURE 7

Répartition de la taille des groupes de bélugas en 1983, 1984, 1987 et 1988 à l'embouchure du Saguenay

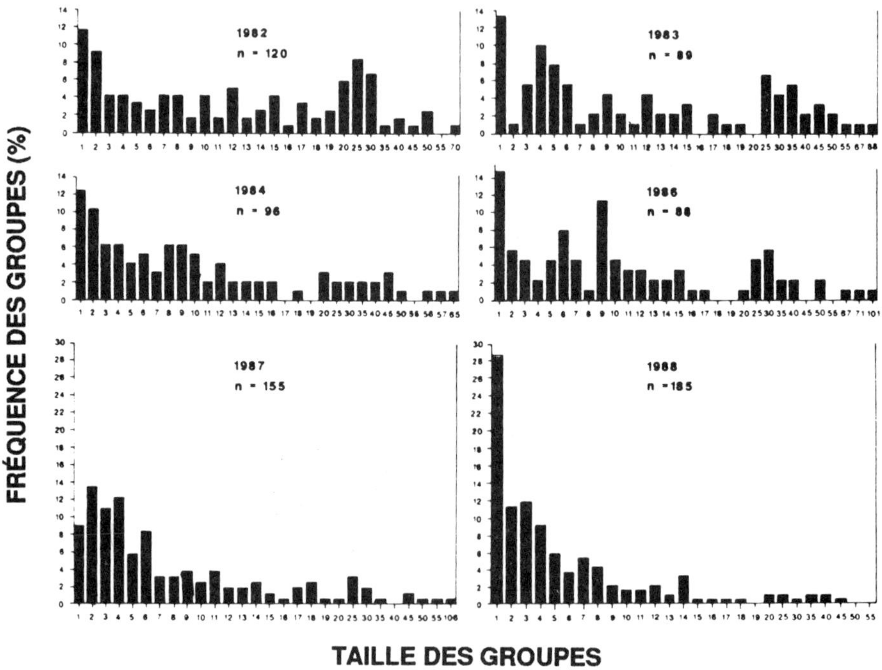

singletons représentaient environ 30% de tous les groupes observés en 1988, tandis que dans les années antérieures ce pourcentage variait entre 11 et 14%. Les groupes de 20 à 50 individus ont progressivement diminué depuis 1982, passant de 31% à 5% en 1988. Même si la définition pratique des groupes a pu varier entre les groupes d'observateurs, soit Sergeant *et al.* et Ketos, la même tendance au fractionnement des groupes de bélugas a été notée pour leurs données respectives. Les pourcentages d'abondance de groupes formés de 20 à 50 animaux ont passé de 31%, à 26%, à 15% de 1982 à 1984, et de même les pourcentages des mêmes types de groupes de bélugas ont passé de 21%, à 9% à 5% de 1986 à 1988.

La détermination des classes d'âge des individus fréquentant le Saguenay a été effectuée avec plus ou moins de succès entre les années 1982 et 1988 (Figure 8). En 1982, 70% des individus n'ont pu être classés, de même qu'en 1986 où ce nombre a atteint plus de 80%. Il semble donc que pour chacune des équipes d'observateurs, la première année d'observation ait été moins fructueuse quant à la détermination des classes d'âge des bélugas.

FIGURE 8

Structure d'âge des bélugas à l'embouchure du Saguenay de 1982 à 1988

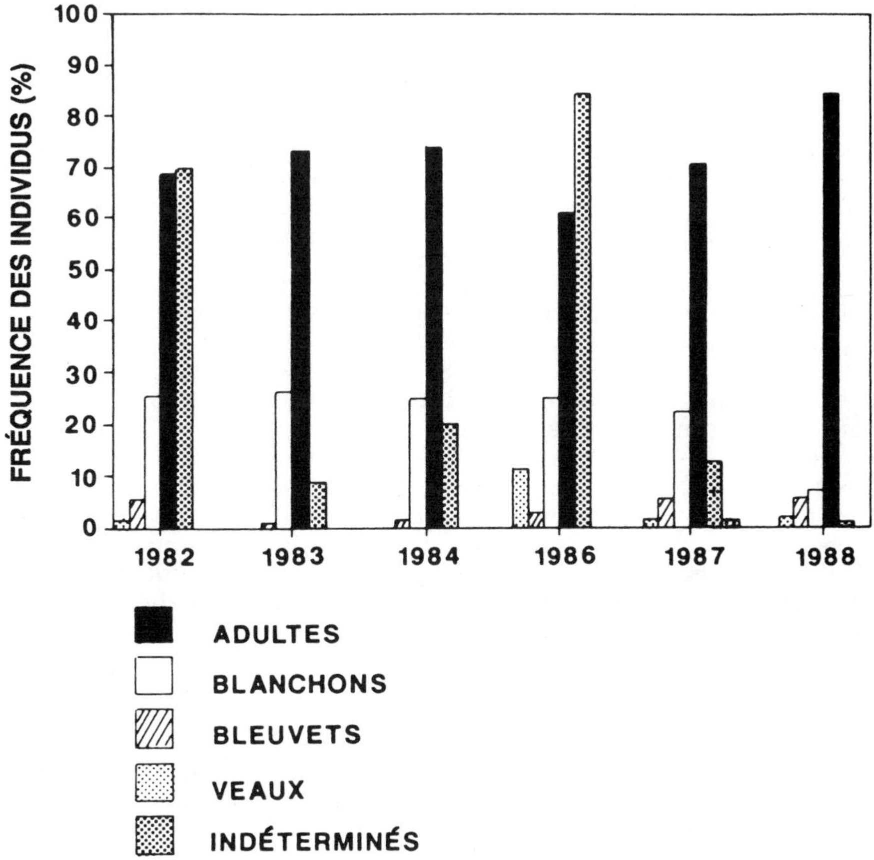

En n'utilisant donc que les années où les classes d'âge ont été assignées avec un certain succès, c'est-à-dire quand il y a eu moins de 20 % de bélugas de classe indéterminée, soit 1983, 1984, 1987 et 1988, on observe que l'abondance des classes d'âge est relativement uniforme pour ces 4 années. Le total des pourcentages des classes d'âge a donc été reporté à 100 % pour ces années afin de pouvoir faire des comparaisons.

La structure d'âge en 1983 et 1984 est presque identique. Les adultes représentaient 72,9 % et 73,7 % du troupeau, les blanchons 26,3 % et 24,8 %, et les bleuvets 0,7 et 1,5 % respectivement. Cependant, aucun veau n'a été vu durant ces 2 années. En 1987 et 1988, les adultes représentaient 70,5 % et 84,9 % du troupeau, les blanchons 22,3 % et 7,2 %, les bleuvets 5,7 % et 5,8 %, et finalement les veaux représentaient 1,4 % et 2,0 % respectivement. Pour ces 2 années, il semble que ce soit la classe des blanchons qui ait subi le plus grand déclin, passant de 22,3 % à 7,2 %, avec une augmentation correspondante d'adultes de 70,5 % à 84,9 %. Par ailleurs, il est intéressant de noter que Pippard et Malcolm (1978) ont remarqué qu'il y avait une prédominance de femelles accompagnées de jeunes dans le troupeau qui fréquentait le Saguenay en 1975 et 1977. Les variations interannuelles de structure d'âge représentent peut-être des tendances au niveau de la population. Même si cela n'est pas le cas, il serait essentiel de comprendre les phénomènes qui font varier la structure d'âge du troupeau qui fréquente le Saguenay afin de déterminer les cibles et les risques de perturbations de cet habitat.

L'information sur la répartition de la taille des groupes a été intégrée à celle de la structure d'âge pour les quatre meilleures années d'observation (Figure 9 : tiré d'un article en préparation). Pour ce, les classes d'âge ont été numérisées à l'aide d'une échelle ordinale (1 = veau, 2 = bleuvet, 3 = blanchon et 4 = adulte), afin de pouvoir calculer l'âge moyen des groupes. On remarque tout d'abord que pour deux paires d'années (1983-1984 et 1987-1988), il y a eu une nette diminution de la proportion des groupes qui avaient un âge moyen entre 3 et 4 ans, accompagnée d'une augmentation de la proportion des groupes composés principalement d'adultes. Par ailleurs, on sait que la récente prédominance des groupes singletons est principalement composée d'adultes dont on ignore évidemment le sexe. Ceci reflèterait donc une diminution dans la proportion de groupes d'âge mixte observés en déplacement à Pointe-Noire. Les groupes de petite taille (1-10 individus) sont les plus variables en terme de classe d'âge, suivis des groupes de 11 à 30 et de plus de 30 individus. Les petits groupes sont donc composés soit d'adultes uniquement, soit d'adultes et de jeunes, soit uniquement de jeunes individus. Puisqu'on a remarqué une augmentation de la fréquence de ces types de groupes, l'unité sociale, qui était composée d'un plus grand nombre d'individus de classes d'âge plus variables, se trouve maintenant réduite en taille et en diversité. Les conséquences de ce morcellement social sont évidemment inconnues et pourraient être importantes pour le succès reproductif de l'espèce.

Pour résumer les changements observés chez les bélugas fréquentant le Saguenay, on note : 1) une importante diminution dans le taux de passage à l'embouchure du Saguenay durant les heures de jour, 2) une réduction de la taille et de la diversité des groupes, et 3) une variation possible dans la structure d'âge du troupeau fréquentant le Saguenay. Les causes de ces changements sont probablement multiples. Nous sommes très certainement en présence de résultats de phénomènes complexes. Cependant, comme mentionné précédemment, la population totale du Saint-Laurent ne semble pas avoir chuté dramatiquement depuis un quinzaine d'années (Sergeant 1986). Il semble plutôt que les

FIGURE 9

Répartition de l'âge moyen par catégorie de taille de groupes de bélugas à l'embouchure du Saguenay en 1983, 1984, 1987 et 1988

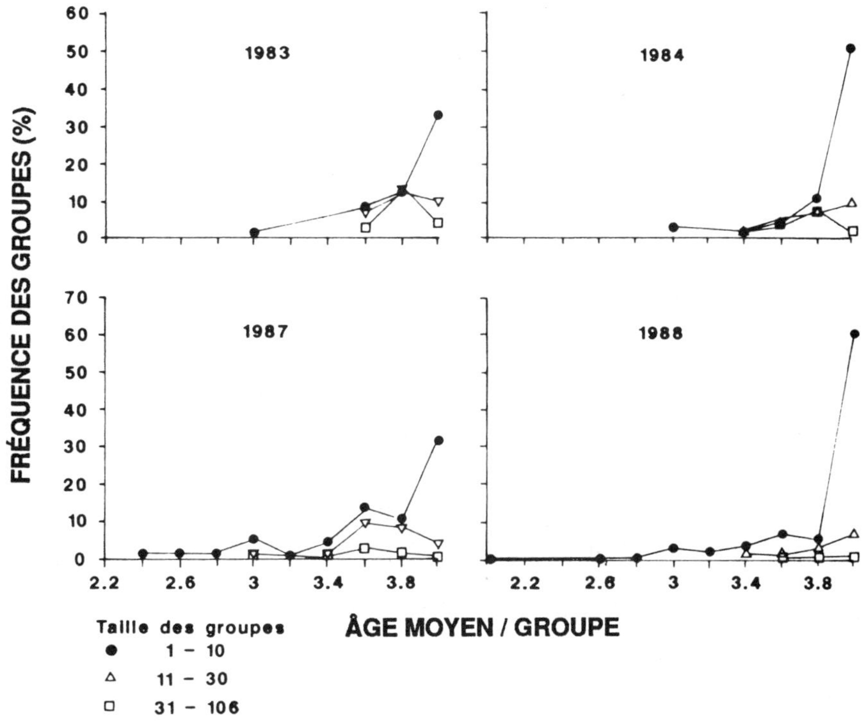

variations observées chez les bélugas à l'embouchure du Saguenay soient causées par une perturbation locale.

Même si les rejets de substances toxiques tels le mercure, et les HAP (Smith and Loring 1981 ; Martel *et al.* 1986) dans les eaux du Saguenay, semblent avoir diminué depuis les années 70, la contamination au niveau du benthos reste élevée et semble affecter principalement les organismes reliés à cet habitat par leur comportement alimentaire, entre autres le béluga. Des études récentes ont révélé de très fortes concentrations en BPC dans les tissus adipeux de bélugas échoués (Massé *et al.* 1986 ; Martineau *et al.* 1987). Il serait extrêmement difficile de démontrer les effets des polluants sur le comportement des bélugas et ne relèverait pas du domaine des recherches qui ont été effectuées à Pointe-Noire.

Il est certain qu'une relation de cause à effet qui s'étend sur une échelle temporelle aussi longue (plusieurs années) est très souvent difficile à prouver. Cependant, lorsque cette même relation est démontrée sur une échelle temporelle beaucoup plus courte (horaire par exemple), la preuve d'une relation de causalité devient plus substantielle. La nature plus détaillée des données prises à Pointe-Noire au cours de 1987 et 1988 permet de vérifier si les facteurs environnementaux tels les marées, l'heure de la journée, et (ou) le passage des bateaux ont une influence sur le passage des bélugas.

Un modèle de coefficients de direction a été élaboré à cette fin (Legendre et Legendre 1984). Dans ce modèle, toutes les relations possibles entre les facteurs environnementaux eux-mêmes (incluant les bateaux), et entre ceux-ci et les passages de bélugas, ont été testées. La direction des relations était fixée à priori, c'est-à-dire qu'il était évident que certains facteurs pouvaient en influencer d'autres mais pas le contraire. Ce genre de modèle permet donc d'exprimer une causalité faible entre les variables. Une telle analyse offre l'avantage de permettre la distinction entre les relations de causalité directe, de causalité indirecte (en passant par une variable intermédiaire), et de non-causalité (variable non incluse dans le modèle).

Dans un premier temps, uniquement les données de 1987 ont été utilisées. Dans ce modèle, les variables suivantes ont été incluses : l'heure, la marée, le vent, l'état de la mer, et le nombre de passages de bateaux (comme pour le nombre de passages de bélugas). Les variables circulaires (marée, vent et heure) ont été transformées et linéarisées afin de pouvoir les inclure dans le modèle. Toutes les variables étaient cumulées ou intégrées, selon le cas, sur des tranches successives d'une heure pour chaque journée d'observation. Les données qui viennent tout juste d'être recueillies en 1988 seront, à leur tour, traitées et analysées de façon identifique (article en préparation). Il est important de souligner que les résultats présentés ici ne sont pas encore révisés.

Le modèle global, celui contenant toutes les combinaisons de relations possibles, a été successivement départi des relations non significatives. Le dernier modèle, celui-ci étant beaucoup plus réduit que le global, montre que cinq facteurs environnementaux influencent de façon significative et directe (Bonneferoni, $p < 0{,}0005$: Legendre et Legendre 1984) et explique un peu plus de 16% de la variation observée des mouvements de bélugas. En 1987, les passages diminuaient avec l'heure du jour ($r = -0{,}26$), augmentaient avec les marées montantes (cosinus de la marée, $r = -0{,}26$), diminuaient avec la saison, ou le mois ($r = -0{,}17$), augmentaient lorsque le vent venait de la côte, *i.e.* du nord (sinus du vent, $r = 0{,}12$), et finalement diminuaient lorsque le nombre total de bateaux circulant dans l'embouchure augmentait ($r = 0{,}25$).

Les effets directs des bateaux et du vent sur les mouvements des bélugas contiennent également des effets indirects provenant de l'effet du mois sur ceux-ci, c'est-à-dire que le mois, facteur intermédiaire, influencait le nombre de bateaux présents ainsi que la direction du vent. Le tableau suivant inspiré de Legendre et Legendre (1984) montre la décomposition des covariations de ces deux triangles.

En d'autres termes, l'effet du mois sur les passages de bélugas est composé d'une covariance causale directe et indirecte. La composante directe (-0,17) est accompagnée d'une composante indirecte (-0,07), elle-même composée de deux routes, celle passant par le vent (-0,26 × 0,12 = 0,03) et l'autre par les bateaux (-0,25 × 0,18 = 0,045).

Dans les relations entre le vent et les bélugas et entre les bateaux et les bélugas, il existe des composantes qui ne sont pas expliquées par le modèle, les covariations non causales (0,05 et 0,17 respectivement). Ces covariations non causales nous indiquent qu'il existerait d'autres variables (peut-être non mesurables) qui auraient influencé les mouvements des bélugas.

Déjà par l'analyse préliminaire des données de 1987, il ressort que plusieurs facteurs environnementaux influencent les passages des bélugas à l'embouchure du Saguenay, y compris le trafic maritime. Celui-ci apparaît comme un facteur négatif sur les mouvements des bélugas, à tout le moins en 1987. Il a été montré, par ailleurs, que les bélugas de l'Arctique canadien réagissaient fortement au trafic maritime occasionné par les vaisseaux brise-glaces (Finley and Davis 1984; Mansfield 1982) et ce, à une échelle de temps de l'ordre de l'heure.

Les facteurs naturels, tels le vent et les marées, mesurés lors de la présente étude n'ont, en toute vraisemblance, pas variés au cours des dernières années. Cependant, le trafic maritime de plaisance, lui, a augmenté de façon importante depuis 1980, passant, pour les mois de juillet, de 4 bateaux/heure à presque 8 bateaux/heure en 1987 (Figure 10: Caron et Sergeant 1989, sous presse), et à plus de 9 bateaux/heure en 1988, (Ketos, données non publiées). Alors que l'effet du trafic maritime sur les passages des bélugas est du même ordre de grandeur que d'autres facteurs physiques du milieu à l'échelle horaire, il est possible que cet effet négatif se soit cumulé sur plusieurs années, ce qui pourrait, au moins en partie, expliquer la chute du taux horaire de passage de bélugas depuis le début des années 1980.

Les trajectoires empruntées par les bateaux sont à l'opposé de celles empruntées par les bélugas, c'est-à-dire que le maximum des passages de bateaux est localisé près de Tadoussac (78%), et relativement peu de bateaux passent près de Pointe-Noire (Figure 11). Puisque les passages de bélugas se font en grande partie le long de la rive ouest du Saguenay, à l'opposé de Tadoussac, il serait important d'empêcher toute augmentation du chevauchement des trajectoires de bélugas et de bateaux afin de réduire l'effet négatif du trafic maritime sur les passages des bélugas.

TABLEAU 1

Décomposition des covariations

Relation totale	Covariation directe	indirecte	Covariation totale	Causale non causale	Covariation
Mois-Sinvent	-0,26	-0,26	0	-0,26	0
Sinvent-Bel	0,18	0,12	0,01	0,13	0,05
Mois-Bel	-0,23	-0,17	-0,07	-0,24	0,01
Mois-Totbat	0,15	0,18	-0,03	0,15	0
Totbat-Bel	-0,08	-0,25	0	-0,25	0,17
Mois-Bel	-0,23	-0,17	-0,07	-0,24	0,01

FIGURE 10

Taux mensuels de passages de bateaux à l'embouchure du Saguenay de 1980 à 1987

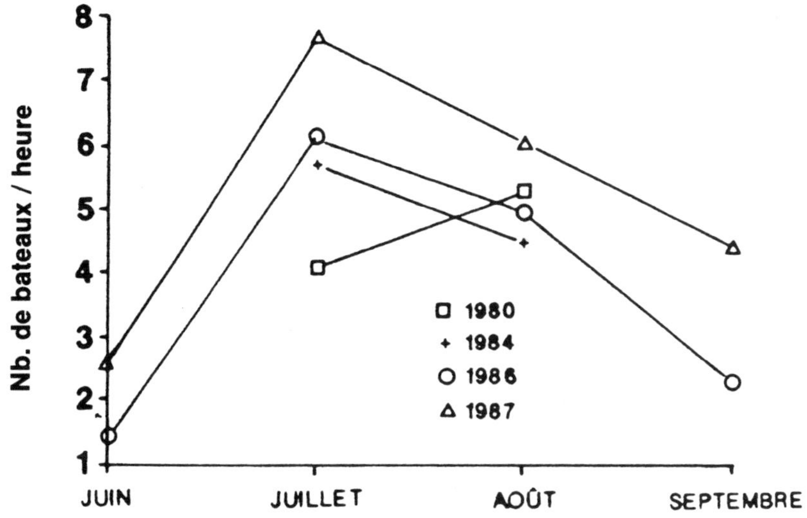

En conclusion, les variations observées du taux de fréquentation, de la taille et de la diversité des groupes et possiblement de la structure d'âge du troupeau qui fréquente le Saguenay sont importantes à deux niveaux. Premièrement au niveau local, si le taux de passage horaire à Pointe-Noire représente le taux de fréquentation du Saguenay par les bélugas, l'utilisation de cet habitat aurait diminué de façon marquée au cours des dernières années, privant les bélugas d'un habitat possiblement très important.

Deuxièmement au niveau de la population, puisque les bélugas du Saguenay font partie de la population du Saint-Laurent, les changements observés dans une aire importante de fréquentation ne peuvent qu'entraîner des changements dans les autres zones, avec des conséquences encore ignorées. Si l'analyse des données de 1988 démontre qu'il existe le même genre de relation entre la fréquentation du Saguenay par les bélugas et le trafic maritime, il serait souhaitable de prévenir la poursuite d'effets négatifs qu'occasionnera une augmentation du trafic maritime à cet endroit, et peut-être également dans d'autres habitats importants du béluga du Saint-Laurent.

FIGURE 11

Trajectoires empruntées par les bateaux lors de leurs déplacements dans l'embouchure du Saguenay en 1987

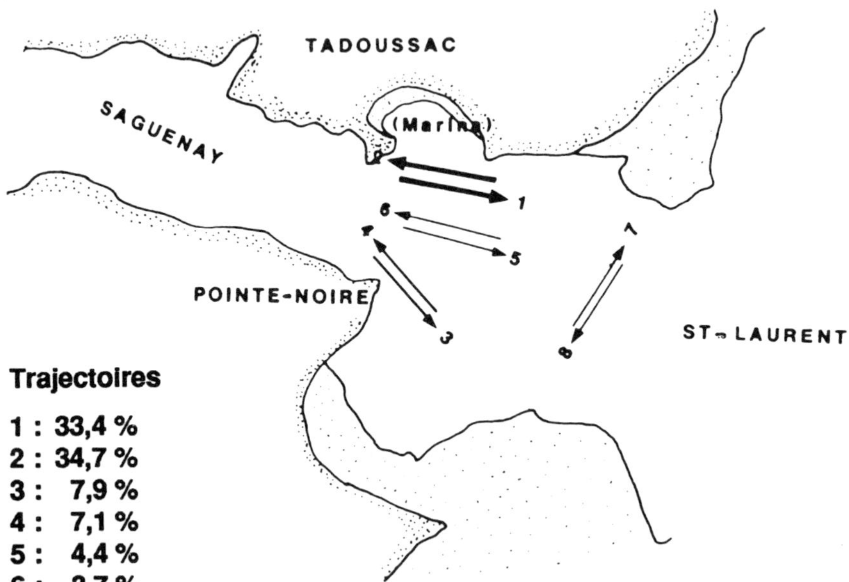

Trajectoires

1 : 33,4 %
2 : 34,7 %
3 : 7,9 %
4 : 7,1 %
5 : 4,4 %
6 : 3,7 %
7 : 4,5 %
8 : 4,1 %

REMERCIEMENTS

Un grand nombre de personnes ont participé au présent projet. En tout premier lieu, les membres du comité exécutif du groupe Ketos qui ont fourni le support logistique et humain afin de trouver les fonds et le personnel nécessaires à la réalisation des trois années d'observation à Pointe-Noire, soit de 1986 à 1988, ainsi que la récolte et l'analyse des données prêtées par le Dr Sergeant pour les années 1982 à 1984, notamment Réjean Gravel (président), Dominique Bouchard (secrétaire), et Dominique Raymond (trésorier). La réalisation et la supervision des trois dernières années d'observations à Pointe-Noire ont été assurées grâce à Johanne Décarie, observatrice à Pointe-Noire et membre du groupe Ketos, à laquelle je dois de très sincères remerciements. Les observateurs de Pointe-Noire pour les trois années sont également remerciés, soit : Daniel Gariépy, François Rioux, Stéphane Barsalou, France Benoît, Pierre Ramet, Kim Marineau, Katherine Ouellette, Patricia Lepage, Annette Bérard, Gabrielle Pelletier, Hélène Dubé, Benoît Robert,

Marie-Claude Lavoie et Éric Richard. Nathalie Desjardins et Jeanne Tremblay ont d'abord été observatrices à Pointe-Noire et ensuite, ont extrait et compilé l'information des notes du Dr Sergeant.

La compilation et la présentation des résultats sur les groupes de bélugas à Pointe-Noire de 1982 à 1988 ont été réalisées en collaboration avec Monica Borobia. L'analyse des coefficients de direction a été réalisée avec la collaboration de Pierre Legendre et Alain Vaudor de l'Université de Montréal.

Plusieurs compagnies et ministères ont participé au financement du projet soit, le ministère de l'Environnement du Québec, Hydro-Québec, Alcan, Voyageur et Imasco et sont par la présente sincèrement remerciés.

BIBLIOGRAPHIE

CARON, L. M. J., and SERGEANT, D. E. « Variation in the Frequency of Passage of Beluga Whales (*Delphinapterus leucas*) at the Mouth of the Saguenay Fjord, Québec, over the Past Decade », in Le naturaliste canadien, 1989.

DRAINVILLE, G. « Le fjord du Saguenay : contribution à l'océanographie », dans Le naturaliste canadien, n° 95 : 809-855, 1968.

FINLEY, K. J., and DAVIS, R. A. Reactions of Beluga Whales and Narwhals to Ship Traffic and Ice-breaking along Ice Edges in the Eastern Canadian High Arctic : 1982-84, Rep. by LGL Limited, King City, Ontario, for Canada Department of Indian Affairs and Northern Development, Ottawa, 1984, 42 p.

LAURIN, J. Étude écologique et éthologique de la population de bélugas (*Delphinapterus leucas*) du fjord du Saguenay, Québec, M. Sc. Thesis, Faculté des arts et des sciences, Université de Montréal, août 1982, MS 145 p., Figs.

LEGENDRE, L., et LEGENDRE, P. *Écologie Numérique*, Masson, Paris et les Presses de l'Université du Québec, 1984, tome 2, 235 p.

MANSFIELD, A. W. « The Effects of Vessel Traffic in the Arctic on Marine Mammals and Recommendations for Future Research », in Canadian Technical Report of Fisheries and Aquatic Sciences, n° 1186, 1982.

MARTEL, L., GAGNON, M. J., MASSE, R., LECLERC, A., and TREMBLAY, L. Polycyclic Aromatic Hydrocarbons in Sediments from the Saguenay Fjord, Canada, Bull. Environ. Cont. Toxicol., n° of cat. 37 : 133-140, 1986.

MASSE, R., MARTINEAU, D., TREMBLAY, L., and BELAND, P. Concentrations and Chromatographic Profiles of DDT Metabolites and Polychlorobiphenyl (PCB) Residues in Stranded Beluga Whales (*Delphinapterus leucas*) from the St. Lawrence Estuary, Canada, Arch. Environ. Contam. Toxicol., n° of cat. 15 : 567-579, 1986.

MARTINEAU, D., BÉLAND, P., DESJARDINS, C., and LAGACÉ, A. Levels of Organochlorine Chemicals in Tissues of Beluga Whales (*Delphinapterus leucas*) from the St. Lawrence Estuary, Québec, Canada, Arch. Environ. Contam. Toxicol. n° 16, 1987.

PIPPARD, L. and MALCOLM, H. White Whales (*Delphinapterus leucas*) : Observations on their Distribution, Population and Critical Habitats in the St. Lawrence and Saguenay Rivers, Dept. of Indian and Northern Affairs, Project C-1632, Contract 76-190, November 1978, MS 160 p.

PIPPARD, L. Patterns of Movement of the St. Lawrence White Whales, Appendices, Tech. Rept. prepared for Canadian Wildlife Service and Canadian Parks Service, November 1985, 225 p.

SERGEANT, D. E. « Present Status of White Whales (*Delphinapterus leucas*) in the St. Lawrence Estuary », in Le naturaliste canadien (Rev. Syst. Ecol.), n° of cat. 113 : 61-81, 1986.

SERGEANT, D. E. and HOEK, W. An Update of the Status of White Whales *Delphinapterus leucas* in the St. Lawrence Estuary, Canada, Biological Conservation, n° of cat. 45 : 287-302, 1988.

SMITH, J. N., and LORING, D. H. Geochronology for Mercury Pollution in the Sediments of the Saguenay Fjord, Québec, Environ. Sci. Technol., n° of cat. 15 : 944-951, 1981.

SOKAL, R. R., and ROHLF, F. J. *Biometry*, San Francisco, W. H. Freeman and Company, 1981, 859 p.

The Impacts of Vessel Traffic on the Behaviour of Belugas

Kerry J. Finley
Environmental Research

The subject of this talk has been modified from the original proposed topic that covered the general impact of shipping on whale migration. This talk focuses specifically on the acoustic effects of vessel traffic on belugas.

Most of my experience on the subject has been with High Arctic whales that experience low levels of vessel traffic compared to the St. Lawrence belugas. I also have considerable experience with hunted populations of belugas. My most recent experience with belugas occurred September 29 while looking out of my hotel room overlooking the Saguenay estuary and wondering what relevance my talk could have to the situation here. At the time there were two freighters in view and a high-speed zodiac with whale-watchers. Undoubtedly the belugas were ensonified but there was nothing unusual about their behaviour — a radically different response than I have observed in High Arctic belugas.

Marine mammals rely heavily on sound for communication and for acquiring information on their surroundings. Besides communicating with each other with sound and hearing ambient noises, many whales use echolocation signals for finding food and for navigation.

Vessel traffic could conceivably affect whales in one of two ways. First, it could increase background noise to the point where signals are masked, thereby interfering with communication and reducing navigational and foraging capabilities. Secondly, high levels of acoustic disturbance could cause detrimental changes in behaviour, such as displacement, thereby resulting in physiological stress. This second category also includes the synergistic effects of stress from noise in relation to other factors. These potential problems have been difficult to address for various reasons.

The beluga produces a remarkable repertoire of sounds, most having tonal properties variously described as whistles, trills, chirps, etc. The frequency range of most beluga vocalizations is between 2 - 8 kHz, with a mean of about 4 kHz — similar to bird songs. These calls are communicative in function, although in the usual cacophony of vocalizing it has been difficult to associate a particular sound with a behaviour.

Belugas also possess a sophisticated echolocation system that operates in a broad frequency range of 2 - 80 kHz. Most of the echolocation frequency is ultrasonic. Higher frequency signals are for examining targets at a few tens of metres — probably useful in the foraging mode. Lower frequency signals may be more useful for navigation. Recent studies by Ridgeway have shown that belugas are capable of locating and diving to targets at depths $>$ 600 m.

Much of what is known about the acoustic sensitivities of belugas has been derived from captive animals. From these studies the audiogram of the beluga has been developed (see figure 1). The audiogram represents the hearing threshold of the whale, that is, the lowest intensity of a pure tone signal at a particular frequency that an animal can detect. The audiogram of the beluga closely resembles that of other odontocete whales that have been tested.

The ocean is a noisy environment where ambient noise is often louder than the hearing threshold. Therefore, to communicate, the signal must be louder than the noise. The hearing ability of a whale is a complex function of several specific abilities or parameters including: 1) the signal-to-noise ratio, 2) the ability to localize the direction from which the sound is arriving, and 3) the ability to discriminate sounds of different frequencies and intensities. An understanding of these factors is necessary to evaluate the ability of a whale to detect ship noises in various circumstances. It is also necessary to evaluate the ability to detect communication and echolocation signals in the presence of masking by natural noise.

Figure 2 shows the generalized audiogram of toothed whales and the average range of underwater ambient noise. In arctic waters, ice contributes much of the low-frequency noise. In more southerly waters, ship traffic contributes a significant part of the energy especially at frequencies $<$ 100 Hz. Thus to some extent whales are preadapted to ship noise — their auditory thresholds are high at low frequencies.

Armed with this knowledge and theory on sound propagation characteristics of arctic waters, a recent impact evaluation of arctic

FIGURE 1

Underwater audiograms of several odontocetes: bottlenose dolphin, *Tursiops truncatus* (Johnson 1968a); white whale, *Delphinapterus leucas* (White et al1978); harbour porpoise, *Phocoena phocoena* (Andersen 1970); killer whale, *Orcinus orca* (Hall and Johnson 1972).

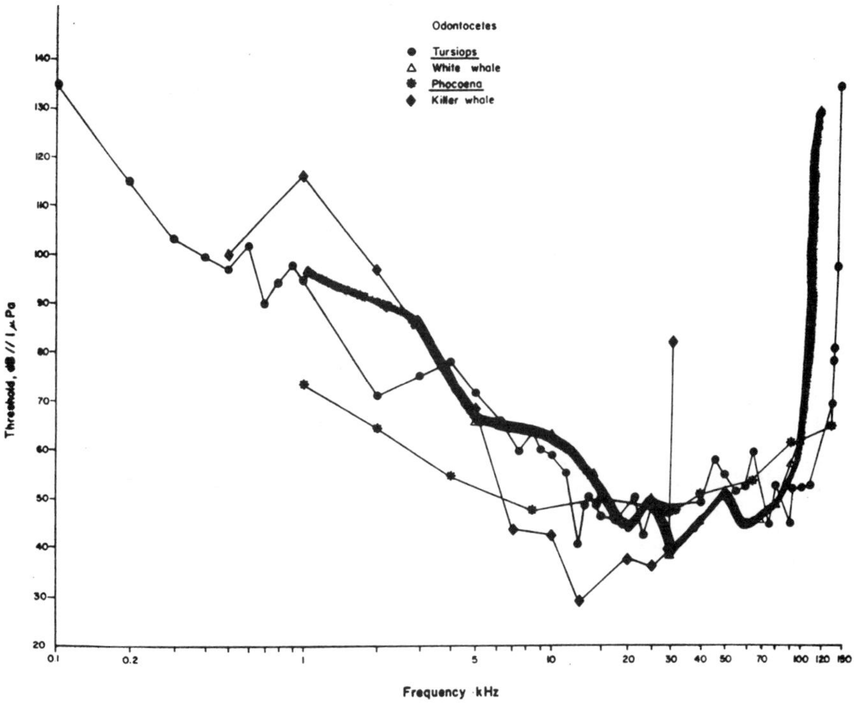

icebreaking predicted that the maximum distance at which a beluga could detect an approaching icebreaker was 5 km. This statement was issued in 1983. In that same year I was conducting the field experiments on the impact of icebreaking activities on the behaviour and distribution of narwhals and belugas. The results were rather surprising in view of the foregoing prediction.

First, more background is necessary. In late June — early July, belugas and narwhals begin migration though Lancaster Sound, the Northwest Passage, toward their summering grounds. If solid ice persists, the whales concentrate along solid ice edges (see figure 3). Their movements are casual — back and forth, and their activity might best be described as waiting — waiting for breakup. At this time of year, the

FIGURE 2

Comparison of average spectrum level noise in Baffin Bay (summer 1972, 1973) and audiograms for seals and toothed whales

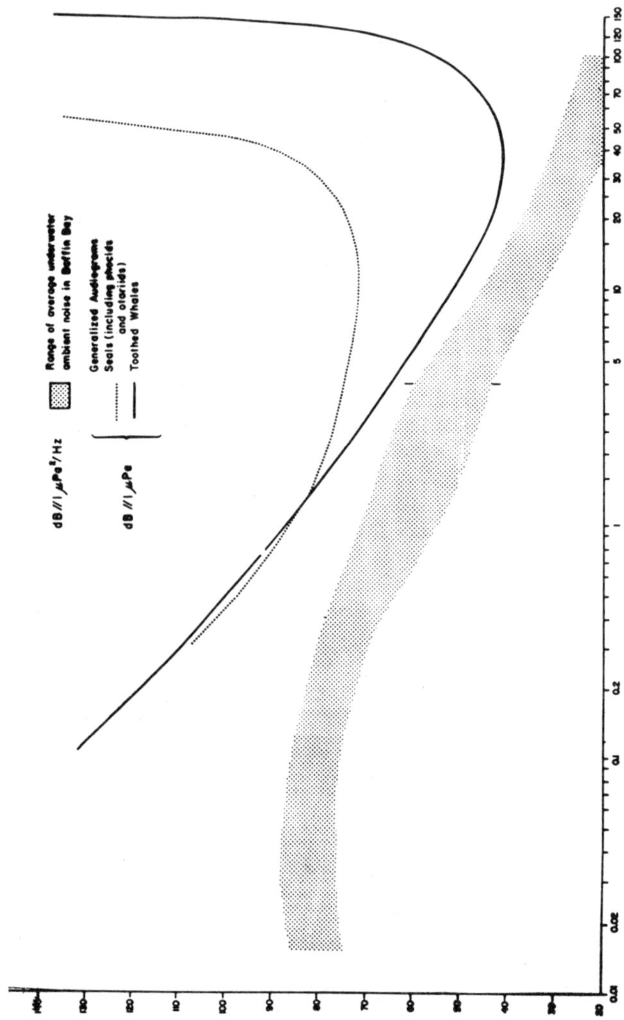

FIGURE 3

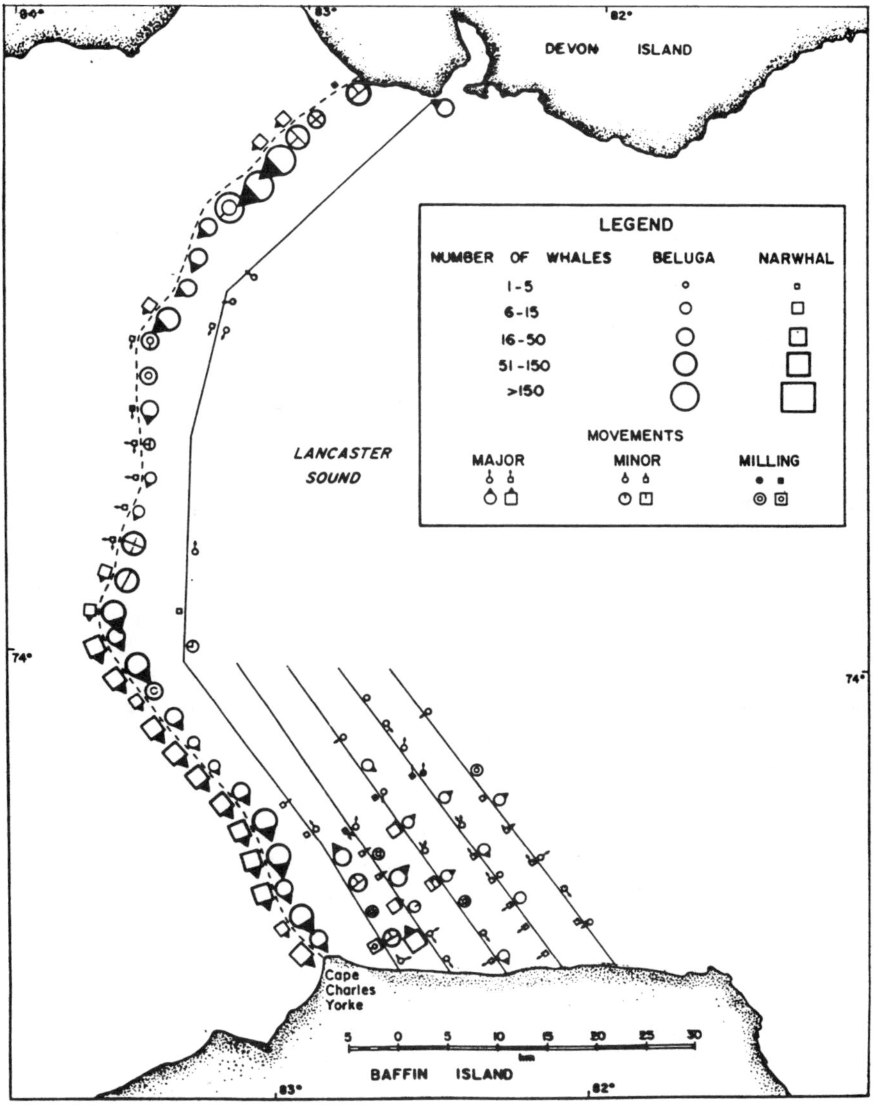

acoustic environment of Lancaster Sound is pristine since there are no sources of vessel traffic. Marine mammal vocalizations contribute much to the ambient background noise.

In 1982 trials were initiated with an icebreaking ore carrier in order to increase the length of the shipping season to a High Arctic mine site. We established a camp on the ice edge to monitor the response of the whales. The study was repeated in two following years and we were able to verify some interesting behavioural responses of the two species.

We were especially surprised at the sensitivity of the beluga. In one case, we had indications that the whales were aware of the ship's approach at a range > 80 km; at that time the whales began emitting broad band pulsive calls. These calls were heard only in situations of disturbance. We were unable to detect any change in the noise levels at the time the whales reacted but spectral analyses revealed a faint tone at 205 Hz. Theoretically this tone should not have been produced by the ship and should not have been detectable by the whale.

As the ship approached to within 40 - 50 km, the whales undertook rapid evasive movements along the ice edge. Herd structure disintegrated and diving patterns became asynchronous. We estimated that the whales achieved speeds in excess of 20 km/h during their panic movement.

In all cases, the passage of the ship caused a major displacement of belugas along the ice edge away from the source of disturbance. Interestingly, the displacement was not always equal on either side of the ship's entry point into the ice. Figure 4 shows the movement usually stopped when the whales reached the nearest shore — in some cases, they travelled nearly 80 km along the ice edge before reaching shore. The greater displacement of whales on the offshore side of the ships is perhaps indicative of their sense of vulnerability in offshore areas. It is well known to Eskimos that belugas seek shelter in ice and (or) shallow water in response to perceived threats — presumably their responses have been shaped by predatory pressure from killer whales.

Belugas were slow to habituate to disturbance by icebreaking ships. In one case, they did not fully reoccupy the ice edge for over a week. When the whales did return, the icebreakers had penetrated 40 km into the ice, but noise levels were considerably higher than that to which the whales had initially reacted, suggesting that the whales had habituated to some extent.

The behaviour of the narwhals in response to the same vessel traffic was dramatically different from the beluga. There was no panic movement away from the ships. Rather, their movements were very subtle — they submerged quietly and slowly dispersed from the area in front of the advancing ship. Other than temporarily ceasing their vocalizing in response to especially loud ship sounds, we could not detect any change in the type of vocalizations that they used. Their displacement was not nearly as great as the beluga and they returned to the area of disturbance even when icebreakers were operating close by.

The strong reactions of belugas that we documented are unprecedented. Why? First, because our research was conducted in a pristine

FIGURE 4

Distribution and directions of movement of narwhals and belugas recorded during survey 2, 28 June 1984 (08 :00-10 :00)

The positions of the MV Arctic (ARC) and CCGS Louis St. Laurent (LSL) at the time of the survey are also indicated.

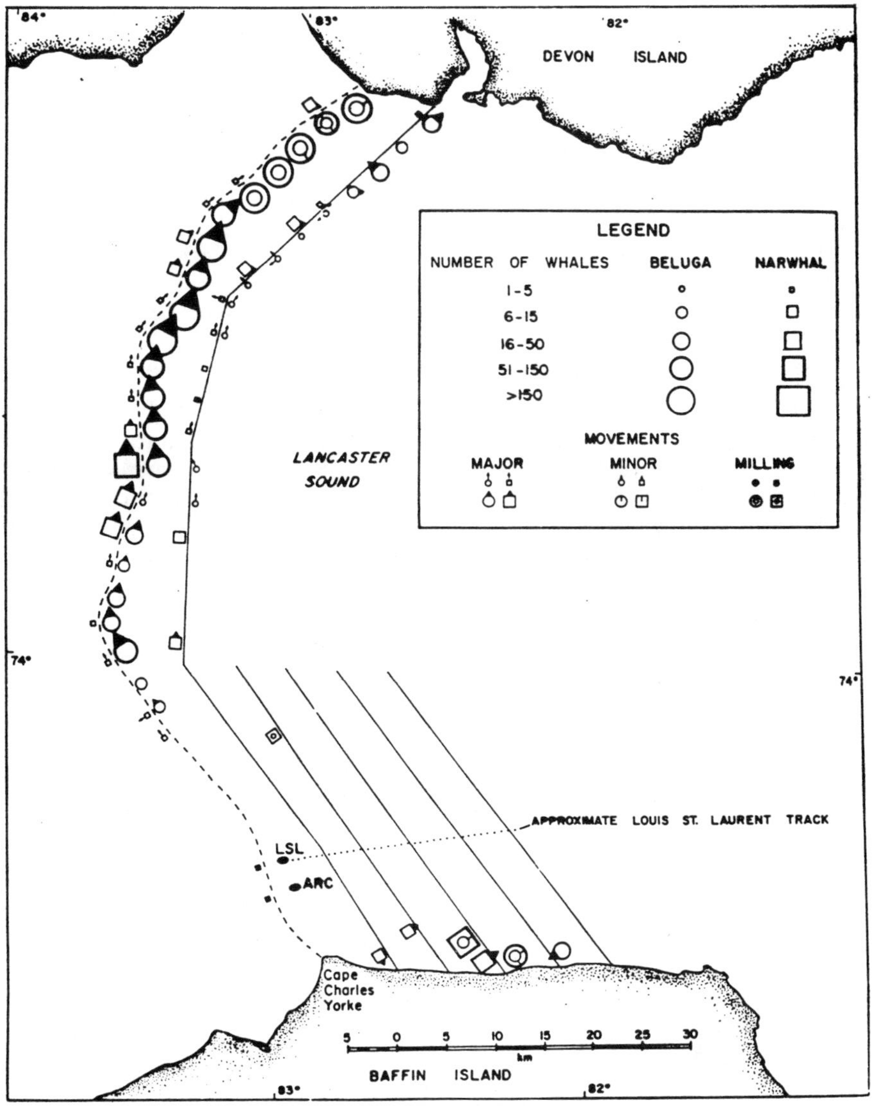

environment with an industrially naive population of whales. High Arctic whales are exposed to very low levels of shipping, so their responses were probably exaggerated relative to southern populations. Secondly, the responses were probably exaggerated because the whales did not have a strong vested interest in remaining in the area.

Where belugas do have a vested interest in remaining in a specific habitat, the question of disturbance becomes more difficult. Certain estuaries appear to constitute critical habitat of the beluga, judging from their long history of use. Wherever I have observed belugas, I have been deeply impressed with their persistence in using certain estuaries — like the Saguenay — often in spite of severe harassment. In the Arctic this harassment usually comes in the form of Eskimo hunters in high-powered boats. In the Saguenay it may be the whale-watchers.

By most accounts, it appears to be difficult to drive belugas from a habitat they are determined to use. The sad history of exploitation of belugas is testimony to this fact. In Alaska, attempts to keep belugas from entering a salmon river by chasing them with power boats and detonating underwater charges have been unsuccessful. In Bristol Bay, Alaska, belugas have been observed feeding amidst a large salmon fishing fleet that is supported by high-powered tender boats.

Belugas in the Mackenzie Delta have been intensively monitored during the last decade in response to concerns about dramatic increases in vessel traffic related to the oil industry. Some short-term reactions were noted but there was no evidence of displacement from preferred areas of the estuary. Similarly, there has been no evidence of displacement of belugas from the Churchill River since it became a shipping centre.

And belugas continue to return to the Saguenay. Most researchers agree that belugas (and most whales) seem to habituate to constant or predictable noises by vessels but that they show aversive reactions to vessels if sudden changes in speed and direction occur close to the animals. Populations of belugas in remote areas react more strongly than those that inhabit areas with high levels of marine traffic.

At present it is difficult to distinguish between habituation and toleration. Animals that tolerate disturbing situations are not necessarily unaffected; they may stay in an area in spite of much industrial noise because there are no alternative areas that meet their needs.

Excessive noise has been shown to adversely affect laboratory animals in various ways. Noise pollution can conceivably act synergistically with other factors to reduce the fitness and survival of free — ranging whales. Populations that are under stress during moult or reproduction may be more susceptible to the effects of additional stress imposed by noise. Populations at the periphery of their ranges may be especially susceptible. No studies have been conducted that would document the presence of noise-induced stress in marine mammals, much less demonstrate long-term population effects.

The Role of Zoo and Aquarium in the Conservation of St. Lawrence Belugas

Stefani Hewlett
Manager, Communications and Development
Vancouver Aquarium

When Mr. Jacques Prescott approached me some time ago with an invitation to participate in this Forum, I agreed

1. because of a personal interest in beluga whales,
2. a desire to participate in a conservation action,
3. and because the Forum seemed to indicate a new approach to environmental problems, an approach which intended to brings together researchers, agencies, groups and industry with common purpose, not something characteristic of the West Coast.

As I interpreted the intent of this Forum, the purpose is not to protest, the purpose is to proceed and identify, where possible, what each group's role might be in guiding the future of the beluga whale in the St. Lawrence River.

So the question is asked: "Is there a role for the captive population ?"

There are some possibilities which I will outline, but first I will define "what is the captive population".

For the purposes of this discussion, I will limit the animals to the North American population, which I am dividing into two different groups.

There are currently 20 beluga whales at five Zoological Parks or Aquariums in the United States and Canada combined; there are 3 in Canada, 17 in the United States (US). They range in age from about 2 to 3 years to at least 19 years in age. There are 13 females and five males.

There are an additional 10 beluga whales maintained at three theme parks in the US. They range in age from 2 to 3 years to at least 11 years of age: seven females and three males.

All whales within the above two groups were acquired from the Hudson Bay, Churchill River area over the past 15 years.

What can a group of varied age and sex animals from a different location contribute to the problem at hand?

In an aside, there were belugas taken from the St. Lawrence early 1900s Pt Barnum.

In 1957, New York Aquarium had 2 males, 1 from Alaska, 1 from St. Lawrence lived well into their 20s.

In 1960, 2 females borned each year, all died 6-8 months.

They are a source of information: all are monitored and can therefore provide background information on belugas which may be of use as a kind of control group:

- growth rates,
- blood values,
- relationship between age/length/and colour change,
- respiration rates,
- metabolic rates,
- hormone levels,
- photographic record to document colour change.

Because these animals can be observed both above and below water, behavioral observations can also make a contribution:

- sexual behavior,
- maternal behavior,
- dominance behavior,
- aggression,
- etc.

It may be possible to link sounds with certain kinds of behavior.

All the whales in the Zoo/Aquarium collection are maintained in groups of at least three animals. Based on studies of other cetacean species, i.e. some dolphins and killer whales, behavior in aquariums is reflective of behavior in the wild and has its greatest benefit in confirming or supporting observations made in the field.

The foregoing as a contribution to beluga whale behavior and biology is in fact passive. It makes available for comparative use data routinely collected or noted.

In a more active way, the captive group are being used to test the usefulness of some kinds of tagging methods such as the beluga bracelet, a flipper band which might be used to identify individuals in the wild over time. The value of using a number of cooperative animals in a controlled environment to refine such techniques is self-explanatory.

Someone asked me recently if it was possible for a breeding program to be established with the captive population to produce animals for reintroduction.

Realistically, the answer is "no" at this time. The majority of the animals are not yet reproductive. The reproduction rate is slow in any case and there are too many unanswered questions: age at weaning, time of independence, social organization.

As Dr. Seal already outlined, while the Zoological Parks and Aquariums have been actively breeding and reintroducing animals into the wild for some endangered species or depleted populations, it is not a realistic expectation for beluga whales now. Even if two, three or four times the number of animals were made available, there is the problem of space.

Housing for cetaceans is extremely expensive. It is not just a bowl filled with water but an extremely complicated life support system. For example, a new beluga facility will begin construction in Vancouver, in January 1989. One million gallons in volume at a cost of 6.5 million dollars. This is for 3 existing whales (that's 2 million per whale). Even if the facility needed only to accommodate animal needs and aesthetic considerations and public spaces were eliminated, it would still cost 1 million dollars per whale to provide the necessary mechanical systems, including pump filtration, chillers, skinners and so on.

Something that is available, potentially useful and portable is the technical expertise available in the personnel at the zoos and aquariums. All these organizations have individuals with many years of practical experience in both the science and the act of handling cetaceans, transport methods and the design of containers.

There might possibly be a place for animal transplants, floating river pins or some other creative alternative that would assist in either the research or rehabilitation plan for the St. Lawrence beluga whales.

The zoos and aquariums holding belugas all have research programs, though not necessary directed at belugas. Perhaps they could pool and redirect some of their resources as a cooperative effort on behalf of beluga conservation.

Some of you may have noticed that when I was describing the captive population, I drew a distinction between animals displayed at theme parks and those at zoological institutions.

This does not suggest any distinction between the quality of facilities or levels of animal care. It does, however, reflect a difference in public presentation.

The zoological institutions all have a natural history approach in their displays to the general public. They all have extensive education programs for school children and they all have zoological societies with programs for members. They are institutions for the public. And they are looked to in their communities as a source of information on the animals they display.

Just the five organizations which exhibit beluga whales have a combined zoological society membership of over 200 000 people. They have an annual visitorship of over 4.3 million people, all ages, all ways of life.

The potential for the zoological institutions to focus attention on beluga whales and deliver a message to the broad general public is enormous. People are fascinated by whales.

To date, the material presented with beluga whales has been oriented toward a natural history approach, centering on general cetacean adaptations and behavior. I submit it is time to update the message.

So, on the subject of beluga whales, what should the Aquariums be telling their 4 million-plus visitors ? What should they be telling the school children ? What should they be telling their members ?

The Aquariums have an enormous potential to communicate, what do you want them to tell the world ?

I think we want them to tell the truth, when visitors to aquarium see beautiful, graceful whales swimming so close, closer than would even be possible under any other circumstances. I think that visitors should know that there is a population of beluga whales in a river known as the St. Lawrence, and that the animals are in trouble.

I think they should hear how effluents, boat traffic, industry, recreation, in other words, how accumulation of everyday human activities can create very real problems for animals. I think they should hear that it is not just the St. Lawrence River but other rivers and coastal oceans as well that are being compromised.

I think they should know there is a solution and I think they should know they are part of the solution.

As the Zoos and Aquariums which exhibit belugas have cooperated with the scientific community and government agencies in the past, I am here to say they are prepared to cooperate in the future in any way that can contribute to the conservation challenge we now face. The captive population can contribute information, expertise and public education.

If we put our collective agencies and efforts toward this problem, if we can solve it and demonstrate to the large community that it can be done, perhaps the beluga whale will become the symbol worldwide for the conservation of aquatic species the way the giant panda has become the recognized symbol for the conservation of endangered terrestrial species!

St. Lawrence Whale Research and Regional Economic Development

E. M. (Ned) Lynas
Ocean Research Information Society

WHALE-WATCHING (ST. LAWRENCE)

Economic Expansion

Since 1982 there has been a phenomenal growth in the business of tourism around the Baie-Sainte-Catherine-Tadoussac sector of the Quebec north shore (Haute-Côte-Nord). This growth also has extended to the Grandes Bergeronnes-Les Escoumins section as well, although not nearly to the same extent. More recently, development has begun to take place in the Sault-au-Mouton-Sainte-Anne-de-Portneuf region.

The major impetus for this growth in tourism comes from an increasing public interest in whale-watching as a recreational and (or) educational activity generally, and the whales of the St. Lawrence in particular. For example, 77% of respondents to a questionnaire, administered by the Association Touristique Régionale (ATR) Manicouagan inc. in 1987, indicated that the reason for their Tadoussac visit was to view the whales as compared to 2% who had come for the hunting and fishing, and 21% for reasons other than the above.

In 1971, Gerald Iles, then with the Montreal Zoological Society, began a series of whale-watching expeditions to the St. Lawrence-Saguenay confluence, using occasional charters out of Rivière-du-Loup. These amounted to little more than one or two per year. In the 1988 season there were 11 whale-watching boats operating regularly out of

TABLE 1

St. Lawrence Whale-Watching
(Tadoussac area)
Net Trips per Boat per Season

Period*	1	2	3	4	5	Total
No. of Days	31	31	30	30	10	132
Allowance for Down Time	-2	-2	-2	-2	-1	-9
Estimated % of Capacity Utilized	98	80	45	55	35	-
Equivalent 100 % Capacity Days	28.4	23.2	12.6	15.4	3.2	82.8
Equivalent 100 % Capacity-Trips**	85.3	50.2	24.5	30.8	6.3	197.1

* 1 = July 15 to August 14
2 = July 1 to July 14, and August 15 to August 31
3 = June 1 to June 30
4 = September 1 to September 30
5 = October 1 to October 10

** Based on 3 trips per day from July 1 to August 14, and an average of 2 trips daily on all other dates.

the Saguenay mouth. I have calculated the equivalent maximum capacity trips per boat for the season at 197 as a first step in determining the dollar value of the season's whale-watching activity. In making the calculation I have allowed for the length of the day, time of season, and downtime for mechanical or meteorological reasons. Maximum capacity for all eleven vessels is 483 persons, and at a cost per person per trip of between 25 $ and 30 $, I estimate the gross income from whale-watching trips themselves at 2.7 $ million approximately. ATR's data (referred to above) suggest that the mean duration of a person-visit in 1987 was 1.35 days, and given mean costs for accommodation, food, etc. that for every dollar spent directly on whale-watching, a further 3.5 dollars was spent ashore. Applying this formula, the overall estimate of gross economic benefit from whale-watching and related activities to the Tadoussac sector becomes 11.2 $ million, approximately.

In the Grandes Bergeronnes-Les Escoumins sector, the activities are less well defined and so are difficult to access. Much of the business being conducted is as a result of spillover from Tadoussac when it is at saturation point from the middle of July to the middle of August. Perhaps no more than 10 to 15 percent of maximum capacity was utilized for the remainder of the season, and so I have estimated very conservatively the gross dollar value from whale-watching at 22 194 $. Applying a 3 : 1 ratio this time (accommodation is lower in Grandes Bergeronnes), the total gross economic input to the sector from all whale-watching-related activities becomes 88 776 $.

Finally, the ferry Le Gobelet d'Argent out of Les Escoumins makes occasional charter trips throughout the season, and the Samuel de Champlain makes irregular excursions for the Société linnéenne from Rivière-du-Loup. I have estimated 2 maximum capacity trips for the former and 17 for the latter, and a gross income from whale-watching of 64 475 $ for the 1988 season. Applying a 3.5 : 1 total spending ratio brings the estimated total gross economic input from these two vessels to 290 137 $.

An overall for the St. Lawrence-Saguenay confluence area as a whole is arrived at by simple addition of the above. This amounts to 11.6 $ million for 1988. Such a sizable infusion of business dollars is one well worth protecting.

At the same time, it is obvious that those involved in the whale-watching phenomenon expect to be able to sustain the present growth level, judging by the amount of ongoing investment in secondary- and tertiary-level services. Amid all the commercialism, however, it is imperative not to lose sight of the resource on which it is predicated : namely, the whales.

Certainly, all the trappings of a good hospitality industry will encourage many visitors to return to the area, but it is the lure of whale-watching on the upper north shore that brings them to the region in the first place, and will continue to do so in the future. In its turn, continued successful whale-watching depends on the reliable summer migration to the St. Lawrence of all but the indigenous beluga population.

This conference is about saving the St. Lawrence beluga whale population. Presently, it is not the object of most whale-watching in the estuary because of the relatively regular summer migrations of rorqual whales. Should these migrations fail for any reason or should the numbers of whales returning be reduced significantly, one effect would be to put enormous pressure on the beluga population. This is already happening on a small scale today. I have observed some trip operators actively seeking out belugas for their clients when at times throughout the season it occurs that rorqual whales are few and far between.

Another consequence of a negative change, particularly in the numbers of large whales, is the risk of an economic slowdown or downturn. No doubt this would be accompanied by various forms of financial stress, except to the degree that it was mitigated by political acceptance of direct beluga-watching. In the event of such a scenario, I have no doubt there would be political pressure to do just that.

So in my opinion, the critical businessman, banker, entrepreneur, and conservative alike should be asking a number of questions, among them the following : 1) how reliable are whale migrations, 2) what brings the various species to the St. Lawrence, 3) what conditions will ensure the reliable return of significant numbers or increasing numbers of animals each season ?

It is axiomatic that the various species come to the St. Lawrence for the fine cuisine. Beyond saying this there really are few ready answers to these questions, because much of the research is as yet only in formulation. Based on what information is available, however, there are some very good indicators and some partial directions to follow which, with your continuing indulgence, I propose to outline.

What follows is a mix of the hypothetical, theoretical, and concrete. I will draw on the work and comments of colleagues and friends, on my

TABLE 2

Energetics

(Key: * = research completed; ** = ongoing research/research in progress; *** = research in development/planning phase; **** = future research.)

TIME/ACTIVITY BUDGETS

(Minke*)
(Beluga**)
(Blue**)
(Finback**)
(Humpback****)

SWIMMING PATTERNS & BEHAVIOURS

Foraging Strategies	Breathing Ecology	Inter/Intra Species & Environmental Interaction: Social Behaviours	Inter/Intra Species & Environmental Interaction: Avoidance Behaviours
(Minke*)	(Minke**)	(Beluga**)	(Beluga**)
(Beluga**)	(Beluga**)	(Finback**)	(Finback**)
(Finback**)	(Finback**)	(Minke***)	(Minke***)
(Blue***)	(Blue***)	(Blue****)	(Blue****)
(Humpback****)	(Humpback****)	(Humpback****)	(Humpback****)

FEEDING, MAINTENANCE, COMPETITIVE & INTERACTION COSTS

ENERGY EXPLOITATION & RECOVERY

PREY	RECYCLED ENERGY	
Hydro-Acoustic Spectra Analysis***	Physical (All Species****)	Thermo-Regulatory (All Species ****)

recent study of the feeding strategies and energetics of minke whales, and on similar work in progress on finback and blue whales, and, to a lesser extent, on belugas.

WHALE-WATCHING (NEW ENGLAND)

Whale-watching in the New England area of the United States predates that in the St. Lawrence by about ten years. Events there in the summer of 1986, and to a lesser extent in 1985 and 1987, underscore the need for a better understanding of the resource that whales represent.

Particularly in 1986, the meteorological condition referred to as the Carolinas High moved out over the Atlantic Ocean during the summer months, changing offshore wind patterns. Coincidental with this, there was a drop in the productivity of the sand launce north of Cape Cod over the Stellwagen Bank. Whether the relationship is correlated or merely causal remains to be established. Regardless, aggregations of humpback whales, which depend heavily on this prey species in the area, moved off along the Great South Channel near Nantucket Island, in order (I must presume) to find sufficient prey densities to optimize their feeding efforts.

A number of consequences attended this move, among them the following: 1) humpback whales seen over the Stellwagen Bank were few and far between, 2) in 1986 and 1987 periods of several weeks passed with no whales being sighted, but otherwise overall species diversity actually increased in the long term (for example, Fred Wenzel of the Mingan Island Cetacean Study and others recorded three blue whale sightings), and 3) media personnel, in their reports to the public, equated the absence of humpback whales, with the absence of whales period.

The consequences of these events were several too. Of three fleet companies operating whale-watching trips out of Provincetown, Massachusetts, each of two retired one vessel at the end of the 1987 season. The Dolphin fleet instituted a once-a-week, eight-hour trip from Provincetown to the Great South Channel to view humpbacks. (Regular trips to Stellwagen take from two to three hours.) Significantly, there no longer is the expectation among customers that they always will see whales when they take a trip. Probably as a direct result, daily capacity has been reduced to 3 000 persons this year, and Gordon Barney, proprietor of the Portuguese Princess, based on mid-August estimates, expects that the reality will see the figure cut by more than a third to 1 700 passengers daily overall for 1988.

VARIABLE DISTRIBUTION IN THE ST. LAWRENCE

The question follows automatically: could similar events take place in the St. Lawrence? They could, of course, anything is possible, but in terms of the St. Lawrence we need to distinguish between system-wide and local variability. Overall, the entire north shore of the St. Lawrence is relatively food-stable as compared to a similar area of the open sea. But it is not immune to perturbations, and virtually anything on a system-wide or local level that adversely affects the prey species on which whales depend, or their ability to effectively exploit that resource, will have an effect on their distribution. These include:

1. A short-term and (or) long-term drop in primary productivity due to natural cyclical phenomena.
2. Increased competition for the available primary and secondary resources from, for example, seals, birds or man.
3. A qualitative deterioration in primary or secondary productivity: *i.e.* the quantitative replacement of one species by another within the same size spectrum having a less efficient energy transfer.
4. A change or deterioration in environmental quality as a result of human habitation and enterprise: for example, changes in temperature and (or) salinity regimes; reduced photosynthetic activity as a result of changes in the runoff ratio of the system; other inhibitions to photosynthetic activity due to water surface contamination or quality.
5. Increased costs to the animals of metabolic maintenance or resource exploitation as a result of competition from commercial and recreational ship traffic and other forms of human use of the shared habitat.
6. A reduction in survivorship, health or longevity due to environmental pollutants.
7. A reduction in reproductive success due to environmental pollutants, or reduced reproductive activity resulting from human development and (or) use of the shared habitat.

Numbers of Whales

Allowing for the relative stability of the St. Lawrence estuary and gulf, the numbers of large whales, in which tourists primarily are interested, are not great on a system-wide basis. Dr. Mitchell, of the Arctic Biological Station, Sainte-Anne-de-Bellevue, has estimated the overall population of finbacks at approximately 1 000 animals. My colleague at the Mingan Island Cetacean Study, Richard Sears, has photo-tagged approximately 200 blue whales. Another favourite of tourists, the humpback whale, is surprisingly few in numbers and largely undetermined. From two to six individuals are sighted each season in the middle estuary. Minke whales and harbour porpoises are ubiquitous, it seems, but of secondary interest to tourists. White-beaked and white-sided dolphins, orca, and pilot whales are seen only very rarely west of Pointe-des-Monts. A source of potential tourist interest because of its uniqueness is the beluga, and my 1985 estimate of approximately 400, plus or minus 83, appears to be standing up well. Not very many individuals for an entire population.

On the local level, numbers are fewer and distribution is not always reliable. Edds and Macfarlane, for example, have reported in the Canadian Journal of Zoology (1987) on approximately a tenfold drop in blue whale sightings off Cap de Bon-Désir from 1975 to 1979. I also have noted an apparent drop in sightings of blues from 1983 to the present at Les Escoumins-Sainte-Anne-de-Portneuf.

On the other hand, I have not heard of anyone failing to see a whale on a trip in the Tadoussac-Les Escoumins area, except during fog. But I have yet to find more than 40 individual finbacks there on any given day, which suggests that this may be some type of maximum. Forty individuals is not a large number of whales when one considers that this is a critical group of animals in the sense that although the local whale-watching industry depends on the romance of the blue whale, it exists by virtue of the day-to-day presence and reality of the finback whale.

The above illustrate well some of the real limits with which the developing whale-watching industry will need to contend. They also underscore the need to husband these resources at all levels. In other

TABLE 3

Reproduction

(Key: * = research completed; ** = ongoing research/research in progress; *** = research in development/planning phase; **** = future research.)

POPULATION DYNAMICS

Adult/Sub-Adult Group Structure	Parenting Behaviours	Reproductive Strategies
(Beluga**)	(Beluga**)	(Beluga***)
(Finback**)	(Finback**)	(Finback***)
		(Minke ****)
		(Blue****)

SURVIVORSHIP

(All Species****)

words, there is every reason to view skeptically such long-term global objectives for the system as further reductions in the ratio of summer to winter runoff. Similarly, those putting forward new concepts for the system, such as that for a krill fishery (now in the feasibility/investigation stage), need to study carefully their impact on the whale-watching industry. The situation of the beluga with respect to overall body burdens of organochloride residues is also a perfect example of a system-wide problem begging attention. At the same time, there is much that needs to be done and that can be done at a local level. The need for research and long-term planning is, of course, obvious. But based on what my research to date has indicated, there also is the need for (as well as the possibility of) immediate self-regulation policy by the industry to minimize its impact on the animals within the shared use habitat at least as a precautionary measure.

Energy Balance

Migrating whale species need to acquire the majority of their annual food supply while on the summer feeding grounds. Dr. Brodie at the Bedford Institute of Oceanography and others have indicated that to do so, rorqual whales must find local heavy concentrations of prey items in order to feed efficiently. Obviously, these are available in the St. Lawrence. Even so, the margin of the cost/benefit balance (that is to say, the benefit to be gained by the whales feeding in a particular location versus the cost of doing so), in general, appears to be a tenuous one.

My work with minke whales in the estuary indicates that on average, 61% of an animal's daily time/energy budget is spent feeding, and a further 23% actively seeking out prey items. (There is nothing in the literature to indicate that night time activity is any different from daytime activity, although it may be somewhat less intense). In the act of feeding, the whale loses a tremendous amount of energy, due not only to the entrapment swimming maneuvers it must make, but also to the force of the inrushing water as it engulfs its prey, and against which it must close its mouth. My colleague Dr. Lamberstein, a mammalian pathologist at Florida State, has concluded that even given the values I have recorded, and assuming a maximum intake of feed with every engulfing strike, the cost/benefit difference for the whale between starvation and survival lies solely in the recoil energy of the ligature governing the mandible.

Finback Behaviour

If this is a realistic assessment of the margin between failure and success, and if it can be generalized to the finback as well, clearly any significant negative change in the energy cost/benefit ratio of one location over another is very important because of the species utility to the industry. Also, it precipitates the question above : what can be done to ensure the return of representative members of the species to the Tadoussac-Les Escoumins area each summer? What is a significant level of change I do not yet know. The subject needs further investigation. In the meantime, I offer the following preliminary findings from my ongoing study of finback behaviour.

I began studying finback feeding techniques and strategies in August 1987. Since that time I have processed in excess of 200 hours of sonar output. In less than 1 % of cases was the target feed found to be deeper than the top 20 metres of the water column. In fact, especially when dealing with euphausiids, as is indicated by Figure 1, the greatest feed density was found within the top ten metres of the water column. (The depth applies equally well to the targets for minke, humpback and beluga whales.) Thus the water surface is not merely an interface where respiration takes place ; it is the active zone where most of the engulfing

FIGURE 1

Finback whale feeding techniques and strategies

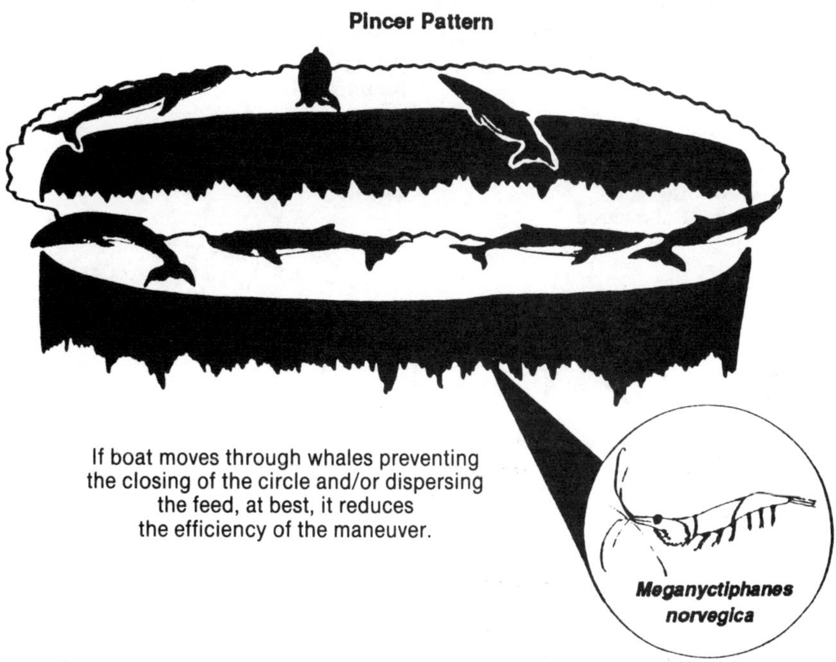

action occurs. It also is the zone most affected by commercial, recreational and whale-watching craft.

Approximately 83 % of all feeding situations so far have been found to involve more than one animal. But whether as individuals or in groups, animals use an elliptical pattern of entrapment and engulfment, the surface manifestations of which take several forms. The most common of these are : 1) a circular, pincer-like movement around the prey with part of the feeding group swimming in one direction while part swims in the opposite direction, 2) a simple 'J'-shaped maneuver, utilized by individuals as well as groups, with prey contained within the curve of the 'J' and most often employed in series, and 3) more complex maneuvers involving double 'J' or 'S' patterns, depending on which side the second part of the maneuver is terminated and used primarily when the prey species is shoaling fish.

Figure 1 represents a pincer pattern. I have observed whale-watching vessels both large and small take a course between the end members of the diverging group, cut straight through and stop at the apex of where the whales appear to be heading. Most often the circle is never closed, and at best the efficiency of the maneuver is sacrificed.

FIGURE 2

Finback whale feeding techniques and strategies

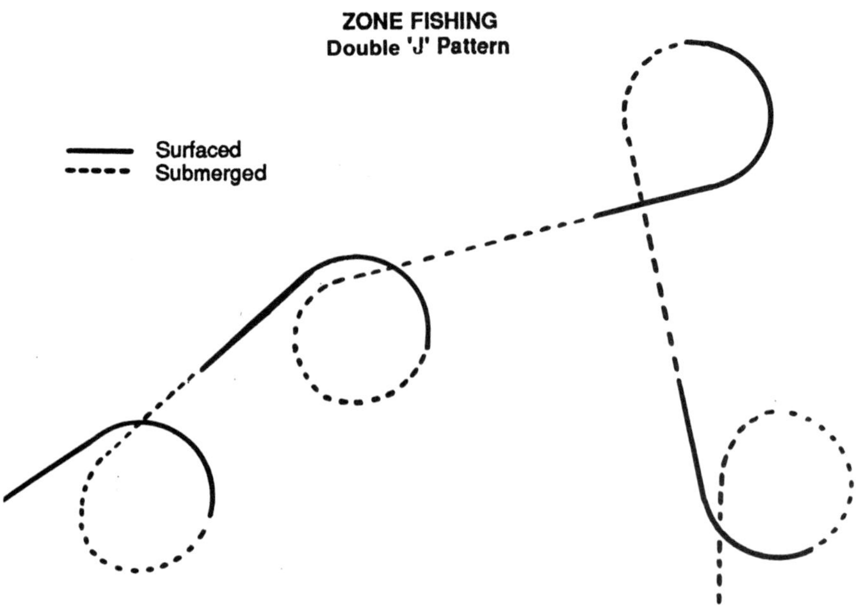

Figure 3 depicts a simple 'J' pattern. Frequently, I have observed boats, especially large boats, take up a position in the water at right angles to where the stem of the 'J' is likely to be formed. Whales either have to dive prematurely beneath the vessel or turn aside from the natural course of the 'J'. In either case, again the efficiency of the maneuver is reduced or, at worst, rendered useless altogether.

Alternately, I have observed vessels, particularly some small vessels, on a converging course with the surfacing animals. As can be seen in Figure 4, this too can reduce or negate completely the effort of the whales, depending upon whether the animals are driving the prey on the same or opposite side as the boat (and incidentally, there is no significant preference shown for one side versus another). If on the same side as the boat, it prevents closure of the entrapment maneuver.

FIGURE 3

Finback whale feeding techniques and strategies

Simple 'J' Pattern

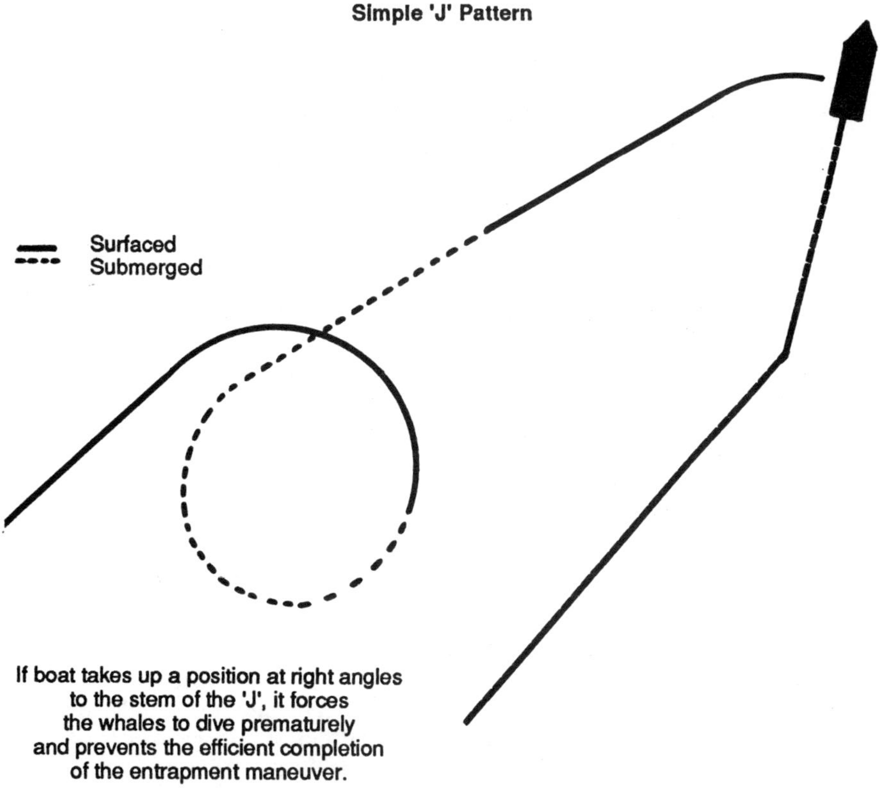

If boat takes up a position at right angles to the stem of the 'J', it forces the whales to dive prematurely and prevents the efficient completion of the entrapment maneuver.

FIGURE 4

Finback whale feeding techniques and strategies

Converging Course

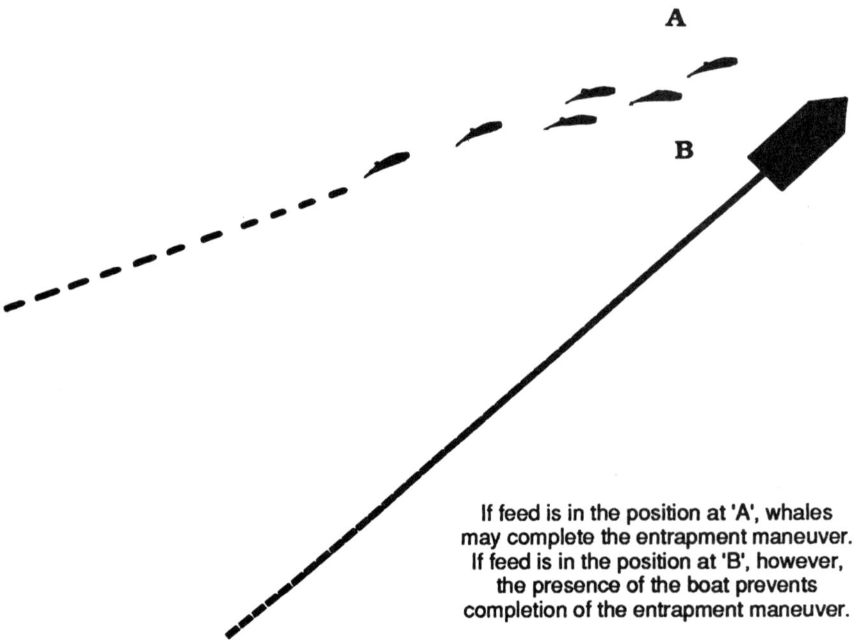

Finally, in Figure 5, is illustrated the double 'J'- or 'S'-shaped maneuver, with the second ellipse utilized to entrap again those prey which escape the primary entrapment maneuver. If a whale-watching vessel sets up at right angles to the direction of the chase, it may interfere with its efficiency. If a vessel runs a converging course in the same direction as the travel of the whales, it may block altogether the closure of the entrapment maneuver, depending on which side the animals are driving their prey.

Two things need to be pointed out at this juncture. The first is that I do not wish to suggest that the captains of any of the whale-watching craft operating in the Tadoussac-Les Escoumins sector of the river are deliberately interfering with the animal's feeding behaviour. I do mean to imply that, being good observers, in all probability they read only too well the surface patterns of the swimming animals, but without comprehending fully the purpose of the maneuvers. The second point I wish to make is that I have illustrated the possible effect of one vessel on a group of feeding whales. More often, several vessels are involved with one

FIGURE 5

Finback whale feeding techniques and strategies

Double 'J' or 'S' Pattern

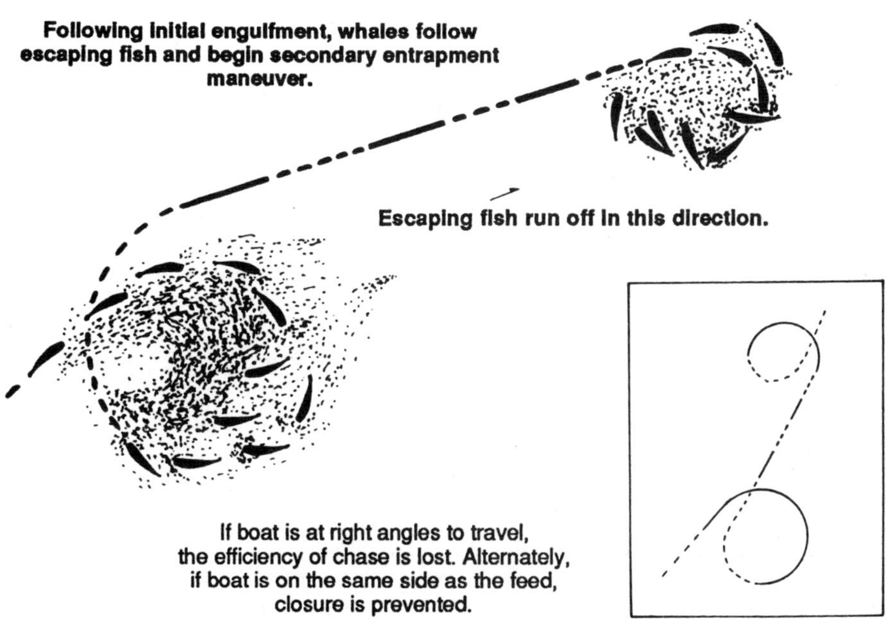

group of animals, and in some cases all the vessels and several pleasure craft can be moving about the area where a single group is fishing.

A mitigation measure that could be effected as readily as the next season by the tour operators is to ensure that: 1) their boat captains recognize the patterns being employed by the whales as important feeding maneuvers, 2) the whale-watching vessels then stand off and allow their completion, and 3) while standing off, let the on-board naturalists explain to the whale-watching tourists exactly why the boats are standing off, what the whales are doing, and why they are doing it. (It is worth emphasizing that at least one of the boats does just this as a matter of policy.)

Once again, it goes without saying that here too, further research work is needed.

Diffusing Development

Finally, having observed the development of organized whale-watching in the Tadoussac-Les Escoumins section of the river virtually from its inception, and the recent, almost exponential growth spurt of the last two years in the Tadoussac area, it is obvious that as maximum capacity is reached, some diffusion of effort and development along the coast is not only desirable but necessary from point of view of the whales as well. While this may be desirable, there has been no research effort that would help in predicting where and when to find whales away from the head of the Laurentian Channel, and other than in Mingan.

Long-Term Research Needs

Indeed, there is no shortage of research work to be done, and I have produced below a flow chart outlining and rationalizing long-term research objectives from the point of view of my own special interests and expertise. I have placed a single star against work I have completed, a pair of stars against work in progress, three stars against research in the planning stage, and four stars against needed future research. As can be seen, the number of items in the needed and planning phases far outstrips the work completed or in progress. Again I emphasize that this is within my own area only.

Research, of course, depends on funding. More importantly, in this case it needs specifically directed funding. In fact, it needs the kind of funding that more properly the community at large should have a hand in directing. In so saying, however, I would like to leave the following thought in mind. In order to best direct the research towards the ongoing development of a viable but sensitive whale-watching industry, and because the north shore communities involved will be the ultimate beneficiaries, I believe they also should take on the responsibility to provide the needed funding. Exactly what mechanisms they might wish to employ I leave to another set of experts.

Trace Metal Concentrations in Surface Sediment of the Saguenay Fjord, Canada [1]

Émilien Pelletier
INRS-Océanologie

INTRODUCTION

The Saguenay Fjord occupies a deep and narrow glacial valley grooved into the Canadian Shield about 160 km northeast of Quebec City (Figure 1) and the up stream region extending along the Saguenay River and is the site of numerous industrial outfalls, anthropogenic metal and organic inputs (Loring and Bewers, 1978). The presence of mercury in the sediment and the biota of the Fjord is well documented (Loring 1975; Loring and Bewers, 1978; Smith and Loring, 1981; Gobeil and Cossa, 1984; Cossa and Desjardins, 1984; Pelletier, Rouleau and Canuel, 1988), nevertheless, few data are available about the presence of other trace metals potentially from anthropogenic origin (Loring, 1976; Barbeau, Bougie and Coté, 1981). The aim of this work is to provide baseline data for some heavy metals usually present in contaminated area and useful to monitor long-term changes in the environmental quality of surface sediment of the Fjord.

Seventeen (17) stations (Figure 1) were sampled in July 1986 using a Macpherson bottom grab (0.1 m^3). Contact of metal with the sample was avoided during sampling and only the superficial layer (0-2 cm) of non-disturbed sediment was sampled with a plastic spoon. The samples (200-300 g in plastic bags) were stored at -25 °C for about

---

1. This manuscript has been previously published in Marine Pollution Bulletin, Volume 19, N° 17, pp. 336-338 (1988).

FIGURE 1

Location of sampling stations in the Saguenay Fjord in eastern Canada

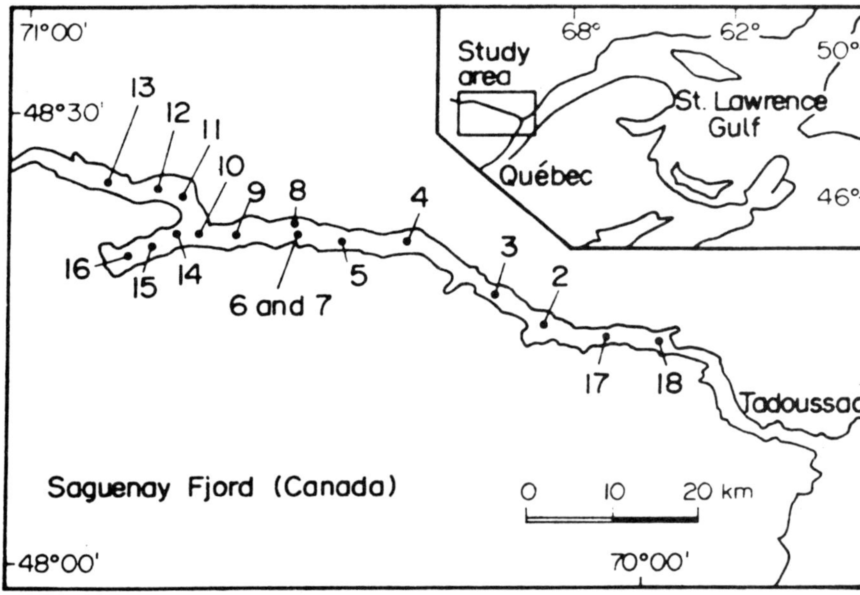

one month before analysis. In the laboratory, sediment samples were dried at 55°C for 72 h, ground and stored in air tight bottles. Mercury was determined by cold vapor atomic absorption (Gobeil and Cossa, 1984) and other trace metals were determined by equipped with graphite furnace (model HGA 500) after digestion of samples in concentrated nitric acid. The number of replicates was two for all analyses but reached four when the first two values disagreed by more than the coefficient of variation in standards given in Table 1. Aqueous standards (BDH Chemicals 1000 ppm) were used for Cd, Cu, Cr and Hg, whereas a standard sediment (no. BCSS-1 from National Research Council of Canada) was used for Zn. The detection limits were respectively 0.02 μg.g-1 for Cd, cr and Hg; 0.07 μg.g-1 for Cu and 3 μg.g-1 for Zn. All blank values were below the limits of detection except for Cd, where the blank value was 0.026 μg.g-1.

Organic matter was determined by loss of weight after calcination of dry sediment at 600°C for 8 h. Organic carbon and nitrogen were determined by CHN analysis (Perkin-Elmer model 240 Elemental Analyser) on dry sediments. Daily standardization provided an accuracy of $\pm$ 0.3% toward a standard sediment for both carbon and nitrogen. Results from analysis of Cr, Cu, Cd, Hg, Zn and % organic matter content, % organic carbon and C/N ration are expressed in Table 1.

TABLE 1

Trace metal concentrations (µgg'dry wt) in surface sediment of Saguenay Fjord

Station No.	Water depth (m)	Sediment[1] type	Cd	Cr	Cu	Hg[2]	Zn	Org.matter (%)	C (%)	C/N ratio
2	249	mud	0.11	55.6	15.8	0.25	160	7.5	2.2	15.4
3	277	mud	.12	71.7	22.3	0.74	169	9.0	2.5	15.8
4	278	mud	0.11	63.7	22.6	0.84	161	10.9	2.9	16.7
5	271	mud	0.24	64.1	22.2	0.70	169	10.7	2.9	17.3
6	278	mud	0.22	61.8	22.4	0.85	166	10.8	2.8	17.0
7	247	mud	0.10	66.3	21.0	0.93	152	10.7	2.8	17.6
8[3]	55	mud	0.16	54.1	20.8	1.20	170	9.3	2.6	20.0
9	243	mud	0.13	61.9	20.5	1.09	155	9.7	2.9	17.5
10	212	mud	0.14	61.8	20.4	0.61	153	9.7	2.8	21.6
11	144	sandy mud	0.16	66.0	18.2	0.44	133	8.8	2.7	19.9
12	100	sandy mud	0.47	45.9	21.4	0.26	232	8.8	2.9	19.7
13	61	muddy sand	0.14	53.3	14.6	0.29	107	8.6	2.8	17.8
14	167	sandy mud	0.10	51.7	21.1	0.66	142	9.2	2.7	20.8
15	150	sandy mud	0.12	51.7	28.1	0.54	156	10.7	3.5	20.5
16	121	sandy mud	0.14	60.9	25.6	0.80	156	12.5	4.4	24.4
17	183	very sandy mud	0.08	55.3	12.1	0.18	115	5.3	1.4	14.4
18	195	muddy sand	0.01	12.3	1.3	0.03	36	0.3	0.04	13.3
Coeff. of variation in standards (%)			4	10	4	10	4	5	0.3	0.9

[1]Sediment classification from Loring (1976)
[2]Data from Pelletier (1989)
[3]Sainte-Rose-du-Nord harbor

Chromium concentrations range from 12.3 to 71.7 μg.g-1 and the average level is 55.7±12.9 μg.g-1. Cr level is slighly higher in muds, (62.3 ± 5.3 μg.g-1) than in sandy muds (53.4±4.6 μg.g-1). Previous data for Cr in surface sediment of the Saguenay are not available for comparaison.

The distribution of cadmium is not clear but concentrations seem to increase from stations 9 to 12. Some stations far from potential industrial inputs (stations 2 to 4 and also 17 and 18) have Cd levels 0.12 μg.g-1, whereas the station 12 reaches 0.47 μg.g-1. For comparison, Cd concentrations observed in sediments from the nearby St. Lawrence estuary range from 0.12 to 0.20 μg.g-1, and vertical profiles provide no evidence for recent anthropogenic contribution (Gobeil, Silverberg, Sundby and Cossa, 1987).

Copper level is very low in muddy sand from station 18 (1.3 μg.g-1) but reaches 28.1 μg.g-1 in anoxic sandy mud from station 15. The average level in mud and sandy mud is 21.0 + 3.7 μg.g-1. Cu concentrations previously reported by Loring (1976) for grab samples collected in 1973-74 range from 6 to 33 μg.g-1, and the mean value reaches 27 μg.g-1 in all muds. The pre-industrial level, as determined by Barbeau, Bougie and Coté (1981) in deep layers, is 21±4 μg.g-1. Copper is linearly correlated to organic matter content ($r = 0.94$, $p < 0.001$) and also to C/N ratio with a lower degree of significance ($r = 0.62$, $p < 0.01$).

The average mercury level observed in all surface samples, (0.61±0.33 μg.g-1) is well above the pre-industrial level (0.1±0.05 μg.g-1) reported by Barbeau, Bougie and Coté (1981). The average Hg level observed in mud from stations 2 to 10 (0.80±0.28 μ.g-1) is in good accordance with previous results (Gobeil and Cossa, 1984) and seems to indicate a steady state of Hg concentrations in surface sediment of the Fjord in the last ten years.

The correlation of Hg to organic matter and organic carbon has been previously discussed by Loring (1976) for surface sediment collected in 1972-74. The exponential relationship observed between Hg and the organic matter (Figure 2) confirms Loring's observations, nevertheless the lack of Hg vs C/N ration linear correlation is new (Figure 2). Stations 3 to 9, all located in the deepest basin of the Fjord, seem to form a cluster (low C/N and high Hg) independent from other stations showing a large range of C/N values and a lower Hg level. This feature could be related to a number of environmental factors: (1) the origin of the organic matter, mostly terrestrial in up stream stations and mainly marine in the muddy samples from the deep basin (Pocklington and MacGregor, 1973); (2) the sedimentation rate which ranges from 0.19 g cm-2 yr-1 in upper stations to 0.07 g cm-2.yr-1 in the deep basin (Smith and Walton, 1980), and also (3) the marked difference in bioturbation rate induced by different worm species and population density observed in shallow and deep stations.

FIGURE 2

Plots of mercury concentrations vs organic matter (%) and C/N ratio in surface sediment

The corresponding station number is given for each value.

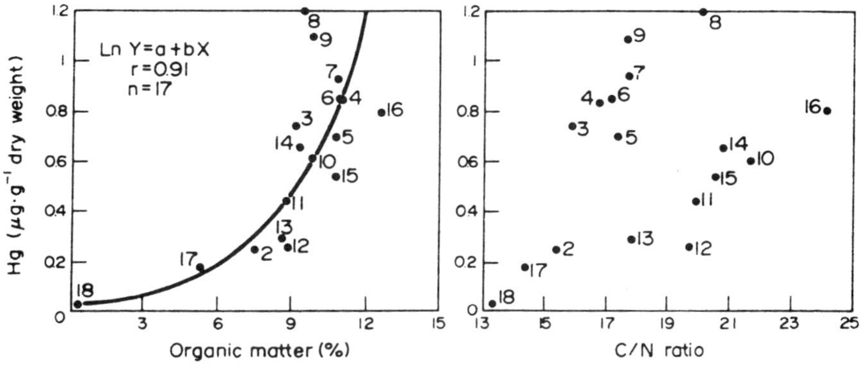

Zinc concentrations vary from 36 μg.g-1 in muddy sand (station 18) to 232 μg.g-1 in sandy mud (station 12). The average Zn level in pre-industrial samples, estimated to 85±20 μg.g-1 by Barbeau, Bougie and Coté (1981), is significantly lower than the average level calculated from Table 1 (148±40 μg.g-1 for all samples). Total Zn concentrations observed by Loring (1976) for surface sediment sampled in 1972-74 ranged from 43 to 145 μg.g-1, with an average of 130 μg.g-1 in muds. The average Zn concentration found in muds in 1986 (excluding stations 13, 17 and 18) is 162±23 μg.g-1, which folds the pre-industrial level and is about 20% higher than Loring's observations. These results support previous conclusions given by Barbeau, Bougie and Coté (1981), as the input of anthropogenic Zn has increased steadily since 1945. The input rate in muds shifted from 2.7 μg.g-1 per year between 1945 and 1968 to 3.3 μg.g-1 per year between 1972 and 1986.

In summary, these results provide confirmation of anthropogenic inputs of mercury and zinc, but no evidence was found for a significant increase of copper level. Both mercury and copper are strongly correlated to the organic matter content (%), but lack of a significant correlation was observed between Hg and C/N ration. The similarity of Cd concentrations found in surface sediment of the Saguenay Fjord and in deep profiles from the St. Lawrence estuary is indicative of an insignificant influence of human activity on present Cd levels in the Fjord. The meaningfulness of chromium data cannot be determined due to the lack of previous data and the restricted number of samples analyzed in the present study.

REFERENCES

BARBEAU, C., BOUGIE, R. and CÔTÉ, J.-E. *Temporal and Spatial Variations of Mercury, Lead, Zinc, and Copper in Sediments of Saguenay Fjord*, Canadian Journal Earth Sciences, N° 18, 1981, pp. 1065-1074.

COSSA, D. et DESJARDINS, C. *Évolution de la concentration en mercure dans les crevettes du fjord du Saguenay (Québec) au cours de la période 1970-83*, Rapport technique canadien hydrogr. science océan, N° 32, 1984, 8 pp.

GOBEIL, C. et COSSA, D. *Profils des teneurs en mercure dans les sédiments et les eaux interstitielles du fjord du Saguenay (Québec) : données acquises au cours de la période 1978-83*, Rapport technique canadien hydrogr. science océan, N° 53, 1984, 23 pp.

GOBEIL, C., SILVERBERG, N., SUNDBY, B. and COSSA, D. *Cadmium Diagenesis in Laurentian Trough Sediments*, Geochim. cosmochim. Acta., N° 51, 1984, pp. 589-596.

LORING, D. H. *Mercury in the Sediments of the Gulf of St. Lawrence*, Canadian Journal Earth Sciences, N° 12, 1975, pp. 1219-1237.

LORING, D. H. *The Distribution and Partition of Zinc, Copper, and Lead in the Sediments of the Saguenay Fjord*, Canadian Journal Earth Sciences, N° 13, 1976, pp. 960-971.

LORING, D. H. and BEWERS, J. M. *Geochemical Mass Balances for Mercury in a Canadian fjord*, Chem. geol., N° 22, 1978, pp. 309-330.

PELLETIER, É., ROULEAU, C. et CANUEL, G. *Niveau de contamination par le mercure des sédiments de surface et des crevettes du fjord du Saguenay en 1985-86*, Revue Inter. Science Eau, N° of cat. 2 : 13-27, 1989.

POCKLINGTON, R. and MACGREGOR, C. D. *The Determination of Lignin in Marine Sediments*, Int. J. Environ. Anal. Chem., N° of cat. 3 : 81-93, 1973.

SMITH, J. N. and LORING, D. H. *Geochronology for Mercury Pollution in the Sediments of the Saguenay Fjord, Québec*, Environ. Sci. Technol., N° 15, 1981, pp. 944-951.

SMITH, J. N. and WALTON, D. H. *Sediment Accumulation Rates and Geochronologies Measured in the Saguenay Fjord using the 210Pb Dating Method*, Geochim. Cosmochim. Acta, N° of cat. 44 : 225-240, 1980.

Principaux intérêts de recherche

Émilien Pelletier
INRS-Océanologie

PROJET 1 : Effets du pétrole dispersé sous la glace
(CRSNG thématique — Toxicologie de l'environnement — Novembre 1987 — Novembre 1990)

L'objectif principal de ce projet vise à répondre à la question pratique suivante : Dans le cas d'un déversement de pétrole en eaux glacées, serait-il avantageux (moins de risques environnementaux) de procéder à une dispersion chimique de la nappe pour éviter les problèmes de fragmentation et de transport à grande distance par les glaces ?

Les objectifs spécifiques de ce projet sont les suivants :

a) Construire un groupe de cinq réservoirs expérimentaux à échelle intermédiaire (3,5 m^3 chacun) particulièrement conçus pour des travaux à long terme à basse température et sous la glace.

b) Développer une méthodologie expérimentale adaptée à ce type de réservoirs (calibration écologique) en comparant périodiquement le comportement des écosystèmes expérimentaux avec le milieu naturel sous toutes les conditions climatiques.

c) Établir le bilan chimique d'une dispersion de pétrole sous la glace en mesurant la contribution individuelle des processus de foculation, de sédimentation et de biodégradation au processus global de vieillissement.

d) Évaluer la capacité de la microfaune subarctique hivernale de survivre et de se rétablir d'un choc toxique majeur entraîné par une dispersion de pétrole (persistance de la toxicité).

e) Mener une étude détaillée du bilan biologique de la dégradation du pétrole dispersé dans des conditions subarctiques en présence de la microfaune de l'estuaire du Saint-Laurent.

PROJET 2 : Indicateurs biochimiques de stress environnemental
(Ministère de l'Environnement du Canada, ministère des Pêches et des Océans du Canada et contrat MAS en cours Juillet 1988 — Mai 1990)

L'objectif de ce projet est de développer un nouveau biotest capable d'évaluer le niveau de toxicité sous-léthale d'un milieu exposé à des contaminations toxiques dissoutes, des sédiments dragués ou des rejets d'usines par l'utilisation en tandem de deux mesures biochimiques, l'une portant sur la fragilité de la membrane lysosomale des cellules digestives et l'autre sur l'activité d'un enzyme-clé du métabolisme énergétique chez *Mytilus edelis* d'abord et ensuite chez d'autres organismes marins.

Les objectifs spécifiques de ce projet sont :

a) Établir la sensibilité de la réponse des deux indicateurs biochimiques en fonction de la nature et de la concentration des différents contaminants.

b) Établir une calibration des réponses des indicateurs biochimiques avec les niveaux de bioaccumulation des contaminants dans les tissus.

c) Vérifier les réponses des indicateurs lors d'une période de récupération après le stress (temps requis pour la remise à zéro des indicateurs).

d) Appliquer le test à au moins une autre espèce marine à déterminer.

e) Appliquer le test à une expérience de terrain.

PROJET 3 : Métabolisme et toxicité des organométalliques
(CRSNG dépenses courantes, recherche fondamentale à long terme)

L'objectif général de ce projet est de comprendre le processus d'intoxication alimentaire par trois organométalliques d'intérêt environnemental (méthylmercure (MM), tributhylétain (TBE) et triéthylplomb (TEP)) et d'évaluer la capacité de détoxification naturelle chez l'étoile de mer, *L. polaris*, afin d'utiliser celle-ci comme modèle dans le biotransfert de contaminants dans une chaîne trophique benthique. Cet objectif global à long terme peut être précisé par l'énoncé d'un groupe d'objectifs spécifiques réalisables sur une période de trois à cinq ans :

a) Déterminer la spéciation de TBE et TEP dans les sédiments marins en développant une méthode d'analyse fine par spectrométrie de masse avec une technique FAB (Fast Atoms Bombardment).

b) Déterminer les cinétiques de biotransfert (digestion, absorption, transport et entreposage) de MM, TBE et TEP chez *L. polaris*.

c) Comparer la toxicité sous-léthale de MM, TBE et TEP chez *L. polaris* par la mesure de la fragilité des membranes lysosomales et la spécificité de la MDH.

d) Déterminer le principal mécanisme de détoxification développé par *L. polaris* pour chacun des trois contaminants : MM, TBE et TEP.

LISTE DES ARTICLES AVEC JURY

BROCHU, C. and PELLETIER, É. *A Microcomputer Program for the Analysis of Hydrocarbon Gas Chromatograms*, Comput. Chem., accepted May 1988.

BROCHU, C., PELLETIER, É., DESNOYERS, J. E. and CARON, G. *The Dispersion of Crude Oil in Seawater : the Role of Synthetic Surfactants*, Oil Chem. Pollut., N° of cat. 3 : 257-279, 1987.

COLOMBO, J. C., PELLETIER, É., BROCHU, C. and CATOGGIO, J. A. *Distribution and Origins of Hydrocarbons in the Rio de La Plata Estuary (Argentina)*. Environ. Sci. Technol., Sudmitted April 1987.

HARROD, J. F. and PELLETIER, É. *Cyclosiloxanes as frameworks for multimetallic compounds ; 2. Synthesis and characterization of some metallocarbonyl substituted cyclosiloxanes*, *Organometallics*, N° 3, 1984, pp. 1064-1069.

LANGFORD, C. H., SAINT-JOLY, C., PELLETIER, É., PERSAUD, L., CROUCH, A. and ARBOUR, C. « A Composite Photocatalyst for Oxidation of Sulfur Dioxide », in *Catalysis on the Energy Scene (1984)*, Kaliaguine, S. and Mahay, A. (eds.), Amsterdam, Elsevier Science Publishers B. V., 1984, pp. 291-296.

LANGFORD, C. H., SAINT-JOLY, C., PELLETIER, É. and ARBOUR, C. *Photo-Oxydation of Sulfur Dioxide by a Polymner Supporterd Porphyrin Onplatinized TiO_2 Particles*, Inorganica Chimica Acta, N° 87, 1984, pp. L31-L32.

LEBEL, J., PELLETIER, É., BERGERON, M., BELZILE, N. et MARQUIS, G. *Le panache du Saguenay*, Canadian Journal of Fisheries and Aquatic Sciences, N° of cat. 40(1), 1983, pp. 52-60.

LEBEL, J. et PELLETIER, É. *Contribution à l'étude du pH et de la saturation en calcite dans l'Estuaire du Saint-Laurent (Canada)*, Atmosphère-Océan, N° of cat. 18(2), 1980, pp. 154-167.

PELLETIER, É. and BROCHU, C. *Study of Oil in Water Dispersion Using a Dynamic Turbidimeter*, Proceedings Oil Spill Conference, 1989.

PELLETIER, É., SAURIOL, F. and WHARF, I. *Preparation and Characterization of New Organomercury(II) Selenolates*, Inorg. Chim. Acta, N° of cat. 138(2) : 99-101, 1987.

PELLETIER, É. and LAROQUE, R. *Bioaccumulation of Mercury in Starfish, Leptasterias Polaris, from Contaminated Food*, Mar. Pollut. Bull., N° of cat. 18 : 482-485, 1987.

PELLETIER, É. and CANUEL, G. *Trace Metal Concentrations in Surface Sediment of the Saguenay Fjord, Canada*, Mar. Pollut. Bull., N° of cat. 19(7) : 336-338, 1988.

PELLETIER, É., ROULEAU, C. et CANUEL, G. *Contamination chronique du fjord du Saguenay par le mercure*, Rev. Inter. Sci. Eau, 1989, sous presse.

PELLETIER, É. *Acute Toxicity of Some Methymercury Complexes to Mytilus edulis and Lack of Selenium Protection*, Mar. Pollut Bull., N° of cat. 19(5) : 213-219, 1988.

PELLETIER, É. *Modification de la bioaccumulation du sélénium chez Mytilus edulis en présence de mercure organique et inorganique*, Canadian Journal of Fisheries and Aquatic Sciences, N° of cat. 43 : 203-210, 1986.

PELLETIER, É. *The Mercury-Selenium Antagonism in Aquatic Organisms ; A review*, Mar. Poll. Res., N° of cat. 18 : 111-132, 1986.

PELLETIER, É. and HARROD, J. F. *Cyclosiloxanes as Frameworks for Multimetallic Compounds ; 3. ^1H NMR Spectra of Some Substituted Methyl Ccyclosiloxanes, Organometallics*, N° 3, 1984, pp. 1070-1075.

PELLETIER, É. and HARROD, J. F. *Mass Spectra of Some Substituted Methylcyclosiloxanes*, Canadian Journal of Chemistry, N° of cat. 61(4), 1983, pp. 762-768.

PELLETIER, É. et LEBEL, J. *La mesure du pH en milieu estuarien sur l'échelle NBS*, Canadian Journal of Fisheries and Aquatic Sciences, N° of cat. 37(4), 1980, pp. 703-706.

PELLETIER, É. et LEBEL, J. *L'alcalinité totale comme indicateur de mélange dans un milieu estuarien*, Canadian Journal Earth. Sciences, N° of cat. 17(8), 1980, pp. 978-984.

PELLETIER, É. and LEBEL, J. *Hydrogeochemistry of Dissolved Inorganic Carbon in the St. Lawrence Estuary (Canada)*, Estuarine and Coastal Marine Science, N° 9, 1979, pp. 785-795.

PELLETIER, É. et LEBEL, J. *Détermination du bore inorganique dans l'estuaire du Saint-Laurent*, Canadian Journal Earth. Sciences, N° of cat. 15(4), 1978, pp. 618-625.

Level and Possible Effects of PCBs and other Organochlorine Contaminants in Arctic and St. Lawrence Belugas

Derek Muir

Research Scientist — Central and Arctic Region
Fisheries and Oceans Canada

INTRODUCTION

The objective of this presentation is to compare types and levels of organochlorine contaminants in arctic belugas, and in other Canadian East coast cetaceans, with those in St. Lawrence belugas. A second objective is to draw some tentative conclusions regarding possible effects on the St. Lawrence beluga population and to make suggestions for the direction of further studies on contaminants.

To understand why PCBs and other organochlorine compounds have accumulated in beluga and other marine mammals requires some information on their properties and uses. The organochlorines are a large class of chemicals which have been produced over the past 40 to 60 years (Table 1).

The insecticides, DDT, toxaphene, chlordane and hexachlorocyclohexane were widely used in the past in agriculture in North America. Use of these chemicals has been banned (DDT, toxaphene, chlordane) or restricted (chlorobenzenes, hexachlorocyclohexanes) in the United States of America (USA), Canada and Western Europe, but large-scale uses of DDT and HCH continues in India and in other developing countries. PCB use was restricted to closed systems in the early 1970s but legislative restrictions did not come into effect until 1979 in the United States (US) and in 1977 in Canada. Prior to that time PCBs were

TABLE 1

Global Production and Use of Major Organochlorines

Organochlorine	Use	Period of manufacture	Estimated total Global production (tonnes)
Polychlorinated biphenyls (PCBs)	Flame retardant	1930-83 (1930-79 USA)	1,2 x 10^6 (0,6 X 10 USA)
DDT	Insecticide	1940-present (1940-74 USA)	1,5 x 10^6
Toxaphene	Insecticide	1947-present (1947-84 USA)	5 x 10^5
Chlordane	Insecticide	1945-present (1945-76 USA)	2,5 x 10^5
Hexachloro-benzene (HCBz)	Fungicides By-products	1915-present	1 x 10^5 (USA)
Hexachloro-cyclohexanes (HC)	Insecticide	1945-present	4 x 10^5

widely used as transformer oils, in other electrical applications and as hydraulic fluids and were disposed of improperly. It is now estimated that 31% of total world PCB production of 1.2×10^6 kgs has been released into the global environment.

PCBs and organochlorine pesticides are characterized by extreme resistence to biodegradation, relatively low vapor pressures, low water solubility and high lipid solubility. Fish and invertebrates are unable to metabolize PCB congeners with greater than 5 chlorines, while mammals and birds can rapidly degrade those congeners with adjacent unsubstituted carbon atoms. Many PCB congeners, particularly those substituted at the 2.4 and 2.4.5 positions, as well as most organochlorine pesticides bioaccumulate in terrestrial and aquatic food chains.

Organochlorines enter the marine environment from disposal, runoff from agricultural land and especially by atmospheric deposition in precipitation and dryfall. Absorption to sedimenting particles and burial will remove some of these hydrophobic pollutants from the water column. Organochlorines can be remitted to the atmosphere by volatilizing from water of surfaces on which they are deposited. Given their resistence to transformation in water, sediments and in the atmosphere, organochlorines can circulate globally. Past uses of the chemicals on farmland in the southern United States (US) (for *e.g.* toxaphene) resulted in transport and deposition in the Great Lakes and in northern Ontario and Québec.

Atmospheric transport is a particularly important source of contaminants for the Canadian Arctic where uses of organochlorine pesticides was negligible and where PCB use was limited to radar installations at, for example, DEW line stations. In the St. Lawrence River drainage area, however, direct use of organochlorine insecticides in agriculture and substantial use of PCBs in urban areas suggest that runoff and disposal would be the major pathways of contamination of the aquatic environment.

Marine mammals, as top predators in marine food chains, are well recognized for the ability to biomagnify PCBs and organochlorine pesticides. Small cetaceans in Eastern Canadian waters, white-beaked dolphins from the Gulf of St. Lawrence, harbour porpoises in the Bay of Fundy, and beluga in the St. Lawrence estuary, have been shown to have high levels (20 to 500 µg/g) of PCBs and DDT related compounds in blubber. Recent surveys of PCBs and chlorinated pesticides in arctic beluga which are reported in more detail elsewhere, permit for the first time, comparisons between levels of pollutants in "healthy" arctic stocks and those in the threatened St. Lawrence stock.

METHODS

Samples: Beluga tissues were obtained by Department of Fisheries and Oceans personnel from animals taken in the Inuit hunt at five locations in the Canadian Arctic between 1983 and 1987. These locations were Grise Fiord (8 males, 7 females), Pangnirtung (5 males, 5 females), Eastern Hudson Bay (8 males, 8 females), Western Hudson Bay (Eskimo Point; 4 males, 4 females), and the Beaufort Sea (Mackenzie Bay; 10 males, 2 females). Additional blubber samples from stranded beluga (4 males, 5 females) in the St. Lawrence estuary during 1986-87 were obtained from Dr. Pierre Béland, Institut national d'écotoxicologie du Saint-Laurent, Rimouski.

Analysis: Determination of PCBs and chlorinated pesticides in beluga blubber followed the methods described by Muir *et al.* Final extracts were analyzed by capillary gas chromatography (60 m × 0.25 mm DB-5 fused silica column) using an electron capture detector and confirmed by GC mass spectrometry. PCBs were identified using a standard mixture of 51 congeners prepared by the National Research Council, Marine Analytical Standards Program (Halifax, Nova Scotia). Organochlorine pesticides were identified and quantitated with authentic standards obtained from the U.S. Environmental Protection Agency. Further details of the extraction and analysis of the beluga samples are given in Muir *et al.*

RESULTS AND DISCUSSION

Comparison between Arctic and St. Lawrence animals: Figures 1 to 4 compare the levels of the four major organochlorine contaminants in beluga blubber from 5 Arctic locations and from the St. Lawrence estuary. In all cases the bars indicate concentration in μg/g (wet weight basis) with males on the left and females on the right. A bar in the upper right of each figure represents 10 μg/g for PCBs, DDT and toxaphene and 1 μg/g for chlordane.

PCBs were 25-fold higher in beluga from the St. Lawrence estuary, for both males and females, than in Arctic animals. Levels of PCBs in Arctic animals were quite similar at all locations averaging about 3 μg/g in males and 2 μg/g in females. Adult female marine mammals usually have lower levels than males because of their ability to excrete the contaminants via lactation. Levels of PCBs were approximately twice as high in male beluga than in females from all sites except for animals from Grise Fiord where only juveniles were analyzed. A similar twofold higher level in males was found in the St. Lawrence animals analyzed in this survey and in a larger survey of PCBs in beluga reported by Martineau *et al.* This result suggests that the St. Lawrence females,

FIGURE 1

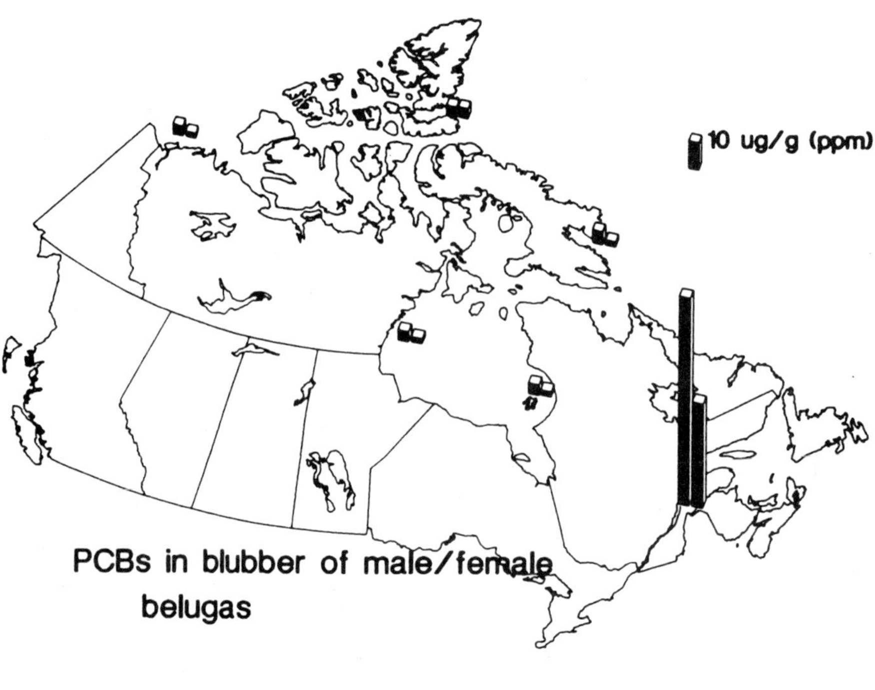

FIGURE 2

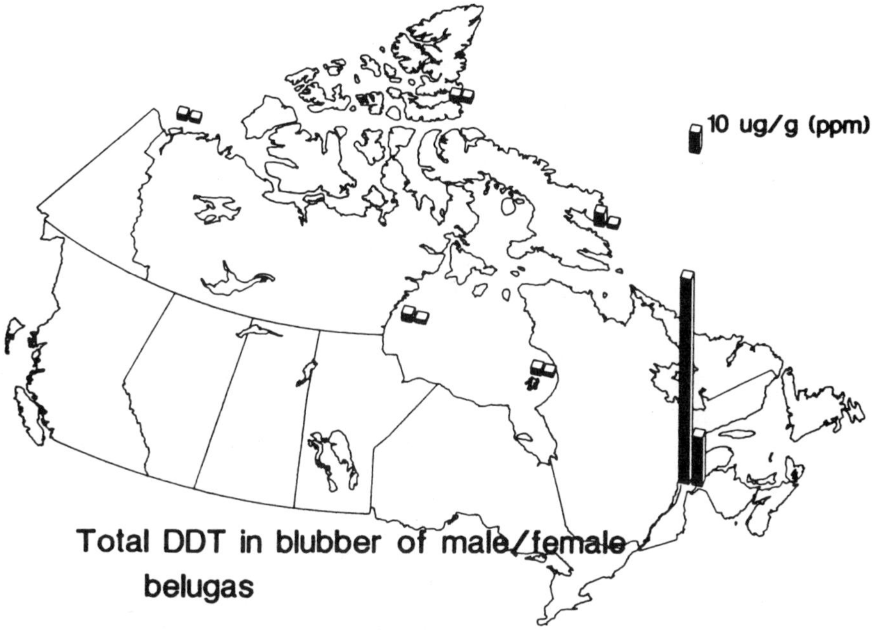

FIGURE 3

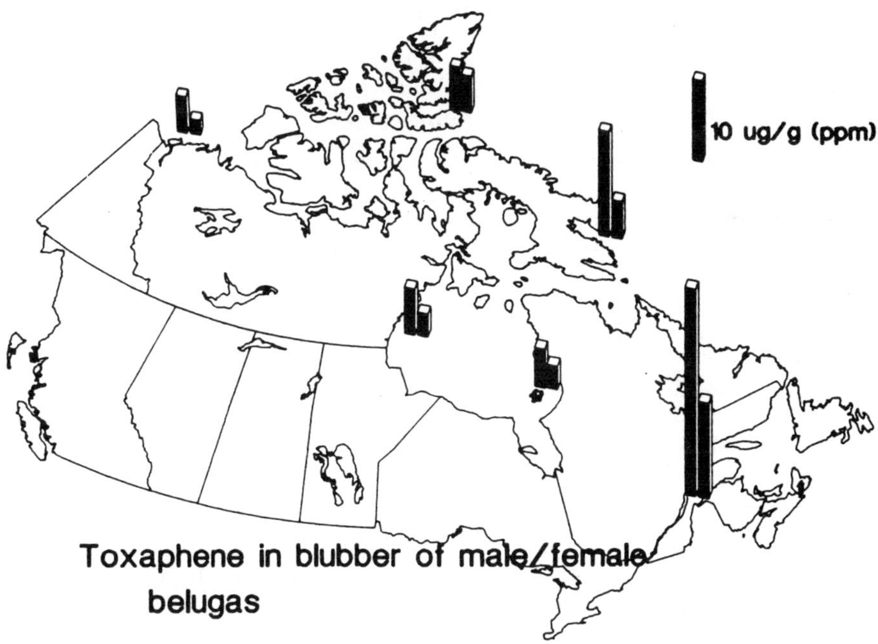

FIGURE 4

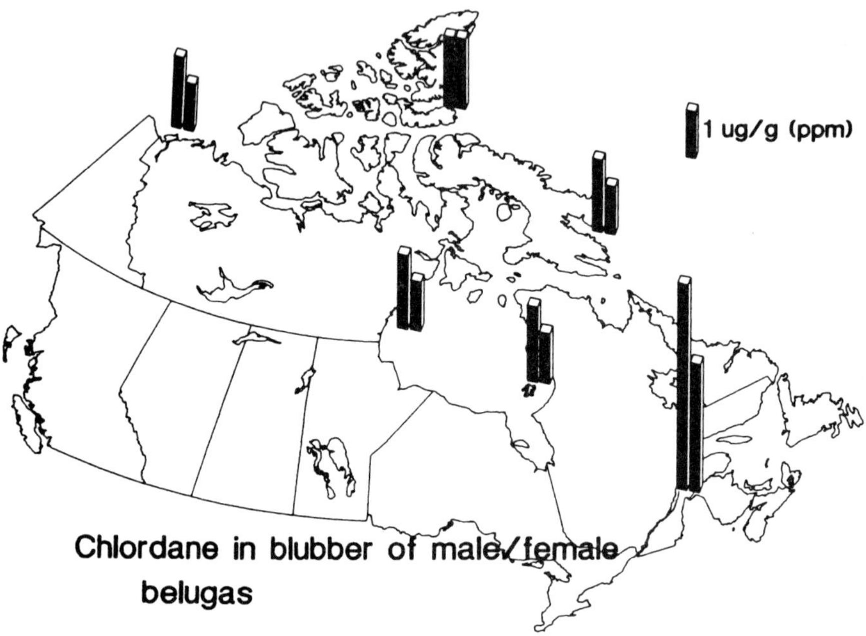

although they died by stranding rather than hunting, have been lactating in the recent past. In another marine mammal population with low reproductive success, the ringed seals in the Baltic Sea/Gulf of Bothnia, pregnant females or "healthy" nonpregnant females has significantly lower levels of PCBs than females with pathological changes in their uteri or males from the same population.

DDT residues in arctic beluga (Figure 2) were similar in all sites, averaging about 3 μg/g in males and 1 μg/g in females. DDT levels were 32 times higher in male St. Lawrence beluga and 19 times higher in females. DDT levels in the St. Lawrence group analyzed for this study were similar to those reported by Martineau *et al.* The major component of DDT in all samples was the persistent metabolite p, p′-DDE.

Toxaphene was the major organochlorine pesticide residue in blubber of arctic belugas averaging approximately 4 μg/g in males and 2 μg/g in females (Figure 3). Belugas from Cumberland Sound had higher levels than other animals. Levels of toxaphene in male and female St. Lawrence belugas were about sixfold higher than in the Arctic stocks.

Chlordane residues in Arctic animals averaged about 2 μg/g in males and 0.8 μg/g in females from all sites except the High Arctic stock (Grise Fiord). Females from the St. Lawrence and High Arctic stocks had similar levels of chlordane while St. Lawrence males had approximately threefold higher levels than the average for all arctic males (Figure 4).

Neither chlordane nor toxaphene were extensively used in the St. Lawrence River watershed, unlike DDT and PCBs. The presence of these compounds in blubber of St. Lawrence beluga is therefore probably the result of long-range transport from agricultural areas of the southern U.S. where these compounds were used extensively for pest control on cotton in the 1960s and 1970s.

Comparisons of St. Lawrence beluga and other East Coast cetaceans: Figures 5 and 6 compare levels of PCBs and DDT reported in white-beaked dolphins and pilot whales from Newfoundland and in harbour porpoises from the Bay of Fundy with those reported by Martineau *et al.* for St. Lawrence beluga. Results are from samples that were collected between 1977 and 1984. Male belugas from the St. Lawrence estuary had significantly higher PCB levels than other male cetaceans surveyed (Figure 5). Female belugas, however, had levels which were not statistically different from those in porpoises or dolphins. DDT levels in male harbour porpoises averaged 103 μg/g versus 91 μg/g in male belugas and 43 μg/g in male dolphins. Clearly, other cetaceans in Canadian East Coast waters are also highly contaminated. Declines in DDT levels have occurred in East Coast seals during the period 1974 to 1982, but little change occurred in average PCB levels in grey or harp seals. Apart from the porpoises, which have been studied extensively, the possible effects of contaminants on East Coast cetaceans have received little study. These comparisons also suggest that other East Coast cetaceans inhabiting Gulf of St. Lawrence waters might prove to be good surrogates for the belugas in terms of studies of contaminant levels and biological effects.

Correlations of contaminant levels with age: DDT and PCB levels in marine mammals are frequently correlated with age, especially in males; therefore comparisons between groups must take into account age differences. The average age of the St. Lawrence beluga in this study was 17.6 years for males and 15.6 years for females, which did not differ greatly from the mean ages of animals from Hudson Bay (13 years for males, 11 years for females) or the Beaufort Sea. Therefore age is unlikely to account for differences in organochlorine contaminant levels between the Arctic and St. Lawrence stocks. PCB and DDT levels in the 4 male belugas analyzed for this study were positively correlated with age. For the Arctic animals, however, there were few statistically significant correlations of organochlorine levels except for Hudson Bay stocks where PCB, DDT and chlordane levels were inversely correlated with age of females, that is, older animals had lower levels because of elimination of lipopholic contaminants by successive lactations. Martineau *et al.* found that PCB and DDT levels in St. Lawrence belugas were positively correlated with age in both male and female adults. In this respect the

FIGURE 5

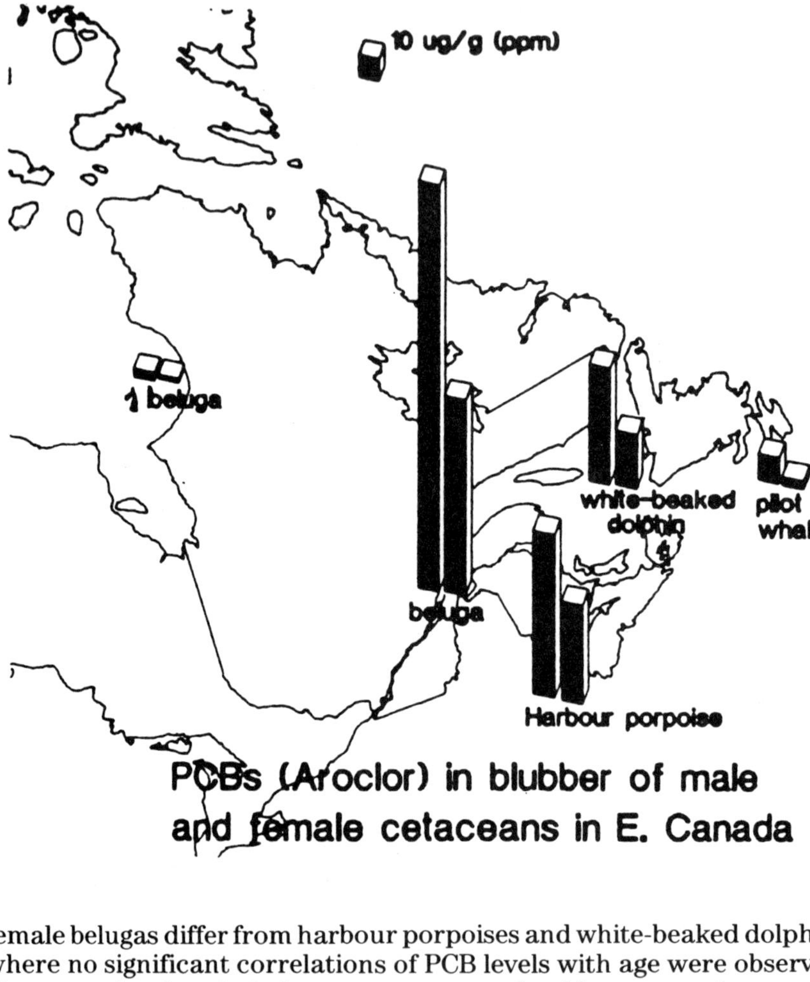

PCBs (Aroclor) in blubber of male and female cetaceans in E. Canada

female belugas differ from harbour porpoises and white-beaked dolphins where no significant correlations of PCB levels with age were observed. However the female belugas were a much older group (mean age 18 years) than the porpoises (2.7 years) or dolphins (3 years). Studies of Antarctic minke whales and of short-finned pilot whales have shown that PCB levels are positively correlated with age of immature females and negatively correlated with age of reproductively active females. Tanabe *et al.* also found evidence for increasing levels in older females which they attributed to reduced number of parturitions in this group. Similar relationships may explain the positive correlation of PCB and DDT levels in female beluga with age.

Possible effects of high PCB levels on beluga: High levels of PCBs in fat (> 50 µg/g in fat) are associated with reproductive failure of laboratory animals fed PCBs and of wild populations of seals and sea lions

FIGURE 6

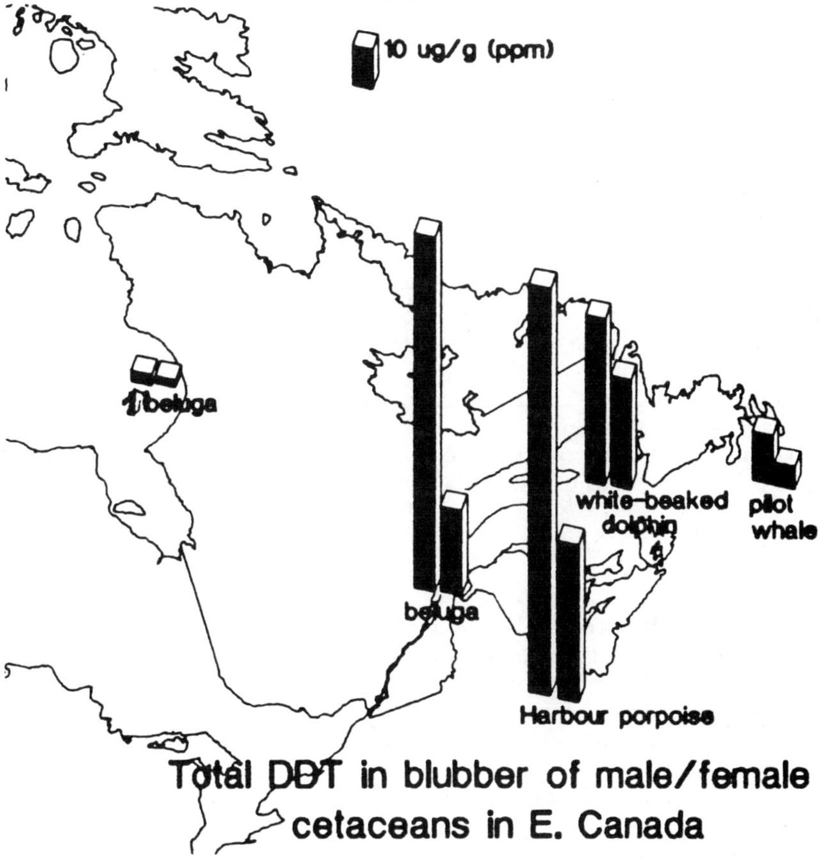

Total DDT in blubber of male/female cetaceans in E. Canada

(Table 2). Numerous studies with mink, which have similar reproductive physiology to marine mammals, indicate reduced whelping success on diets of fish similar to those consumed by seals. Perhaps the most convincing demonstration of the effects on marine mammals is the work of Reijnders, who showed that captive harbour seals fed a diet of North Sea fish showed poor reproductive success (4 pregnant animals out of 12 ovulating) in comparison with a control group fed Atlantic Ocean fish (10 pregnant out of 12).

The reproductive failure in seals and mink took the form of abortion or resorption of the embryo. The exact cause was not known but could be due to hormonal disturbance of direct embryo toxic effect of PCBs or cocontaminants such as dioxins.

Reijnders concluded that tenfold higher levels of PCBs in wild harbour seals from the Dutch Wadden Sea than in the same species from

TABLE 2

Some Effects Attributed to Organochlorines in Marine Mammals

Species	Location	Effect	Chemical/level
Ringed seal	Baltic Sea	Reproductive failure uterine occlusions	PCBs > 70 ug/g
Harbour seal	Dutch Wadden	Reproductive failure	PCBs > 100 ug/g
Sea lions	California	Abortions	DDE > 500 ug/g PCBs > 100 ug/g

the German/Danish coasts were strongly correlated with the reduced reproductive success of the Dutch seal population.

CONCLUSIONS

The hypothesis of PCB-induced reproductive failure of St. Lawrence belugas put forward by Martineau *et al.* is supported by comparisons with Arctic stocks and, especially by recent studies on harbour seals fed fish contaminated with these chemicals. Other organochlorines (chlordanes, toxaphene) are probably of lesser concern because, in contrast to PCBs and DDT, levels of these compounds in St. Lawrence animals are only threefold to sixfold greater (in males) than in "healthy" arctic stocks.

There is evidence from the much lower PCB and DDT levels in St. Lawrence females than in males that, although they had died from stranding, the animals had been eliminating the organochlorines by lactation. Although little can be said about the frequency of lactations, the ratio of organochlorines in males to that in females was similar in Arctic and St. Lawrence animals.

Levels of PCBs and DDT in St. Lawrence belugas are within the range observed for other small cetaceans, especially in the case of females, from eastern Canadian waters. Other cetaceans may therefore be at risk due to PCB contamination of their food chains.

Further work on contaminants should make use of samples of other cetaceans from the Gulf of St. Lawrence which may be available due to strandings or nettings.

Other trace toxic contaminants such as dioxins, furans and coplanar PCBs should be surveyed. There is a need to investigate temporal trends in organochlorine levels in food chain organisms of the beluga and to link contaminant levels to biochemical measurements, *e.g.* hormones, mixed function oxidase enzymes, in marine mammals.

ACKNOWLEDGMENTS

This presentation would not have been possible without the contributions of the following individuals and organizations. Cathy Ford and Bert Grift, Fisheries and Oceans (DFO), Winnipeg carried out organochlorine analyses. Dr. Ross Norstrom and Mary Simon, Canadian Wildlife Service, Hull, provided GC-mass spectrometry confirmation of organochlorine residues. Dr. Rob Stewart and Patt Weaver, DFO, Winnipeg provided samples, information and advice on belugas from Eskimo Point, Pangirtung, Grise Fiord and Mackenzie Bay. Dr. Tom Smith and Bill Doidge, DFO, Sainte-Anne-de-Bellevue, provided samples, ages and additional information on beluga from Eastern Hudson Bay. Dr. Pierre Béland, Institut national d'écotoxicologie du Saint-Laurent, Rimouski, provided St. Lawrence beluga samples and information.

REFERENCES

ADDISON, R. F., BRODIE, P. F., ZINCK, M. E. and SERGEANT, D. E. *DDT has Decline More than PCBs in Eastern Canadian Seals During the 1970s*, Environ. Sci. Technol. n° of cat. 18 : 935-937, 1984.

AGARWAL, H. C., KAUSHIK, C. P. and PILLAI, M. K. K. *Organochlorine Insecticide Residues in the Rainwater in Delhi, India*, Water Air Soil Pollut. n° of cat. 32 : 293-300, 1987.

BERGMAN, A., OLSSON, M. and REUTERGARDH, L., Lowered Reproduction Rate in Seal Population and PCB; *A Discussion of Comparability of Results and Presentation of Some Data from Research on the Baltic seals*, Intern. Coun. Explor. Sea, Marine Mammals Committee, 1981, 17 p.

BIDLEMAN, T. F., CHRISTENSEN, E. J., BILLINGS, W. N. and LEONARD, R. *Atmospheric Transport of Organochlorines in the North Atlantic Gyre*, J. Mar. Res. n° of cat. 39 : 443-464, 1981.

DELONG, R. L., GILMARTIN, W. G. and SIMPSON, J. G. *Premature Births in California Sea Lions*. Association with High Organochlorine Pollutant Residue Levels, Science, n° of cat. 181 : 1168-1170, 1973.

EISENREICH, S. J. "The Chemical Limnology of Nonpolar Organic Contaminants : Polychlorinated Biphenyls in Lake Superior", in *Sources and Fates of Aquatic Pollutants*, Hites, R. A. and Eisenreich, S. J. (eds), Washington, D. C. Adv. Chem. Ser. 216, American Chemical Society, 1987, pp. 393-470.

GASKIN, D. E., FRANK, R. and HOLDRINET, M. *Polychlorinated Biphenyls in Harbor Porpoises (*Phocoena Phocoena L.*) from the Bay of Fundy, Canada,* *and Adjacent Waters, with Some Information on Chlordane and Hexachlorobenzene Levels*, Arch. Environ. Contam. Toxicol, n° of cat. 12 : 211-219, 1983.

GASKIN, D. E. "Environmental Contaminants and Trace Elements : Their Occurence and Possible Significance in Cetacea", in *The Ecology of Whales and Dolphins*, Gaskin, D. E., London, Heinemann Educational Books, 1982, pp. 393-433.

GRANT, D. L. In : *PCBs, Human and Environmental Hazards*, Boston, Butterworth Publ., 1983, pp. 383-392.

HOLDEN, A. V. *Pollutants and Seals — a Review*, Mammal Rev, n° of cat. 8 : 53-66, 1978.

HOLTZ, A., SHARPE, M. A., CONSTABLE, M. and WILSON, W. *Removal of Contaminants from Distant Early Warning Sites in Canada's Arctic*, Edmonton, Alberta, Environmental Protection Service, 1987.

MARTINEAU, D., BÉLAND, P., DESJARDINS, C. and LAGACÉ, A. *Levels of Organochlorine Chemicals in Tissues of Beluga Whales (*Delphinapterus leucas*) from the St. Lawrence Estuary*, Quebec, Canada, Arch. Environ. Contam. Toxicol, n° of cat. 16 : 137-147, 1987.

MUIR, D. C. G., FORD, C. A., STEWART, R. E. A., SMITH, T. G., ADDISON, R. F. and BÉLAND, P. *Organochlorine Contaminants in Beluga (*Delphinapterus leucas*) from the Canadian Arctic*, manuscript in preparation.

MUIR, D. C. G., NORSTROM, R. J. and SIMON, M. *Organochlorine Contaminants in Arctic Marine Food Chains : Accumulation of Specific Polychlorinated Biphenyls and Chlordane-Related Compounds*, Environ. Sci. Technol, n° of cat. 22 : 1071-1079, 1988b.

MUIR, D. C. G., WAGEMANN, M. R., GRIFT, N. P., NORSTROM, R. J., SIMON M. and LIEN, J. *Organochlorine Chemical and Heavy Metal Contaminants in White Beaked Dolphins (*Lagenorhynchus Albirostris*) and Pilot Whales (*Globiccephala Melaena*) from the Coast of Newfoundland*, Canada, Arch. Environ. Toxicol. Chem., n° of cat. 17 : 613-629, 1988a.

National Academy of Sciences. *Polychlorinated Biphenyls*, Washington, D. C., National Academy of Sciences, 1979, 182 p.

RAPAPORT, R. A. and EISENREICH, S. J. *Historical Atmospheric Imputs of High Molecular Weight Chlorinated Hydrocarbons to Eastern North America*, Environ. Sci. Technol., n° of cat. 22 : 931-941, 1988.

REIJNDERS, P. J. H. *Reproductive Failure in Common Seals Feeding on Fish from Polluted Coastal Waters.* Nature, n° of cat. 324 : 456-457, 1986.

REIJNDERS, P. J. H. *Organochlorine and Heavy Metal Residues in Harbour Seals from the Wadden Sea and Their Possible Effects on Reproduction*, Neth. J. Sea Res., n° of cat. 14 : 30-65, 1980.

RICE, C. P., SAMSON, P. J. and NOGUCHI, G. E. *Atmospheric Transport of Toxaphene to Lake Michigan*, Environ. Sci. Technol., n° of cat. 20 : 1108-1116, 1986.

TANABE, S., LOGANATHAN, B. G., SUBRAMANIAN, An. and TATSUKAWA, R. *Organochlorine Residues in Short Finned Pilot Whales ;* Possible Use as Tracers of Biological Parameters, Mar. Pollut. Bull., n° of cat. 18 : 561-563, 1987.

TANABE, S., MIURA, S. and TATSUKAWA, R. *Variations of Organochlorine Residues with Age and Sex in Antarctic Minke Whales*, Mem. Natl. Inst. Polar Res., Spec. Issue, n° of cat. 41 : 174-181, 1986.

TANABE, S. *PCB Problems in the Future: Foresight from Current Knowledge*, Environ. Pollut., n° of cat. 50: 5-28, 1988.

VOLDNER, E. C. and ELLENTON, G. *Production, Usage and Atmospheric Emissions of Priority Toxic Chemicals with Emphasis on North America*, Report ARD-88-4 prepared for the International Joint Commission, Dowmsview, Ontario, Atmospheric Environment Service.

The Role of Biotransformation in the Toxicity of Marine Pollutants

Mark E. Hahn and John J. Stegeman
Department of Biology
Woods Hole Oceanographic Institution

INTRODUCTION

A large number of chemical contaminants can be found in marine and freshwater environments (Clark, 1986; Connell and Miller, 1984). Some of the most important classes of marine pollutants are shown in Table 1. The toxicity of many of these compounds is well known from studies in experimental animals. Two classes of marine pollutants, polycyclic aromatic hydrocarbons and polychlorinated biphenyls, have been suggested as having an important impact on the St. Lawrence beluga population (Masse *et al.*, 1986; Martineau *et al.*, 1987, 1988). Polycyclic aromatic hydrocarbons (PAHs), such as benzo(a)pyrene, are potent carcinogens in humans and other animals (Stegeman, 1981). Polychlorinated biphenyls (PCBs) are members of a group of ubiquitous environmental contaminants, the halogenated aromatic hydrocarbons, many of which produce similar toxic effects. There are 209 possible PCB compounds, or congeners, containing from 1 to 10 chlorine atoms; large quantities of mixtures of PCBs were used commercially and released into the environment. (The presence of PCBs in beluga whales from the St. Lawrence estuary is discussed by Muir. Two other types of halogenated aromatic hydrocarbons chlorinated dibenzofurans (PCDFs) and chlorinated dibenzo-p-dioxins (PCDDs) are also of potential concern due to their presence in sediments and biota in the Laurentian Great Lakes (Baumann and Whittle, 1988) and in cetaceans (Ono *et al.*, 1987).

TABLE 1

Some Marine Pollutants

Hydrocarbons	
	• Polycyclic Aromatic Hydrocarbons (PAH) e.g. Benzo[a]pyrene
	• Petroleum Hydrocarbons
Halogenated Hydrocarbons	
	• Halogenated Aromatic Hydrocarbons
	- Polychlorinated biphenyls (PCB) - Polychlorinated dibenzofurans (PCDF) - Polychlorinated dibenzo-*p*-dioxins (PCDD)
	• Organochlorine Pesticides e.g. DDT
Heavy Metals	
	e.g. Hg, Cd

Although the PCDDs and PCDFs are generally present in the environment at much lower levels than the PCBs, there are toxic effects observed in wildlife. There are 75 possible PCDD congeners and 135 possible PCDF congeners; however, only a few of the many possible congeners are dominant in environmental samples. For all of the halogenated aromatic hydrocarbons (PCBs, PCDDs, PCDFs) the toxicity of the individual congeners varies tremendously depending on the number and position of the chlorine substituents (Poland and Knutson, 1982).

The toxicity of PAHs and halogenated aromatic hydrocarbons has been well documented from studies in experimental animals. Examples of the kinds of effects that have been observed following exposure of animals to these compounds are : decreases in growth rates, neurotoxicity (seen also with many organochlorine pesticides), hepatotoxicity; altered functioning of the immune system (which can lead to increased susceptibility to viral or bacterial infection), endocrine dysfunction (changes in the levels and function of various hormones), and impaired reproductive ability (Poland and Knutson, 1982; Safe, 1984). In addition, some of these compounds are teratogenic, *i.e.* they produce birth defects in the offspring of exposed parents, and chronic exposure to some chemicals, particularly PAHs, may lead to tumors in certain organs.

THE ROLE OF BIOTRANSFORMATION IN MECHANISMS OF TOXICITY

It is important to know the mechanism by which these pollutants produce toxicity. Knowing how a chemical produces its toxic effects provides strong evidence for causality. This is especially helpful with regard to effects observed in wildlife, since often the best evidence we have is circumstantial, *i.e.* correlations between the presence of a particular contaminant and some effect, such as a reduced reproductive rate. Knowing the mechanism of toxicity can help us design tests to predict the potential for other chemicals to produce similar effects. It can also lead to the selection and use of sensitive biochemical indicators to detect the presence and effects of certain classes of chemicals in wildlife. In addition, knowledge of mechanisms of toxicity provides increased confidence in the extrapolation of results from one species to another, especially when used in conjunction with information on the comparative biochemistry and physiology of the systems involved.

What are the mechanisms by which chemicals produce toxicity? The toxic effects of a chemical are observed at the level of the individual organism. However, these effects can be traced back to events occurring at the cellular level. Figure 1 shows a diagram of a cell, which has been exposed to a chemical ("X"). After entering the cell, some of the chemical may be stored; PAHs and PCBs, for example, are very lipophilic (fat-soluble) and so tend to become associated with tissues that possess a high lipid content. There are two ways in which chemicals are able to produce toxicity. Some chemicals produce toxicity directly, by interaction with essential cellular macromolecules (such as proteins, lipids, and nucleic acids) and disrupting their normal functions. Depending on the chemical properties of the toxicant, it may interact with one or more of these components, resulting ultimately in some toxic effect on the organism.

Other chemicals, however, are not toxic in their initial form, but must first be transformed to a toxic derivative of metabolite, which then goes on to produce toxicity. This biotransformation can be performed by various enzymes in the cell, depending on the specific chemical involved. The major enzyme system involved in these reactions is cytochrome P-450, a group of related enzymes found in many different species of animals, plants, and bacteria (Nebert and Gonzalez, 1987; Nelson and Strobel, 1987). In addition to its ability to transform chemicals to derivatives that are more toxic than the original compound (bioactivation), cytochrome P-450 can also detoxify chemicals, usually by converting them to metabolites that are more water-soluble and therefore more easily excreted. Thus, the ability of a compound to be metabolized by P-450 is an important determinant of the persistence and toxicity of that compound in an organism.

FIGURE 1

The role of biotransformation in the toxicity of xenobiotic chemicals

Chemical X may produce toxicity directly, by interacting with essential cellular macromolecules (e.g. proteins, lipids, nucleic acids) and disrupting their normal functions, or X may require activation by cytochrome P-450 to a toxic metabolite, Y, before toxicity can occur.
Cytochrome P-450 may also detoxify X by metabolizing it to Z, which is more water-soluble and thus more easily excreted. See text for additional details.

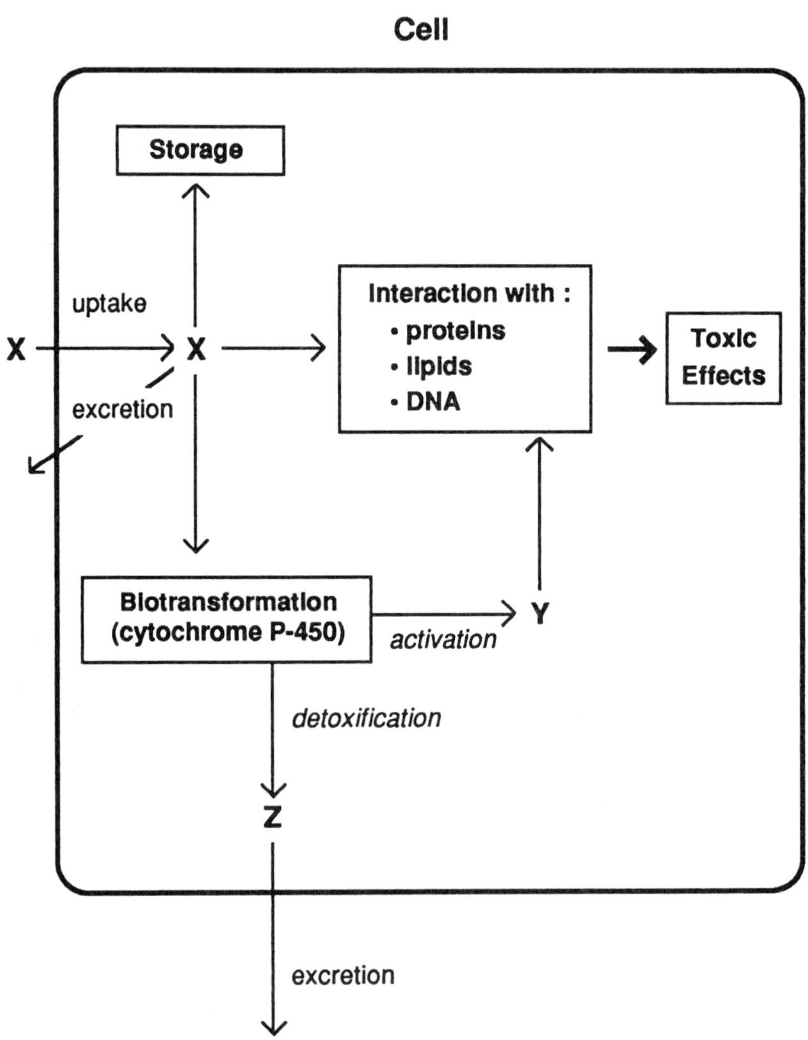

Although the highest levels of cytochrome P-450 are found in the liver, it is also present in many other organs as well, including the lung, kidney, intestine, and adrenal. Cytochrome P-450 is not a single enzyme, but rather a group of related enzymes (isoenzymes); for example, more than 10 P-450 isoenzymes have been identified in the livers of rats. As mentioned earlier, cytochrome P-450 can either detoxify a chemical or activate it to a toxic metabolite. Which of these occurs with a given chemical is determined chiefly by the properties of the chemical and by the form of P-450 involved.

The classic example of a compound that is bioactivated to a toxic metabolite is the PAH benzo(a)pyrene. Before it can exert its well-known carcinogenic effect, benzo(a)pyrene must first be metabolized by cytochrome P-450. Reactions catalyzed by P-450 are known as monooxygenase reactions, because they involve the insertion of an oxygen atom into the compound being metabolized. Benzo(a)pyrene is metabolized by P-450 to form a diolepoxide derivative, a reactive metabolite that then binds tightly to specific components of the DNA, producing a mutation that leads eventually to the formation of a tumor. At the same time, other benzo(a)pyrene molecules are being converted to less toxic metabolites that are rapidly excreted from the organism, preventing the accumulation of this chemical. (The binding of benzo(a)pyrene metabolites to DNA is discussed in more detail in the paper by Shugart.)

CYTOCHROME P-450 IN MARINE FISH

Our laboratory has been studying the cytochrome P-450 system of fish, focusing on the marine fish scup, or porgy (*Stenotomus chrysops*), which is found along the United States Atlantic coast from Cape Cod, Massachusetts, south to Cape Hatteras, North Carolina. We have isolated several forms of P-450 (designated P-450 A, B, C, D, and E) from the livers of scup (Table 2) (Klotz *et al.*, 1983, 1986). We have focused our attention on P-450E, which is similar to a form of P-450 (P-450IA1) found in terrestrial mammals (rats, mice, humans) that is involved in the metabolism of many pollutants and chemical carcinogens.

One way in which cytochrome P-450 forms are characterized is by the rates at which they metabolize different compounds. Shown in Table 2 are the rates at which several forms of scup P-450 metabolize three compounds: the PAH benzo(a)pyrene (aromatic hydrocarbon hydroxylase (AHH) activity); ethoxyresorufin, a synthetic substrate that is commonly used to characterize P-450 enzyme activity (ethoxyresorufin O-deethylase (EROD) activity); and testosterone (testosterone hydroxylase activity). In comparison with the other four forms, P-450E is very efficient at metabolizing benzo(a)pyrene and ethoxyresofurin; these two monooxygenase activities are often used and indicate the

TABLE 2

Cytochrome P-450 Isoenzymes in the Marine Fish Scup (*Stenotomus chrysops*)

Isoenzyme or Fraction	Monooxygenase Activities (nmol/min/nmol P-450)		
	Benzo[a]pyrene hydroxylase (AHH)	Ethoxyresorufin O-deethylase (EROD)	Testosterone hydroxylase
P-450A	0.16	n.d.	0.80
P-450B	0.001	---	0.07
P-450C	0.001	n.d.	---
P-450D	0.001	---	0.15
P-450E	0.90	7.1	0.04

n.d. = not detectable. Source Klotz *et al.* (1983, 1986).

amount of functional P-450E in a tissue sample. In contrast, testosterone is metabolized poorly by P-450E.

Induction of P-450E

The induction (increase in amount) of P-450 isoenzymes by various chemicals has been studied extensively in laboratory animals. Scup P-450E is inducible by some of the same compounds that are effective inducers in mammals. These compounds include polycyclic aromatic hydrocarbons such as three-methylcholanthrene and B-naphthoflavone, and halogenated hydrocarbons, including polychlorinated biphenyls (both PCB mixtures and some of the individual congeners) and a chlorinated dibenzofuran (2, 3, 7, 8-TCDF) (Table 3).

An example of the induction of P-450E by tetrachlorobiphenyl and tetrachlorodibenzofuran is shown in Figure 2. Both of these compounds produce a 20-fold increase in the rate of metabolism of ethoxyresorufin (EROD activity). These compounds also increase the total amount of cytochrome P-450 in the livers of the fish. However, many different forms of P-450 are present in these fish. In order to specifically measure the amount of P-450E, we use the technique of immunoblotting or "Western blotting". This method uses a specific antibody to P-450E as a probe to selectively identify P-450E in a mixture of P-450s and other cellular proteins (Park *et al.*, 1986; Kloepper-Sams *et al.*, 1987). First, proteins in the mixture are separated according to size by electrophoresis,

TABLE 3

Compounds that Induce P-450E in Scup

Polycyclic Aromatic Hydrocarbons (PAH)	
	3-Methylcholanthrene (3MC) 3-Naphthoflavone (BNF)
Halogenated Aromatic Hydrocarbons	
	Aroclor 1254/1242 (PCB mixture) 3,4,3',4'-Tetrachlorobiphenyl (3,4,3',4'-TCB) 3,4,5,3',4',5'-Hexachlorobiphenyl 2,3,7,8-Tetrachlorodibenzofuran (2,3,7,8-TCDF)

Data from Stegeman *et al.* (1981), Kloepper-Sams *et al.* (1987), Gooch *et al.* (1988), and Hahn & Stegeman (unpublished).

FIGURE 2

Induction of EROD activity, total P-450, and P-450E in scup

Scup were treated with a single intraperitoneal injection of corn oil (control), 3,4,3',4'-tetrachlorobiphenyl (TCB ; 100 μg per kg body weight), or 2,3,7,8-tetrachlorodibenzofuran (TCDF ; 3.1 μg per kg body weight), and killed after 5 days. The livers were isolated and measurements made on the microsomal fraction (100,000 g pellet) as described elsewhere (Gooch *et al.*, 1988). The number of fish in each group were : control (3), TCB (3), TCDF (2).

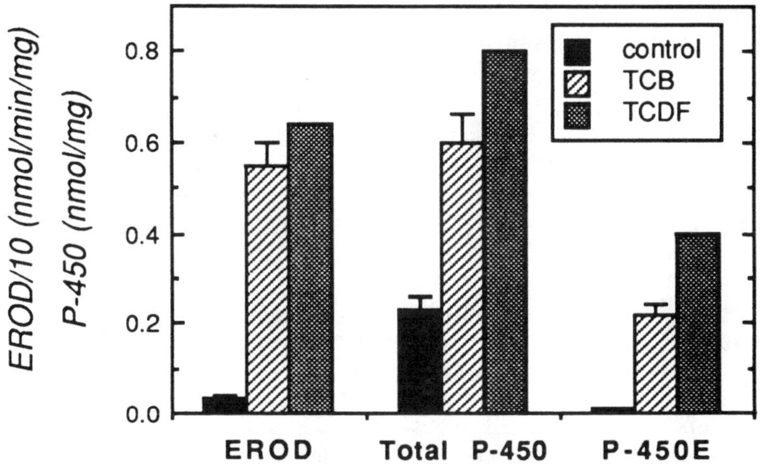

and then transferred to a piece of nitrocellulose paper. The antibody is then used to identify and stain only P-450E. The amount of P-450E present is proportional to the intensity of the stain ; by comparing the staining in the sample to that of known amounts of P-450E, we can determine the amount of P-450E in the sample. In untreated fish, only a small proportion of the total P-450 present is P-450E. In fish treated with tetrachlorobiphenyl or TCDF, however, the amount of P-450E is increased dramatically (Figure 2) in agreement with the elevated EROD activity.

ENVIRONMENTAL INDUCTION

Using these two techniques (immunoblotting and measurements of monooxygenase activities), we have detected apparent induction of P-450E in untreated fish sampled directly from the ocean, in association with elevated levels of environmental contaminants, particularly PCBs. One example of this "environmental induction" was seen in a deep-sea fish, the rattail *Coryphaenoides armatus* (Stegeman *et al.*, 1986). These fish were sampled from two sites in the western North Atlantic : near Hudson Canyon, off New York, and near Carson Canyon, off Newfoundland. Immunoblot analysis indicated elevated levels of a protein homologous to P-450E in the livers of fish from Hudson Canyon as compared to fish from Carson Canyon. Measurements of monooxygenase activities confirmed these results ; the rates of metabolism of both ethoxyresorufin and benzo(a)pyrene were higher in the Hudson Canyon fish. Chemical analysis of the livers from these same fish showed that PCB levels were much higher in the Hudson Canyon fish (mean of 2.73 ppm) than in Carson Canyon fish (mean of 0.36 ppm) (Stegeman *et al.*, 1986). Similarly, other studies in our laboratory have demonstrated elevated levels of P-450E in coastal and estuarine fish in association with elevated levels of PCBs and PAHs (Stegeman *et al.*, 1981, 1987, 1988 ; Elskus & Stegeman, 1988 ; Susani, 1987). Similarly, other laboratories have reported elevated monooxygenase activities in fish and other animals from contaminated environments (Payne *et al.*, 1987 ; Spies *et al.*, 1982 ; Foureman *et al.*, 1983 ; Varanasi *et al.*, 1986 ; Ellenton *et al.*, 1985).

CYTOCHROME P-450 IN MARINE MAMMALS

Since this forum is concerned with the future of the beluga whale and the possible effects of environmental contaminants on the health of these animals, we need to consider the role that the cytochrome P-450 system might play in the toxicity of these chemicals in the beluga. Unfortunately, very little is known about biotransformation reactions in marine mammals, especially cetaceans. However, the structural and functional similarities between the cytochrome P-450s of terrestrial mammals and fish (Heilmann *et al.*, 1988; Stegeman and Kloepper-Sams, 1987; Klotz *et al.*, 1983) suggest that this system has been conserved to some degree during evolution. Most of the limited number of investigations of cytochrome P-450 in marine mammals have dealt with pinnipeds (Engelhardt, 1982; Addison and Brodie, 1984; Addison *et al.*, 1986); these studies have generally indicated that monooxygenase activities (*e.g.* EROD, AHH) in seals resemble those found in other mammalian species.

The only published studies on P-450 in cetaceans have dealt with the minke whale, *Balaenoptera acutorostrata* (Goksoyr *et al.* 1986, 1988). Some of these studies were performed in our laboratory in collaboration with Dr. Anders Goksoyr (University of Bergen, Norway). Cytochrome P-450 was detected in the livers of both adult and fetal whales, with higher levels in the adults (Goksoyr *et al.*, 1988). The hepatic P-450 concentration in adult minke whales (0.35 nmol/mg protein) was similar to that found in untreated fish (scup), but somewhat less than that found in scup that had been induced with three-methylcholanthrene, or untreated rats (*e.g.* Stegeman and Kloepper-Sams, 1987). Minke whale kidneys also contained P-450, but at a lower level than the livers. Both ethoxyresorufin O-deethylase (EROD) and benzo(a)pyrene hydroxylase (AHH) activities were detected in the liver samples, suggesting that these whales possess a form of cytochrome P-450 similar to scup P-450E and the related forms in terrestrial mammals (collectively known as cytochrome P-450IA1; Nebert *et al.*, 1987). Since whales were not sampled from different sites, it is not possible to determine whether these activities represent basal or induced levels. However, analysis of the liver from one of these whales showed a PCB concentration of 0.23 ppm (Goksoyr *et al.*, 1988), which is lower than levels found in beluga whales from the St. Lawrence estuary (mean levels of 2.6 ppm, range of 0.23-8.6 ppm, Martineau *et al.*, 1987) or "environmentally induced" fish (2.73 ppm, Stegeman *et al.*, 1986).

In addition to enzyme activities, we also used immunoblotting to look for a P-450 protein related to P-450E in these whales. A monoclonal antibody to scup P-450E was able to identify a related P-450 in rats (Kloepper-Sams *et al.*, 1987), suggesting that it could also be used in whales. Using this antibody, we detected a P-450E homologue in the livers, but not the kidneys, of adult minke whales. We also found small amounts of this P-450 in the livers of fetal whales. These results strongly suggest that whales possess a form of P-450 related to the PAH- and PCB-inducible forms (P-450IA1) found in terrestrial mammals and in marine and freshwater fish.

In contrast, when immunoblots were performed using polyclonal antibodies raised against a phenobarbital-inducible form of rat P-450 (PB-4; Waxman and Walsh, 1983), no related P-450 isoenzymes could be detected in the whales. In addition, pentoxyresorufin O-deethylase activity (PROD, a monooxygenase activity specific for phenobarbital-inducible P-450s) could not be detected in these samples (B. R. Woodin, T. Tautz, and J. J. Stegeman, unpublished observations). These results are intriguing in light of the suggestion by other investigators that whales are deficient in the phenobarbital-inducible forms of P-450 (Tanabe *et al.*, 1988).

SUMMARY AND CONCLUSIONS

The importance of knowing the mechanisms of toxicity of environmental pollutants cannot be overemphasized, especially with regard to identifying the chemicals and specific effects responsible for changes in wildlife populations. Cytochrome P-450-mediated biotransformation reactions play an important role in the mechanisms of toxicity of many environmental pollutants. Cytochrome P-450 isoenzymes can be involved in the bioactivation of compounds to toxic metabolites that produce toxicity by interacting with essential cellular macromolecules. However, these enzymes can also detoxify many compounds and hasten their excretion. In addition, some forms of P-450 are involved in the synthesis and degradation of endogenous compounds such as steroid hormones; disruption of these reactions can also lead to toxic effects, such as impaired reproduction.

Cytochrome P-450 can be induced by many environmental contaminants, including many that have been found at high levels in beluga tissues and in the St. Lawrence estuary. This response may be useful as a sensitive indicator of the exposure of wildlife populations to these chemicals. Although the overall toxicological significance of this "environmental induction" is not yet known, for some compounds (*e.g.* PCBs, PCDDs, PCDFs) there is a good correlation between their ability to induce some forms of P-450 (*e.g.* P-450IA1) and their toxic potency (Poland and Knutson, 1982; Safe 1984, 1986).

Little is known about cytochrome P-450 and the biotransformation of environmental pollutants in cetaceans, due to the difficulty in obtaining fresh tissues from these animals. Clearly, however, they possess a form of forms of cytochrome P-450 that are similar to those of other vertebrate species, including terrestrial mammals and marine fish. It is quite likely, based on phylogenetic relationships (Nelson and Strobel, 1987), that P-450 enzymes in cetaceans will more closely resemble those of terrestrial mammals than those of fish. However, since cetaceans and fish share the same environment, including food sources, they are exposed to the same pollutants. Thus, information gained from studies of P-450 in fish may be of some relevance in predicting the effects of environmental contaminants on the cytochrome P-450 system of whales. In particular, the presence of induced levels of certain forms of P-450 in fish and other animals from polluted marine environments suggests that similar induction may also be occurring in marine mammals, including the St. Lawrence belugas, that are exposed to these pollutants. There is a need for further characterization of cetacean P-450 isoenzymes and their inducibility. Knowledge of the ability of these isoenzymes to catalyze biotransformation reactions involving both endogenous and xenobiotic compounds may help us to understand which of the many pollutants found in the marine environment are responsible for effects seen in beluga whales and other cetaceans.

ACKNOWLEDGMENTS

We would like to thank Dr. Jacques Prescott for the opportunity to participate in the Forum for the Future of the Beluga. We are grateful to Dr. Anders Goksoyr for providing the samples of minke whales tissues. We are also grateful for the contributions and helpful comments of the members of Dr. Stegeman's laboratory, including Adria A. Elskus, Jay W. Gooch, Pamela J. Kloepper-Sams, Michael J. Moore, Terry Tautz, and Bruce R. Woodin. M. E. Hahn was supported by a SURDNA Postdoctoral Fellowship in Marine Biomedical Research.

REFERENCES

ADDISON, R. F. and BRODIE, P. F. *Characterization of Ethoxyresorufin O-Deethylase in Grey Seals* Halichoerus Grypus, Comp. Biochem. Physiol., n° of cat. 79C: 261-263, 1984.

ADDISON, R. F., BRODIE, P. F., EDWARDS, A. and SADLER, M. C. Mixed Function Oxidase Activity in the Harbour Seal (Phoca Vitulina) from Sable, N. S. Comp. Biochem. Physiol., n° of cat. 85C: 121-124, 1986.

BAUMANN, P. C. and WHITTLE, D. M. *The Status of Selected Organics in the Laurentian Great Lakes: an Overview of DDT, PCBs, Dioxins, Furans, and Aromatic Hydrocarbons*, Aquatic Toxicol., n° of cat. 11: 241-257, 1988.

CLARK, R. B. *Marine Pollution*, New York, Oxford University Press, 1986, 215 p.

CONNELL, D. W. and MILLER, G. J. *Chemistry and Ecotoxicology of Pollution*, New York, John Wiley & Sons, 1984, 444 p.

CONNEY, A. H. *Pharmacological Implications of Microsomal Enzyme Induction*, Pharmacol. Rev., n° of cat. 19: 317-366, 1967.

ELLENTON, J. A., BROWNLEE, L. J. and HOLLEBONE, B. R. *Aryl Hydrocarbon Hydroxylase Levels in Herring Gull Embryos from Different Locations on the Great Lakes*, Environ. Toxicol. Chem., n° of cat. 4: 615-622, 1985.

ELSKUS, A. A. and STEGEMAN, J. J. *Induced Cytochrome P-450 in* Fundulus Heteroclitus *Associated with Environmental Contamination by Polychlorinated Biphenyls and Polynuclear Aromatic Hydrocarbons* (submitted for publication), 1988.

ENGELHARDT, F. R. *Hydrocarbon Metabolism and Cortisol Balance in Oil-Exposed Ringed Seals*, Phoca Hispida, Comp. Biochem. Physiol., n° of cat. 72C: 133-136, 1982.

FOUREMAN, G. L., WHITE, N. B. and BEN, J. R. *Biochemical Evidence that Winter Flounder (*Pseudopleuronectes Americanus*) Have Induced Hepatic Cytochrome P-450 Dependent Monooxygenase Activities*, Can J. Fish. Aquat. Sci., n° of cat. 40: 854-865, 1983.

GOKSOYR, A., ANDERSSON, T., FORLIN, L., STENERSEN, J., SNOWBERGER, E. A., WOODIN, B. R. and STEGEMAN, J. J. *Xenobiotic and Steroid Metabolism in Adult and Fœtal Piked (Minke) Whales*, Balaenoptera Acutorostrata, Mar. Environ. Res., n° of cat. 24: 9-13, 1988.

GOKSOYR, A., SOLBAKKEN, J. E., TARLEBO, J. and KLUNGSOYR, J. *Initial Characterization of the Hepatic Microsomal Cytochrome P-450 System of the Piked Whale (Minke)* Balaenoptera Acutorostrata, Mar. Environ. Res., n° of cat. 19: 185-203, 1986.

GOOCH, J. W., ELSKUS, A. A., KLOEPPER-SAMS, P. J., HAHN, M. E. and STEGEMAN, J. J. *Effects of Ortho and Non-Ortho Substituted Polychlorinated Biphenyl Congeners on the Hepatic Monooxygenase System in Scup* Stenotomus Chrysops, Toxicol. Appl. Pharmacol., (in press).

HEILMANN, L. J., SHEEN, Y.-Y., BIGELOW, S. W. and NEBERT,D. W. *The Trout P450IA1 : cDNA and Deduced Protein Sequence, Expression in Liver, and Evolutionary Significance*, n° of cat. DNA 7: 379-387, 1988.

KLEINOW, K. M., MELANÇON, M. J. and LECH, J. J. *Biotransformation and Induction : Implications for Toxicity, Bioaccumulation and Monitoring of Environmental Xenobiotics in Fish*, Environ. Health Perspect, n° of cat. 71: 105-119, 1987.

KLOEPPER-SAMS, P. J. and STEGEMAN, J. J. *The Temporal Relationships Between Cytochrome P-450E Protein Content, Catalytic Activity and mRNA Levels in the Teleost* Fundulus Heteroclitus *Following Treatment with B-Naphthoflavone*, Arch. Biochem. Biophys., 1988, (in press).

KLOEPPER-SAMS, P. J., PARK, S. S., GELBOIN, H. V. and STEGEMAN, J. J. *Specificity and Cross-Reactivity of Monoclonal and Polyclonal Antibodies Against Cytochrome P-450E of the Marine Fish Scup*, Arch. Biochem. Biophys., n° of cat. 253: 268-278, 1987.

KLOTZ, A. V., STEGEMAN, J. J. and WALSH, C. *An Aryl Hydrocarbon Hydroxylating Hepatic Cytochrome P-450 from the Marine Fish* Stenotomus Chrysops, Arch. Biochem. Biophys., n° of cat. 226: 578-592, 1983.

KLOTZ, A. V., STEGEMAN, J. J., WOODIN, B. R., SHOWBERGER, E. A., THOMAS, P. E. and WALSH, C. *Cytochrome P-450 Isozymes from the Marine Teleost* Stenotomus Chrysops*: Their Role in Steroid Hydroxylation and the Influence of Cytochrome* b_5, Arch. Biochem. Biophys., n° of cat. 249: 326-338, 1986.

MARTINEAU, D., BELAND, P., DESJARDINS, C. and LAGACE, A. *Levels of Organochlorine Chemicals in Tissues of Beluga Whales (*Delphinapterus Leucas*) from the St. Lawrence Estuary, Quebec, Canada*, Arch. Environ. Contam. Toxicol., n° of cat. 16: 137-147, 1987.

MARTINEAU, D., LAGACE, A., BELAND, P., HIGGINS, R., ARMSTRONG, D. and SHUGART, L. R. *Pathology of Stranded Beluga Whales (*Delphinapterus

Leucas) *from the St. Lawrence Estuary, Quebec, Canada*, J. Compt. Pathol., n° of cat. 98 : 287-311, 1988.

MASSE, R., MARTINEAU, D., TREMBLAY, L. and BELAND, P. *Concentrations and Chromatographic Profile of DDT Metabolites and Polychlorobiphenyl (PCB) Residues in Stranded Beluga Whale* (Delphinapterus leucas) *from the St. Lawrence Estuary*, Canada, Arch. Environ. Contam. Toxicol., n° of cat. 15 : 567-579, 1986.

NEBERT, D. W., ADESNIK, M., COON, M. J., ESTABROOK, R. W. *et al. The P450 Superfamily : Recommended Nomenclature*, n° of cat. DNA 6 : 1-11, 1987.

NEBERT, D. W. and GONZALEZ, F. J. *P450 Genes : Structure, Evolution, and Regulation*, Ann Rev. Biochem., n° of cat. 56 : 945-93, 1987.

NELSON, D. W. and STROBEL, H. W. *Evolution of Cytochrome P450 Proteins*, Mol. Biol. Evol., n° of cat. 4 : 572-593, 1987.

ONO, M., KANNAN, N., WAKIMOTO, T. and TATSUKAWA, R. *Dibenzofurans a Greater Global Pollutant than Dioxins ? Evidence from Analyses of Open Ocean Killer Whale*, Mar. Poll. Bull., n° of cat. 18 : 640-643, 1987.

PARK, S. S., MILLER, H., KLOTZ, A. V., KLOEPPER-SAMS, P. J., STEGEMAN, J. J. and GELBOIN, H. V. *Monoclonal Antibodies to Liver Microsomal Cytochrome P-450E of the Marine Fish* Stenotomus Chrysops *(Scup) ; Cross-Reactivity with 3-methylcholanthrene Induced Rat Cytochrome P-450*, Arch. Biochem. Biophys., n° of cat. 249 : 339-350, 1986.

PAYNE, J. F., FANCEY, L. L., RAHIMTULA, A. D. and PORTER, E. L. *Review and Perspective on the Use of Mixed Function Oxygenase Enzymes in Biological Monitoring*, Comp. Biochem. Physiol., n° of cat. 86C : 233-245, 1987.

POLAND, A. and KNUTSON, J. C. 2,3,7,8 *Tetrachlorodibenzo-p-dioxin and Related Halogenated Aromatic Hydrocarbons : Examination of the Mechanism of Toxicity*, Ann. Rev. Pharmacol. Toxicol., n° of cat. 22 : 517-554, 1982.

SAFE, S. *Polychlorinated Biphensyls (PCBs) Biochemistry, Toxicology, and Mechanism of Action*, CRC Crit. Rev. Toxicol., n° of cat. 13 : 319-395, 1984.

SAFE, S. *Comparative Toxicology and Mechanism of Action of Polychlorinated Dibenzo-P-Dioxins and Dibenzofurans*, Ann. Rev. Pharmacol. Toxicol., n° of cat. 26 : 371-399, 1986.

SPIES, R. B. and RICE, D. W. *Effects of Organic Contaminants on Reproduction of the Starry Flounder* Platichthys Stellatus *in San Francisco Bay*, Marine Biol., n° of cat. 98 : 191-200, 1988.

SPIES, R. B., FELTON, J. S. and DILLARD, L. *Hepatic Mixed Function Oxidases in California Flatfishes are Increased in Contaminated Environments and by Oil and PCB Ingestion*, Marine Biol., n° of cat. 70 : 117-127, 1982.

STEGEMAN, J. J. "Polynuclear Aromatic Hydrocarbons and their Metabolism in the Marine Environment", In GELBOIN, H. V. and Ts'o, POP (eds.), *Polycyclic Hydrocarbons and Cancer*, New York, Academic Press, 1981, vol. 3, pp. 1-60.

STEGEMAN, J. J. and KLOEPPER-SAMS, P. J. *Cytochrome P-450 Isozymes and Monooxygenase Activity in Aquatic Animals*, Environ. Health Perspect., n° of cat. 71 : 87-95, 1987.

STEGEMAN, J. J., KLOEPPER-SAMS, P. J. and FARRINGTON, J. W. *Monooxygenase Induction and Chlorbiphenyls in the Deep-Sea Fish* Coryphaenoides Armatus, Science, n° of cat. 231 : 1287-12, 1986.

STEGEMAN, J. J., KLOTZ, A. V., WOODIN, B. R. PAJOR, A. M. *Induction of Hepatic Cytochrome P-450 in Fish and the Indication of Environmental Induction in Scup*, Aquatic Toxicol., n° of cat. 1 : 197-212, 1981.

STEGEMAN, J. J., TENG, F. Y. and SNOWBERGER, E. A. *Induced cytochrome P-450 in Winter Flounder (*Pseudopleuronectes Americanus*) from Coastal Massachusetts Evaluated by Catalytic Assay and Monoclonal Antibody Probes*, Canadian Journal of Fisheries and Aquatic Sciences, n° of cat. 44 : 1270-1277, 1987.

STEGEMAN, J. J., WOODIN, B. R. and GOKSOYR, A. *Apparent Cytochrome P-450 Induction as an Indication of Exposure to Environmental Chemicals in the Flounder* Platichthys Flesus, Mar. Ecol. Prog. Ser., n° of cat. 46 : 55-60, 1988.

SUSANI, L. C. *The Use of Biochemical Probes to Characterize Field Populations of Winter Flounder* Pseudopleuronectes Americanus, M. S. Thesis, Massachusetts Institute of Technology, 1987, 81 p.

TANABE, S., WATANABE, S., KAN, H. and TATSUKAWA, R. *Capacity and Mode of PCB Metabolism in Small Cetaceans*, Mar. Mam. Sci., n° of cat. 4 : 103-124, 1988.

VARANASI, U., REICHERT, W., STEIN, J., BROWN, D., SANBORN, H. R. *Hepatic Cytochrome P-450 Isozymes and Aryl Hydrocarbon Hydroxylase in English Sole (*Parophyrs Vetulus*)*, Biochem. Pharmacol., n° of cat. 35 : 2967-2971, 1986.

WAXMAN, D. J. and WALSH, C. *Cytochrome P-450 Isozyme 1 from Phenobarbital Induced Rat Liver: Purification, Characterization, and Interactions with Metyrapone and Cytochrome* b_5. Biochemistry, n° of cat. 22 : 4846-4855, 1983.

Organochlorine Pollutants in the Marine Environment: Analytical Assessment of the Contamination of the Beluga Whale (*Delphinapterus leucas*) from the St. Lawrence Estuary — Canada by DDT and PCB Residues

Robert Massé, Daniel Martineau and Pierre Béland
INRS-Santé, Faculté de médecine vétérinaire de l'Université de Montréal
and Department of Fisheries and Oceans Canada

INTRODUCTION

The status of marine mammal populations has become a subject of high interest and concern in recent years. Legislation and international agreements have been formulated with the objective of safeguarding these populations. Elevated levels of DDT and PCB are known to occur in blubber of cetaceans (1-3). It is generally accepted that lipophilic pollutants such as DDT and PCB accumulate in animal tissues with a high content of lipids. Although the bioaccumulation and magnification mechanisms are not completely understood, apparently, DDT and PCB levels tend to proportionately increase with the trophic level and metabolic rate of the organisms. A great number of marine mammals, such as the beluga whale of the St. Lawrence estuary, are at the end of their complex food web and this makes them very vulnerable to organic chemical pollution.

The St. Lawrence beluga whale population is the southernmost stock of an essentially Arctic species. Isolated from other beluga populations, it is centered at the confluence of the St. Lawrence and Saguenay rivers. It was recently given an endangered population status (4), the only Canadian whale stock to be so identified. Recent surveys indicated that the beluga population of the St. Lawrence estuary comprises about

350 whales (5,6). It is a remnant of large groups that lived there as recently as the last century and which number has been estimated to be about 5000 whales (7). Whale hunting alone cannot account for the drastic decline of the beluga population in the St. Lawrence estuary, since commercial and sport hunting of all whales were banned by the Canadian government in 1973. Therefore, one can question whether organochlorine contaminants and/or other environmental pollutants have contributed to the decline of this marine species in the St. Lawrence estuary.

This assumption is supported by the fact that reproductive impairment induced by PCBs and DDT or its metabolites has been experimentally verified in various mammals and bird species (8-10).

The aim of the present study was to determine the concentrations and molecular profiles of DDT, DDE and PCB residues in blubber, kidney, liver and lung tissues and in milk of stranded beluga whales collected in the St. Lawrence estuary during the summer-autumn seasons of 1983 and 1984. Interestingly, a transitional cell carcinoma of the urinary bladder was diagnosed in one animal (11). This study reports the gas chromatographic and mass spectrometric characterization and quantitation of PCB congeners and DDT metabolites in various tissues of beluga whales from this marine ecosystem.

MATERIALS AND METHODS

Sampling of the biological tissues, extraction and cleanup procedure of the organochlorine residues and gas chromatographic and mass spectrometric analysis of the organic extracts are described elsewhere (12).

RESULTS AND DISCUSSION

High-resolution glass capillary gas-chromatographic analysis of blubber, liver, lung, kidney and milk samples from beluga whales showed more than 20 peaks corresponding to tetra through heptachlorobiphenyls. Characteristic gas-chromatographic profiles of blubber and liver tissue extracts are shown in Figures 1 and 2 with the peak identified according to the numbering scheme proposed by Ballschmiter and Zell (13). The specific chlorine content of each of the PCB congeners and DDT metabolites was determined by gas chromatography-mass spectrometry analysis.

Although there were significant differences among the organochlorine compound concentrations measured in these various tissues, the PCB patterns showed great similarities as far as the identity of the organochlorine congeners are concerned. Indeed, these patterns resemble

FIGURE 1

High-resolution gas chromatogram of a beluga whale blubber extract

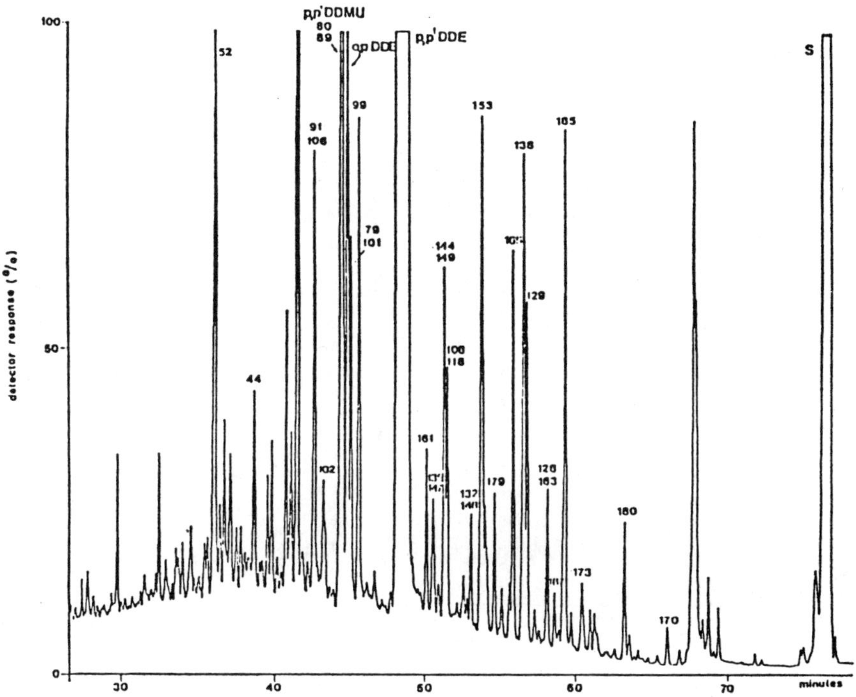

those of Aroclors 1254 and 1260, since several PCB congeners including nos. 52, 99, 138 and 180 are among the major components of both Aroclor 1254 and 1260 mixture and the beluga whale tissue extracts.

Table 1 shows the concentrations of PCB, *p,p'*-DDE and ΣDDT measured in the tissue samples and their respective n-hexane extractable lipid contents. The most striking facts of these data were the concentrations of *p,p*-DDE which were higher than those of PCB in all whales with the exception of those measured in the liver and kidney tissues from whales nos. 1 and 3. However, *p,p*-DDE was the most abundant individual organochlorine compound detected in each tissue.

Comparisons between the concentrations of organochlorine compounds (expressed per unit weights of wet tissue) in the various beluga whale tissues showed no significant relationship which could enable us to rationalize their relative distribution.

FIGURE 2

High-resolution gas chromatogram of a beluga whale liver extract

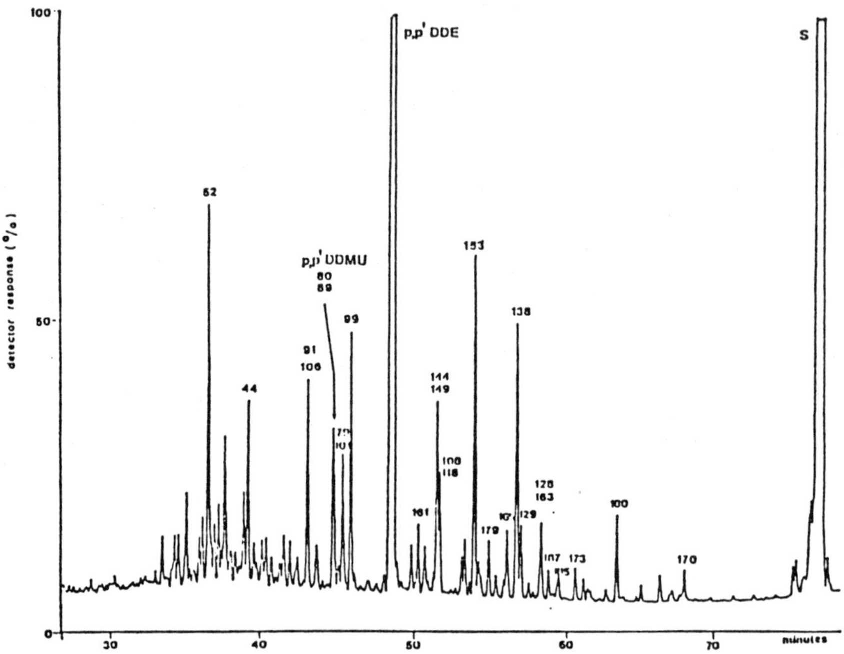

It is possible that the high *p,p'*-DDE/ΣDDT ratios (Table 1) reflect the timing and persistence of the contamination to which the beluga whale was exposed and probably indicates a lifetime exposure to DDT. Furthermore, the *p,p'*-DDT to *p,p'*-DDE ratios were very low, ranging from 0.02 ppm to 0.04 ppm. These data were in accordance with those (0.03 ppm to 0.07 ppm) reported by O'Shea *et al.* (2) in several species of small cetaceans from the Pacific and South Atlantic oceans. Long-term accumulation of the persistent metabolite *p,p'*-DDE in marine ecosystems, metabolic transformation of *p,p'*-DDT in the marine biota as well as the lack of recent input of *p,p'*-DDT (general use of which in North American ended in 1972) may contribute to these low ratios.

The differences in organochlorine concentrations from one tissue to another as well in a given whale and between several whales may be related to factors such as: the fat content of the tissues, blood flow differences in the highly perfused organs (e.g. liver, kidney, lung) and to individual and organic specific metabolic activities. Recent studies concerning the disposition of PCB have shown important variations in pharmacokinetics relative to the extent of chlorination, position of the chlorine atoms and the mammalian species tested (14,15).

TABLE 1

Organochlorine Residues in Beluga Whale Tissues[a]

Animal	Age[b]	Tissue	Fat%[c]	PCBs	p,p'-DDE	ΣDDT[d]	p,p'/DDE/ΣDDT	PCB/ΣDDT
1 Male	33	Blubber	96	72.15 ± 5.77	89.25 ± 8.03	103.75 ± 9.34	0.86	0.69
		Liver	23	2.55 ± 0.20	2.41 ± 0.22	2.54 ± 0.23	0.95	1.00
		Lung	12	0.56 ± 0.05	0.78 ± 0.07	0.82 ± 0.07	0.95	0.68
		Kidney	20	0.68 ± 0.05	0.44 ± 0.04	0.45 ± 0.04	0.98	1.44
2 Male	44[+]	Blubber	96	59.09 ± 4.73	66.23 ± 5.96	76.08 ± 6.85	0.87	0.77
		Liver	21	0.61 ± 0.05	0.93 ± 0.08	1.01 ± 0.09	0.92	0.60
		Lung	5	0.21 ± 0.02	0.30 ± 0.03	0.32 ± 0.03	0.94	0.65
		Kindney	21	0.77 ± 0.06	0.94 ± 0.08	0.98 ± 0.09	0.96	0.78
3 Male	30	Liver	21	0.49 ± 0.04	0.30 ± 0.03	0.32 ± 0.03	0.94	1.53
		Kidney	20	10.03 ± 0.80	2.68 ± 0.24	3.38 ± 0.30	0.79	2.97
4 Female	46	Milk	45	1725 ± 138	1879 ± 169	2046 ± 184	0.92	0.84

a) Concentrations were calculated per unit weights of wet tissue in µg/g (ppm); b) These numbers indicate the of concentric dentine layers measured on longitudinal sections of teeth, adopting the standard of two dentine layers per year (Sergeant 1973; Brodie 1982); the actual number of dentine layers (age) in two whales (+) is greater than those measured since some dentine layers could not be measured due to the wear of the teeth; c) The fat of the tisues was derined as follows: dry weight of the hexane soluble lipids/dry weight of the tissue X100; d) ΣDDT = p,p'-DDE, o,p-DDE, p,p'-DDT, o,p-DDT, p,p'-DDHU, p,p'-DDD.

Although great differences were observed in organochlorine concentrations, the PCB profiles from blubber, liver, kidney and lung tissue extracts were qualitatively similar (Figures 1, 2). None of the PCB patterns from liver, lung, and kidney samples reflects organ-specific metabolism, which could have given rise to PCB organ-specific profiles. However, quantitative differences were observed in the organochlorine profiles, suggesting that organ-specific retention of some PCB congeners occurs in the beluga whale. It is likely that the qualitative and quantitative differences in the PCB profiles are not solely related to the respective lipid content of the tissues, but also to the specific nature of the lipids which varies from one tissue to the other. In fact, it was not possible to determine whether the general PCB profile associated with the beluga whale tissues results from some specific metabolic activities including distribution, elimination and retention processes or was mainly influenced by the characteristic PCB content of the marine organisms which are part of its diet.

Comparison of our data with the chromatographic profiles by Ballschmiter *et al.* shows that the PCB patterns found in cod (*Gadus morhua*) from the North Atlantic gives very good correlation with those obtained from the beluga whale tissues. Indeed, PCB congeners nos. 52, 91, 99, 108, 118, 128, 138, 144, 149, 153, 163 and 180 were among the most abundant chlorinated biphenyls detected in the cod-liver oil as in the beluga whale blubber, liver, lung, kidney tissues, and milk sample.

The data also showed that the PCB pattern found in the beluga whale tissues resemble that of commercial Aroclor 1260. Indeed, several PCB congeners including nos. 101, 138, 149, 153, 170, 180 and 185 are among the major components of both Aroclor 1260 and beluga whale tissue extracts. In addition, some of the Aroclor 1254 minor and major congeners such as nos. 44, 52, 79, 99, 101, 105, 138, 149, 153, 170 and 180 were also detected in these marine mammals. Three PCB congeners can be used to determine the probable source of the PCBs observed in the beluga whale tissues. Indeed, congener nos. 138, 153 and 180 are the most abundant and most persistent PCB congeners observed in these samples. Thus, their presence in the beluga whale tissues can be attributed to Aroclor 1254 and 1260. The latter commercial mixtures have probably gained access into the marine environment from leaks, spills, waste disposal and atmospheric transport.

The data indicate that the most persistent PCB congeners are primarily penta—, hexa— and heptachlorobiphenyls with 2,3,4, and 2,4,5, 2,3,4,5, and 2,3,4,5,6 substitution patterns. Interestingly, the most abundant penta—, hexa— and heptachlorobiphenyls (nos. 99, 106, 138, 153, 173, 180, 185 and 187) possess chloro substituents at the 2,4,5 position on at least one of the two phenyl rings. Aromatic rings with this 2,4,5 substitution pattern do not bear adjacent unsubstituted carbon atoms and are therefore resistent to metabolic transformations (17).

Our results also suggest that the chlorinated PCBs that contain a 2,3,4-trichlorophenyl group (nos. 89, 105, 108, 128, 132, 138 and 170) are also resistent to environmental breakdown and metabolism. Consequently, their bioaccumulation in the beluga whale tissues is not unexpected.

TOXICOLOGICAL IMPLICATIONS

It is noteworthy that several of the PCB congeners detected in the beluga whale tissues, including the prominent 2,2′,3,4,4′-5-hexa—(no. 138) and 2,2′,4,4′,5,5′-hexachlorobiphenyls (no. 153) are aryl hydrocarbon hydroxylase (AHH) inducers (18). Since these compounds are not metabolized and persist indefinitely in the beluga whale tissues, the integrated total exposure to these AHH inducers may be significant. The beluga whale live in an area of the St. Lawrence estuary located at the mouth of the Saguenay River where the waters are contaminated by polyclic aromatic hydrocarbons (19). Thus, it is likely that the beluga whale is exposed to PAH as well as the marine organisms of its food web. The potential biological effects which are likely to result from the combined exposure to organochlorine residues and PAH have never been investigated in cetaceans, although they were studied in various mammalian and marine species (20,21).

CONCLUSION

The results presented herein clearly indicate that beluga whales of the St. Lawrence estuary are severely contaminated by DDT metabolites and PCB residues. As expected, the higher levels were found in the blubber. Considerable variations in the concentrations of *p,p′*-DDE and PCB were observed with respect to age, sex of the whales, and lipid content of the tissues. The qualitative profiles of PCB in the various tissues were very similar, indicating the age and persistence of the contamination. Several compounds which are known to be AHH inducers are among the major PCB congeners detected in each tissue and identified in Aroclors 1254 and 1260.

REFERENCES

1. AZIEU, C. L. and DUGUY, R. *Océanologica Acta*, 2, 107-120, 1979.
2. O'SHEA, T. J., BROWNELL, D. R., CLARK Jr., WALKER, W. A., GAY, M. L. and LAMONT, T. G. *Pesticide Monitoring Journal*, 14, 35-46, 1980.
3. AGUILAR, A. and JOVER, L. *Report International Whale Commission*, 32, 299-301, 1982.
4. COOK, F., and MUIR, R. *Canadian Field-Naturalist*, 98, 63-70, 1984.

5. PIPPARD, L. *Canadian Field-Naturalist*, 99, 438-450, 1985.
6. BÉLAND, P., MICHAUD, R. and MARTINEAU, D. *Rapport technique canadien science halieutique aquatique*, in press.
7. REEVES, R. R. and MITCHELL, E. *Naturalist Canadian*, 111, 63-121, 1984.
8. HEATH, R. G., SPANN, J. W. and KREITZER, J. F. *Nature*, 224, 47-48, 1969.
9. AULERICH R. J. and RINGER, R. K. *Archives Environmental Contamination Toxicology*, 6, 279-292, 1977.
10. ANDERSON, D. W., JEHL, J. R., RISEBROUGH, R. W., WOODS Jr., L. A., DEWESSE, L. R. and EDGECOMB, W. G. *Science*, 190, 806-808, 1975.
11. MARTINEAU, A., LAGACÉ, R., MASSÉ, R. and MORIN, M. *Canadian Veterinary Journal*, 26, 297-302, 1985.
12. MASSÉ, R., MARTINEAU, D., TREMBLAY, L. and BÉLAND, P. *Archives Environmental Contamination Toxicology*, in press.
13. BALLSCHMITER, K. and ZELL, M. *Fresenius Z. analytische Chemie*, 302, 20-31, 1980.
14. SPARLING, J. and SAFE, S. *Chemosphere*, 9, 129-137,1980.
15. SIPES, J. G., SLOCUMB, M. L., CHEN, H-S. G. and CARTER, D. E. *Applied Pharmacology*, 62, 317-324, 1982.
16. BALLSCHITER, K., BUCHEST, H., BIHLER, S. and ZELL, M. *Fresenius Z. Analytische Chemie*, 306, 323-339, 1981.
17. MATTHEWS, H. B. and DEDRICK, R. L. *Annual Reviews Pharmacology Toxicolgy*, 24, 85-103, 1984.
18. PARKINSON, A., SAFE, S., ROBERTSON, L., THOMAS, P. E., RYAN, D. E., REIK, L. and LEVIN, W. *Journal Biological Chemistry*, 258, 5967-5976, 1983.
19. PICARD-BÉRUBÉ, M. and COSSA, D. *Marine Environmental Research*, 10, 63-71, 1983.
20. STEGEMAN, J. J. In : *Polyclic hydrocarbons and cancer*, H. V. Gelboin and P. O. P. TS'0 eds., Academic Press, New York, pp. 1-60, 1981.
21. SAFE, S. *CRC Critical Reviews Toxicology*, 13, 319-395, 1984.

Aperçu général des HAP au Québec

Jean-Yves Saucier et Gaétan Duchesneau
Direction de la protection, région de Québec
Ministère de l'Environnement du Canada

Dans le cadre de ce Forum international pour l'avenir du béluga, il fait plaisir de vous donner un aperçu général du dossier des HAP au Québec.

Depuis quelque temps, on s'intéresse beaucoup aux HAP à cause des propriétés réputées cancérigènes pour les animaux, les mammifères et possiblement les humains ainsi qu'aux propriétés mutagènes et tératogènes de certains hydrocarbures aromatiques polycycliques.

En tout premier lieu, je voudrais vous présenter les principales caractéristiques de ce contaminant ainsi qu'un sommaire de nos connaissances actuelles de cette substance toxique.

DÉFINITION ET PROPRIÉTÉS PHYSIQUES

Les hydrocarbures aromatiques polycycliques (HAP) sont des composés organiques formés d'atomes de carbone et d'hydrogène et contenant plus de deux anneaux du benzène. On estime à près d'une centaine le nombre de substances qui composent la famille des HAP et le benzo(a)pyrène est celle qui est la plus connue et la plus étudiée.

Les HAP ont des points de fusion et d'ébullition élevés et ont une faible solubilité dans l'eau. Ils sont reconnus comme ayant une très

Hydrocarbures aromatiques polycycliques

- Composés organiques
- Formés exclusivement d'atomes de carbone et d'hydrogène
- Structure moléculaire renferme deux ou plusieurs anneaux benzéniques
- Plus de 100 molécules différentes
- La plus simple est le naphtalène (2 anneaux)
- Ils proviennent de la combustion incomplète de substances organiques

Propriétés physiques

- Ce sont d'habitude des solides cristallins colorés
- Peu solubles dans l'eau
- Point de fusion élevé (175^0 C)
- Point d'ébullition élevé (400^0 C)
- Tension de vapeur faible
- Affinité d'adsorption à la surface des particules
- Les HAP sont habituellement associés aux matières particulaires en suspension dans l'air et dans l'eau

grande affinité d'adsorption à la surface des particules. Ainsi, on les retrouve habituellement associés aux matières particulaires en suspension dans l'air et dans l'eau.

SOURCES D'ÉMISSION

Les HAP ne sont pas produits intentionnellement comme c'était le cas pour les BPC, le Mirex ou le DDT ; ils proviennent essentiellement de la combustion incomplète des matières organiques. Les émissions de HAP dans l'atmosphère proviennent principalement des procédés industriels fonctionnant dans les industries métallurgiques, les usines de ferro-alliage et les alumineries. Le chauffage au bois et la combustion d'essence ou de carburant diesel dans les véhicules moteurs sont aussi des sources importantes de HAP.

Secteurs industriels (sources fixes)

1 -	Métallurgie:	• ferro-alliages • sidérurgie • alumineries	
2 -	Incinérateurs:	• municipaux • pathologiques • industriels	• chaudières à écorces • scieries T.P. burners
3 -	Autres:	• raffineries • industries d'asphalte • créosote	

Sources diffuses

- Chauffage au bois
- Transports
- Incendies de forêts
- Autres (combustion à ciel ouvert)

EFFETS SUR LA SANTÉ

On croit généralement que le phénomène de la bioaccumulation des HAP dans l'organisme n'est pas significatif mais que leur biotransformation est une étape essentielle pour induire la formation de tumeurs supposément cancéreuses. Le foie est généralement l'organe principal où s'effectue cette biotransformation. Une théorie veut que certains enzymes transformeraient les HAP présents dans l'organisme en métabolites dont certains auraient des propriétés mutagènes et cancérigènes.

En 1983, l'Agence internationale pour la recherche sur le cancer a évalué le potentiel cancérigène des HAP. Elle a conclu que 14 molécules de HAP étaient cancérigènes chez les animaux ; l'évidence était limitée ou inadéquate pour 29 autres molécules de HAP.

CONTAMINATION DU MILIEU

Air

On rapporte la présence de benzo(a)pyrène dans l'air ambiant de grands centres urbains au Canada, aux États-Unis et en Europe. Au Québec, on en retrouve dans l'air ambiant de Montréal-Est, de Jonquière et de La Baie. On constate toutefois que la concentration en benzo(a)pyrène mesurée à Jonquière est nettement supérieure aux concentrations mesurées en milieu urbain et est plus élevée que celles que l'on retrouve près d'autres sources importantes. On note cependant que la concentration dans l'air ambiant de Jonquière a considérablement diminué ces dernières années.

Eau

Étant donné leur faible solubilité dans l'eau et leur grande affinité d'adsorption à la surface des particules, on retrouve habituellement une concentration relativement faible de HAP en solution dans l'eau. Ainsi, dans le fleuve Saint-Laurent et dans la rivière Saguenay, on rapporte des concentrations en benzo(a)pyrène inférieures à 1,0 nanogramme par litre. La Commission mixte internationale recommande que la concentration dans l'eau où s'alimentent les poissons soit inférieure à 10 nanogrammes par litre.

Concentration de HAP dans l'eau (ng / 1)

	B(a)P	HAP totaux	Référence
Rivière Saguenay (en aval de Arvida)	1.0	124	Rapport Marsan 1985
	0.8	81	" "
	0.4	101	" "
Fleuve Saint-Laurent (Ile d'Orléans)	N.D.	36	Env. Canada 1983
Recommandation	10	-	Commission mixte internationale 1983

Sédiments

À cause de leurs propriétés physiques et chimiques, les HAP se concentrent préférentiellement dans les sédiments et les boues de traitement. Ainsi, en 1983, on notait dans le Saguenay des concentrations importantes de benzo(a)pyrène dans les sédiments près des effluents industriels. À cet endroit, l'objectif de 1 000 nanogrammes par gramme suggéré par la Commission mixte internationale était nettement dépassé. Les autres analyses effectuées dans le fjord du Saguenay démontraient toutefois que cet objectif était rencontré.

Ressources halieutiques

En ce qui concerne la contamination de la ressource halieutique, étant donné que la bioaccumulation des HAP dans l'organisme n'est pas

Concentration de HAP dans divers sédiments (ng/g)

	B(a)P	HAP totaux	Référence
Rivière Saguenay (500 pi. en aval Alcan)	1928	34054	Rapport Marsan 1985
Rivière Saguenay (1200 pi. en aval Alcan)	2436	20132	Rapport Marsan 1985
Rivière Saguenay (aval de Arvida)	524	7397	Réseau de surveillance MENVIQ - 1983
Baie des Ha! Ha!	174	2046	Rapport Martel 1985
Fjord du Saguenay (Cap Trinité)	271	3783	Rapport Martel 1895
Lac Saint-François	100	960	Réseau de surveillance MENVIQ - 1985
Lac Saint-Louis	200	3890	Réseau de surveillance MENVIQ - 1985
Fleuve Saint-Laurent (Repentigny)	130	1210	Réseau de surveillance MENVIQ - 1985
Fleuve Saint-Laurent (Québec-Bassin Louise)	345	8616	Réseau de surveillance MENVIQ - 1987
Norme	1000		Commission mixte internationale

un phénomène significatif, il est normal qu'on ne retrouve aucune concentration élevée de HAP dans la chair de poisson du Saguenay et du fleuve Saint-Laurent, de Québec à Tadoussac. De plus, des analyses effectuées sur le foie, les reins, les muscles et le gras des bélugas n'ont démontré aucune valeur élevée de HAP dans ces mammifères.

Cependant, ceci n'est pas une indication que les HAP n'ont pas laissé de séquelles dans ces organismes car la biotransformation est une étape essentielle pour induire la formation de tumeurs. En effet, des études effectuées sur trois cerveaux de bélugas par le Dr Lee Shugart du Tennessee nous laissent croire que ceux-ci auraient été exposés au benzo(a)pyrène et auraient possiblement biotransformé cette substance en métabolites.

CONTRIBUTION DU MINISTÈRE DE L'ENVIRONNEMENT DU CANADA

Depuis quelques mois, la direction de la protection du ministère de l'Environnement du Canada prépare un inventaire des sources d'émission de HAP au Québec tant au niveau de l'atmosphère qu'à celui des effluents et des lieux où sont rejetés les déchets industriels pouvant contenir des HAP. Cet inventaire servira à identifier des secteurs prioritaires en terme de quantités de contaminants et de localisation des sources d'émission. On procédera aussi à l'examen des techniques de contrôle et des coûts à envisager.

De plus, en collaboration avec le ministère des Pêches et des Océans du Canada, le ministère de l'Environnement du Canada a élaboré un plan d'action pour la survie du béluga en tenant compte des connaissances actuelles.

Ce plan d'action, tout comme celui du plan d'action du Saint-Laurent, vise à diminuer et contrôler les rejets de substances chimiques toxiques pouvant nuire au béluga et aux autres espèces.

Contribution d'Environnement Canada

- Inventaire des sources de HAP au Québec
- Évaluation des technologies de contrôle des HAP
- Plan d'action interministériel (survie du béluga)
- Plan d'action du Saint-Laurent -
Centre Saint-Laurent
- Nouvelle loi sur la protection de l'environnement
- Liste des substances toxiques prioritaires (HAP)

L'adoption récente de la nouvelle loi canadienne pour la protection de l'environnement est aussi un atout important pour la protection des espèces menacées. Même s'il n'est pas évident que les HAP affectent de façon dramatique les bélugas du golfe, ces substances sont suffisamment préoccupantes pour la santé et pour l'environnement.

Des recommandations sont présentement faites pour les placer en tête de la liste des substances à réglementer en vertu de la Loi. Nous croyons donc que ces substances méritent un traitement de faveur puisqu'elles sont comme les BPC, les pesticides et les métaux lourds, une menace pour notre environnement.

Problèmes pathologiques décelés chez les bélugas du Saint-Laurent

Daniel Martineau
Institut d'écotoxicologie du Saint-Laurent
et Cornell University

Un récent article publié en août 1988 dans la revue scientifique *Science* (voir annexe) rapporte une diminution dramatique du troupeau de phoques communs habitant la mer du nord. Les opinions émises sur l'origine de cette épidémie sont diverses. Un second article paru une semaine plus tard dans *Nature*, une autre revue scientifique bien connue, rapporte que la cause probable de l'épidémie est le virus du distemper canin. Ce rapport est convaincant puisque les anticorps spécifiques pour ce virus apparaissent et augmentent lors de l'apparition des signes cliniques chez des phoques capturés. La vitesse à laquelle s'est répandue l'épidémie laisse cependant les chercheurs perplexes.

Au moment où ces lignes paraîtront, une explication satisfaisante aura peut-être été trouvée. Quoiqu'il en soit, une littérature abondante étaye la contamination des phoques communs de cette région par les organochlorés (OC) (pour une revue de la littérature, voir la revue *Archives of Environmental Contamination and Toxicology*, 16 : 137-147). Bien que, chez tous les mammifères et oiseaux étudiés, l'affaiblissement du système immunitaire par les OC soit démontré, l'immunosuppression causée par ces composés n'a pas été étudiée en laboratoire chez les mammifères marins. Par contre, ces effets ont été étudiés chez plusieurs animaux de ferme et chez la plupart des animaux de laboratoire.

Dans le cas des animaux de ferme, ces études répondent à des besoins économiques ; les expériences sur les animaux de laboratoire visent à connaître, par extrapolation, les dangers auxquels sont soumis les humains exposés à ces substances. Les mammifères marins ne sont pas inclus dans ces préoccupations. Néanmoins, ces animaux sont des mammifères et comme tels, ils sont potentiellement sensibles aux effets de substances dont la toxicité a été clairement démontrée pour tous les mammifères et oiseaux exposés expérimentalement.

Nous avons retrouvé de hautes concentrations des mêmes contaminants dans 26 carcasses de bélugas échoués sur les rives du Saint-Laurent. Nous avons déterminé en outre :

1. la présence de 6 tumeurs chez 6 animaux parmi les 15 que nous avons examinés (deux de ces tumeurs affectaient la vessie et une était maligne) ;
2. la présence d'infections sévères et généralisées, causées par des bactéries opportunistes et donc, suggestives d'immumosuppression ;
3. la contamination de 3 carcasses sur 3 carcasses testées pour le benzo(a)pyrène, un puissant carcinogène.

En conclusion, les sources de ces contaminants sont connues et la réduction à très court terme de l'émission d'organochlorés et d'hydrocarbures aromatiques polycycliques dans l'environnement de ces animaux doit être l'élément le plus important dans tout plan visant à leur survie.

ARTICLE DE LA REVUE *SCIENCE*

By August 1988, 7 000 of the 16 000 harbor seals (over 60 % of the population in certain localities) previously found off the coasts of Denmark, Sweden, Norway, West Germany and Denmark have been wiped out. Two suspect viruses have been discovered in the carcasses. However, various lesions are found throughout the body and affect many organs of the seals ; many bacterial infections, not seen in the past, affect the pups. Abortions are often observed ; umbilical cords do not heal. The fear is that the seals may be suffering from a suppression of the immune system and that this may be directly linked to the discharge of toxic waste in the North Sea, perhaps to polychlorinated biphenyls (PCBs). Minnie Courtney, a marine biologist at the University of London who has carried out widespread studies into the impact of organochlorines on the environment, reports high concentrations of these compounds found in the bodies of seals (partly as a result of their position at the top of the food chain). These high concentrations are known to significantly reduce their fertility.

The extent to which chemical pollution can be blamed as the primary cause of the outbreak of the disease among the harbor seal is hotly debated. Albert Osterhaus, head of the Department of Immunobiolgy at the National Institute of Public Health and Environmental Hygiene at Bilthovn in the Netherlands had initiated an international project to establish a global inventory of the viruses found in aquatic animals only a few months before the disease outbreak. He was one of the first to provide positive identification of the presence of the two viruses mentioned above. He is cautious about drawing overhasty conclusions, certainly without further research, into the difficult area of measuring the effects of low levels of exposure to toxic chemicals on the immune system.

Ottmar Wasserman, professor of toxicology at the University of Kiel, points out that PCBs have been shown to impair the immune system in other mammals, such as mice, rabbits, and pigs. In the absence of any direct data, "we have to take the scientifically clear evidence we have from mammals and apply it to seals", he says.

By contrast, a spokesman for Brittain's Ministry of Agriculture, Food and Fisheries said "there were no grounds for thingking that the seal deaths were related to chemical pollution".

Spurred by the widespread public concern that seals, particularly baby seals, seldom fail to generate, politicians reacted quickly; German, Danish, British and Swedish governments have undertaken already research to investigate effects of environmental factors, including pollutants, on the immune system of seals. Unfortunately, for most of the seals in the Netherlands and around the Baltic sea, the results of the research will come too late.

Source : *Science*, Août 1988.

Detection and Quantitation of Benzo(a)Pyrene-DNA adducts in Brain and Liver Tissues of Beluga Whales (*Delphinapterus leucas*) from the St. Lawrence and Mackenzie Estuaries

Lee R. Shugart
Environmental Sciences Division
Oak Ridge National Laboratory

INTRODUCTION

The rationale underlying the strategy of measuring levels of chemicals which become covalently attached to cellular macromolecules as a bioassay for genotoxicity is based on the current understanding of the mode of action of chemicals once they become bioavailable (1).

The metabolism of organic chemicals is a relatively complex phenomenon and detoxification by cellular mechanisms is not always complete, sometimes resulting in highly reactive electrophilic metabolites that react with nucleophilic centers in macromolecules such as lipids, proteins, DNA and RNA. Binding with DNA can cause formation of altered bases that can be repaired, be innocuous, or result in alterations which become fixed and are transmitted to daughter cells. Current research suggests that damage to DNA that goes uncorrected is probably one of the initial stages in chemical carcinogenesis (2-5).

Given that genotoxic agents exert their activity through irreversible reactions with nucleophilic atoms to form adducts, the amount of metabolite bound to cellular DNA could provide a basis upon which to estimate exposure and possibly, to assess the risk connected with that exposure (1,6-8).

It should be noted that there are few analytical techniques available for the detection and quantitation of chemical adducts in the DNA of living organisms. The reasons for this are: a) the analytical technique often has to accommodate the unique chemical and (or) physical properties of the individual chemical or its metabolite; b) the percentage of total chemical that becomes attached to the DNA in the target tissue is quite small because most of the parent compound is usually detoxified and excreted; c) not all adducts that form between the genotoxic agent and DNA are stable or are involved in the development of subsequent deleterious events in the organism; and d) the amount of DNA available for analysis is often quite limited.

Recently (9), I demonstrated a sensitive and specific analytical method for the detection of benzo(a)pyrene B(a)P bound to cellular DNA. This technique was used to analyze DNA for adducts to B(a)P of several stranded beluga whales from the St. Lawrence estuary (10) as well as the DNA of beluga whales from the Mackenzie estuary.

METHODOLOGY

Whale tissue

Whale brain tissue from three stranded beluga whales from the St. Lawrence estuary was provided by Dr. P. Béland, Fisheries Ecology Research Center, Rimouski, Quebec. Whale brain and liver tissue from four beluga whales from the Mackenzie estuary was provided by Patt Weaver, Freshwater Institute, Winnipeg, Manitoba.

DNA preparation

DNA isolation was accomplished by: a) homogenizing the tissue in 1 *N* NH_4OH/0,2% Triton X100; b) partitioning of nucleic acids with chloroform/isoamyl alcohol/phenol (24/1/25-v/v), and; c) desalting by passage through a molecular sieve column (Sephadex G50). Further purification was accomplished by enzymatic depolymerization of RNA and spermine precipitation of DNA (9).

DNA concentration was determined with bisbenzamide (Hoechst dye 33258), which forms a stable, fluorescent product with DNA (11).

Benzo(a)pyrene binding to DNA

A sensitive HPLC method coupled with fluorescence detection was used (9). Essentially the technique consists of the acid-induced removal of the benzo(a)pyrene adduct from the DNA as the strongly fluorescent-free tetrols which are then separated and quantitated. The technique not only allows femtomole quantities of B(a)P adducts to be detected, but also measures only the adducts that are formed between the DNA and the "ultimate" carcinogenic form of B(a)P (2-5), the diolepoxide (B(a)PDEE).

RESULTS AND DISCUSSION

Analyses for B(a)P adducts in the DNA of brain tissue from three stranded beluga whales from the St. Lawrence estuary and in the DNA of brain and liver tissues from four whales from the Mackenzie estuary were performed using the fluorescence/HPLC assay (Table 1). Values obtained for the St. Lawrence belugas were 2,15, 0,98, and 0,73 adducts of B(a)PDE per 10 nucleotides of DNA. No detectable adducts were found in the DNA of the belugas from the Mackenzie estuary.

The data obtained are important for several reasons. First, they provide evidence that the whales from the St. Lawrence estuary had been exposed to B(a)P, and had metabolized it to B(a)PDE, which subsequently became covalently bound to the DNA of the brain tissue. Over the past several years a strong and convincing argument has developed for a causal relationship between the carcinogenic potency of B(a)P and the amount bound to an organism's DNA as a result of cellular metabolism (2-5). This is reinforced by the premise that the integrity of DNA is essential for survival. Alterations, if left uncorrected, could trigger a sequence of events that culminates in the appearance of

TABLE 1

Detection of Benzo(a)Pyrene Adducts in DNA of Beluga Whales (*Delphinapterus leucas*)

Sample	Tissue	B(a)P Adduct binding*	Formation level**
St. Lawrence			
Estuary #1	Brain	206	2,15
#2	Brain	94	0,98
#3	Brain	69	0,73
Mackenzie			
Estuary #1-#4	Brain	none detected***	
#1-#4	Liver	none detected***	

* B(a)P adducts to DNA expressed as nanograms of tetrol 1-1 per gram of DNA. St. Lawrence data taken from Martineau *et al.* (1988).

** Level of adduct formation expressed as B(a)P adducts per 10^7 DNA nucleotides.

*** Detection limit is 10 picograms of tetrol (see Shugart *et all.*, 1983).

an overt malignancy. Second, the level of adducts detected approaches found in animals, both terrestrial and aquatic, exposed under controlled laboratory conditions to carcinogenic doses of B(a)P(12-15).

Third, cells in brain tissue are known to have slow turnover rates and lack or have very low capacity for excission repair of DNA damage. Therefore, significant accumulation of DNA adducts could occur in this tissue from long-term chronic exposure to environmental levels of B(a)P too low to induce neoplasia (16).

Several notes of caution are advisable in assessing and interpreting the data presented. First, the sparseness of samples examined precludes a definitive statement about the status of the DNA of the whales in the population from which they were taken. Second, the data provide neither an insight as to the source of B(a)P exposure (water, food, air, etc.) of these animals, nor information as to the type of exposure (acute vs chronic). Third, although it would seem reasonable to relate B(a)PDE adduct levels in the DNA of the whales from the two different estuaries to the level of B(a)P in their respective environments, it should be noted that the health of an animal may influence the formation of adducts. In this regard, the whales from the Mackenzie estuary were hunted animals and not known to be diseased at the time of their capture, while the whales from the St. Lawrence estuary were diseased animals that had beached.

ACKNOWLEDGEMENT

A preliminary report of this investigation was presented at the Seventh Biennial Conference on the Biology of Marine Mammals, Miami, FL, December 5-9, 1987.

The Oak Ridge National Laboratory is operated by Martin Marietta Energy Systems, Inc., under contract De-AC05-840R21400 with the U.S. Department of Energy. Support for this research was funded in part by the ORNL Director's R&D Fund.

This is publication N° 3192 of the Environmental Sciences Division of the Oak Ridge National Laboratory.

REFERENCES

1. WOGAN, G. N. and GOREUCK, J. *Chemical and Biochemical Dosimetry to Exposure to Genotoxic Chemicals*, Environ. Health Perspec., n° of cat. 62: 5-18, 1985.
2. GELBOIN, H. and T'SO, P. O. P. (eds.). *Polycyclic Hydrocarbons and Cancer*, Molecular Biology and Environment, New York, Academic Press, 1978, p 408.

3. WEINSTEIN, I. B. *Current Concepts on Mechanisms of Chemical Carcinogenesis*, Bull. N. Y. Academy of Med., n° of cat. 54 : 336-383, 1978.

4. HARVEY, R. *Polycyclic Hydrocarbons and Cancer, American Scientist*, n° of cat. 72 : 386-393, 1982.

5. PHILIPS, D. H. *Fifty Years of Benzo(a)Pyrene*, Nature, n° of cat. 303 : 468-472, 1983.

6. PERERA, F., POIRIER, M., YUSPA, S., NAKAYAMA, J., JARETZKI, A., CURNEN, M., KNOWLES, D. and WEISTEIN, I. B. *A Pilot Project in Molecular Cancer Epidemiology : Determination of B(a)P-DNA Adducts in Animal and Human Tissue by Immunoassays, Carcinogenesis*, n° of cat. 3 : 1405-1410, 1982.

7. HOEL, D., KAPLAN, N. and ANDERSON, M. *Implication of Nonlinear Kinetics on Risk Estimation in Carcinogenesis*, Science, n° of cat. 219 : 1032-1037, 1983.

8. HARRIS, C. C. *Future Directions in the Use of DNA Adducts as Internal Dosimeters for Monitoring Human Exposure to Environmental Mutagens and Carcinogens*, Environ. Health Perspec., n° of cat. 62 : 185-191, 1985.

9. SHUGART, L. R., HOLLAND, J. and RAHN, R. *Dosimetry of PAH Carcinogenesis : Covalent Binding of B(a)P to Mouse Epidermal DNA. Carcinogenesis*, n° of cat. 4 : 195-198, 1983.

10. MARTINEAU, D., LAGACE, A., BELAND, P., HIGGINS, R., ARMSTRONG, D. and SHUGART, L. R. *Pathology of stranded beluga whales (Delphinapterus leucas) from the St. Lawrence estuary*, Quebec, Canada, J. Comp. Pathol, 1988.

11. DOWNS, T. R. and WILFINGER, W. W. *Fluorometric Quantitation of DNA in Cells and Tissue*, Anal. Biochem., n° of cat. 131 : 538-548, 1983.

12. VARANASI, U., STEIN, J. E. and HOM, T. *Covalent Binding of B(a)P to DNA of Fish Liver*, Biochem. Biophys. Res. Commun., n° of cat. 103 : 780-787, 1981.

13. STOWERS, S. J. and ANDERSON, M. W. *Ubiquitous Binding of B(a)P Metabolites to DNA and Protein in Tissue of Mouse and Rabbit*, Chem-Biol. Interact., n° of cat. 51 : 151-166, 1984.

14. SHUGART, L. R. and KAO, J. *Examination of Adduct Formation in Vivo in the Mouse Between B(a)P and DNA of the Skin and Hemoglobin of the Red Blood Cells*, Environ. Health Perspec., n° of cat. 62 : 223-226, 1985.

15. SHUGART, L. R. *Analysis of Adduct Formation in Bluegill Sunfish Between B(a)P and DNA of the Liver and Hemoglobin of the Erythrocyte*, Aquatic Toxicol., n° of cat. 9 : 319-325, 1987.

16. STOWERS, S. J. and ANDERSON, M. W. *Formation and Persistence of B(a)P Metabolite-DNA Adducts*, Environ. Health Perspec., n° of cat. 62 : 31-39, 1985.

"The submitted manuscript has been authored by a contractor of the U.S. Government under contract N° DE-AC05-840R21400. Accordingly, the U.S. Government retains a nonexclusive, royalty-free license to publish or reproduce the published form of this contribution, or allow others to do so, for U.S. Government purposes."

Les conférences des organismes environnementaux et socio-économiques

Corporation municipale de Tadoussac

Jacques Boulianne
Maire

INTRODUCTION

Faisant suite à votre initiative, il nous fait plaisir en tant qu'organisme public que représente la Corporation municipale de Tadoussac de vous présenter un court mémoire représentant notre position sur ce sujet.

Notre exposé ne se veut en aucune façon un aspect scientifique de la question, laissant cet aspect aux diverses personnalités compétentes, mais profitons de l'occasion pour vous faire part de nos commentaires et suggestions.

1. CONCILIER PRÉSERVATION DE L'ENVIRONNEMENT ET DÉVELOPPEMENT ÉCONOMIQUE

Nous attendions avec impatience la position gouvernementale sur la protection de notre faune marine et aquatique, de sorte que la préparation d'un plan de survie pour le béluga et qui pourrait par la même occasion s'appliquer aux autres mammifères marins, nous apparut comme une solution de départ excessivement intéressante.

Nous pensons qu'il est urgent de passer aux actes et de ne pas démontrer seulement une intention populairement politique.

Nous respectons le point de vue des groupes écologiques et adhérons à la majeure partie de leurs revendications, mais il faut que ce soit d'abord et avant tout pour la préservation de cette ressource qu'est le béluga aux mêmes titres que les autres mammifères marins, poissons, mollusques et invertébrés du Saguenay et du Saint-Laurent. Le béluga sert de cheval de bataille pour la préservation de l'environnement, mais c'est l'ensemble de l'écosystème de notre secteur qui se doit d'être protégé.

Il faut concevoir que nous vivons une confrontation entre préservation de l'environnement et développement économique. Les croisières d'observation ont eu un impact économique extraordinaire non seulement pour notre municipalité, mais aussi pour la plupart des municipalités de Charlevoix et de la Haute Côte Nord. Les retombées économiques sont en termes de millions et nos efforts de promotion et marketing ne commencent qu'à produire certains fruits. Nous vivons actuellement un phénomène autant national que québécois, le touriste étranger. Nous faisons face cependant à de très nombreux problèmes environnementaux et il faut que des mesures de protection exceptionnelles s'appliquent au transport des touristes, ainsi qu'au dérangement des animaux observés.

Ainsi, il n'est pas rare de voir de petites embarcations surchargées de touristes ne respectant pas les mesures de sécurité. Nous avons été chanceux de ne pas avoir eu d'accidents qui tournent à la tragédie.

L'implantation d'aires d'approche peut s'avérer une solution, mais cela nécessitera des mesures de contrôle supplémentaires pour les contrevenants. Actuellement les entreprises commerciales font leur possible pour éviter de déranger les animaux, mais les petites embarcations continuent de s'approcher à des distances qui peuvent s'avérer perturbatrices.

2. LE PLAN DE SURVIE DU BÉLUGA

Nous acceptons avec joie les actions du plan de survie du béluga et aimerions faire les commentaires suivants :

Promotion d'un parc marin pour sa création à l'embouchure du Saguenay

Il est essentiel que cette aire de protection pour l'ensemble des mammifères marins soit déterminée, approuvée et publicisée une fois pour toutes, pour favoriser la conservation, la préservation et la reproduction des espèces concernées. Il faut que cette aire de protection soit le plus possible scientifique et raisonnable et non une aire politique.

Nous croyons que les développements des stations terrestres du Cap de Bon-Désir, des dunes de sable de Tadoussac, des installations de la Pointe-Noire et de la Baie Sainte-Marguerite pourraient permettre de causer moins de dérangement aux bélugas.

Il est capital que la gestion administrative d'un éventuel parc marin soit confiée aux instances régionales pour faire respecter les lois provinciales et fédérales sur ce sujet et poursuivre les contrevenants à la réglementation concernant la circulation, le dérangement et l'analyse scientifique du comportement des espèces. Il serait bien de faire une zone, contrôler l'émission des permis de croisière, contrôler la circulation maritime, mais si le centre de contrôle est à 100 milles ou 150 milles de la zone concernée, ceci ne sera qu'un coup d'épée dans l'eau ; comme nous l'avons déjà vécu dans d'autres situations similaires.

Nous souscrivons à l'idée d'un développement du béluga par un reconditionnement génétique ou par une analyse poussée d'implantation d'un troupeau de bélugas arctiques. L'idée de croisements génétiques entre ces deux espèces qui furent isolées par évolution peut peut-être accroître éventuellement la démographie de cette population qui serait renforcée et serait peut-être plus résistante face aux agents de pollution.

Nous sommes conscients de l'évolution de la pollution en notre province et des mesures de contrôle que diverses instances veulent prendre pour diminuer le stade critique auquel notre secteur fait face. Nous sommes cependant réalistes et ne croyons pas aux effets démultiplicateurs d'enraiement des facteurs polluants, alors que nous faisons face à un problème d'ordre mondial.

Nous croyons cependant que la création d'un parc marin et des mesures appropriées de contrôle des rejets industriels et des eaux provenant des grandes cités ne peuvent qu'avoir un effet positif à long terme, mais nous exprimons certaines réserves sur ce sujet. Qu'il nous suffise de mentionner le nombre de municipalités du Lac-Saint-Jean et du Saguenay dont plusieurs villes et villages qui n'assainissent pas encore leurs eaux. Nous sentons cependant des efforts en ce sens et croyons que l'avenir deviendra prometteur.

CONCLUSION

En conclusion, en tant que maire de la municipalité de Tadoussac, j'ai été très heureux d'accueillir chez nous les participants au Forum international pour l'avenir du béluga. Mais, après trois jours de discussions et d'exposés sur toutes les facettes du problème de survie du béluga, nous en sommes à la clôture de ce Forum, à nous poser encore la question :

Que faisons-nous demain, chacun de notre côté, pour assurer la survie de cette espèce ? Bien sûr, nous, en tant que représentants municipaux, sommes prêts à faire notre part, à favoriser l'éducation et la sensibilisation des citoyens à la conservation de ce patrimoine, à offrir des facilités d'observation des ressources marines, dans le cadre de nos moyens limités. Et nous le ferons. Mais, vous, demain, qu'allez-vous faire ? Quelle sera votre contribution, à chacun de vous ?

C'est la question fondamentale, à laquelle vous êtes maintenant invités à répondre. Autrement le discours n'aura pas de suite.

Association touristique régionale de Manicouagan

André Blais
Directeur au Développement

L'Association touristique régionale de Manicouagan s'inquiète depuis fort longtemps de l'ensemble de la problématique environnementale de son territoire. Bien que son mandat concerne d'abord et avant tout le développement de l'industrie du tourisme en région, il faut reconnaître que l'environnement, la nature, les paysages et les différents systèmes écologiques ont un impact très concret sur le monde du tourisme. En effet, la qualité visuelle d'une région touristique représente sans aucun doute l'élément majeur d'attrait des clientèles touristiques et également de leur rétention en région.

À ce propos, le « plan de développement touristique de la région de Manicouagan » qui vient juste d'être déposé, confirme d'une façon non équivoque que notre avenir touristique repose sur la présence de phénomènes naturels et d'écosystèmes environnementaux reliés à la faune et à la flore régionale. Il importe donc de présenter notre environnement et surtout de veiller à ce que les éventuels développements touristiques de ces phénomènes ne mettent pas en péril la qualité des habitats que l'on retrouve dans le milieu.

Nous croyons qu'il soit possible d'allier adéquatement les notions de protection et de mise en valeur des produits touristiques régionaux. À titre d'exemple, nous citons le cas de Pointe-aux-Outardes, où déjà en 1978, l'ATR de Manicouagan faisait des représentations auprès des différentes instances gouvernementales : fédérale, provinciale et municipale afin que soit protégé l'immense marais salin qui abrite quelque

175 espèces d'oiseaux. Il ne s'agissait pas non plus d'interdire complètement l'accès à ce milieu fragile, mais au contraire d'en assurer sa protection et sa mise en valeur sur le plan touristique. Après dix années d'efforts et de sensibilisation auprès des populations locales et régionales, ce site est devenu maintenant un « parc régional », les espèces y sont protégées et des aménagements légers y ont été réalisés afin que les citoyens et visiteurs puissent observer et interpréter de façon adéquate cet écosystème particulièrement fragile.

Nous sommes convaincus qu'il est réaliste de penser que cette forme de développement puisse s'appliquer aux autres attraits naturels de la région et particulièrement aux mammifères marins. L'ATR de Manicouagan reconnaît toute l'importance que représente la présence de ces animaux sur le plan touristique. Les baleines constituent dans les faits l'« achalandeur » touristique majeur de notre région et si on désire développer ce produit touristique, encore faut-il s'assurer que ces mammifères marins puissent résister aux différentes pressions qu'exerce l'homme sur leur habitat, et survivre. Il importe donc d'œuvrer à leur sauvegarde tout en favorisant leur mise en valeur par des mesures bien adaptées aux conditions particulières qui régissent leur mode de vie. À cet effet, l'ATR de Manicouagan s'associe déjà avec les différents organismes et ministères, afin d'élaborer conjointement des processus de développement tenant compte de ces particularités.

Comme organisme régional, nous faisons des représentations pour mettre en place un parc marin à la confluence du Saint-Laurent-Saguenay, sans oublier toutefois le rôle fondamental de ce parc qui consiste à protéger la ressource et l'habitat. Nous préconisons également un développement axé sur l'observation terrestre et sur tout autre moyen visant à atténuer le stress que provoque chez le mammifère marin, spécifiquement le béluga, un achalandage non contrôlé des embarcations de croisières qui sillonnnent leurs habitats. Une partie déjà de ce problème de « harcèlement des mammifères marins » est en voie de règlement grâce aux normes édictées par le ministère des Pêches et des Océans du Canada concernant les croisières aux baleines.

Il reste cependant l'épineux problème de la pollution qui affecte l'ensemble de l'habitat de ces mammifères. L'ATR de Manicouagan s'associe aux organismes et intervenants qui réclament des mesures plus sévères en matière de pollution, en précisant que l'industrie touristique est une industrie en pleine expansion et que l'on doit y investir financièrement autant que dans les autres industries du Québec. Cet investissement ne vise pas nécesssairement des infrastructures et des complexes hôteliers, mais peut être consenti à la sauvegarde de l'environnement car il représente somme toute le meilleur atout de notre devenir touristique. Si le milieu est bien protégé et que les écosystèmes sont maintenus, ils constitueront alors une ressource naturelle renouvelable et en ce sens les sommes d'argent consenties directement à la protection de l'environnement, seront comptabilisées comme un investissement touristique à long terme, et cela pour le mieux-être des générations futures. Il nous appartient en tant que collectivité de léguer un héritage environnemental sain et amélioré à ceux qui nous suivront.

Association touristique régionale de Charlevoix

Charles Roberge

Permettez-moi tout d'abord de remercier la Fondation pour la sauvegarde des espèces menacées (FOSEM) et le comité organisateur du Forum international pour l'avenir du béluga de nous avoir invité à prendre la parole à ce Forum.

Ce Forum est une occasion unique de rencontre et d'échange mais également de concertation et de prise de décision.

Mon allocution se veut brève mais claire. Ce sera néanmoins un « discours fleuve »...

La côte de Charlevoix est bordée sur toute sa longueur par le majestueux fleuve *Saint-Laurent*. Ce cours d'eau, qu'on appelle chez nous « la mer »...

Nous parlerons donc de ce fleuve et de toutes les richesses qu'il nous apporte ainsi que de l'amour et du respect qu'on doit lui porter quand on sait que devant Charlevoix se trouve la « pouponnière » des bélugas du Saint-Laurent.

Il existe toute une gamme d'activités autour du fleuve Saint-Laurent. C'est ainsi que Charlevoix est résolument tournée vers l'avenir. En plus d'être l'initiatrice de la coalition pour le parc marin Saint-Laurent—Saguenay, l'association touristique de Charlevoix a participé à plusieurs actions visant à redonner l'accès et la jouissance du fleuve aux gens de Charlevoix et aux touristes.

Dans ce contexte, notre présence à cette table ronde apparaît des plus pertinentes du fait de la place importante qu'occupe, dans notre préoccupation et notre réalité, la protection du béluga et de son habitat et la place qu'occupent aussi de façon plus générale, les mammifères marins dans le produit touristique de la région de Charlevoix.

C'est ainsi qu'on évalue globalement qu'en 1988, près de 45 000 visiteurs de Charlevoix ont fait des croisières d'observation des baleines (Baie-Sainte-Catherine), engendrant une activité économique de plus de 10 millions de dollars.

La force de vente des quelque 2 000 chambres d'hôtellerie et 1 000 emplacements de camping constituant l'offre structurée la plus importante qui sert à diriger la clientèle sur des activités touristiques à caractère marin (croisière, centre d'interprétation).

Pour l'industrie touristique régionale, les croisières d'observation aux mammifères marins ont permis de favoriser l'étalement saisonnier tout en augmentant fortement les taux d'occupation des établissements hôteliers en basse saison (juin, septembre, octobre) créant ainsi de nouveaux emplois.

Défi : créer des emplois dans la conservation.

Ainsi, les croisières ont permis de structurer l'industrie touristique de Charlevoix, elles contribuent de plus à positionner la région de Charlevoix en tant que destination-séjour pour une clientèle nationale et internationale.

Cette ressource naturelle exceptionnelle à la fois unique et fragile voit sa survie menacée. Par ailleurs, à l'ATR de Charlevoix nous sommes conscients que la création d'un parc marin national à l'embouchure du Saguenay doit être un moyen privilégié afin d'assurer la protection des ressources marines du fleuve.

Déjà en 1987, nous avions inscrit ce projet de parc marin à titre de projet majeur dans le plan de développement touristique régional. Depuis ce temps, les principales études préalables à la réalisation du projet ont été déposées. À la lecture et à l'analyse de ces documents plusieurs questions nous viennent à l'esprit.

Dans un premier temps, je vais traiter de l'étude biophysique. En 1981, le Service canadien des parcs a fait une étude préliminaire qui a révélé que l'embouchure du Saguenay était très représentative de toutes les espèces marines de la région de l'estuaire et du golfe Saint-Laurent, ce qui en faisait un bon candidat pour l'aménagement d'un parc marin.

De plus, la carte des écosystèmes publiée en complément de l'étude biophysique met en évidence le fait que l'estuaire du Saint-Laurent constitue le milieu écologique le plus représentatif et le plus diversifié de toute l'aire définie par le ministère de l'Environnement du Canada.

Le fleuve Saint-Laurent, dans sa partie de l'estuaire localisée à l'embouchure du Saguenay, constitue donc à notre avis, le cœur même du futur parc marin. L'ATR de Charlevoix considère que le scénario n° 5 de l'étude biophysique devrait être l'aire minimum retenue pour l'établissement de ce parc marin (cela comprend la portion du fleuve Saint-Laurent comprise entre Les Escoumins et Saint-Siméon incluant l'Île aux Lièvres et quelques autres îles ainsi que la rivière Saguenay de son embouchure jusqu'au Cap-à-l'Est).

En adoptant le scénario n° 5, nous nous assurons que le parc marin puisse constituer réellement un élément représentatif de l'estuaire du Saint-Laurent. Or, dans le scénario actuellement véhiculé par le Service canadien des parcs, la place occupée par le Saint-Laurent est beaucoup trop restreinte. Dans ce scénario là, la portion du Saguenay reste intacte mais la portion Saint-Laurent est réduite de façon dramatique.

Je vais aborder maintenant l'étude socio-économique « Étude de faisabilité d'un parc marin au Saguenay—Lac-Saint-Jean ». Ceux qui ont eu la chance d'en obtenir une copie et qui ont eu le courage et le temps de le lire (1 000 pages) constatent qu'il s'agit d'un document qui malgré sa longueur demeure à notre avis incomplet.

Déjà dans l'introduction du volume, on peut lire que le mandat du consultant se limite à des études statistiques en excluant toute enquête sociale sur le sujet.

En effet, le lecteur est confronté à une description de la réalité économique de la région du Saguenay—Lac-Saint-Jean (dans son entier jusqu'à Chibougamau). Or, cette description de plus d'une centaine de pages est précédée par une note au lecteur mentionnant qu'on exclut Charlevoix, Tadoussac et le reste de la Côte-Nord, alors que la réalité du parc marin s'y retrouve.

Encore dans l'introduction, le lecteur constate avec stupéfaction qu'on mentionne et je cite : « Chicoutimi—Jonquière constitue le cœur de la région à l'étude ». Retrouverons-nous les infrastructures et les emplois dans cette région située à plus de 100 km des baleines et du fleuve ?

L'objet de toute cette masse de papier est précisé un peu plus loin : « Elle constitue la deuxième phase de l'étude de faisabilité pour l'implantation d'un parc marin au Saguenay—Lac-Saint-Jean. »

Donc, après avoir espéré un parc marin d'estuaire, nous en sommes maintenant à un parc marin de lac. On pourrait sans doute y faire des croisières d'observation des dorés et des brochets.

Mais de façon plus sérieuse, nous croyons qu'il est possible (à la lumière de la création des parcs de Bruce Peninsula et South Morisby) de réaliser la jonction entre la protection du milieu naturel et les intérêts socio-économiques de la région concernée. Les gouvernements du Canada et du Québec ont tout le loisir de créer une jonction entre l'actuel parc provincial du Saguenay et le futur parc marin national Saint-Laurent-

Saguenay en s'associant le dynamisme des intervenants régionaux, regroupés au sein de la coalition pour le parc marin.

Nous sommes activement impliqués dans le dossier pour la création d'une réserve mondiale de la biosphère dans Charlevoix. Il s'agit d'une nouvelle génération d'espaces naturels protégés où on intègre les préoccupations des populations locales, où on tente de réconcilier écologie et développement, économie et environnement.

Le projet vise à intégrer la région de Charlevoix, de Petite-Rivière-Saint-François jusqu'à Port-au-Saumon, dans le réseau international des réserves de la biosphère de l'UNESCO qui en compte près de 270 dans plus de 70 pays.

Nous invitons les autorités du Service canadien des parcs à étudier ce concept révolutionnaire et inventif où un être humain n'est pas considéré comme un intrus, au contraire...

Autrement dit, comme dans la réserve de la biosphère de Charlevoix, on veut être plus que de la visite dans le futur parc marin, on veut pouvoir y habiter et y vivre.

Somme toute, créer un parc marin c'est construire un gros bateau. Il nous apparaît clair à la lecture des études biophysique et socio-économique qu'en misant sur une option Saguenay de façon trop exclusive, en marginalisant en quelque sorte l'industrie touristique de Charlevoix, le bateau risque de partir à la dérive et d'aller s'échouer... sur les rives d'un lac...

Comment réconcilier ce projet de parc marin avec le plan Saint-Laurent et la série de mesures essentielles à la survie du béluga? En reconnaissant, comme le fait le Fonds mondial pour la nature (Canada), une large portion du fleuve Saint-Laurent en tant que zone marine naturelle d'intérêt exceptionnel (Les Escoumins à l'île-aux-Coudres). En accordant ainsi une place importante à l'estuaire du Saint-Laurent dans ce projet de parc marin, on remet donc le navire à flots...

Nous, l'ATR de Charlevoix, croyons fermement que le parc marin du Saguenay (tel qu'il a été conçu par les planificateurs) doit se transformer en parc marin national Saint-Laurent—Saguenay.

D'après nous, il est temps que chez les fonctionnaires, on comprenne qu'un parc marin ça ne se crée pas uniquement à partir d'un bureau à Québec ou à Ottawa mais plutôt en association avec le milieu régional. À cet effet, nous demandons (comme Mme Pippard l'a mentionné dans sa conférence de jeudi) que la population soit consultée à toutes les étapes du processus de conception et d'implantation du parc marin et non pas quand tout est décidé.

Nous croyons également qu'il faut reconnaître en les intégrant dans ce projet de parc marin, les expertises telles celles développées par la Société linnéenne du Québec (Pointe-Noire) et le centre écologique de Port-au-Saumon qui possède une vaste expérience dans le domaine des écosystèmes marins. Nous pensons que ce dernier pourrait s'avérer un lieu propice pour l'établissement d'un centre sur le milieu marin.

Pour terminer, nous proposons que l'entente Canada-Québec sur la zone périphérique du parc provincial du Saguenay puisse servir (avec de nouveaux budgets) au développement des infrastructures du futur parc marin. De plus, nous souhaitons que les intervenants soient des partenaires au comité de gestion de l'entente.

Finalement, nous considérons que ce parc marin doit être représentatif des deux habitats estuariens du Saint-Laurent et du Saguenay pour le béluga. En outre, comme dans les études, la partie Saint-Laurent semble généralement avoir été oubliée, nous demandons que soit rétabli dans sa priorité le majestueux fleuve Saint-Laurent pour le développement du parc et son appellation.

Longue vie au béluga dans ce futur parc marin Saint-Laurent—Saguenay.

Société touristique du fjord

Guy Girard
Directeur général

C'est dans la foulée de la mise en valeur du fjord du Saguenay qu'a été créée au printemps de 1985 la Société touristique du fjord. Structure intermunicipale vouée au développement touristique, la Société a comme principal mandat d'informer, de stimuler et d'aider les promoteurs privés, les organismes et les municipalités du Bas-Saguenay dans leurs projets de nature touristique. De plus, la Société est l'interlocuteur privilégié des gouvernements dans le cadre du programme d'aide spécifique à la zone périphérique de dix millions de dollars de l'Entente auxiliaire Canada-Québec sur le développement touristique.

La zone périphérique du parc du Saguenay que dessert la Société comprend les onze municipalités suivantes : Saint-Fulgence, Sainte-Rose-du-Nord, Sacré-Cœur, Tadoussac, Baie-Sainte-Catherine, Ferland-Boileau, Saint-Félix-d'Otis, Rivière-Éternité, l'Anse-Saint-Jean, Petit-Saguenay et La Baie, ainsi que la MRC du Fjord du Saguenay.

CE QUI MENACE LE BÉLUGA ET LES AUTRES MAMMIFÈRES MARINS

Grâce aux travaux de recherche réalisés au cours des dernières années, nous sommes maintenant en mesure de connaître les principaux facteurs (chasse, destruction d'habitats, pollution, etc.) qui ont pu conduire le béluga du Saint-Laurent au bord de l'extinction. Certains de ces facteurs sont maintenant contrôlés et d'autres sont en voie de l'être, nous y reviendrons plus tard. Pour l'instant, nous ne pouvons que déplorer les erreurs passées et espérer qu'elles servent d'exemples à ne pas répéter à l'avenir.

L'IMPORTANCE DE SAUVEGARDER L'ESPÈCE

Dans le contexte du parc du Saguenay qui est un parc de conservation, ainsi que dans celui de sa zone périphérique dont la vocation est vouée essentiellement au plein air (randonnée, nautisme, pêche, etc.) et à l'interprétation, des valeurs comme le respect de l'environnement et de la faune, dont les mammifères marins, sont évidemment des éléments très importants auxquels nous souscrivons. D'ailleurs, le Plan d'actions concerté (Office de planification et de développement du Québec ; 1984) prévoit que le développement du Bas-Saguenay doit s'effectuer en harmonie avec le milieu naturel considérant qu'il constitue l'essence même de notre produit touristique.

Comme vous le savez, les croisières d'observation des mammifères marins sont très populaires et constituent maintenant le fer de lance de l'industrie touristique à l'embouchure du Saguenay. En effet, entre 50 000 et 60 000 personnes ont pris le départ des quais de Tadoussac et de Baie-Sainte-Catherine cette année. Les retombées économiques générées par cette activité sont non seulement très importantes pour Tadoussac et Baie-Sainte-Catherine, mais s'étendent également aux régions de Charlevoix, de la Haute-Côte-Nord et du Saguenay. En plus de mettre la région de l'embouchure du Saguenay sur le circuit touristique québécois, les croisières attirent de plus en plus une clientèle internationale et contribuent à allonger substantiellement la saison touristique unique et exceptionnel pour la latitude auquel nous nous trouvons et par surcroît dans l'estuaire du Saint-Laurent, soit à quelques heures des grands centres.

Pour ces raisons, nous réaffirmons l'importance de protéger tous les mammifères marins, et notamment, de poser à très court terme les actions qui permettront de sauvegarder le béluga.

LES ACTIONS À POSER

N'ayant pas la prétention d'être des spécialistes en ce qui concerne les mammifères marins, notre intervention portera presque essentiellement sur le Plan d'action interministériel pour favoriser la survie du béluga, préparé conjointement par les ministères des Pêches et des Océans du Canada et de l'Environnement du Canada.

Considérant que les principaux facteurs ayant contribué à rendre plus rare le béluga sont : la chasse, la destruction des habitats, la pollution et le dérangement, nous sommes globalement en accord avec les actions proposées dans le Plan. Selon nous, il renferme l'essentiel des mesures à adopter pour solutionner le problème une fois pour toutes. Nous reprendrons ici quelques actions que nous jugeons particulièrement importantes ; par la suite nous vous ferons part de nos suggestions.

ACTIONS PORTANT SUR LE CONTRÔLE DES SUBSTANCES CHIMIQUES TOXIQUES

L'adoption de la loi canadienne sur la protection de l'environnement qui réglemente sévèrement les rejets de substances toxiques, la mise en place d'un programme de dépollution industrielle, sont à notre avis les éléments les plus importants du plan de survie. La pollution industrielle étant sans aucun doute le principal facteur ayant contribué au déclin de l'espèce, il faut donc y consacrer l'essentiel des ressources.

ACTIONS PORTANT SUR LE CONTRÔLE DES FACTEURS DE DÉRANGEMENT

La préparation d'un plan annuel de conservation, comprenant des directives sur l'observation des bélugas et des cétacés, est une initiative fort louable, mais on devra accroître la surveillance pour s'assurer du respect de la Loi. Ces directives ayant été élaborées en collaboration avec les représentants de l'industrie d'observation des baleines, ces derniers sont conscients du problème et collaborent généralement très bien. La situation est différente avec les plaisanciers, qui par inconscience ou en raison de la méconnaissance du problème, harcèlent fréquemment les baleines.

Concernant les normes de survol pour les aéronefs, nous croyons également qu'une surveillance plus stricte devrait être exercée. Les chasseurs CF-18 de la base de Bagotville effectuent presque quotidiennement des vols à basse altitude au-dessus du Saguenay et à son embouchure. Nous avons commencé récemment à les sensibiliser aux désagréments qu'ils causent aux cétacés et aux touristes. Il n'y a pas de doute que l'implantation d'un parc marin national tel qu'il a été préconisé pourrait contribuer substantiellement à réduire les facteurs de dérangement.

ACTIONS PORTANT SUR L'ACCROISSEMENT DE LA CONNAISSANCE

Nous sommes évidemment favorables à l'accroissement des activités de recherche sur le béluga et les autres cétacés, car bien des questions restent sans réponse pour l'instant. Un projet de recherche a particulièrement attiré notre attention : il s'agit de l'examen de la possibilité de renforcer la population de bélugas par l'introduction d'individus de l'Arctique. Selon nous, cette idée devrait être mise en branle rapidement. Il est évident que si l'on attend de comprendre en détail tout ce qui s'est passé, ce qui prendra encore plusieurs années, il sera impossible d'inverser le processus d'extinction.

ACTIONS ADDITIONNELLES SUGGÉRÉES PAR LA SOCIÉTÉ TOURISTIQUE DU FJORD

Au plan de survie proposé, nous aimerions voir ajouter parmi les actions à réaliser à court terme les éléments suivants :

1) La mise en place de facilités d'observation des bélugas à partir de la rive, notamment à l'aire de séjour de la baie Sainte-Marguerite. Cette activité s'intègre bien aux formes de mise en valeur prévues par le parc du Saguenay et serait accessible à toutes les clientèles. Cette façon d'observer les bélugas ne les dérangerait aucunement ; de plus, on rendrait accessible une fenêtre sur le magnifique fjord.
2) Soutenir la consolidation et le développement de centres d'interprétation. Nous pensons alors à la halte côtière de Pointe-Noire à Baie-Sainte-Catherine, opérée par la Société linnéenne du Québec et au Centre d'interprétation des mammifères marins de Tadoussac, de la Société d'interprétation du milieu marin de la Haute-Côte-Nord, dont la première version a débuté ses opérations cette année.

CONCLUSION

Avec ces ajouts qui favoriseraient l'accroissement des connaissances sur le milieu marin et l'éducation à la conservation, nous estimons que le plan de survie devrait atteindre les objectifs souhaités. Toutefois, son rythme de mise en œuvre nous inquiète beaucoup. Il faut se rappeler que le béluga a été déclaré espèce menacée en 1983 et que peu à peu on a commencé à prendre des mesures pour corriger la situation. Le plan de survie du béluga n'a toutefois été déposé qu'en juin 1988, soit cinq ans après que l'espèce fut déclarée en voie d'extinction. Il ne faut surtout pas que l'on prenne encore cinq ans pour mettre en œuvre les éléments majeurs et coûteux du plan, comme le programme de dépollution industrielle. Les gouvernements fédéral et provincial doivent donc consentir les ressources humaines et financières nécessaires à sa mise en œuvre. Nous demandons donc que le plan de dépollution du Saint-Laurent dans lequel sont inclus le plan de survie du béluga, le parc marin national, etc., soit enrichi et mis en œuvre très rapidement.

Concernant la création du parc marin national, nous espérons que les gouvernements du Canada et du Québec arriveront rapidement à une entente, car c'est un élément crucial du plan de survie au même titre que la dépollution. Avec un parc marin, on pourrait assurer une aire protégée pour les bélugas et les autres mammifères marins, où la surveillance serait plus intensive. Le parc fournirait également des moyens additionnels d'apprécier et de connaître les ressources marines de l'estuaire du Saint-Laurent, en plus de contribuer au développement de l'industrie touristique régionale. Bien que ce Forum porte sur l'avenir du béluga, il ne faut pas oublier que d'autres espèces de baleines sont possiblement menacées. Nous espérons que les intervenants concernés s'en préoccupent afin qu'on évite les problèmes que nous vivons présentement avec le béluga.

En terminant, nous voudrions remercier la Fondation pour la sauvegarde des espèces menacées, ainsi que tous les individus, entreprises ou organismes impliqués, pour l'excellent travail accompli depuis plusieurs mois pour l'organisation du Forum. C'est la répétition de ce genre d'événements, qui fera que tous nous serons d'ici quelques années conscientisés à un développement économique respectueux de l'environnement.

Coalition pour le parc marin Saguenay-Saint-Laurent

Pierre Tremblay

C'est avec plaisir qu'à titre de porte-parole de la coalition pour le parc marin Saguenay-Saint-Laurent, je m'adresse à vous.

Les bélugas et le parc marin ont un enjeu commun : leur survie, qui elle-même est soumise à notre capacité d'améliorer l'habitat marin de l'estuaire en réduisant la pollution et en agrandissant les frontières de cette zone où les bélugas pourront vraiment survivre et où le parc marin établira ses limites.

Pour réussir dans ce projet, il est essentiel d'obtenir la collaboration effective des intervenants des milieux politique, économique et scientifique.

Durant le Forum, chercheurs et porte-parole de groupes environnementaux et scientifiques nous ont donné une belle preuve que tous ces spécialistes se sentent concernés par l'état de santé du fleuve et de ses habitants. Cet échange d'information et la poursuite des recherches fondamentales sont parmi les principales clefs pouvant conduire les bélugas hors de l'emprise de la pollution.

Un autre moment de concertation efficace fût celui où la coalition pour le parc marin Saguenay-Saint-Laurent s'est constituée.

Cette concertation s'est réalisée sous l'initiative de l'ATR Charlevoix et d'autres intervenants de ce comté, non pas par agressivité envers le Service canadien des parcs ou encore par peur de ne pas voir se concrétiser de vains espoirs, mais plutôt positivement, pour assurer aux régions limitrophes de Manicouagan, Saguenay et Charlevoix ainsi qu'au

Canada tout entier que le futur parc marin ne serait pas un projet moindre que ce qui a pu se faire au pays tels Bruce Peninsula et South Morisby, et que ce parc de conservation devant protéger et mettre en valeur un échantillon du fleuve, de type de l'estuaire, pourrait s'établir sur des bases solides, qui ne seraient pas à l'image actuelle du troupeau de bélugas du Saint-Laurent : petits, faibles, presque condamnés à l'avance.

La création de notre coalition qui regroupe plus de vingt-sept municipalités, groupes environnementaux et groupes de développement économique, constitue une première fort originale. Ailleurs, pareil groupe s'est déjà formé pour, principalement, s'opposer au projet de parc.

La coalition, solidement appuyée par le milieu régional, a pour but premier de hâter la création d'un véritable parc marin, dont les frontières minimales correspondent à ce maximum proposé par le Service canadien des parcs dans son document intitulé « Étude de faisabilité d'un parc marin au Saguenay-Lac-Saint-Jean ». La coalition d'ailleurs préfère de beaucoup l'appellation parc marin Saguenay-Saint-Laurent.

Les limites minimums de notre projet s'étirent, dans l'axe fluvial, de Les Escoumins à Port-au-Saumon y incluant l'Île aux Lièvres et, dans l'axe de la rivière Saguenay, de Tadoussac jusqu'à La Baie. Puisqu'on parle là de minimum, il ne faudrait pas fermer la porte à une extension pour le futur.

De plus, nous proposons qu'une zone de conservation s'établisse de l'Île aux Coudres à Rivière-du-Loup, incluant Les Escoumins ainsi que tout le Saguenay.

Voilà, au strict minimum, l'aire où pourront s'établir et se développer tant le parc marin que les bélugas et ce, dans un milieu où la pollution devra régresser et lâcher son emprise.

Mais pour satisfaire cette dernière et indispensable condition, il nous faut compter avec la sincérité inébranlable et tenace de tous les partenaires gouvernementaux, tant les politiciens d'aujourd'hui que les fonctionnaires de demain. Notre projet en est un de société.

Pourrons-nous être assez sincères dans cette démarche pour sortir des sentiers battus des négociations fédérales-provinciales où chacun est habile à donner le blâme à l'autre pour justifier le blocage des négociations ? Serons-nous assez convaincus pour innover dans les relations ministères concernés et intervenants régionaux, où pour l'un, un certain mépris, et pour l'autre, un esprit de clocher trop vif empêchent une véritable concertation et une saine collaboration ?

Voilà peut-être pourquoi, du côté fédéral, on a fait faire une étude aussi incomplète, banale pourrait-on dire, à mettre sur les tablettes pour ce qui est de l'étude socio-économique et aussi insatisfaisante pour ce qui est des scénarios d'aménagement de ce parc marin.

Voilà peut-être pourquoi il n'y a pas eu encore de consultation de ce milieu vraiment concerné par ce projet, lequel, tout petitement ficelé, est bien en-dessous des aspirations et des besoins des intervenants régionaux, des groupes environnementaux et des bélugas eux-mêmes.

Voilà peut-être pourquoi, dans les négociations fédérales-provinciales, nos fonctionnaires manquent d'imagination ; l'un étant convaincu à l'avance qu'il se fera dire non ; l'autre ne voulant pas céder un pouce de terrain : tous deux se demandant de quelle juridiction relève le cadavre d'un béluga échoué.

Pourtant, nous avons tous un si beau, si grand projet : doter l'estuaire du Saint-Laurent d'un meilleur habitat pour sa faune et sa flore, y établir une large zone de conservation où on pourra mieux lutter contre la pollution et les pollueurs, y incarner le parc marin devant être à la hauteur du prestigieux Saint-Laurent, véritable aorte de toute l'Amérique du Nord. Tourisme et environnement sont aujourd'hui deux réalités associées.

On doit beaucoup à la Société linnéenne et aux actuels bâteliers pour la sensibilisation du grand public au monde marin du fleuve Saint-Laurent et à ses mammifères. Serions-nous à Tadoussac aujourd'hui si les croisières d'observation des baleines n'avaient pas permis à plus de 150 000 personnes ces dernières années d'être plus sensibilisées aux richesses du fleuve et de son estuaire ? Mais il faut faire plus...

Où trouver l'énergie pour dire « Il en est assez de ces querelles stériles » et inventer un cadre de gestion opérationnel où s'associeraient les gouvernements fédéral et provincial, les instances régionales, l'entreprise privée et les groupes locaux ? Qui le premier va briser ce cercle et décider de faire ce qu'il faut pour avoir un parc marin important, en établir la cogestion, lui conserver une seule image forte qui intégrerait en un tout, fleuve et fjord, parc provincial du Saguenay et entreprises privées, croisiéristes, Société linnéenne, Pointe-Noire, Petit-Saguenay, centre écologique de Port-au-Saumon, Cap de Bon-Désir, et tant d'autres ?

Comme vous le voyez, il nous reste un parc marin à inventer, des bélugas à sauver.

Nous croyons que la coalition pour le parc marin Saguenay-Saint-Laurent doit continuer à contribuer dans l'avancement des idées et qu'elle est la seule capable en ce moment, d'intégrer l'action des intervenants régionaux aux actions des gouvernements supérieurs et des responsables du projet du parc.

Nous affirmons que le développement du parc marin n'est donc pas la seule responsabilité des gouvernements fédéral et provincial et que ces derniers doivent immédiatement associer la coalition et ses membres à l'ensemble de la démarche.

Nous demandons des preuves tangibles que ce projet de parc n'en est pas un de papier, que, fidèles à leur réputation, nos gouvernements sauront s'associer au secteur privé de la zone concernée ainsi qu'à la coalition.

Nous proposons que, devant un manque évident d'imagination et un manque probable de ressources, l'on tienne une véritable consultation sur les véritables problèmes, sur les vrais enjeux, avant qu'à Québec et à Ottawa, nos représentants ne manquent de motivation.

La coalition affirme haut et fort sa volonté de voir créer ici un parc marin. La coalition et ses membres veulent, par là, sécuriser le politicien : oui maintenant, les régions du Saguenay, de Manicouagan et de Charlevoix veulent ce parc. Il ne faudrait pas mettre de côté ce dynamisme régional et se priver, dans certaines officines, du vent frais qu'apportent les régions riveraines.

Vingt-sept organismes et municipalités désirent collaborer activement à la concrétisation d'un projet moteur pour nos régions touristiques, lequel projet trouve sa justification dans cette double réalité du tourisme et de l'environnement.

Notre démarche est sincère et durera longtemps, et ce, autant pour la création du parc que pour la sauvegarde du béluga. Nos gouvernements devront aussi prouver leur sincérité dans cette action et nous démontrer que demain, ils ne dévieront pas de cet objectif.

Nous désirons contribuer, car, en fait, les plus proches voisins des marsouins, ce sont nous, les habitants riverains de la côte et du fjord et de Charlevoix ; nous qui y vivons en permanence depuis l'arrivée du malouin Jacques Cartier qui avait reconnu le béluga autour de l'Île aux Coudres.

Mais, puisque ces derniers et nous-mêmes sommes là pour rester, puisque le parc marin devra être créé et que la coalition et ses membres pourront y collaborer, sûrs de l'aimable collaboration de tous les intervenants, nous proposons que le béluga soit l'emblème animalier du parc marin.

Qu'avec toute cette bonne volonté et cette grande sincérité, on puisse réserver les fonds requis au développement du projet de sauvegarde du béluga et de création du parc marin ainsi que de son aménagement à même l'entente Canada-Québec sur la zone périphérique du fjord Saguenay, le fonds régional de l'Office de planification et de développement du Québec (OPDQ), le plan de développement régional (fédéral, provincial) Saguenay-Lac-Saint-Jean-Charlevoix, le plan Saint-Laurent, le budget du parc provincial Saguenay, le programme PADEL (Programme d'aide au développement des équipements de loisirs) et tant d'autres programmes normalisés disponibles qui rendront possible ce projet, seulement, mais seulement si, bien sûr tous et chacun sont bien sincères dans cette démarche.

Je vous remercie de votre attention tout en vous assurant de notre engagement total à cette cause.

Club nautique de Tadoussac

Thomas Maher
Commodore

C'est avec plaisir que je participe à ce Forum international pour l'avenir du béluga.

Pour nous qui habitons la merveilleuse région du Saguenay, qui partageons avec les bélugas le même territoire et certains éléments de leur habitat, ces assises sont l'occasion d'une profonde réflexion sur l'avenir du béluga mais aussi sur notre propre survie.

Comme le béluga, comme les autres espèces animales, comme les arbres et la flore en général de la vaste région du Saguenay, nous subissons les effets nocifs et de plus en plus meurtriers des pluies acides et de sources importantes de pollution des usines de transformation des pâtes et papiers et de l'aluminerie situées en amont. Jour après jour, les courants descendants du Saguenay charrient une énorme quantité de matières toxiques qui polluent l'habitat du béluga et des autres espèces dont les poissons et les crustacés que nous retrouvons sur nos tables. Les essais menés par le ministère des Pêches et des Océans du Canada, en collaboration avec un groupe de pêcheurs de la région, afin de commercialiser les stocks de crevettes et de crabes du Saguenay, au cours du mois de juin 1988, ont permis de conclure que ces produits sont impropres à la consommation.

Les vents dominants de l'ouest nous forcent également, en même temps que le béluga, à respirer une quantité indescriptible de produits chimiques qui causent aussi chez l'homme un nombre croissant de cancers, de malformations congénitales et de malaises de toutes sortes. D'ailleurs, les statistiques nationales indiquent qu'un fort pourcentage des décès dans notre région sont dus aux différents problèmes de santé dont souffre également le béluga. Voilà pour vous rassurer sur la grande solidarité entre les humains et les bélugas de la région du Saguenay.

Les bélugas sont plus chanceux. On les compte depuis plus de 15 ans, on les identifie et les analyse par des croisements de données scientifiques de plus en plus sophistiquées. Ils profiteront probablement jusqu'à leur extinction des recherches d'une imposante brochette de spécialistes de toutes sortes qui arrivent aux mêmes conclusions : il y en a moins qu'il y a dix ans, qu'il y a cinq ans même, et même qu'on n'en voit presque plus.

Tous les sujets traités par les conférenciers qui, tour à tour, au cours des derniers jours, nous ont entretenu de la question, ajoutent une preuve scientifique à cette démarche de mort mais uniquement pour le béluga. N'est-ce pas là un motif suffisant pour nous rendre un peu jaloux et peut-être même un peu inquiets ? Ne devons-nous pas faire le même diagnostic pour les humains ?

Cette délicate question a été traitée avec plus de pertinence par mon amie, Leone Pippard, dont les recherches et son acharnement à répéter le même cri d'alarme, depuis plusieurs années, ne sont sans doute pas étrangers à la tenue de ces assises où sont réunies autant de personnes compétentes pour en discuter.

Comme citoyen de cette région (je suis né à Tadoussac, j'y ai vécu mon enfance), c'est avec nostalgie que je me rappelle les merveilleuses expéditions de pêche à la truite sur le Saguenay accompagnées de centaines de bélugas que nous appelions alors « marsouins » et qui comme les arbres de la forêt nous semblaient immortels.

La venue de Mme Leone Pippard en 1973 fut pour nous le début d'une prise de conscience lente mais profonde de la valeur de notre milieu et de ses richesses.

Le marsouin de notre enfance est devenu béluga. Nous apprîmes que souvent on en trouvait échoués sur les plages, morts d'une maladie inconnue. On nous apprit aussi que l'eau du Saguenay, qui nous semblait limpide, est très polluée, que les truites de mer sont impropres à la consommation, etc., bref, que nous devrions nous préoccuper de notre environnement.

Le célèbre commandant Cousteau est venu nous dire que nous avions le privilège de posséder l'un des plus beaux fjords au monde ; que l'eau des profondeurs est la même qu'on retrouve dans les régions arctiques emprisonnées dans d'impressionnantes fosses très profondes laissées par le passage du glacier.

D'autres naturalistes nous apprirent que le phénomène observé au jusant à l'embouchure du Saguenay permet le mélange des eaux profondes du fjord et des eaux de surface du Saint-Laurent et favorise la croissance de micro-organismes, de petits crustacés et de petits poissons dont les baleines se nourrissent. Nous savons aujourd'hui que le mélange est aussi composé des produits chimiques des Grands Lacs, du Saint-Laurent et du Saguenay, de tous les déchets qui résultent de l'activité humaine.

Les gibarts de notre enfance sont alors devenus Rorqual bleu, Rorqual commun et Petit Rorqual.

Comme commodore de la marina de Tadoussac et aussi comme administrateur des Croisières du Grand Fleuve qui opèrent trois navires sur le Saint-Laurent et le Saguenay, notre mission se situe dans le prolongement de l'émerveillement que nous avons connu et que nous désirons faire découvrir aux nombreux touristes qui nous visitent grâce en très grande partie à la présence des mammifères marins à proximité de nos rives.

En effet, selon une étude effectuée en 1987 par l'Association touristique régionale de Manicouagan, plus de 49 % des touristes qui ont visité notre région cette année-là ont déclaré qu'ils sont venus voir les baleines.

On estime qu'au cours de l'été 1988, plus de 100 000 visiteurs auront ajouté la région de Tadoussac à leurs souvenirs de vacances. Un bon nombre reviendront et tous raconteront à leurs amis les merveilles et les beautés naturelles qu'ils ont découvertes en plus de l'accueil chaleureux que leur réservent les résidents.

L'industrie des croisières d'observation des mammifères marins sur le fjord Saguenay a remplacé très avantageusement les regrettés bateaux blancs de la Canada Steamship Lines.

Toutes ces splendeurs que plusieurs d'entre nous connaissions depuis plus longtemps et que d'autres viennent à peine de découvrir, dont le Saint-Laurent, le fjord Saguenay, les animaux qui l'habitent et la flore qu'ils recèlent, constituent la matière première de l'industrie touristique de cette grande région située à l'est de Québec. Sur les deux rives du Saint-Laurent et du Saguenay des centaines de petits commerces et de petites entreprises en dépendent et sont les principaux créateurs d'emplois et le moteur économique de ces régions du Québec. On évalue à plus de 25 millions de dollars cette industrie reliée à la vie du Saint-Laurent et du Saguenay.

La menace qui plane sur la survie du béluga, plane-t-elle aussi sur les autres espèces, sur la flore et sur notre vie ? Je dois vous avouer que les messages que nous donne la nature et que tous ici dans vos travaux de recherche et d'analyse semblez confirmer, nous inquiètent grandement.

La tâche à accomplir nous semble immense et nécessite une grande concertation.

Il nous semble que quelques projets d'envergure pourraient davantage motiver tous et chacun d'entre nous. Ce Forum en est un. Je fais le vœu que cette conférence devienne permanente et que tous ceux qui y participent, continuent le dialogue ouvertement autour de la création du parc marin. Cette tâche de renverser la vapeur, de changer le destin que nos habitudes polluantes ont tracé pour le béluga et les autres espèces dont nous-même mérite-t-elle toute notre attention ? Ne doit-on pas en parler ensemble plus souvent et très ouvertement ?

Devant l'ampleur de la tâche, on hésite à prendre les moyens, on procède à des analyses, on en prévoit d'autres pour les prochaines années. Monsieur Ronald Reagan, l'ex-président des États-Unis, croit qu'il faudra investir dans la recherche sur les pluies acides, le gouvernement canadien aussi. Nous prévoyons procéder à la dépollution du Saint-Laurent, etc. Alcan prendra des moyens aussi, mais où sont les plans d'action ? Quand seront-ils prêts ? Dans dix ans ? Ou quinze ans ? Tout naturellement, la réponse nous viendra de ceux qui, croit-on, prendront les moyens, les autres bien sûr.

Mais chacun d'entre nous, quel est notre plan d'action ?

Peut-on ensemble discuter d'un échéancier de réalisation du projet de parc marin ? Peut-on ensemble réaliser le vaste projet de dépollution du Saint-Laurent et de ses rives ? Peut-on ensemble arrêter le processus de destruction de notre propre habitat ? La réponse, nous l'espérons sera OUI.

Nous croyons qu'il faut donner le feu vert à la création du parc marin, encourager la recherche, promouvoir des activités de vulgarisation et d'information auprès du public comme le fait le Groupe de recherche et éducation sur le milieu marin (GREMM) auprès de la clientèle touristique qui vient voir les baleines afin que ces visiteurs deviennent eux aussi des partenaires de ce vaste projet.

1. Nous favorisons une meilleure connaissance du milieu en accueillant les touristes et en fournissant des équipements de qualité dont les bateaux de croisière.
2. Nous participons depuis trois ans au comité de consultation du ministère des Pêches et des Océans du Canada et à plusieurs comités voués au développement touristique.
3. Nous sommes partenaires avec le GREMM dans la création d'un Centre d'interprétation des mammifères marins à Tadoussac.

4. Nous demandons qu'un comité du milieu participe aux travaux de création d'un parc marin.
5. Nous n'utiliserons plus de verres de styromousse à la marina et sur nos navires à compter de 1989.

Nous vous assurons de notre collaboration.

Corporation des Pilotes du Bas-Saint-Laurent

Jean-Yves Roy
Président

Les pilotes du Saint-Laurent, comme vous le savez sans doute, ont depuis le tout début de la Nouvelle-France guidé les navires sur le Saint-Laurent et le Saguenay.

Les connaissances du pilote se sont pendant longtemps transmises par un apprentissage qui a évolué, mais qui subsiste encore aujourd'hui.

En effet, le pilote contemporain est d'abord un marin d'expérience qui, à la suite de ses études à l'Institut de marine, a dû naviguer pendant de nombreuses années et obtenir un brevet de capitaine avant d'entreprendre un apprentissage de trois ans lui permettant d'obtenir, à la suite d'examens rigoureux, son brevet de pilote pour la circonscription de pilotage de Québec, c'est-à-dire le Saint-Laurent de Les Escoumins à Québec et le Saguenay jusqu'à La Baie et Chicoutimi.

Ce n'est qu'à la suite de ce long cheminement que le pilote peut enfin exercer sa profession et remplir son rôle qui est d'assurer une navigation sûre et efficace des navires qui sillonnent le Saint-Laurent et le Saguenay.

Tout ce processus se déroule sous l'autorité de l'Administration de pilotage des Laurentides, société d'État relevant du ministère des Transports du Canada, qui a pour mission d'administrer le pilotage dans les eaux en question.

Les pilotes sont des entrepreneurs privés regroupés en corporation et ils fournissent les services de pilotage conformément à un contrat de services avec l'Administration de pilotage des Laurentides.

Traditionnellement, le pilotage a été une affaire entre gouvernement, armateurs et pilotes. De nos jours, nous croyons que le pilotage, dont la principale raison d'être est d'assurer la sécurité de la navigation dans nos eaux, devrait intéresser toute la population et surtout ceux qui habitent près du fleuve et en vivent.

Les citoyens, de plus en plus conscients de la nécessité de protéger l'environnement des fleuves et la vie en général, s'intéresseront sûrement de plus en plus à la sécurité de la navigation qui est la première et la meilleure mesure de protection de l'environnement en ce qui concerne le transport maritime.

Le Saint-Laurent et le Saguenay sont et demeureront encore bien longtemps d'extraordinaires voies de pénétration du continent. Nous croyons que cette utilisation peut très bien coexister avec toutes les autres sans nuire à la survie des fleuves ni des espèces qui y vivent. Nous sommes convaincus que cette coexistence est possible en autant que nous prenions certaines précautions pour prévenir la pollution pouvant découler du transport maritime, élément essentiel à notre développement économique.

À cet égard, nous les pilotes du Bas-Saint-Laurent sommes très conscients de notre rôle « de protecteur » de nos deux grands cours d'eau, très conscients de notre devoir d'assurer une navigation efficace. Nous nous devons de ne jamais oublier que la sécurité de la navigation demeure notre premier souci, notre principale raison d'être.

Nous sommes aussi très conscients qu'en nous opposant farouchement à tout relâchement des normes imposées aux navires, aux navigateurs et aux pilotes eux-mêmes, nous défendons les intérêts du public en général, du fleuve et de tout ce qui y vit ainsi que nos propres intérêts. C'est donc dire que nous avons des intérêts communs... C'est probablement pourquoi il n'y a pas longtemps on accusait les pilotes de considérer le fleuve comme leur propre domaine. Je crois que nous, comme tous les citoyens, ne sommes que les fiduciaires des fleuves, des rivières et de toute la biosphère et que comme tels, nous devons nous efforcer de remettre tout cela à nos « enfants » en aussi bon et même, si possible, en meilleur état que c'était quand on nous l'a confié.

Voilà vraiment le défi que toute humanité se doit de relever.

Je vous remercie de votre attention !

Ultramar Canada

Raynald Archambault

Ultramar se fait un plaisir de participer à ce Forum et d'y apporter un soutien financier. Si on le fait, c'est parce qu'on a le sens du devoir, qu'on se sent une responsabilité. Nos activités industrielles, notamment à Saint-Romuald, touchent en effet le fleuve. Je pense qu'indirectement nous rejoignons les préoccupations entendues depuis deux jours, c'est-à-dire la survie du béluga. En effet, ce qui se passe dans l'industrie touche indirectement l'ensemble de la population, l'ensemble de la faune, l'ensemble de la flore.

Je dois vous dire ici qu'Ultramar est engagée au point de vue environnement, et qu'il s'agit d'un engagement réel. Quand nous réalisons nos activités de raffinage, et nos autres activités industrielles et commerciales, nous voulons que cela se fasse avec beaucoup de soins et en protégeant l'environnement, c'est-à-dire avec un impact minimal sur l'environnement. Il est bien certain qu'il y a des incidents, comme celui du 8 mai 1988 où le navire polonais « Czantoria » déversait accidentellement 2 000 barils de pétrole brut. Mais là encore on a des moyens pour intervenir et nous prenons nos responsabilités pour faire en sorte que les dégâts soient minimisés.

Ce que nous proposons en terme d'apport à la survie du béluga se situe surtout au niveau de la prévention. Si nous faisons de la prévention dans nos usines et dans le déroulement de nos activités, si nous faisons en sorte qu'il y ait un minimum de pollution, je pense que, indirectement, nous contribuons. Il s'agit peut-être d'une action un peu indirecte, mais je pense qu'on a entendu depuis quelques jours qu'elle peut être considérée comme assez pertinente.

Par ailleurs, nous faisons aussi beaucoup d'investissements, même s'il y a des gens qui ont semblé douter des investissements industriels dans le contrôle de la pollution, dans la prévention. Je dois vous dire qu'à la raffinerie de Saint-Romuald, par exemple, nous avons déjà réalisé vingt-sept projets en cinq ans qui ont coûté plus de cinq millions de dollars. Et nous avons aussi des projets de remplacement de réservoirs dans les stations de service. Vous allez me dire que nous sommes loin du béluga. Mais rappelons-nous que s'il y a fuite, cela peut atteindre les rivières. Ces efforts que fait Ultramar, il faut vous dire que l'industrie pétrolière en général les fait également.

Je dois vous dire aussi que nous comptons participer pleinement au programme d'assainissement industriel qui vient d'être annoncé. Nous y participons déjà en respectant toutes les normes qui sont déjà en place, mais nous savons qu'il faut faire plus. Nous sommes tout à fait d'accord avec le Ministère pour contribuer et ainsi participer à cette nouvelle évolution vers le mieux-être. Concrètement, nous allons donc continuer à essayer de réduire à la source, à recycler les produits, à disposer des résidus d'une façon correcte. On se rappellera, entre autres, à ce sujet là, le projet que nous développons avec l'Université Laval sur la réduction des résidus, la récupération des huiles qu'on retrouve dans des solides huileux.

La gestion environnementale est une dimension importante chez nous. Le département que je dirige en est la preuve. Nous avons des critères qui veulent que, par exemple, nous fassions le contrôle à la source, le recyclage au maximum, les stockages en toute sécurité des résidus produits, pour en disposer plus tard avec des moyens aussi corrects au point de vue environnemental qu'efficaces au point de vue économique. Vous comprendrez alors que les objectifs de la Commission Brundtland nous plaisent, car ils associent économie et environnement.

Maintenant, laissez-moi vous dire un mot de l'APCE, parce qu'il s'agit d'un sujet pertinent dans les discussions en cours. L'Association pétrolière pour la conservation de l'environnement canadien est une association sans but lucratif à participation volontaire qui regroupe huit grandes compagnies de pétrole. Cette association étudie les questions de santé et d'environnement reliées à la fabrication et à la distribution des produits pétroliers. C'est par le biais de cette association, que l'on appelle PACE en anglais et APCE en français, que les compagnies pétrolières tentent de résoudre les problèmes associés à leur activité. L'association a déjà plusieurs comités au travail, une trentaine de projets actifs, et elle dépense plusieurs centaines de milliers de dollars. Je dirais aussi qu'elle subventionne des études pour plusieurs millions de dollars par année. Elle amène les gens à travailler ensemble, ce qui est important puisque je pense que c'est en regroupant les forces qu'on va réussir à répondre aux besoins environnementaux et à améliorer la protection de l'environnement.

Le fait d'être regroupé au sein de l'APCE a apporté plus d'efficacité dans le traitement et dans la résolution des problèmes. À ce sujet, si je peux apporter une suggestion, je crois que ce mode de fonctionnement où l'on crée une association très volontaire, où l'on groupe toutes les forces, est peut-être un modèle à explorer pour résoudre le problème d'association. Je vois ici énormément de bonne volonté, énormément d'organismes qui travaillent ensemble, qui ont tous la même préoccupation. Mais on sait que le processus décisionnel est souvent un peu difficile car il y a beaucoup de monde impliqué. L'industrie pétrolière a trouvé ce moyen, une association à base volontaire, pour agir. Je pense que je veux offrir ce modèle comme point de discussion. Rappelez-vous aussi que l'industrie pétrolière est déjà en avance sur les normes, et qu'elle fait tout ce qu'elle peut faire au point de vue environnemental pour prévenir. Je pense enfin qu'elle souscrira certainement à ce projet de parc marin, car tout ce qui peut amener un mieux-être, nous y croyons.

Alcan

Robert Salette
Vice-président régional

Depuis trois jours déjà, le nom d'Alcan revient souvent sur le tapis ; tantôt pour parler de notre présence au Forum, tantôt pour parler de nos activités industrielles, particulièrement au Saguenay-Lac-Saint-Jean.

Notre présence ici, à la commandite et à l'organisation de ce Forum, relève de notre motivation de participer à un projet révélateur. Il nous faut écouter, comprendre ce que les chercheurs, ce que les intervenants impliqués dans la survie des bélugas ont à dire et aussi ce qu'ils proposent pour assurer la survie du troupeau présent dans le Saint-Laurent et, à voir avec quel intérêt vous avez participé et en constatant la qualité des échanges, force m'est de réaliser que ce Forum s'imposait peut-être depuis longtemps.

On a qualifié de « courageuse » notre présence. D'autres ont été plutôt cyniques. Non, je crois plutôt que notre présence ici au Forum tient davantage de notre maturité. Une maturité qui ouvre la porte, je crois, à notre volonté ferme d'être un partenaire, rejoignant ainsi la philosophie d'intégration des dimensions économiques et environnementales telles qu'elles ressortent du rapport Brundtland.

Partenaire

Une des dimensions à cette réalité de partenariat repose obligatoirement sur la compréhension des règles auxquelles chacun doit se plier.

Par exemple, les scientifiques que nous avons entendus ces deux derniers jours ont des règles et des contraintes avec lesquelles ils doivent vivre ; souvent le manque de ressources financières, des équipements pas toujours à la fine pointe, une méthodologie remise en question, des jugements critiqués par des pairs, et tout cela dans une recherche de la pure vérité.

Quant à nous, de l'industrie, les règles du jeu sont économiques, environnementales et sociales, alors que la continuité est une nécessité réelle dans un contexte comme le nôtre. Il devient de plus en plus évident que chacun a besoin de l'autre car nous sommes en situation d'interdépendance.

Des exemples

Dans un passé pas si lointain, les entreprises se suffisaient à elles-mêmes. Celles qui se dotaient de ressources professionnelles de qualité avaient un net avantage sur leurs concurrents. Dans ce modèle, nous avons chez nous réalisé des progrès importants, même au niveau des vieilles salles de cuves d'électrolyse, les Soderberg, où des améliorations significatives ont été apportées tant au niveau des conditions de travail qu'au niveau des émissions et ce, tout en amorçant la reconstruction progressive de nos vieilles installations. Je mentionne ici quelques exemples : le nouveau centre de calcination de l'alumine, le nouveau four de cuisson des anodes, l'usine pour la production de fluorure d'aluminium, sans oublier l'usine de Grande-Baie. Toutes ces usines modernes intègrent dans leur conception même les paramètres de protection de l'environnement et les concepts de qualité de vie au travail.

Aujourd'hui, les problèmes rencontrés et l'évolution des valeurs nous indiquent qu'il faut avoir une vision plus globale de la société. Nous rejoignons en ce sens le ministre Lincoln et Jacques Prescott qui y ont également référé. Je pense que c'est là une chose partagée par tous ici présents. Cette vision, cette approche globale, nous ouvrent la porte à une meilleure intégration des connaissances, à une intégration d'un plus grand nombre de paramètres.

Du reste, dans le domaine de la santé, notre association avec les représentants de nos employés, l'Institut de recherche en santé et en sécurité du travail (IRSST) et la contribution d'experts reconnus de différentes universités nous ont permis d'atteindre plus rapidement une crédibilité sur les résultats et ainsi apporter les correctifs appropriés. C'est là, comme je le disais, un exemple d'un partenariat constructif, orienté vers la recherche de solutions.

Je tiens, de plus, à souligner que ces études ont été régulièrement diffusées à nos employés et leurs représentants, à la communauté et à la presse. Ces études ont été publiées dans le milieu scientifique puis communiquées à l'industrie de l'aluminium à travers le monde.

Dans cette évolution de la société, il m'apparaît plus important de regarder vers l'avenir en intégrant ces nouvelles valeurs. La prise de conscience collective de la dégradation de notre environnement alors que nous la croyons encore réversible, nous offre l'opportunité de mettre sur pied un programme d'action où nous avons tous un rôle à jouer.

J'aurais pu m'attarder sur les 200 millions de dollars investis chez nous depuis le début des années 70, dans le domaine de l'assainissement de l'air, ou des 150 millions de dollars engagés dans celui de l'assainissement des rejets liquides ou encore des mesures prises quant à la gestion de nos déchets et résidus. Mais ce qui nous réunit ici c'est demain.

C'est pourquoi, chez nous, des améliorations techniques appliquées à nos vieux procédés, même si elles sont extrêmement utiles, ne sont pas suffisantes. Elles ne s'adressent qu'à court terme et il faut aller vers la reconstruction : l'usine Laterrière, dont on vient une seconde fois de devancer l'échéancier, n'est que le premier jalon de ce programme de remplacement progressif du système Soderberg. Déjà, lors de l'assemblée des actionnaires d'avril 1988, à une question d'un journaliste, notre président François Senécal-Tremblay, signifiait l'arrêt de mort du système Soderberg.

Le Forum

Il y a quelques années, la société Alcan a été associée à la problématique de la disparition du troupeau de bélugas du Saint-Laurent.

Notre première action fut de nous interroger sur l'état général du troupeau et sur les causes du problème. Vous admettrez que nous ne sommes pas des spécialistes dans ce domaine. Nous avons pris l'initiative de faire établir un premier bilan des connaissances disponibles partagé lors de rencontres avec les groupes qui sont ici présents.

C'est conjointement que nous avons perçu le besoin d'améliorer les connaissances sur le béluga, le Forum en est une expression vivante. Certains aspects d'ailleurs de la problématique sont nouveaux.

Nous croyons important de soutenir concrètement les initiatives qui favoriseront une amélioration des connaissances de l'espèce et de son habitat. Le béluga fait partie de notre patrimoine collectif; c'est pourquoi nous devons tous ensemble appuyer les efforts de ceux qui ont la responsabilité de mettre en place un plan de survie pour ce troupeau de mammifères du Saint-Laurent. Ensemble, nous sommes certains que nous pouvons accomplir beaucoup de choses.

Finalement, j'aimerais reprendre avec vous certains éléments qui m'apparaissent primordiaux.

En premier lieu, je reviens sur la question des HAP. Nos engagements sont fermes et précis. Nous fermerons nos salles de cuves Soderberg.

L'usine Laterrière, présentement en construction au coût de 750 millions de dollars, remplacera 200 mille tonnes de production équivalentes à Jonquière, dès sa mise en opération progressive.

En deuxième lieu, en ce qui concerne les bélugas, nous en sommes rendus à l'étape où nous croyons fermement qu'il est primordial d'élargir et d'enrichir le modèle de relations entre nous. Il faut établir des mécanismes soutenus, des « vases communicants » qui nous permettront de construire ensemble, au cours des années à venir, le type de société que l'on voudra bien se donner. Cela demande un échange suivi d'idées, d'informations, d'hypothèses, de plans, de projets auxquels nous pourrons tous participer. Brisons ensemble les barrières établies dans le modèle antérieur. Faisons confiance au comité de suivi afin d'établir les mécanismes appropriés.

Nous nous sommes déjà engagés, avec le Fonds mondial pour la nature et le ministère des Pêches et des Océans du Canada, dans le programme de recherche en toxicologie du Dr Béland. À l'intérieur du plan de suivi du béluga les domaines de recherche, d'interprétation, de sensibilisation sont des éléments que nous entendons privilégier.

Il n'y a, à notre avis, qu'une seule façon de construire cette société que nous désirons collectivement. C'est pour cette raison que nous avons signé, en tant qu'entreprise, le rapport du Groupe canadien de travail sur l'environnement et l'économie. C'est aussi pour cette raison que nous avons accepté d'emblée l'invitation du ministre Lincoln à faire partie de la table ronde québécoise.

Comme membre à part entière de la communauté, nous manifestons ainsi notre respect pour le milieu qui nous accueille.

Je vous remercie, vous pouvez compter sur Alcan !

Hydro-Québec

Richard Verdon
Conseiller en recherche

PRÉOCCUPATIONS D'HYDRO-QUÉBEC FACE À L'AVENIR DU BÉLUGA

1. INTRODUCTION

Les aménagements hydroélectriques des tributaires de milieux marins, de même que les traversées sous-fluviales de câbles d'alimentation électrique sont susceptibles d'avoir un effet sur les populations de mammifères marins et en particulier de bélugas. Au cours des dernières années, Hydro-Québec a réalisé plusieurs études sur les populations de bélugas. Les études les plus importantes ont porté sur les populations de bélugas de la Baie-d'Hudson. Cependant quelques études récentes ont permis d'approfondir nos connaissances sur la distribution et les déplacements des bélugas du Saint-Laurent.

2. LES AMÉNAGEMENTS HYDROÉLECTRIQUES

Parmi les préoccupations d'Hydro-Québec face à l'avenir du béluga, l'aménagement hydroélectrique des rivières et leur effet potentiel sur la dynamique des estuaires représentent une priorité. Dans cette optique, plusieurs études portant sur l'utilisation des estuaires par les bélugas ont été entreprises par la vice-présidence Environnement (Breton-Provencher 1979, Painchaud 1982, Painchaud et Hayeur 1982). Toutefois, les études les plus importantes ont porté sur la population de bélugas de la région de Kuujjuarapik (Poste-de-la-Baleine), puisque tous les projets futurs d'aménagement des tributaires du Saint-Laurent sont localisés à l'extérieur de la zone actuelle de distribution du béluga.

Les études réalisées ont quand même permis une meilleure compréhension de la biologie et du comportement du béluga, de même que de l'utilisation qu'il fait des estuaires et ces résultats sont d'un grand intérêt pour la survie des bélugas du Saint-Laurent. La distribution des bélugas est très souvent corrélée aux milieux estuariens. Les températures relativement élevées que l'on y retrouve semblent les y attirer plus que tout autre facteur. Toutefois, la proximité des ressources alimentaires, les faibles profondeurs et les abris contre les tempêtes exercent probablement un certain attrait sur les bélugas dans les estuaires documentés.

À l'instar de la population de bélugas du Saint-Laurent, la population de bélugas de la région de Kuujjuarapik a connu un important déclin depuis le siècle dernier. Une étude historique révèle que des milliers de bélugas fréquentaient jadis la région, alors qu'on en compte maintenant environ 400. Leur décroissance numérique est grandement corrélée à la chasse commerciale dont ils furent l'objet, puisqu'aucune autre activité humaine nuisible n'avait cours dans cette région.

Dans l'estuaire du Saint-Laurent, la population de bélugas n'est pas menacée par les futurs projets d'aménagement hydroélectrique, qui seront localisés à l'extérieur de la zone de distribution actuelle des bélugas. Il y a quelques décennies, le béluga fréquentait la région du banc de Manicouagan. L'aménagement hydroélectrique de cette rivière au cours des années 60 ne peut être tenu responsable du déclin de cette sous-population, qui a décliné jusqu'à l'extinction au cours des années 30 et 40 ; il semble probable que la surexploitation par la chasse soit à l'origine de cet état de fait (Sergeant dans Painchaud et Hayeur 1982).

3. LES TRAVERSÉES SOUS-FLUVIALES

Les traversées sous-fluviales de câbles d'alimentation électrique peuvent affecter les populations de bélugas si des travaux de dynamitage en eau sont nécessaires.

Dans le cadre du projet de traversée du câble sous-marin de l'Île aux Coudres, on a réalisé une étude de la distribution du béluga dans la partie amont de l'estuaire du Saint-Laurent (Institut national d'écotoxicologie du Saint-Laurent inc., 1987). Des inventaires aériens effectués en août et septembre 1987, entre l'Île aux Oies et les îles de Kamouraska, ont révélé que cette partie de l'estuaire était fréquentée par une forte proportion de la population totale de bélugas du Saint-Laurent. Le Passage de l'Île aux Coudres, situé entre cette île et la rive nord du fleuve, semble peu fréquenté par cette espèce au cours de cette période. Selon plusieurs observateurs, toutefois, ce secteur est visité régulièrement par les bélugas au printemps.

Bien qu'il soit peu probable que du dynamitage soit effectué lors de la réalisation du projet de l'Île aux Coudres et que le béluga soit peu susceptible de fréquenter le secteur des travaux à cette période, Hydro-Québec a néanmoins préparé un plan de surveillance pour la protection du béluga, afin de s'assurer qu'il n'y ait aucun risque pour l'espèce (Huot et Couture, 1988). L'objectif de ce plan de surveillance est, dans l'éventualité qu'il soit nécessaire d'effectuer du dynamitage durant les travaux, de s'assurer qu'il n'y ait aucun béluga dans un rayon de 5 km du lieu d'impact, de façon à ce que le comportement du béluga ne soit affecté d'aucune façon.

En vertu du plan de surveillance, la journée même du sautage, la surveillance débutera par un survol général en hélicoptère d'une zone qui s'étend bien au-delà des 5 km et ce, au moins trois heures avant le sautage. Par la suite, la zone de surveillance est diminuée aux 5 km prescrits et les entrées est et ouest du Passage de l'Île aux Coudres feront l'objet d'une surveillance accrue. Si la surveillance montre qu'il n'y a aucun risque pour le béluga, un comité d'experts, sous l'autorité du ministère de l'Environnement du Québec, autorisera le sautage.

4. CONCLUSION

En vertu du principe 2 de sa politique d'environnement, adoptée en 1984, Hydro-Québec gère à la source les implications environnementales de ses activités. Dans le cas des espèces rares ou menacées, telles que le béluga du Saint-Laurent, l'entreprise accepte de déployer des efforts particuliers pour le maintien des populations. C'est pourquoi, des mesures particulières ont été adoptées dans le cadre du projet de l'Île aux Coudres, ce qui devrait éliminer tout risque de perturbation pour l'espèce.

RÉFÉRENCES

BRETON-PROVENCHER, M. *Projet Grande-Baleine*: études océanographiques dans la Baie-d'Hudson, étude de la population de bélugas de la région de Poste-de-la-Baleine (Nouveau-Québec), rapport présenté à la direction Environnement d'Hydro-Québec, 1979, 93 p.

HUOT, J. G. et COUTURE, M. *Projet Île aux Coudres* : plan de surveillance pour la protection du béluga, Hydro-Québec, Distribution et projets, 1988, 8 p.

INSTITUT NATIONAL D'ÉCOTOXICOLOGIE DU SAINT-LAURENT INC. *Distribution du béluga (*Delphinapterus leucas*) dans la partie amont de* *l'estuaire du Saint-Laurent* (secteur Île aux Coudres), rapport présenté à Hydro-Québec, 1987, 36 p.

PAINCHAUD, J. *Synthèse des connaissances sur la fréquentation des estuaires par les bélugas*, étude présentée à la direction Environnement d'Hydro-Québec par le groupe Dryade, 1982, 122 p.

PAINCHAUD, J. et HAYEUR, G. *Compte rendu de l'atelier sur l'utilisation des estuaires par les bélugas et sur les effets possibles de projet Grande-Baleine sur les troupeaux des estuaires touchés*, Hydro-Québec, direction Environnement, 1982, 75 p.

Société linnéenne du Québec

Benoît Gauthier
Comité de recherche et développement

INTRODUCTION

Bref rappel de l'implication de la Société linnéenne (SLQ) depuis 10 ans. Heureux de fêter cet anniversaire dans le présent contexte où tant d'intervenants de qualité et d'enjeux sont présents.

1. PRÉOCCUPATIONS PASSÉES DE LA SLQ EN CE QUI CONCERNE LES BÉLUGAS

1.1 Rappel des grands traits historiques

a) avant 1671 : préhistoire
b) 1671-1953 : prélèvements réguliers des bélugas sur la rive sud et la rive nord du Saint-Laurent (272 ans) ;
c) 1953-1979 : période de déclin (25 ans) ;
d) 1979-1988 : mise en place d'un écosystème de conservation tant sur la rive sud que sur la rive nord du Saint-Laurent et le long du Saguenay.

1.2 Contribution de la Société linnéenne

Au sein de la Société linnéenne, le projet de conservation des bélugas du Saint-Laurent et du Saguenay a débuté en 1981. Il s'inscrivait dans un plus vaste programme de sensibilisation du public au monde des baleines, amorcé en 1979 par des croisières régulières sur le Saint-Laurent. Ce très gros programme devait d'ailleurs nous mériter le prix du Gouverneur général du Canada en conservation en 1982.

En ce qui a trait strictement aux bélugas, le projet comprenait deux étapes en vue d'en arriver ultimement à la création d'un parc marin.

a) *Étape d'alerte positive (1981-1982)*

Il s'agit d'informer le public régional et national des dangers encourus par la petite population des bélugas (émissions radiophoniques, articles de journaux, posters, livrets, chandails, expositions, etc.).

Cette étape a connu un franc succès et plusieurs ministères se sont impliqués, tant au provincial qu'au fédéral. Les mises d'argent étaient à chaque fois réduites (moins de 5 000 $) pour chacune des années considérées.

Nous croyons qu'au cours de ces deux années, le public régional et national a évolué vers un sens accru de conservation. De plus, les fonctionnaires du gouvernement fédéral ont eu le temps de préparer une stratégie de surveillance et de connaissance préliminaire des bélugas.

Nous estimons que cette étape fut bénéfique pour les bélugas eux-mêmes quant aux aspects du braconnage et du harcèlement.

b) *Étape de sensibilisation et d'éducation (1983-1988)*

Des milliers de citoyens étaient désireux d'en apprendre plus sur la biologie et l'écologie des bélugas. Pour répondre à ce désir légitime, nous avons jugé très important d'assurer une présence de qualité auprès du public intéressé. Ainsi, en mai 1982, la Société linnéenne a soumis le projet d'une halte côtière au Service canadien des parcs avec une partie nautique. L'entente concernant la halte côtière fut signée en juin 1983 pour une période d'au moins 5 ans.

b.1 *Partie nautique*

Un bateau effectue des croisières régulières. À son bord, un naturaliste interprète la vie maritime et dirige le bateau de manière à ne pas harasser les bélugas.

Nous pensons que cette étape a permis d'atteindre les objectifs suivants :

a) plus de données pour les gestionnaires et chercheurs du ministère des Pêches et des Océans du Canada qui ont été présents à bord ;
b) des milliers de personnes informées ;
c) moins de petits bateaux indisciplinés.

b.2 *Partie terrestre*

Cette partie rattachée à la halte côtière de Pointe-Noire visait cinq objectifs :

a) aider les chercheurs qui étudient les bélugas en leur offrant un hébergement et un site d'observation ;
b) informer des milliers de personnes ; (1984-1988 : 46 000 visiteurs) ;
c) aider les ministères à se coordonner entre eux et avec le public ;
d) obtenir un parc marin pour les bélugas ;
e) susciter une halte côtière à Cap de Bon-Désir.

En conclusion, un scénario complet de conservation a été mis en branle par la Société linnéenne qui s'est répété et amplifié constamment si on considère les 46 000 visiteurs à Pointe-Noire (1984-88) et les dizaines de milliers d'excursionnistes seulement en 1988.

2. COMMENTAIRES SPÉCIFIQUES SUR LE PLAN D'ACTION DU MINISTÈRE DES PÊCHES ET DES OCÉANS DU CANADA (13 JUIN 1988)

2.1 La Société linnéenne se dit pleinement d'accord avec l'idée d'implanter un parc marin optimal pour les estuaires du Saint-Laurent et du Saguenay.

2.2 Accroissement des connaissances (p. 7, pt IV) : nous suggérons un plus grand effort afin de bien comprendre cette espèce « estuarienne ».

2.3 Rôle du public

- (p. 3, a.1) consultation trop limitée au seul dérangement des bélugas ;
- (p. 4, pt IV) information limitée à une monographie ;
- manque des sommes d'argent pour actualiser l'information à l'attention du public selon une action à court terme ;

- il convient d'associer tant les populations de la rive nord que de la rive sud du Saint-Laurent où se trouvaient la plupart des pêches prospères des bélugas.

3. RÔLE DE LA SOCIÉTÉ LINNÉENNE DANS L'APRÈS-FORUM POUR L'AVENIR DES BÉLUGAS : RECOMMANDATIONS

Considérant que la sensibilisation, l'information et l'éducation du public ont démontré leurs effets positifs dans la dynamique de la protection et préservation des bélugas, la Société linnéenne juge important de présenter les recommandations et les engagements suivants.

La Société linnéenne recommande :

1) qu'un contrat soit élaboré à court terme entre le ministère des Pêches et des Océans du Canada, le Service canadien des parcs et la Société linnéenne du Québec en vue d'actualiser l'information sur les bélugas dans le cadre de la halte côtière de Pointe-Noire ;
2) que le public, incluant la Société linnéenne, soit associé à la dynamique d'évaluation du plan d'action prévue pour avril 1989 par le ministère des Pêches et des Océans du Canada.

La Société linnéenne s'engage :

3) de concert avec la Fondation linnéenne, à créer, à promouvoir et à décerner un prix « Vadim Vladykov », pour la recherche, la vulgarisation et la conservation des mammifères marins y incluant les bélugas des zones côtières du Québec ;
4) à faciliter la recherche sur les bélugas, les mammifères marins et leur habitat tant sur la rive nord que sur la rive sud du Saint-Laurent à la halte côtière de Pointe-Noire et sur le bateau de croisière Samuel de Champlain ;
5) à travailler, de concert avec le Conseil du loisir scientifique du Saguenay-Lac-Saint-Jean et le Musée du fjord à la Baie, à la réalisation d'une exposition itinérante sur les bélugas ;
6) à stimuler la création artistique, les activités culturelles et scientifiques à caractère muséologique autour de la thématique des mammifères marins y incluant les bélugas.

Enfin, la Société linnéenne recommande :

7) que la halte côtière de Pointe-Noire devienne le premier centre international sur l'interprétation des bélugas à l'intérieur du futur parc marin et que des sommes d'argent soient disponibles, engagées à cet effet.

CONCLUSION

La Société linnéenne va bientôt fêter 60 ans d'existence. Elle se dit prête à entreprendre un autre long terme avec la même énergie rayonnante que celle dégagée depuis les dix dernières années.

La Société Duvetnor ltée

Jean Bédard
Président

PRÉSENTATION

Fondée en 1979, la Société Duvetnor ltée (sans but lucratif) a pour objet principal la conservation des milieux naturels dans l'estuaire du Saint-Laurent. Elle possède en biens immobiliers deux des trois îles du Pot à l'Eau-de-Vie (25 ha) ainsi que l'Île aux Lièvres (900 ha) ; elle exerce également un droit de regard dans la gestion de l'archipel des îles Les Pèlerins (200 ha, appartenant à la Société pour la conservation de l'archipel Les Pèlerins) ; enfin, elle gère et effectue des aménagements sur certaines des îles appartenant au ministère de l'Environnement du Canada et faisant partie de la Réserve nationale de la faune des îles de l'estuaire. Duvetnor tire ses revenus de la cueillette et de la mise en marché du duvet d'un abondant canard de mer, l'Eider à duvet.

ACTIONS PRÉVUES PAR DUVETNOR POUR LA CONSERVATION DU BÉLUGA

En faisant l'acquisition de l'Île aux Lièvres, grâce à la collaboration de plusieurs organismes publics et privés [1], notre corporation croit avoir

---

[1] La Fondation habitat faunique Canada, Canards illimités Canada, l'Office de planification et de développement du Québec, le ministère du Loisir, de la

déjà posé un geste concret en vue de la conservation du béluga. Le territoire entourant la pointe ouest de cette île revêt une importance particulière pour le béluga durant les mois de mai et juin surtout. En plus de vouer à la conservation ces îles importantes de l'estuaire maritime, Duvetnor entend aussi y effectuer des observations sur le comportement de ce mammifère marin : des observations scientifiques sont d'ailleurs en cours depuis août 1988 à partir de l'extraordinaire plate-forme terrestre que constitue la pointe ouest de l'Île aux Lièvres.

Duvetnor a également pour mandat de développer le souci de conservation et de respect du milieu naturel au sein de la population québécoise. C'est dans cet esprit que la corporation a entrepris d'organiser une exposition d'envergure sur la recherche océanographique dans l'estuaire du Saint-Laurent. Intitulée « Parlez-moi du fleuve », cette exposition est parrainée par le programme Sciences et Culture Canada et par plusieurs organismes du milieu scientifique (le ministère des Pêches et des Océans du Canada, le ministère de l'Environnement du Québec, le ministère de l'Agriculture, des Pêcheries et de l'Alimentation et le Groupe interuniversitaire de recherches océanographiques du Québec) ; elle sera inaugurée dans la gare fluviale de Rivière-du-Loup en mai 1989. Elle comprendra huit exhibits portant sur les principaux thèmes de recherche scientifique en cours dans l'estuaire ; le problème des contaminants et des effets de ces substances sur le béluga sera certainement incorporé à la thématique et ceci constitue un second geste concret visant à la conservation par le biais de la sensibilisation du public.

Après quatre mois d'été à Rivière-du-Loup, l'exposition deviendra itinérante et circulera dans le milieu scolaire (cegeps, polyvalentes) de la région estuarienne pendant tous les mois d'hiver.

Chasse et de la Pêche, la Fondation de la faune du Québec, la Société canadienne pour la conservation de la nature et la Société québécoise de protection des oiseaux.

Canadian Nature Federation

B. Theresa Aniskowicz
Coordinator of Conservation Programs

CANADIAN NATURE FEDERATION COMMITMENT AND HISTORY

The St. Lawrence beluga is one of the highest conservation priorities of the Canadian Nature Federation. We have addressed the issue to date through a combination of public awareness and advocacy.

Our involvement began in 1979 when we published an article by Leone Pippard in *Nature Canada* raising the alarm about the impending threat to the white whales. This was three years before the St. Lawrence beluga was classified as an endangered species by the Committee on the Status of Endangered Wildlife in Canada.

In 1987, we stepped up our involvement. The St. Lawrence beluga moved to the forefront of our public awareness activities. It was selected as one of four species to form part of our "Species in Danger" mini-poster series, published in 1987 in *Nature Canada*. This series was then combined into one poster that was circulated to thousands of school classrooms around the country through the "Operation Lifeline" program, in which we are a partner with World Wildlife Fund (Canada). The poster also was distributed to over 12 000 teachers when it was inserted into *Classroom* magazine.

During "National Wildlife Week" in 1988, the Canadian Nature Federation (CNF) had the opportunity to participate in a wildlife supplement to *Maclean's* magazine. We chose to supply a quarter-page colour photograph of the St. Lawrence beluga with a caption identifying the whales as one of Canada's most endangered species as part of our contribution. Just one month ago, we distributed by mail 85 000 informational brochures on the plight of the beluga.

This commitment to public awareness was furthered with the latest issue of *Nature Canada*, which has been distributed to all registrants at this conference. The St. Lawrence beluga and the pollution of the St. Lawrence River are given front-cover treatment, backed up by an excellent article by Pierre Béland.

Public awareness, by itself, is not enough. The activities that have just been described have been complemented every step of the way by our advocacy work. The CNF is a strong supporter of a protected habitat for the St. Lawrence beluga and has communicated that desire frequently to both the federal and provincial governments.

In late 1987, we joined forces with seven other national conservation organizations to present the Honourable Tom McMillan with common protected areas priorities. This informal caucus, organized by World Wildlife Fund (Canada), placed the Saguenay estuary near the top of its list and worked closely with the Minister's office on these issues.

While we are a national organization based in Ottawa, we have strong local contacts on this issue. Our involvement has at all times benefitted from the sound advice and cooperation of two of our directors, Benoît Gauthier (currently our Québec Vice-President) and CNF President-elect, Jacques Prescott. We have also benefitted from the excellent work of our Québec provincial affiliate, l'Union québécoise pour la conservation de la nature.

These introductory remarks serve to demonstrate the commitment of the Canadian Nature Federation to protection of the St. Lawrence beluga. We believe that such protection can be achieved by a combination of three things : a protected habitat, education and interpretation, and a crackdown on polluters.

PROTECTED HABITAT NECESSARY

While the Canadian Nature Federation strongly believes that a protected habitat for the beluga is necessary, it cannot be looked upon in isolation. The creation of a marine park should not be viewed as anything other than one component of a strategy to save the beluga. For a protected area to be viable, we feel that three things are necessary.

Firstly, the boundaries of a marine park should embrace all critical habitat of the species. This will require some flexibility in the boundaries to adapt to developments in our knowledge of the behaviour and distribution of the whales. Secondly, and following from this point, the establishment and management of such an area should be in harmony with other conservation initiatives and should be part of a comprehensive conservation strategy for the region.

Thirdly, the CNF feels that protected areas are not truly viable unless they are supported and respected by the citizens of the region in which they are located. For this reason, we have supported the involvement of the Haida people in the development and management of South Moresby National Park and of native peoples, in general, in the development and management of new parks in areas that fall within aboriginal homelands. This principle should not only apply to native peoples. In an area such as the Saguenay estuary, which has been settled and travelled for hundreds of years, the citizens of the region must be fully involved in the development and management of a protected area such as a marine park.

Therefore, we fully support the objectives of the Coalition for the Saguenay-St. Lawrence Marine Park. Further, we have recently urged the Honourable Tom McMillan and the Honourable Yvan Picotte to ensure that the public has full opportunity for input into the establishment of the park and the development of its master plan.

EDUCATION AND INTERPRETATION

Securing a protected habitat for the St. Lawrence beluga is only a first step in ensuring its survival as a species. In our opinion, another component of success is changing attitudes all along the St. Lawrence and Saguenay rivers. This requires that a high priority be assigned to public education and interpretation both locally and upstream.

The St. Lawrence beluga provides a case study of wildlife as an indicator of environmental health. That message should be aggressively communicated to all peoples who reside along the affected waterways and to all visitors to the region. The Société linéenne du Québec, and others, are doing excellent work with the resources available to them. These programs must be expanded.

While we are pleased to see the federal and provincial agreement, and associated funding, for the cleanup of the St. Lawrence River that has recently been announced, we are disappointed that there is little reference to education and interpretation and no funds are allocated for those purposes. We were shocked by the response received from the Prime Minister's Office when we communicated this concern. His staff advised us that education was a provincial responsibility and therefore should be addressed by the Government of Québec, displaying a complete lack of awareness of this issue!

At the local level, programs must be expanded and funded to educate citizens of the region as to how their actions directly impact upon the beluga and other wildlife species. For a park to be successful, it must be seen as more than an economic incentive. Residents, and tourists, must know why the wildlife is important to them. That message can only be communicated through continued and enhanced education and interpretation programs. Many similar programs have been highly successful. One of particular relevance is the work of Dr. Kathy Blanchard of the Québec Labrador Foundation in protecting seabird populations along the North Shore of the St. Lawrence River.

Of equal importance are educational and awareness programs targeted upstream on the two rivers. The problems faced by the belugas are comparable to the effects of acid rain. The polluters, whether they be corporations, municipalities, private citizens or whatever, must be identified at source and dealt with through a combination of education and enforcement. They must be shown how they are directly or indirectly contributing to a serious problem and urged to react by whatever means is most appropriate to the situation. Long-term success in this endeavour means more than pointing fingers and levying fines.

DEALING WITH POLLUTERS

The previous steps can only be effective if they are taken in the context of an overall restoration of the health of the St. Lawrence River. Cleaning up the river is only one component of a long-term solution to the problems faced by the beluga and other wildlife. Strong pressure should be brought to bear to eliminate pollution at source. Our enemy in this case is the burden of proof. Everyone agrees that the St. Lawrence is in bad shape yet no one is stepping up to accept the blame. This is unacceptable.

Industries, governments and individuals who are discharging pollutants into the environment must accept responsibility for their actions. Whether a direct cause and effect relationship can be established between a particular substance and a decline in belugas, or other wildlife, is irrelevant. If the commitment to sustainable development that is currently being voiced at all levels is real, then it follows that any substance considered toxic, or of unknown consequences, should not be discharged. That is the moral obligation of all agents who have the potential to directly or indirectly pollute our environment. A strong effort must be expended to ensure that the principles of sustainable development are being embraced and implemented all along the St. Lawrence and Saguenay rivers.

Of course, where polluters can be definitely shown to be having an adverse effect on the environment, retribution should be swift and harsh. Such industries, governments or individuals must be dealt with to the full extent of the law. As research produces more chemicals and tells us more about the effects of existing ones, we must be prepared to upgrade our laws rapidly to ensure the highest level of environmental protection. The state of the St. Lawrence today is proof that negotiation and persuasion with polluters is not effective unless it is backed up by a sincere commitment to enforcement. We must put our collective foot down and cease excusing or tolerating violations.

CONCLUSION

In summary, the Canadian Nature Federation believes that a strategy for the protection of the St. Lawrence beluga requires the following components:

a) creation of a protected habitat, such as a marine park, that is established and managed to be complementary with other protected areas and conservation initiatives in the region;

b) involvement of local citizens in the development of the marine park and its management plan;

c) expansion and funding of public awareness and interpretive programs aimed at the local population and tourists;

d) establishment and funding of public awareness and educational programs targeted upstream to increase sensitivity to the downstream consequences of actions and promote the concept of sustainable development;

e) acceleration of research into the sources, and effects, of pollutants in the St. Lawrence and Saguenay rivers; and

f) the dealing with individuals and organizations that wilfully contribute to the deterioration of the St. Lawrence and Saguenay rivers, and their associated flora and fauna, to the full extent of the law.

The St. Lawrence beluga is a bellwether for Canadian wildlife. We can find no better indicator of a wildlife species that acts as a "canary" to indicate the state of environmental health. We have ignored the beluga's message for far too long and, were it not for the efforts of a few conservationists dedicated to protecting the whale, might still be ignoring it today. We hope that society's awakening is not too late for the St. Lawrence beluga.

The Canadian Nature Federation is commited to working with governments, industry and the people of Québec to help ensure the survival of the St. Lawrence beluga. No matter what the outcome, this lesson must not be lost and wildlife species must cease to be sacrificed on the altar of our ignorance.

Fédération québécoise de la faune

Léo-Paul Quintal
Président

INTRODUCTION

La Fédération québécoise de la faune est heureuse de vous présenter sa position concernant le plan d'action interministériel pour favoriser la survie du béluga du Saint-Laurent. La Fédération québécoise de la faune représente environ 200 000 chasseurs et pêcheurs sportifs au Québec, regroupés dans 11 conseils régionaux et 250 associations locales. Les principaux buts de la Fédération québécoise de la faune sont de défendre la conservation de la faune et de ses habitats ainsi que les droits de l'ensemble des chasseurs et pêcheurs sportifs du Québec.

La Fédération québécoise de la faune est membre de la Fédération canadienne de la faune. Cette dernière, tout comme la Fédération québécoise de la faune, a adopté les grands principes de la Stratégie mondiale de conservation en adhérant à l'Union internationale pour la conservation de la nature (UICN). Nous tenons à vous rappeler les trois objectifs fondamentaux de cette Stratégie :

— maintenir les processus écologiques et les systèmes entretenant la vie ;
— préserver la diversité génétique ;
— veiller à l'utilisation durable des espèces et des écosystèmes.

La Fédération québécoise de la faune défend aussi le principe de la diversité faunique intégrale (DFI) des écosystèmes.

Le Québec est l'un des rares endroits au monde dont les eaux intérieures sont fréquentées régulièrement par les cétacés. Donc, il s'agit d'un joyau mondial du patrimoine faunique. Nous nous devons de protéger et de conserver cet habitat unique au monde.

L'aire de distribution des bélugas en Amérique du Nord est surtout concentrée dans les eaux froides de l'Arctique.

La population de bélugas du Saint-Laurent constitue la limite méridionale de l'aire de répartition de cette espèce. Le déclin de la population de bélugas avant le début des années 1970 est surtout relié à la surexploitation de cette espèce par une chasse commerciale abusive.

Il ne faudrait pas oublier que, durant cette même époque, les habitats essentiels du béluga ont diminué et furent fortement perturbés. La disparition du banc de bélugas de la région de l'estuaire de Manicouagan est un exemple de la perturbation des habitats essentiels de cette espèce. Le harnachement des rivières Bersimis, Manicouagan et des Outardes au profit d'Hydro-Québec a entraîné de graves modifications du régime hydrique et du bilan thermique de l'eau.

Actuellement, la survie du béluga est remise en question par une piètre qualité de l'eau due à une contamination par des substances toxiques et par des facteurs de dérangement directs ou indirects de cette espèce dans ses habitats essentiels.

Il est donc regrettable de constater que l'état de santé de la population de bélugas du Saint-Laurent nous montre des faits troublants révélés par des autopsies pratiquées sur les carcasses de bélugas échouées. Les scientifiques observent des lésions encore jamais rapportées chez les cétacés : cancer de la vessie, anévrisme disséquant de l'artère pulmonaire, fibrose de la rate, etc. Il est étonnant de constater que le cancer de la vessie découvert chez les carcasses de bélugas échouées s'avère le même que celui dont souffrent 77 travailleurs de l'usine Alcan, d'après les statistiques publiées par Greenpeace Québec.

Les chercheurs ont également découvert dans les tissus et le gras de ces mammifères marins des concentrations élevées de 15 types de contaminants organiques dont les HAP et de neuf différents métaux lourds.

Pour la Fédération québécoise de la faune, le béluga représente donc le symbole de la dégradation du Saint-Laurent, une ressource stratégique et vitale pour le Québec.

La Fédération québécoise de la faune tient à intervenir dans le cadre de ce Forum pour éviter que le béluga du Saint-Laurent vienne rejoindre la longue liste des espèces disparues au cours des dernières années.

CRITIQUE DU PLAN DE SURVIE DU BÉLUGA ET RECOMMANDATIONS DE LA FÉDÉRATION QUÉBÉCOISE DE LA FAUNE

Avant d'aborder plus précisément certains aspects spécifiques du plan de survie du béluga du Saint-Laurent, la Fédération québécoise de la faune tient à vous souligner certains constats généraux face à l'ensemble des actions élaborées dans le cadre de ce plan.

Tout d'abord, il s'agit du financement du plan de survie du béluga. La Fédération québécoise de la faune se pose la question suivante: combien le gouvernement fédéral est-il prêt à investir pour financer l'ensemble des actions comprises dans ce plan ? Lors de la signature, en juin dernier, de l'entente fédérale-provinciale sur la dépollution du Saint-Laurent, il a été annoncé que le gouvernement fédéral consacrerait 110 millions de dollars pour les cinq prochaines années dans ce dossier. Cette entente est composée de quatre grands volets dont celui de la conservation. Le gouvernement fédéral a prévu débourser un budget de 20 millions de dollars pour le secteur conservation. Ce volet « conservation » regroupe trois programmes:

1° Création d'un parc marin au confluent du Saguenay et du Saint-Laurent.

2° Création, protection et amélioration de réserves fauniques le long du Saint-Laurent.

3° Élaboration et mise en œuvre de plans de survie pour les espèces les plus menacées, en particulier le Béluga, le Faucon pèlerin, le Canard noir, la Sarcelle à ailes bleues, le Bar rayé et l'Esturgeon noir.

La Fédération québécoise de la faune s'interroge aussi sur la part du 20 millions de dollars qui sera allouée au plan de survie du béluga du Saint-Laurent. La Fédération québécoise de la faune doute que les sommes accordées au volet « conservation » dans le cadre de cette entente soient suffisantes, non seulement pour le plan de survie du béluga mais aussi pour la création du parc marin et les autres actions prévues.

D'autre part, la Fédération québécoise de la faune aurait aimé que le plan de survie contienne aussi une évaluation budgétaire, c'est-à-dire la répartition des sommes d'argent accordées aux différentes catégories d'action (exemple : accroissement de la connaissance, contrôle du dérangement, contrôle des substances toxiques, etc.). Cela aurait permis aux différents intervenants dans le cadre de ce Forum international de connaître les véritables intentions du gouvernement fédéral et d'amener certaines précisions sur les priorités accordées par celui-ci à différents aspects du plan de survie.

Enfin, le plan de survie du béluga demeure silencieux au niveau de la collaboration entre le fédéral et le gouvernement du Québec quant à l'application de certains aspects. La Fédération québécoise de la faune est consciente que certaines actions prévues dans ce plan interministériel ont fait l'objet de négociations entre le fédéral et le provincial lorsqu'il y a eu l'entente sur la dépollution du Saint-Laurent. On pense, entre autres, à la création du parc marin et à la dépollution industrielle. Cependant, pour la coordination des activités de recherche sur le béluga et l'implantation de certains moyens au niveau législatif, on connaît très peu les intentions des deux paliers de gouvernement et leur niveau de collaboration à ce sujet.

SECTION 1

Aspects légaux du plan de survie du béluga

La Fédération québécoise de la faune considère que les aspects légaux contenus dans le plan de survie du béluga sont nettement insuffisants. Est-ce que cela dénote le manque de volonté du Gouvernement d'agir fermement dans ce dossier ? Le document fait mention uniquement de la loi canadienne sur la protection de l'environnement ainsi que la possibilité d'y inscrire certains produits toxiques dont les HAP dans la liste des substances à être réglementées. Il faut indiquer que dans l'annexe 1 de la loi canadienne sur la protection de l'environnement, on retrouve déjà les BPC et le Mirex qui sont toutes les deux interdites dans le commerce, la fabrication et le traitement. La Fédération québécoise de la faune se demande combien de temps sera nécessaire pour inscrire les produits toxiques visés dans la liste des substances à réglementer. La Fédération québécoise de la faune souligne aussi que cette procédure peut ouvrir la voie à de formidables batailles d'experts. On n'a qu'à penser à l'actuel débat sur l'impact des HAP provenant des alumineries sur la santé des bélugas. Donc, cela peut prendre plusieurs années avant que le Gouvernement décide de réglementer ces substances et il sera peut-être trop tard pour sauver la population de bélugas du Saint-Laurent.

Pour la Fédération québécoise de la faune, le béluga représente le symbole de la dégradation et de la pollution du Saint-Laurent. Nous sommes convaincus que le béluga représente probablement la pointe de l'iceberg de la contamination des différentes chaînes alimentaires dans le fleuve. Nous proposons donc l'application intégrale de l'article 33 de la loi fédérale sur les pêcheries donnant aux divers paliers de gouvernement les pouvoirs pour procéder à des actions en justice obligeant les industries polluant l'habitat des poissons et, par le fait même, celui des bélugas, de cesser leurs activités polluantes.

Selon les experts en droit de l'environnement, la loi fédérale sur les pêcheries constitue la pièce maîtresse de la législation fédérale en matière de contrôle de la pollution des eaux.

D'autre part, nous constatons, jusqu'à présent, que les deux paliers de gouvernement ont mis en place une stratégie de dépollution industrielle basée sur une négociation avec l'industrie. Nous nous interrogeons sur cette façon de procéder.

Cette stratégie fut maintes fois dénoncée par des groupes environnementaux dont la Fédération québécoise de la faune. Ces organismes se sont toujours interrogés sur la façon dont le Gouvernement peut espérer négocier la réduction d'émission de polluants dans les cours d'eau en mettant de côté les outils légaux et législatifs. Dans un essai sur l'élaboration des politiques en matière d'environnement (Commission de réforme du droit 1984), T. Schrecker stipule que la réglementation en matière d'environnement résulte souvent de négociations entre le Gouvernement et les industries responsables de la pollution. Les préoccupations économiques de ces dernières dominent les aspects de protection de la santé humaine et de l'environnement. Aujourd'hui, nous sommes devant les faits accomplis et nous constatons l'échec de cette stratégie. Il est encore temps d'agir et l'application de l'article 33 de la loi fédérale sur les pêcheries demeure un outil privilégié.

L'intervention du gouvernement fédéral dans ce cadre pourrait forcer le gouvernement du Québec à agir plus rapidement surtout au niveau de sa réglementation sur les normes de rejet des polluants toxiques. Dans son programme de réduction des rejets industriels, le ministère de l'Environnement du Québec prévoit l'insertion dans les règlements concernés des normes de rejet pour les polluants toxiques, à partir de 1992. La Fédération québécoise de la faune trouve ce délai trop long, en particulier pour les HAP qui contaminent les bélugas et souhaite que le Gouvernement procède plus rapidement. Il faut indiquer ici qu'actuellement seulement trois secteurs spécifiques de l'industrie sont encadrés légalement par le Ministère au niveau du contrôle des effluents industriels. Il s'agit des usines de pâtes et papiers, des raffineries de pétrole et des usines de béton bitumineux.

Il est important que le ministère de l'Environnement du Québec réglemente de nouveaux secteurs industriels. La priorité devrait être accordée aux secteurs industriels qui, par leurs rejets, menacent en particulier la population de bélugas du Saint-Laurent. La Fédération québécoise de la faune pense, entre autres, au secteur de l'aluminerie.

En avril 1983, le Comité sur les espèces fauniques menacées d'extinction au Canada (CSEFMEC — COSEWIC) a décidé de donner le statut de population menacée à la population de bélugas vivant dans le Saint-Laurent. La Fédération québécoise de la faune tient à préciser que le ministère de l'Environnement du Canada aurait pu intervenir en utilisant l'article 9 de la loi de la mise en valeur et de la conservation de la faune. Cet article permet au Ministre de prendre toutes les mesures qu'il juge nécessaires pour protéger toutes espèces d'animaux sauvages menacées d'extinction. La Fédération québécoise de la faune considère que le Ministre peut se prévaloir de ce pouvoir discrétionnaire. La Fédération québécoise de la faune reconnaît aussi que la typologie utilisée dans le cadre de cette Loi pour les espèces menacées d'extinction ne correspond pas à celle utilisée par le COSEWIC. Malgré cela, le Ministre aurait pu tout de même intervenir pour amener des correctifs permettant la protection des bélugas du Saint-Laurent. Le plan de survie ignore complètement la loi de la mise en valeur et de la conservation de la faune et plus particulièrement cet article.

La Fédération québécoise de la faune souhaite que les ministères de l'Environnement du Canada et des Pêches et des Océans du Canada examinent soigneusement la possibilité d'utiliser ou de modifier la loi de la mise en valeur et de la conservation de la faune afin d'avoir en main un outil légal permettant de sauver des espèces menacées telles que le béluga. Toutefois, cette étude devra tenir compte des législations provinciales actuelles ou futures (exemple : Québec) dans ce domaine.

Rappelons-nous qu'en 1983, le groupe de travail pour la protection des habitats a remis un volumineux rapport qui révélait qu'aucune loi ni règlement n'ont été adoptés au Québec avec l'intention spécifique de protéger les habitats fauniques. Le rapport Sarrazin avait déjà identifié une liste de buts à atteindre dans le cadre d'une politique sur la protection des habitats fauniques. Un des items les plus pertinents était d'éviter aux espèces animales d'être un jour mises en danger au Québec à cause d'une détérioration de leur habitat.

D'autre part, la loi 15 adoptée dernièrement par le gouvernement du Québec modifie la loi de la mise en valeur et de la conservation de la faune, en ajoutant un chapitre concernant la protection des habitats fauniques.

Cette modification permet au ministère du Loisir, de la Chasse et de la Pêche du Québec d'effectuer des inventaires et de cartographier les habitats fauniques essentiels d'un certain nombre d'espèces. La Fédération québécoise de la faune croit qu'il serait très pertinent que les ministères de l'Environnement du Canada et des Pêches et des Océans du Canada collaborent étroitement avec le ministre du Loisir, de la Chasse et de la Pêche du Québec dans le cadre d'un projet de recherche et de cartographie permettant d'identifier les habitats essentiels du béluga du Saint-Laurent. Étant donné que ce mandat existe déjà au niveau de la loi québécoise sur la mise en valeur et de la conservation de la faune et que déjà, dans les actions à moyen ou long termes concernant l'acquisition de connaissances, il est prévu dans le plan de survie un tel programme de recherche, la Fédération québécoise de la faune n'entrevoit pas de problèmes pour appliquer cette proposition.

Enfin, la Fédération québécoise de la faune espère que la future loi québécoise sur les espèces menacées présentée conjointement par le ministère de l'Environnement du Québec et le ministère du Loisir, de la Chasse et de la Pêche du Québec aura des dents, empêchant la destruction d'habitats essentiels d'espèces menacées d'extinction et (ou) leur surexploitation. La Fédération québécoise de la faune considère que cette loi devrait prévoir des mesures préventives afin de ne pas attendre qu'une espèce vivante possède le statut d'espèce en danger d'extinction avant d'agir.

La Fédération québécoise de la faune souhaite qu'après l'adoption de cette loi, le gouvernement du Québec procède rapidement pour amener une réglementation spécifique concernant les habitats essentiels du béluga afin de les protéger contre : les opérations de dragage qui pourraient avoir un potentiel de dérangement élevé sur les bélugas du Saint-Laurent, le passage de câbles sous-marins à des fins de transport d'électricité, la construction de barrages hydroélectriques ayant un impact sur la productivité primaire des estuaires, etc.

La Fédération québécoise de la faune propose également que cette loi donne le pouvoir à des citoyens et à des regroupements d'intervenir devant les tribunaux pour obtenir des injonctions afin d'empêcher la destruction d'habitats essentiels d'espèces menacées d'extinction. La Fédération québécoise de la faune exige aussi que les sanctions et amendes soient très sévères contre les infractions aux règlements et dispositions de la loi.

SECTION 2

Dépollution industrielle

Dix ans après la publication du rapport final du Comité d'étude sur le Saint-Laurent, ce dernier conserve encore la réputation d'être le cours d'eau le plus pollué en Amérique du Nord. Pourtant, le Comité d'étude sur le Saint-Laurent avait localisé les principales zones détériorées par les substances toxiques, pour le couloir fluvial situé entre Cornwall et Montmagny. Ce vaste territoire englobe le lac des Deux Montagnes, les rivières des Prairies et des Mille Îles. Les travaux du Comité avaient permis d'établir les priorités d'action basées principalement sur l'importance des sources de contamination. Le Comité d'étude sur le Saint-Laurent avait également déterminé les moyens légaux applicables aux interventions sur ces sources de contamination. Leur recommandation d'adopter des mesures pour limiter les rejets industriels dans le fleuve (mesures devant être conçues en fonction de la meilleure technologie pratique en tenant compte des exigences de l'environnement) fut complètement oubliée et laissée sur les tablettes par les deux paliers de gouvernement. Bien sûr, certaines industries le long du Saint-Laurent ont mis sur pied des programmes de dépollution. Il s'agit d'une infime minorité face à la majorité de pollueurs industriels.

Ces dernières années, le rapport « Le Saint-Laurent, ressource nationale prioritaire » (juin 1985), soulignait que parmi tous les problèmes de pollution du Saint-Laurent, celui des substances toxiques ou dangereuses demeure le plus critique. Malgré tous ces avertissements et ces recommandations, le Saint-Laurent continue à être un égout à ciel ouvert.

L'annonce de l'entente fédérale-provinciale sur la dépollution du Saint-Laurent nous réjouit puisqu'on consacrera un budget de 14 millions de dollars pour la protection des eaux du fleuve et un budget de 55 millions de dollars pour la recherche dans le domaine des technologies environnementales s'appliquant à des problèmes de pollution industrielle particuliers au fleuve. Ceci nous laisse entrevoir un avenir meilleur pour cette ressource stratégique et vitale pour le Québec.

La mise en place d'un nouveau programme de réduction des rejets industriels par le ministère de l'Environnement du Québec qui intègre dans ses priorités la dépollution du Saint-Laurent nous permet encore une fois de nous réjouir. Souvenons-nous que plus de la moitié des usines visées par ce programme déversent leurs effluents dans le Saint-Laurent ou un bon nombre les rejettent dans ses tributaires.

En ce qui a trait au plan de survie du béluga, il reprend les grandes lignes de l'entente fédérale-provinciale sur la dépollution du Saint-Laurent. Cependant, la Fédération québécoise de la faune tient à indiquer que les deux paliers de gouvernement ne devraient pas oublier de se servir de certains moyens légaux ou de légiférer lorsqu'ils rencontreront la moindre résistance des industries polluantes. De plus, la Fédération québécoise de la faune précise qu'elle étudie actuellement la possibilité d'intervenir par différents moyens, et en particulier par des actions légales, pour obliger certaines industries à réduire leurs rejets de polluants dans le Saint-Laurent. Dans la section précédente, la Fédération québécoise de la faune demandait également au ministère de l'Environnement du Québec de procéder le plus rapidement possible à la réglementation de certaines substances toxiques qui contaminent les tissus des bélugas.

La Fédération québécoise de la faune siège actuellement au sein du groupe directeur pour le projet de mise en valeur du Saint-Laurent et fera la recommandation suivante : « que le Gouvernement mette en place une planification à long terme du développement futur d'industries situées le long de l'axe du Saint-Laurent et de ses principaux tributaires ».

Cette planification s'avère essentielle si l'on veut éviter de se retrouver avec certains types d'industries qui ne répondraient pas aux exigences d'une utilisation durable de cette ressource et d'éviter certains conflits d'utilisation.

SECTION 3

Contrôle du dérangement

En ce qui concerne le contrôle du dérangement, la Fédération québécoise de la faune est d'accord avec la plupart des propositions présentées dans le plan de survie du béluga. Cependant, la Fédération québécoise de la faune aimerait apporter certaines modifications mineures et de nouvelles propositions. Le plan de survie suggère, au niveau des actions à moyen et à long termes, d'accroître la surveillance dans certaines aires fréquentées par les bélugas. La Fédération québécoise de la faune propose que l'accroissement de la surveillance dans certaines aires fréquentées soient déjà appliquées dans le cadre des actions à court terme. Étant donné l'augmentation de la navigation de plaisance dans ce secteur, la Fédération québécoise de la faune trouve important que des mesures de surveillance additionnelles soient prises dès la première année de la mise en application du plan de survie.

La Fédération québécoise de la faune considère important de maintenir les activités d'observation des baleines, car elles permettent d'éduquer la population du Québec et les touristes étrangers à la précarité et aux problèmes de survie de ces mammifères marins. D'un autre côté, au niveau des excursions touristiques pour l'observation des baleines, la Fédération estime important de continuer la préparation des plans annuels de conservation des bélugas et des cétacés en collaboration avec les organismes et regroupements du milieu. Les résultats sont très encourageants et démontrent le respect de ce code d'éthique par les responsables de ces activités touristiques. Néanmoins, la Fédération québécoise de la faune propose que le ministère des Pêches et des Océans du Canada étudie la possibilité d'implanter un moratoire pour toute nouvelle entreprise d'excursion d'observation de baleines. La Fédération québécoise de la faune est inquiète de voir que certains organismes voudraient développer des excursions d'observation de baleines dans le secteur de Rivière-du-Loup.

Il s'agit d'une expansion qui peut amener une prolifération de nouvelles entreprises de ce genre dans différents secteurs et peut provoquer le dérangement des bélugas dans ses habitats essentiels auxquels on observait auparavant peu de dérangement.

L'émission de permis pour l'observation des baleines est intéressante mais la proposition de la Fédération québécoise de la faune vise à étudier la possibilité d'émettre un nombre limité de permis afin de contrôler parfaitement le dérangement par ce type d'activités. D'ailleurs, le rapport « Le Saint-Laurent, ressource nationale prioritaire » s'interrogeait sur les conséquences de la popularité croissante de ce genre d'excursions, il recommandait un certain contrôle de ces activités.

En ce qui a trait à la navigation de plaisance, la Fédération québécoise de la faune formule le même genre de recommandations. La Fédération québécoise de la faune propose au ministère des Pêches et des Océans du Canada d'étudier la possibilité d'implanter un moratoire pour la construction ou l'agrandissement de marinas pour la navigation de plaisance à proximité et à l'intérieur des zones protégées (habitats essentiels) pour le béluga. La Fédération québécoise de la faune sait pertinemment que les activités de navigation de plaisance sont un facteur non négligeable de dérangement des cétacés et des bélugas.

Les membres de la Fédération québécoise de la faune ont accueilli avec joie l'annonce de la création d'un parc marin au confluent du Saguenay qui permettra d'assurer une aire protégée où la surveillance de ce mammifère sera plus intensive. La Fédération québécoise de la faune a appuyé publiquement tous les groupements et associations qui préconisent de protéger cet environnement marin dans le cadre des compétences constitutionnelles respectives de chaque palier de gouvernement. La Fédération québécoise de la faune souhaite fortement que les responsables de la création du parc marin développent plusieurs attraits touristiques à l'intérieur de ce parc tout en respectant les objectifs de conservation de la nature.

Nul doute que la création du parc marin protégera une partie des habitats essentiels du béluga. Pour les autres zones à protéger, la Fédération québécoise de la faune réitère sa proposition (formulée dans la section 1 de cette partie) concernant la délimitation de ces habitats essentiels et de leur intégration au niveau de la réglementation de la loi sur la mise en valeur et de la conservation de la faune.

SECTION 4

Programmme de recherche et d'éducation

Le plan de survie du béluga du Saint-Laurent nous présente un programme de recherche fort élaboré et composé de nombreux projets. Malheureusement, on ne nous fournit pas une première évaluation des coûts de ces recherches. Cela nous aurait permis d'avoir une idée de l'importance qu'on accorde à certains projets.

La Fédération québécoise de la faune considère que la plupart de ces recherches répondent à un besoin pressant d'acquisition de nouvelles connaissances nous permettant de mieux cerner la problématique de la survie des bélugas du Saint-Laurent. Cependant, ces recherches ne doivent pas nuire à la mise en place d'actions permettant déjà d'améliorer l'habitat et, en particulier, la qualité de l'eau du Saint-Laurent. La Fédération québécoise de la faune désire vous faire remarquer que l'élaboration de programmes de recherche dans certains dossiers conduit malheureusement à justifier l'inaction des gouvernements et des industries polluantes (exemple : cas des pluies acides entre le Canada et les États-Unis). La majorité des projets de recherche présentés dans le plan de survie répondent à nos objectifs, mais il y a une exception où la Fédération québécoise de la faune tient à manifester son profond désaccord. Il s'agit d'une étude portant sur l'examen de la possibilité scientifique de renforcer la population de bélugas par l'introduction d'individus de l'Arctique. La Fédération québécoise de la faune trouve inacceptable que cette proposition soit intégrée dans les actions à court terme avant même d'attendre les résultats de l'évaluation des caractères génétiques de cette population. Cette dernière recherche nous permettrait de répondre à la question suivante : Est-ce que la population de bélugas du Saint-Laurent possède un code génétique différent de celui de l'Arctique (détermination d'une sous-espèce) ?

Si cette hypothèse était vérifiée scientifiquement, nous pouvons conclure que le remplacement de la population de bélugas du Saint-Laurent par des individus de l'Arctique irait à l'encontre du deuxième principe de la Stratégie mondiale de conservation. Ce principe expose l'importance de préserver la diversité génétique des espèces vivantes. Nous croyons que cette restauration de la population de bélugas ne peut être utilisée qu'en dernier recours. Avant d'établir des bélugas de l'Arctique dans le fleuve, il faut également que nous possédions des garanties au niveau de la qualité de l'eau pour ne pas leur faire subir le même stress qu'à la population précédente.

D'autre part, la Fédération québécoise de la faune souhaite fortement que le programme de recherche développé dans le plan de survie profite non seulement aux différents ministères et institutions universitaires mais aussi à des organismes (exemple : Kétos) et des chercheurs indépendants.

La Fédération québécoise de la faune profite de l'occasion pour rendre hommage à madame Leone Pippard qui fut la première à sensibiliser la population québécoise à la survie des bélugas. Elle a initié de nombreuses activités d'éducation et des recherches importantes qui sont reconnues dans le milieu scientifique canadien.

Le volet « éducation » du plan de survie s'avère le parent pauvre. Pourtant, il pourrait se concevoir de nombreux projets qui soutiendraient les activités des groupes à but non lucratif voués à la conservation des cétacés et des bélugas. La Fédération québécoise de la faune déplore cet oubli important et propose que les deux ministères fédéraux réévaluent la possibilité d'implanter un programme d'éducation particulier à la problématique du béluga et des cétacés, auprès de l'ensemble de la population québécoise. Ce programme pourrait être fait en collaboration avec le ministère du Loisir, de la Chasse et de la Pêche. Le volet « éducation » ne comprend que l'intention des deux ministères de publier certains documents d'information et de sensibiliser les amateurs de navigation de plaisance.

PARTICIPATION DE LA FÉDÉRATION QUÉBÉCOISE DE LA FAUNE AU PLAN DE SURVIE DU BÉLUGA

La Fédération québécoise de la faune continuera à suivre l'évolution du dossier de la survie du béluga du Saint-Laurent par le biais de la revue *Faune Québec*, revue officielle de la Fédération québécoise de la faune consacrée principalement à la conservation de la faune et de ses habitats. La création du parc marin fera aussi l'objet de certains articles à l'intérieur de la revue. Par le programme d'éducation en sécurité et en conservation de la faune (PESCOF), la Fédération québécoise de la faune, conjointement avec le ministère du Loisir, de la Chasse et de la Pêche, participe à l'élaboration de la Semaine de la conservation de la faune. Le thème de la dernière semaine de la conservation fut celui des espèces menacées au Québec. Une brochure et différents dépliants furent distribués dans le milieu scolaire québécois.

Depuis environ un an, la Fédération québécoise de la faune a mis en opération la Fondation héritage faune. La Fondation héritage faune possède, entre autres, les buts et les objectifs suivants :

- Promouvoir, susciter et soutenir tous les projets d'aménagements fauniques, aquatiques ou terrestres ;
- Promouvoir, susciter et soutenir des études et recherches, programmes d'éducation publique portant sur l'amélioration de l'environnement et l'assainissement des eaux ;
- Offrir des bourses d'études et de recherches à des étudiants et chercheurs au niveau universitaire dont les travaux se rapportent à la faune ;
- Encourager et soutenir des recherches pour l'amélioration des cheptels de la faune terrestre et aquatique.

Le directeur de la Fondation héritage faune et actuel président de la Fédération québécoise de la faune, M. Léo-Paul Quintal, vous annonce son intention de demander au Conseil d'administration de la Fondation d'étudier la possibilité de financer un projet de recherche sur le béluga dès l'année prochaine.

World Wildlife Fund

Arlin Hackman

Thank you for inviting World Wildlife Fund (WWF) to participate in the Forum. I am pleased to be here for several reasons. First, we believe this Forum is an important step in developing a plan of action to ensure the survival of the beluga. Such a plan should also improve future prospects for other life forms in the St. Lawrence River basin, ourselves included. Second, WWF believes the many complex challenges we face in restoring health to the beluga and its habitat require that all organizations represented here today, though differing in responsibility and resources, must work together in making the survival plan work. Third, we support the proposed marine park as a major element of the survival plan and the park needs a push from this meeting.

WWF Canada is a branch of the world's largest private conservation organization. Based in Switzerland with offices in 23 countries, our international network has raised over $ 200 million for 5 000 projects in 130 countries. Funding priorities are based on the expert scientific advice of our sister organization, the International Union for the Conservation of Nature and Natural Resources (IUCN).

Founded twenty years ago in Montreal, WWF Canada has funded roughly $ 1 million worth of projects in Quebec, including the Pointe-Noire project of the Société linnéenne and the acquisition of Île aux Lièvres by Société Duvetnor ltée. Yesterday we announced our support for the work of Dr. Pierre Béland. Our involvement with the St. Lawrence River belugas stretches back over ten years to the early field studies conducted by Leone Pippard. Since then we have supported a local workshop on the marine park proposal and worked with the Coalition parc marin Saint-Laurent-Saguenay to ensure that regional concerns are addressed in government plans for the park.

WWF believes further research is needed to understand and resolve the many problems facing the beluga. We also believe it is essential to take whatever action we can right now. The most important such step is the establishment of the marine park.

In itself, the park will not clean up the Saguenay or the St. Lawrence rivers. It will not prevent all future disturbance of the marine habitat. What it can do, with your involvement and support, is this:

a) provide a measure of habitat protection from physical disturbance;
b) establish long-term environmental goals for the marine environment and set up monitoring programs to measure the success or failure of other elements of the beluga strategy in achieving these objectives;
c) link together other conservation programs already existing along the Saguenay and St. Lawrence Rivers, so that we move toward an overall conservation plan for the region. These include the Parc Saguenay, national and private wildlife reserves in the St. Lawrence River islands as well as the proposed biosphere reserve at Île aux Coudres;
d) stimulate regional development that is compatible with the conservation goals of these programs, so that local communities have a direct economic interest in ensuring that the wildlife and marine environment of the region are protected.

Most important of all, a marine park will set public expectations about the survival of the beluga and the quality of the marine environment. These expectations will be a powerful incentive for all agencies to meet their responsibilities for implementing the rest of the beluga survival plan, especially pollution control.

In the past two days we have all become more aware than ever about the technical complexity of responding to the environmental challenge represented by the beluga. There will be endless possibilities and excuses for inaction. In my view, the marine park is the single most important tool for focusing public concern to ensure that procrastination does not become the main element of the beluga strategy.

Over the past several years, the marine park has gained broad support within and outside the region. The most important sign of this support has been the formation of the Coalition parc marin Saint-Laurent-Saguenay. Based on this support, the federal and provincial ministers formally agreed to discuss the creation of a marine park as one element of the St. Lawrence Plan announced by the Prime Minister on June 3, 1988 in Montreal.

So what is the problem ? Quite simply, the negotiations have turned into a classic struggle for control between various federal and provincial agencies. Since the debate is going on behind closed doors, it is difficult to know what arguments and positions are being put forward or rejected. So it is difficult to know what it will take to break the deadlock. What we can say, and must forcefully respond to, is that with every passing day both governments are failing to serve the mandate they have received from the public to establish a marine park. After all, if we can't achieve resolution of this issue, with all the positive attractions it holds, what are the prospects for other tougher decisions we will need to make on behalf of the beluga?

I believe the first message we should transmit to the outside world from this discussion today is that we are all united in our support for establishment of a marine park through federal-provincial cooperation as a key element of the beluga survival strategy. WWF is therefore pleased to support the proposed communiqué to the Prime Minister of Canada and the Premier of Quebec which has been circulated this morning.

The Canada Environment Minister, Tom McMillan, indicated his willingness to take a new cooperative approach in establishing the marine park when he spoke at the June 3, 1988 St. Lawrence Plan ceremony in Montreal. The agreement he signed last week to establish Grasslands National Park in Saskatchewan contains provisions which show that he is serious about this.

Yesterday Québec Environment Minister, Clifford Lincoln, encouraged everyone to avoid squabbling over administrative details and to focus instead on partnership in meeting the conservation challenge of the park.

Let's help them get on with the job.

Fédération canadienne de la faune

Louis Lemieux
Président

La Fédération canadienne de la faune (FCF) est un organisme national sans but lucratif voué à la conservation et à l'utilisation avisée de la faune, de la flore et des ressources naturelles du Canada. Créée en 1961, la FCF est aujourd'hui le plus important organisme voué à la conservation avec 500 000 membres et supporteurs. Un organisme voué à la conservation des ressources naturelles de chaque province et territoire est également affilié à la FCF.

La FCF s'occupe des problèmes portant sur les espèces et les habitats menacés d'extinction depuis plusieurs années. La première liste officielle des espèces canadiennes menacées d'extinction, que nous avons publiée en 1976, a entamé les démarches pour la création ultérieure du Comité sur le statut des espèces fauniques menacées d'extinction au Canada, en 1978. Nous sommes toujours un membre actif de ce comité. La FCF a parrainé à elle seule le rapport de Peter Pearse publié récemment et intitulé *Relever le défi*, qui recommande la création d'une nouvelle politique pour la pêche en eau douce au Canada. Nous avons également participé activement à un large éventail de questions portant sur les parcs nationaux et de prises de décision, notamment le soutien que nous avons apporté récemment à la création d'un parc national à South Moresby, Colombie-Britannique, et la présentation de commentaires au comité législatif étudiant le projet de loi C-30, concernant la Loi sur les parcs nationaux.

INTRODUCTION

La FCF se préoccupe sérieusement de la situation précaire de la population de bélugas du Saint- Laurent et de la condition générale de ce fleuve. Comme suite à plusieurs années de surexploitation et, plus récemment, à la destruction de son habitat causée par la pollution, le béluga du Saint-Laurent est presque devenu une espèce déracinée. Le béluga retient l'attention de beaucoup de Canadiens, car sa lente disparition symbolise la mort du fleuve lui-même.

Dans le cadre de cette présentation, la FCF fait plusieurs recommandations pour accroître les chances de survie du béluga du Saint-Laurent. Nous nous concentrons sur la nécessité d'utiliser les lois fédérales et provinciales pour interdire les déversements de déchets toxiques dans le fleuve, et pour créer des règlements de lutte contre la pollution, pour toutes les entreprises polluantes. Nous recommandons également au gouvernement fédéral de faire des recherches pour l'élaboration de nouvelles techniques de destruction des déchets toxiques actuels, ou d'appuyer ce genre de recherches, dans le but de reconstituer l'habitat du béluga. Enfin, nous appuyons la création d'un parc marin national et nous recommandons une réglementation de la circulation maritime, afin de protéger l'habitat fragile du béluga. Nous croyons fermement que seule la mise en œuvre de ces recommandations permettra au béluga de survivre dans le Saint-Laurent.

1. LUTTE CONTRE LA POLLUTION

Le gouvernement fédéral a dévoilé récemment un plan de 110 millions de dollars pour le nettoyage du Saint-Laurent. Dans le cadre de ce plan, on prévoit l'identification des industries polluant le Saint-Laurent et l'évaluation des déchets produits par chaque industrie. On prévoit également la recherche de nouvelles techniques de lutte contre la pollution.

La FCF appuie ce genre de recherches, mais sait bien que plusieurs importants pollueurs du Saint-Laurent et du Saguenay ont déjà été identifés. Nous croyons qu'on doit immédiatement venir à bout des sources de pollution identifiées, en utilisant les règlements en vigueur qui découlent de la loi fédérale sur les pêcheries et de la loi québécoise sur la qualité de l'environnement.

L'article de la loi fédérale sur les pêcheries stipule qu' « il est interdit d'exploiter des ouvrages ou entreprises diminuant ou faisant disparaître les qualités biologiques de l'habitat des poissons ou rompant son équilibre d'une manière préjudiciable ». Par ailleurs, l'article 31 stipule qu' « il est interdit à qui que ce soit de déposer ou de permettre que l'on dépose une substance nocive dans les eaux ».

De façon similaire, l'article 20 de la nouvelle loi québécoise sur la qualité de l'environnement limite l'émission, le dépôt, le rejet ou le déversement dans l'environnement de contaminants ayant des effets nocifs sur la santé des humains et sur la bonne condition des ressources naturelles. L'article 25 de la même loi autorise les hauts fonctionnaires à ordonner aux responsables d'activités polluantes de cesser ou de limiter ces activités.

La FCF croit que cette loi doit être utilisée afin de réduire considérablement la pollution du Saint-Laurent. Une loi inutilisée ne sert à rien.

> La FCF recommande que les règlements actuels découlant de la loi fédérale sur les pêcheries et de la loi québécoise sur la qualité de l'environnement soient mis en application afin de limiter et de réduire la pollution du bassin fluvial du Saint-Laurent. Plus précisément, la FCF recommande que les gouvernements s'assurent que soient éliminés la pollution organochlorée provenant des sources ponctuelles, et l'écoulement d'hydrocarbures polyaromatiques dans le Saint-Laurent, d'ici 1993. Afin d'atteindre ces objectifs, la FCF recommande également que les gouvernements accroissent les dépenses consacrées à la mise en vigueur de la réglementation actuelle de lutte contre la pollution.

La FCF sait également qu'il existe des règlements découlant de la loi fédérale sur les pêcheries, d'après lesquels sont établies des normes de lutte contre la pollution pour les industries minière et papetière, pour les raffineries de pétrole et pour les déversements de mercure. Les plus récents rapports de conformité préparés par ces industries et présentés au gouvernement fédéral indiquent que, dans plusieurs cas, on ne satisfait pas aux normes établies. La FCF croit que ces industries doivent immédiatement se conformer à ces normes, en installant des systèmes de lutte contre la pollution ou en améliorant les systèmes actuels.

> La FCF croit que les industries, réglementées par les normes actuelles de lutte contre la pollution en vertu de la loi fédérale sur les pêcheries, qui ne se conforment pas aux normes en vigueur, devraient payer des amendes d'une valeur égale à l'installation de systèmes de lutte contre la pollution.

La FCF croit également qu'on doit accroître le nombre de règlements de lutte contre la pollution, afin d'englober toutes les industries et toute autre source ponctuelle et non ponctuelle de pollution. Ces règlements devraient faire partie de la loi fédérale sur les pêcheries ou de la loi canadienne sur la protection de l'environnement, au niveau fédéral, et de la loi québécoise sur la qualité de l'environnement, au niveau provincial. Les règlements devraient entrer en vigueur d'ici cinq ans et les budgets devraient être accrus pour une mise en application adéquate de ces règlements.

La FCF recommande la création, d'ici 1993, de nouveaux règlements pour le contrôle absolu des polluants des cours d'eau et des nappes d'eau. Les règlements devraient faire partie de la loi sur les pêcheries ou de la loi canadienne sur la protection de l'environnement, au niveau fédéral, et de la loi québécoise sur la qualité de l'environnement, au niveau provincial. Les gouvernements doivent accroître leur budget pour assurer la mise en vigueur de ces futurs règlements.

La pollution du Saint-Laurent n'est pas le seul résultat de déversements directs de déchets industriels dans ce fleuve, et la FCF approuve les recherches fédérales prévues pour localiser davantage des sources de pollution en amont. Il est très probable qu'une partie de la contamination provient de sources polluantes qui se déversent dans le Saint-Laurent par les Grands Lacs. Il faut donc imposer des normes de lutte contre la pollution à toutes les industries situées le long des Grands Lacs, semblables à celles imposées aux industries situées le long du Saint-Laurent.

D'ailleurs, des négociations doivent avoir lieu avec les États-Unis pour s'assurer que les industries polluantes situées aux États-Unis le long du Saint-Laurent et des Grands Lacs soient régies par les mêmes règlements que les industries situées au Canada.

La FCF recommande que le gouvernement fédéral amorce des négociations avec la province de l'Ontario et le gouvernement des États-Unis, pour s'assurer que des règlements de lutte contre la pollution soient préparés et mis en vigueur pour toutes les industries polluantes le long des Grands Lacs et du Saint-Laurent.

2. PROTECTION DE L'HABITAT DU BÉLUGA

2.1 Destruction des déchets toxiques

Afin de reconstituer l'habitat du béluga du Saint-Laurent, il faut que les gouvernements élaborent de nouvelles techniques de destruction des déchets toxiques qu'on trouve dans le Saint-Laurent et le Saguenay. À l'heure actuelle, la communauté scientifique canadienne connaît mal le traitement efficace des contaminants toxiques qui polluent nos lacs et nos rivières.

Des plans récents du ministère de l'Environnement du Canada prévoient l'entreposage de contaminants toxiques provenant du canal Lachine, dans des contenants de plastique situés en bordure du canal. Ce plan, nommé le « nettoyage » du canal Lachine, n'est en réalité qu'un projet qui retarde la solution réelle du problème, et qui le transmet aux futures générations. Il faut élaborer des techniques de destruction immédiate des déchets toxiques.

La FCF recommande que tous les gouvernements entament ou appuient financièrement des recherches pour l'élaboration de nouvelles techniques de destruction des déchets toxiques.

La FCF est également préoccupée par les plans fédéraux de nettoyage par dragage des ports de Québec, de Montréal et de Trois-Rivières, qui ne feront qu'accroître la contamination toxique du Saint-Laurent. Rien n'a encore été prouvé de façon concluante, mais on croit qu'en draguant le lit du fleuve, les concentrations de contaminants polluant l'eau pourraient s'accroître au lieu de diminuer.

> La FCF recommande que le gouvernement remette à plus tard ses plans de nettoyage à la drague, jusqu'à ce que soit prouvé de façon certaine que le dragage est la meilleure solution pour entreprendre la décontamination des cours d'eau et des nappes d'eau.

Idéalement, on a besoin d'une technique nous permettant de recueillir les contaminants des déchets toxiques et de les réduire en éléments biodégradables qu'on pourrait ensuite remettre dans l'environnement. À l'heure actuelle, le Conseil national de recherches et Énergie atomique du Canada, entre autres, ont élaboré des méthodes de destruction des BPC. C'est un point de départ. On devrait étudier soigneusement ces techniques et les incorporer aux plans gouvernementaux de nettoyage du Saint-Laurent.

2.2 Parc marin national

La FCF croit que l'habitat du béluga du Saint-Laurent pourrait être grandement protégé, si un parc marin national était créé au confluent du Saint-Laurent et du Saguenay. La FCF appuie sérieusement l'initiative récente du Service canadien des parcs pour la création de ce parc. Un parc marin national favoriserait la préservation du béluga et la conservation de toutes les autres espèces fauniques vivant dans cette zone, en attirant l'attention du public et des gouvernements vers cette région.

La FCF a déjà écrit au ministre fédéral de l'Environnement pour lui recommander d'allouer 7,5 millions de dollars pour entamer la création et le fonctionnement du parc au cours des cinq premières années. Nous pressons également le Ministre de mettre le parc en service d'ici deux ans.

> La FCF recommande que des 110 millions de dollars consacrés au plan de nettoyage du Saint-Laurent, 7,5 millions soient alloués à la création du parc marin national au confluent du Saint-Laurent et du Saguenay, pendant les cinq premières années de fonctionnement de celui-ci. La FCF recommande également que le parc soit créé d'ici 1991.

La FCF appuie la politique du Service canadien des parcs, favorisant la consultation et la participation du public vivant dans la région et des organismes gouvernementaux et non gouvernementaux intéressés, lors de la préparation des politiques de gestion du parc.

2.3 Identification des zones d'habitat fragile

La FCF appuie fermement les plans du gouvernement fédéral visant à identifier les zones d'habitat fragile du béluga du Saint-Laurent, et à limiter la circulation maritime et les excursions d'observation des baleines dans cette région. Les navires pourraient avoir des effets néfastes sur la population de baleines. Les zones fragiles doivent donc être identifiées. Par ailleurs, les périodes critiques du cycle biologique du béluga doivent être identifiées (par exemple : naissance, soins donnés aux veaux, reproduction) et des restrictions comparables doivent être imposées à la circulation maritime au cours de ces périodes. Les restrictions doivent rester en vigueur jusqu'à ce qu'il soit évident que ces activités n'ont pas d'effet néfaste sur la taille et la santé de la population de bélugas.

> La FCF recommande que le gouvernement fédéral appuie les recherches visant à identifier les zones fragiles de l'habitat du béluga et les périodes critiques du cycle biologique du béluga du Saint-Laurent. La circulation maritime devrait être limitée dans ces régions, et pendant les périodes critiques, jusqu'à ce qu'il soit évident qu'elle n'a pas d'effet néfaste sur la taille et la santé de la population de bélugas.

CONCLUSION

En conclusion, la FCF désire réaffirmer en tout premier lieu, que les règlements actuels de lutte contre la pollution, découlant de la loi fédérale sur les pêcheries et de la loi québécoise sur la qualité de l'environnement, doivent être appliqués, afin de restreindre sévèrement la pollution d'organochlorés provenant de polyaromatiques dans le bassin fluvial.

Selon la FCF, si l'on veut éliminer, d'ici 1993, la pollution et toutes les sources de pollution du bassin fluvial du Saint-Laurent, des règlements de lutte contre la pollution doivent être établis, tant au niveau fédéral qu'au niveau provincial. On doit imposer aux industries polluantes qui commettent des infractions aux règlements actuels, des amendes équivalant au coût d'installation de dispositifs de lutte contre la pollution.

Afin de reconstituer l'habitat du béluga, le gouvernement fédéral devrait entreprendre, ou appuyer, le développement de techniques visant à détruire les contaminants de déchets toxiques existants. De plus, l'habitat du béluga devrait être protégé par la création d'un parc marin national, d'ici 1991, et par la limitation de la circulation maritime dans les régions en question, et au cours des périodes critiques du cycle biologique du béluga.

La FCF appuie les plans actuels des gouvernements canadien et québécois pour le nettoyage du Saint-Laurent. Nous sommes convaincus, toutefois, que nos recommandations doivent être implantées pour atteindre les objectifs de dernier recours pour sauvegarder l'habitat du béluga, et pour permettre la survie de cette population dans le Saint-Laurent.

Nous désirons vous remercier de nous avoir accordé le temps de cette présentation, et de demander aux organismes non gouvernementaux de continuer à prendre part aux décisions concernant l'avenir de la population de bélugas du Saint-Laurent.

Groupes environnementaux de la Sagamie

Martine Bourgeois, Suzanne Tremblay, Cyprien Gaudreault, Jean Désy et Jean-Guy Renaud

PARTICIPANTES ET PARTICIPANTS DU FORUM DU PREMIER ESPOIR

Sur les causes environnementales probables de la diminution du béluga et les solutions possibles à sa survie :

— Comité d'environnement d'Alma
— Comité d'environnement de Chicoutimi
— Comité d'environnement de La Baie
— Conseil régional de l'environnement
— États généraux de l'environnement

Nous avons déjà fait publiquement nôtre, il y a quelques mois déjà, la citation de madame Leone Pippard, l'une des héroïnes de cet événement qu'est le Forum, et qui s'énonce ainsi :

> Dans l'ensemble, il faut simplement comprendre qu'il ne s'agit pas seulement de la survie du béluga du Saint-Laurent (et du Saguenay), mais de la détérioration de la qualité environnementale de tout le système Saint-Laurent.

Ce point d'ancrage qui relie le béluga en danger à tout son environnement, à tout notre environnement, a servi également d'amorce à la réflexion de cinq groupes environnementaux de la région du Saguenay-Lac-Saint-Jean : trois comités locaux et un conseil régional de l'environnement, auxquels se greffe une structure récente issue de la Table sectorielle en environnement du Conseil régional de concertation et de développement du Saguenay-Lac-Saint-Jean, et baptisée : Les États généraux de l'environnement. Le processus des états généraux est en cours, dont le momentum ultime se tiendra le 26 novembre prochain.

Partant de ses pratiques et de ses mandats spécifiques, chaque groupe a formalisé un état de situation relié à la problématique qui nous réunit actuellement. Tout n'est pas dit dans ces quelques pages, loin de là, ni nécessairement confectionné avec les plus récentes données. C'est davantage une synthèse visuelle que nous proposons autour de trois environnements mieux connus dont l'état de dégradation nous apparaît logiquement lié à la misère existentielle du béluga. Notre rôle n'est pas d'y développer des liens de cause à effet irréfutables mais de faire émerger des intuitions proches du gros bons sens, partagées par n'importe quelle citoyenne ou citoyen de cette planète, de ce pays.

Voici donc dans l'ordre, d'amont en aval les ébauches environnementales du Lac-Saint-Jean, du Haut-Saguenay et de La Baie.

Une double conclusion dégagera quelques pistes d'action.

PARC MARIN ET SOUS-COMITÉ RÉGIONAL DU SUIVI

Les scientifiques du Forum ont fait ou feront peut-être la lumière sur la nature exacte des liens qui unissent cette violence faite quotidiennement à l'environnement et la survie hypothétique du béluga.

Pour notre part, en tant que Conseil régional de l'environnement (CRE), c'est cependant moins le « pourquoi » que le « quoi faire » qui nous préoccupe. Et dans cette veine, nous partageons l'avis de plusieurs autres organismes régionaux et nationaux qui voient dans le projet du parc marin fédéral un levier de grande puissance pour fermer rapidement les vannes de pollution grandes ouvertes qui vomissent, en amont du Saguenay et du Saint-Laurent, des milliers de tonnes de poison dans la baignoire et condamnent à coup sûr toute chance de survie du béluga et même toute vitalité économique du parc.

En mars 1987, nous soumettions au Service canadien des parcs un mémoire qui soulevait précisément cette problématique, en plus de celle, tout aussi déterminante, de la gestion de ce parc en devenir : s'agira-t-il du modèle technocratique si bien connu depuis plus de 100 ans, ou d'un type participatif de gestion impliquant des collectivités locales et les scientifiques régionaux, entre autres ?

Une étude spécifique de la firme Logimer a rassuré le Service canadien des parcs sur la dynamique à long terme des écosystèmes et des pratiques environnementales des entreprises et des municipalités ayant des incidences sur la viabilité socio-économique d'un tel projet.

Dieu les entende! Quant à la deuxième question, la réponse demeure toujours aussi évasive que le modèle emprunté à la réserve de la biosphère du lac Watertons. Mieux que rien, mais rien de mieux, il faudra très bientôt s'asseoir et élaborer les principes d'une représentativité régionale équitable des intérêts socio-économiques et environnementaux en jeu : tâche éminemment délicate, mais indispensable.

Par ailleurs, dit le proverbe : « Aide-toi et le ciel t'aidera ». De notre côté, c'est-à-dire du côté amont du Saguenay, source proche et immédiate de tant de maux, nous polissons un outil d'intervention sociale d'une performance prometteuse dont nous parlions au début : *Les États généraux de l'environnement.* Il s'agit d'un partenariat intéressant de plus d'une vingtaine d'organismes régionaux impliqués dans la défense et... la pollution de l'environnement dont notamment les compagnies Price et Alcan qui ont décidé d'agir. Ces états généraux produiront un constat relativement précis de notre environnement, des acteurs en jeu, des programmes et mesures à l'œuvre et tout cela par le vaste brassage social qui interrogera et interpellera à la base des centaines de citoyennes et citoyens instruits d'un premier constat, déjà disponible.

Pourquoi alors ne pas profiter de cet événement hors de l'ordinaire pour prolonger la vie de cette structure, et l'associer au grand comité du suivi de l'actuel Forum ? Pour encadrer activement, en quelque sorte, les entreprises sur le chemin de la restauration de leur passif environnemental, dans toute la région du Saguenay-Lac-Saint-Jean.

C'est ainsi qu'un organisme pan-régional issu de très nombreux secteurs de la société sagamienne pourrait susciter et maintenir la coordination et « le dynamisme » nécessaires à la réalisation d'un magnifique projet collectif: la quête d'une harmonie perdue entre l'Homme producteur et le Capital nature, entre une région et son parc, sa flore, sa faune... dont bien sûr, ses précieux bélugas!

Société pour vaincre la pollution

Daniel Greene
Président

LE BÉLUGA DU SAINT-LAURENT, VICTIME DE TOXIQUES VENUS D'AILLEURS

La Société pour vaincre la pollution n'est pas très fière de vous annoncer aujourd'hui que nous sommes victimes d'un autre type de pollution transfrontalière. En plus des pluies acides, c'est maintenant le Saint-Laurent qui nous amène les polluants de nos amis américains. Le libre-échange a déjà commencé et se poursuit sous forme toxique.

En 1985, la Société pour vaincre la pollution a pris connaissance du rapport de la Sous-commission sur la qualité des eaux, publié par l'organisme international « La Commission mixte internationale ». Ce rapport a identifié 42 zones dans le bassin Saint-Laurent-Grands Lacs ; ces zones ont été identifiées à cause de la gravité de la dégradation environnementale dont elles sont victimes. La 42e zone du rapport est celle de Massena. Massena est juste face à Cornwall, dans l'État de New York. Cette zone est fortement affectée par les opérations passées et présentes des industries lourdes de la région. Elle est située à moins de cinq kilomètres de la frontière Québec-New York.

De 1956 à 1986, la compagnie General Motors de Massena des États-Unis opérait une fonderie pour faire des blocs-moteurs, à Massena. Plus de 1 700 tonnes métriques de boues contaminées au BPC ont été produites par General Motors depuis 1973. La compagnie General Motors, qui a maintenant fermé ses portes, a été obligée de payer une amende de 400 000 $ pour avoir mal entreposé des BPC. Il s'agit de la plus forte amende jamais imposée à une compagnie pour la mauvaise gestion de BPC aux États-Unis. General Motors elle-même admet qu'elle a mal géré des tonnes et des tonnes de boues contaminées au BPC.

Aujourd'hui toute la région de Massena, située tout près du Québec, accuse des incroyables concentrations de BPC, les plus fortes en Amérique du Nord. Le site d'enfouissement de General Motors, qui occupe une partie importante de la rive du fleuve à Massena, a fait l'objet d'une enquête menée par le gouvernement américain. Cette enquête confirme que ce site est une source importante de BPC pour le Saint-Laurent. D'autres substances très toxiques telles que le dibenzo furanne, des substances comme le toxafenne, le mirex, encore plus dangereuses que les BPC, ont été trouvées dans les sédiments de ce site.

Une autre étude sur le site de déchets dangereux de la compagnie General Motors, situé à quelques mètres de la rive du Saint-Laurent, a trouvé que ce site contient des BPC à des concentrations incroyables de 340 000 parties par million de BPC. Nous savons qu'une concentration supérieure à 50 parties par million est considérée comme dangereuse. Ce site de la compagnie General Motors est loin d'être étanche. Il y a des écoulements de BPC importants du site de Massena et les BPC ont déjà fortement contaminé l'environnement de ce secteur du fleuve. Par exemple, une tortue confinée dans ce site avait une concentration de 835 parties par million. Cette tortue était plus BPC que tortue. Cette tortue, comme nos bélugas, était tellement contaminée qu'il a fallu l'entreposer dans un site de déchets dangereux.

Devant la contamination importante des poissons et de la faune, il a fallu émettre des avis recommandant aux enfants de moins de 15 ans et aux femmes enceintes et à celles, qui allaient peut-être l'être, de s'abstenir de consommer du poisson de cette région. Le niveau de contamination par les BPC dans la région de Massena est peut-être le plus élevé de tout le Saint-Laurent. Les concentrations de BPC dans les sédiments varient de 200 à 5 000 parties par million. Et cela se passe, je le répète, à cinq kilomètres de la frontière québécoise. La zone la plus contaminée couvre une superficie d'à peu près 125 000 mètres carrés. D'après les estimations, on évalue qu'il y a au moins 135 à 400 tonnes métriques de BPC pur à cet endroit. Et puisqu'il n'y a, d'après les analyses, que peu de BPC au fond dans les sédiments, qu'ils sont seulement en surface, on peut conclure que les BPC s'accumulent peu dans cette région là et qu'ils s'acheminent vers le Québec au fur et à mesure qu'ils sont déversés.

De plus, il y a les compagnies Reynolds et Alcoa qui sont deux alumineries. Les données préliminaires que j'ai obtenues des États-Unis m'indiquent que les concentrations de benzo(a)pyrène dans cette zone-là atteignent des sommets de 313 parties par million. Les concentrations les plus élevées qu'on a trouvé dans le Saguenay se situent entre 2 et 3 parties par million.

Les bateaux de la voie maritime passent juste à côté de la zone contaminée. Si jamais il arrive une avarie, si jamais un navire perd le contrôle et rentre dans la zone sédimentaire contaminée, il est possible que des tonnes et des tonnes de BPC soient tout d'un coup mobilisées. Les courants étant assez forts dans cette région, les BPC vont poursuivre leurs cours jusqu'au Lac Saint-François et continuer jusqu'à la région du Lac Saint-Pierre et encore plus loin. Donc, on peut augmenter d'un coup, de façon incroyable, la contamination du fleuve par des B(a)P et par des BPC.

Recommandations de la SVP

Ce que nous demandons est très simple. Des études préliminaires du ministère de l'Environnement du Canada ont déjà prouvé qu'il y a un certain transport de BPC vers le Québec. Or nous avons ici un cas patent de pollution transfrontalière dont nous sommes victimes. Ce qu'il faut faire, premièrement et rapidement :

1) Entreprendre, le plus tôt possible, un programme d'échantillonnage des eaux à la frontière Québec-New York afin de quantifier la pollution transfrontalière dont le Québec est victime.

2) Exiger, auprès des autorités américaines, un droit de participation des gouvernements du Québec et du Canada dans la préparation et l'exécution du plan d'action de réhabilitation environnementale de la zone contaminée de Massena.

3) Demander, en vertu du Traité des eaux limitrophes de 1909 entre le Canada et les États-Unis, que l'Entente sur la qualité des eaux des Grands Lacs-fleuve Saint-Laurent soit amendée afin d'y inclure la section québécoise du Saint-Laurent.

Sans tout ceci le Québec, le fleuve, et ultimement les bélugas du Saint-Laurent vont rester victimes de contamination sans possibilité de représentation.

TABLEAU 1

Les superficies des zones sédimentaires contaminées dans le fleuve Saint-Laurent

Secteur du fleuve	Superficie totale (km^2)	Superficie contaminée (km^2)	% de la superficie contaminée
Lac St-François à Repentigny	250	182.6	73%
Verchères au Lac St-Pierre	456	162.9	35%
Trois-Rivières à Cacouna	2 721	680	25%
Tadoussac à Percé	19 126	1 910	10%

Greenpeace

Lyne Brissette

Greenpeace est heureux d'avoir la chance de faire cette présentation au Forum international pour l'avenir du béluga.

Les dangers de la contamination chimique ont été adéquatement décrits en 1962 lors de la publication du livre de Rachel Carson intitulé *Silent Spring*.

On se retrouve aujourd'hui, 26 ans plus tard, après de très nombreux désastres environnementaux et humains mettant en cause des produits chimiques et nous n'avons toujours pas compris la règle de base :

1) Si l'on ne peut prouver qu'un produit ou sous-produit chimique est inoffensif pour l'environnement, alors il ne devrait en aucun cas être émis. Certains produits chimiques, comme les hydrocarbures halogénés ne devraient pas être fabriqués du tout. En ce qui concerne les industries, le défi est d'implanter des systèmes ne permettant pas d'émissions ou de déversement.

En ce qui concerne le Canada, le Québec et les bélugas, il faudrait tout d'abord ;

a) Que le Canada adhère formellement à la recommandation de la Commission mixte internationale de déversement des contaminants dans les Grands Lacs et qu'il applique une politique persuasive pour faire cesser la contamination des eaux canadiennes par les États-Unis.

b) Le Québec doit devenir un signataire de « L'entente sur la qualité de l'eau des Grands Lacs », afin d'ajouter les pressions nécessaires pour mettre fin à la pollution originant de l'Ontario et des États-Unis.

c) Le Canada et le Québec doivent s'engager à mettre fin à la pollution par dioxine et organochlorés par le secteur du blanchiment, dans l'industrie des pâtes et papiers, et cela d'ici quatre ans. À cause de la proximité entre le territoire du béluga et des utilisateurs de chlore, il faudrait fortement considérer l'analyse de dioxine chez le béluga.

d) Il faut que l'on fasse respecter les lois anti-pollution existantes. (On a, par exemple, un outil puissant, l'article 33.2 de la loi fédérale des pêcheries qui n'est à peu près pas utilisé au Québec). Ce Forum couronne des efforts de 13 ans par une véritable armée de citoyens (ceci incluant des bureaucrates) et organismes non gouvernementaux. Cependant, tout le temps qu'il a fallu pour à peine en arriver à ce qui se passe aujourd'hui, et le fait que plusieurs suggestions énoncées aujourd'hui ont déjà été faites il y a 5 ou 10 ans, montrent qu'il y a une brèche dans nos structures institutionnelles et politiques. Cette brèche est que les décisions sont prises par des personnes qui ne sont pas en mesure de les prendre, et qui ne devraient en aucun cas prendre des décisions.

Ceci nous amène à notre point 2 :

2) Il y a un besoin de mécanismes viables qui pourront assurer que les questions fondamentales, que les idées visionnaires et que les orientations possibles puissent être discutées, travaillées et mises en application avec la collaboration la plus large possible d'experts et de citoyens. Le peu d'implication des citoyens et des experts dans le processus de développement du parc marin est un exemple criant de cette lacune. La coalition (représentée par M. Pierre Tremblay) a déjà fait valoir clairement ce point de vue.

Plus spécifiquement au Québec, nous avons récemment formulé au ministre de l'Environnement du Québec quelques recommandations sur le processus d'évaluation des impacts sur l'environnement :

— que le ministre de l'Environnement utilise son pouvoir (en vertu de l'article 6.3 de la loi sur la qualité de l'environnement) pour tout projet qui aurait des conséquences environnementales. On veut éviter des exclusions à cause de technicalités ;

— il faut que des ressources financières soient octroyées aux groupes et citoyens pour qu'ils participent maximalement aux audiences publiques. Actuellement les citoyens investissent leur propre temps et argent. Si on veut un mécanisme véritablement efficace, il faut donner des moyens ;

— que les analyses d'experts du Ministère sur l'étude d'impact du promoteur soient rendues publiques avant la tenue de la période d'information d'audiences publiques.

Pour revenir à tous ces paliers administratifs impliqués, nous voulons ajouter :

3) qu'il y a actuellement une confusion empêchant une prise en charge adéquate et directe dans le dossier du béluga et de la création du parc marin à cause des responsabilités gouvernementales partagées, de juridictions confuses et de rivalités fédérales-provinciales. Il y a un besoin de réévaluation des présents mandats et des engagements clairs doivent être pris à partir desquels le gouvernement ou un département gouvernemental sera responsable pour un aspect ou des aspects de la dépollution du Saint-Laurent, de l'évaluation des effets de la dégradation environnementale et de l'application des lois environnementales. Quand chaque mandat et ses responsabilités subséquentes seront définies, ce département gouvernemental sera responsable pour l'élaboration de politiques claires et de plans d'action (et cela avec la participation des citoyens). Un premier pas nécessaire serait d'évaluer la faisabilité de mettre sur pied un système de révision par le public afin de s'assurer que les mandats soient remplis.

4) Le béluga retient actuellement plus d'attention gouvernementale à cause des pressions qui ont été mises sur nos gouvernements. Cependant, cette préoccupation croissante ne signifie pas que l'on tient également compte de toutes les autres facettes de l'écosystème du Saint-Laurent. Peu de recherches ont été faites sur les effets des contaminants ou de la modification de l'habitat pour plusieurs espèces de poissons, oiseaux, plantes et mammifères le long du Saint-Laurent et du Saguenay, et un peu partout au Québec. Un de ces exemples est que l'on possède très peu d'information sur les effets possibles des contaminants sur une espèce hautement menacée, la Baleine bleue, qui passe une partie de son cycle annuel dans le Saint-Laurent.

Toutes ces recommandations ne peuvent reposer que sur la base d'un engagement viscéral de nos gouvernements pour la protection de notre environnement et pour permettre la participation des citoyens dans les débats sur l'environnement et le développement. Il apparaît clairement qu'un tel engagement n'existe pas présentement au Canada ou au Québec.

Les décisions fondamentales sont prises davantage par les compagnies engagées à augmenter leurs profits et les gouvernements ayant une vision à court terme. Les progrès sont lents à venir mais l'ampleur du problème auquel le Canada et le monde doivent faire face nécessite une intervention d'urgence.

Ketos

Réjean Gravel

L'intervention de KETOS se divise en trois parties.

A. Les **recommandations** portent sur des questions liées directement ou indirectement à nos travaux. Elles touchent :

   a) les limites du parc marin du Saguenay et ses habitats critiques,
   b) la circulation maritime,

   et sont dans l'ensemble établies en fonction de l'implantation d'un parc marin, quoique pas exclusivement. KETOS les juge prioritaires et souhaite qu'elles soient étudiées avec attention.

B. Les **engagements** décrivent les actions que KETOS entend mener dans le cadre du mandat de recherche et d'éducation qu'il s'est donné pour préserver le troupeau de bélugas du Saint-Laurent.

C. Les **suggestions** sont des propositions plus générales, qui nous paraissent raisonnables, et que nous souhaitons soumettre à la réflexion des participants. Si le temps nous manque, nous n'en ferons pas mention dans notre intervention, quitte à les reprendre lors de la table ronde de l'après-midi, si l'occasion s'en présente.

Vous trouverez ci-joint la liste de nos recommandations, engagements et suggestions. La plupart se fondent sur le résumé du rapport de faisabilité intitulé Points saillants. Il se pourrait que nous supprimions ou modifions certaines propositions quand nous aurons terminé nos consultations, mais le sens de notre intervention et les sujets que nous aborderons ne changeront pas.

A. RECOMMANDATIONS

1. Limites du parc et habitats critiques

Les habitats critiques du béluga doivent jouir d'une protection absolue pour donner au troupeau le maximum de chances de récupérer. Par habitats critiques nous entendons les zones de forte fréquentation où le béluga se livre présumément à des activités vitales telles la mise bas et l'alimentation. L'étude de faisabilité semble donner un sens assez large à l'expression si l'on en juge par la carte 2, page 33 du rapport final d'Environnement Canada — Service canadien des parcs : « Étude de faisabilité reliée à la création d'un parc marin national à la confluence du Saguenay et du Saint-Laurent », juin 1988.

Nous recommandons donc :

a) que la navigation soit interdite dans les zones classées habitats critiques du béluga et que toute activité humaine susceptible de perturber le milieu marin y soit strictement réglementée ;

b) qu'on classe dès à présent dans cette catégorie :
   - la baie Sainte-Catherine
   - le couloir sud de l'embouchure du Saguenay, le long de la Pointe-Noire, sur une distance de 500 m vers le large et d'une dizaine de kilomètres vers l'amont ;

c) que les abords de l'Île aux Lièvres et la baie Sainte-Marguerite soient inclus dans le parc marin et classés parmi les habitats critiques ;

d) qu'un effort spécial soit fait, particulièrement mais non exclusivement à l'intérieur des limites du parc, pour situer les autres habitats critiques du béluga, dans le Saguenay et dans le Saint-Laurent ;

e) qu'on fasse remonter la limite du parc à Saint-Fulgence.

2. Circulation maritime

Les croisières constituent un outil pédagogique précieux : rien ne sensibilise plus efficacement le public au sort des cétacés. Or, la survie du béluga passe par une large mobilisation populaire. Donc, les croisières doivent se poursuivre.

KETOS ne voit pas de problème fondamental à ce qu'elles soient assurées par l'entreprise privée : au contraire, cela lui semble un bon moyen d'intégrer le parc au milieu socio-économique régional.

Cette activité s'est toutefois développée de façon un peu désordonnée ces dernières années, engendrant des risques de harcèlement involontaire dans certains habitats critiques, la baie Sainte-Catherine et le couloir sud du Saguenay particulièrement. Nous recommandons donc :

a) que tous les départs d'excursion soient centralisés à Tadoussac pour mettre fin à la navigation dans la baie Sainte-Catherine ;

b) à défaut, que soit promulgué un règlement au moins aussi rigoureux que les normes actuelles sur les limites de vitesse et les couloirs de navigation dans la baie Sainte-Catherine et l'embouchure du Saguenay ; que ce règlement prévoit des sanctions dissuasives ; et qu'un système de surveillance intensive soit mis sur pied pour qu'il devienne clair que les règles doivent être respectées ;

c) sans porter atteinte aux droits acquis de longue date, qu'on limite le nombre des bateaux d'excursion et le nombre des sorties quotidiennes à Tadoussac ; qu'on organise plutôt des départs à partir de quais situés plus à l'est afin de minimiser les risques de harcèlement involontaire ;

d) si l'industrie des croisières continue de se développer, qu'on encourage l'emploi de plus gros bateaux pour les excursions afin d'éviter la prolifération des petites embarcations ;

e) que seuls les résidents de la municipalité de Baie-Sainte-Catherine aient le droit d'utiliser le quai de la baie Sainte-Catherine et que tout autre aménagement marin y soit prohibé ou très réglementé ; qu'ils ne puissent y amarrer que des petites embarcations à usage personnel et qu'un permis spécial leur soit délivré à cet égard ; qu'ils soient tenus d'emprunter un couloir spécifique pour entrer dans la baie ou en sortir et qu'ils ne puissent y circuler autrement ;

f) que les autorités compétentes créent un programme de sensibilisation des plaisanciers ; la clientèle du port de Tadoussac en sera évidemment la principale cible, mais tous les quais et ports de la région devraient en bénéficier tôt ou tard.

B. ENGAGEMENTS

1. Recherche

KETOS s'engage à respecter les axes prioritaires de recherche qui seront dégagés par les organisateurs du Forum, dans la mesure où ils correspondent à ses domaines de compétence. Notre groupe est prêt à collaborer de toutes les manières possibles à la recherche sur le béluga en échangeant des informations, en créant des projets conjoints, etc.

Nous estimons que la contamination du milieu est le domaine de recherche le plus essentiel à la survie du béluga à l'heure actuelle. Toutefois, la question des habitats critiques nous paraît également vitale à moyen terme. Or, nous disposons d'une base de données intéressante sur certains d'entre eux et nous avons toutes les compétences voulues pour mener ce type de recherche. Nous avons donc l'intention de poursuivre et d'élargir nos travaux dans ce domaine, et notamment de collaborer à la détermination des habitats critiques à l'intérieur et aux environs du parc marin.

2. Éducation

KETOS est très actif dans la région de Montréal, où il s'emploie à diffuser les connaissances scientifiques sur les cétacés du Saint-Laurent et à sensibiliser la population aux menaces qui pèsent sur eux. Il intensifiera cet effort au cours de l'année qui vient et s'efforcera d'entretenir l'intérêt pour le béluga qu'a éveillé le Forum dans l'opinion publique.

Il a également l'intention d'offrir des services d'animation à bord du traversier Saint-Siméon-Rivière-du-Loup l'été prochain.

C. SUGGESTIONS

1. Impact socio-économique

a) *Scénarios*

Le parc ne doit pas être une simple étiquette destinée à attirer les touristes, une coquille vide : si l'infrastructure et les ressources nécessaires ne sont pas là, l'afflux des visiteurs aggravera la situation du béluga au lieu de l'améliorer en accroissant le harcèlement, le bruit, etc.

Le scénario 1 nous semble donc insuffisant, car il n'offre aucune garantie de durée ni de progrès.

b) *Traverse Baie-Sainte-Catherine-Tadoussac*

Une augmentation du nombre ou de la fréquence des traversées serait un facteur perturbant dont il est difficile de mesurer l'impact, mais dont on ne peut que s'inquiéter, sachant que le béluga fréquente moins le Saguenay.

Pour pallier l'éventuelle congestion du traversier (à moyen terme), il faudrait organiser un système de réservations et implanter des structures d'accueil à Baie-Sainte-Catherine. On pourrait entre autres donner plus d'ampleur aux installations de Pointe-Noire.

c) *Intégration au milieu*

La direction du parc ne doit rien négliger pour susciter la participation et l'intérêt du milieu régional. Cette participation peut donner à un parc un dynamisme remarquable, même et surtout lorsque les ressources permanentes sont limitées, comme ce sera le cas pour le parc marin du Saguenay. La direction du parc doit faire office de chef de file et d'arbitre, mais donner le plus de marge de manœuvre possible à l'initiative locale.

2. Qualité du milieu

La dépollution du Saguenay et plus encore, celle du Saint-Laurent, est une tâche de très longue haleine, vu la toxicité de leurs sédiments. Une partie de l'épuration se fera naturellement, mais l'homme aura encore beaucoup à faire pour assainir complètement cet habitat.

KETOS s'est réjoui d'apprendre que la situation s'améliorait, mais estime qu'il ne suffit pas de moins polluer. La création du parc devrait s'accompagner d'une concertation entre tous les riverains (entreprises, municipalités, etc.) qui ont une part de responsabilité dans la pollution du Saguenay, et de l'élaboration d'un plan de dépollution des effluents, avec échéancier et engagements financiers précis. La création du parc ne doit pas servir de prétexte aux autres intervenants pour ralentir leur action et s'en remettre à l'État. Nous souhaitons vivement que là comme ailleurs, la direction du parc assume un rôle de chef de file et de coordonnateur, voire d'arbitre.

3. Limites du parc

Nous avons été surpris de constater que les limites préliminaires du parc n'englobent pas la zone de Les Escoumins ; il nous semble que la beauté de ses falaises sous-marines justifie largement sa préservation.

4. Pêche commerciale

Le rapport préliminaire prône le maintien de la pêche commerciale à l'intérieur du parc. Sans y être opposés, nous suggérons d'adopter une formule d'extinction des droits qui interdirait le transfert des permis, sauf à un descendant direct. Les détenteurs des permis actuels pourraient poursuivre l'exploitation, mais seraient tenus de vendre leur permis aux autorités à leur retraite, à moins qu'un de leurs enfants ne reprenne l'entreprise.

Union québécoise pour la conservation de la nature

Harvey L. Mead
Président

LA PROBLÉMATIQUE DU BÉLUGA

L'Union québécoise pour la conservation de la nature (UQCN) est un organisme sans but lucratif dont une des priorités est l'adoption de mesures pouvant constituer une stratégie de conservation pour le Québec. L'UQCN regroupe 4 000 membres individuels ainsi que 80 organismes membres ayant des intérêts divers dans le domaine de la conservation. Parmi les organismes affiliés on peut compter plusieurs des intervenants à ce Forum. De plus, l'UQCN publie *Franc-Nord*, magazine de vulgarisation dans les domaines de l'environnement et des sciences naturelles ; un numéro hors série de *Franc-Nord* est le magazine officiel de ce Forum.

L'UQCN, dans ce contexte, cherche à intégrer et à appuyer les efforts de ses organismes membres plutôt que de les doubler. De plus, elle joue un rôle aux niveaux provincial et national permettant de développer un cadre pour ces efforts.

Ces quelques notes permettront de situer l'Union québécoise pour la conservation de la nature dans le dossier de la sauvegarde du béluga et la création d'un parc marin national dans l'estuaire du Saint-Laurent. Elles seront divisées en trois groupes de commentaires : le passé, les préoccupations actuelles, les actions à entreprendre.

LE PASSÉ

Depuis environ dix ans l'UQCN, au début agissant directement avec ses organismes membres actuels, s'implique dans le dossier du Saguenay. Un projet fédéral d'implantation d'un parc national terrestre et marin dans la région, vers la fin des années 1970, était l'objet d'un effort embryonnaire d'appui de la part d'un comité *ad hoc*.

La proposition de création d'un parc provincial terrestre était l'objet de mémoires du Club des ornithologues du Québec et de la Société linnéenne entre autres. L'absence de préoccupation pour le béluga était signalée, entre autres par le biais de commentaires sur le projet d'implantation d'infrastructures majeures à la baie Sainte-Marguerite.

Depuis le lancement du magazine *Franc-Nord* en 1984, plusieurs articles ont porté sur la région.

LES PRÉOCCUPATIONS ACTUELLES

L'UQCN voit la problématique du béluga dans celle du système Saint-Laurent. Les causes des impacts sur l'habitat du béluga, ainsi que sur le béluga lui-même, proviennent en bonne partie maintenant d'activités industrielles à l'extérieur de la région immédiate ou relèvent de décisions prises par les gouvernements fédéral et provincial. Des efforts pour contrôler ces impacts nécessiteront des démarches complexes et variées, adaptées au contexte socio-économique et politique des différents intervenants, démarches complétées par des programmes majeurs d'éducation.

On peut donc dire que, dans ce dossier, les préoccupations actuelles de l'UQCN, comme organisme provincial mais en tenant compte des préoccupations plus régionales ou plus sectorielles de ses affiliés et des autres intervenants, se résument en une seule : le constat du besoin d'une stratégie de conservation pour le Saint-Laurent.

LES ACTIONS À ENTREPRENDRE

Consciente de cette situation, et connaissant l'importance des gestes posés déjà par de nombreux intervenants du milieu, l'UQCN a mis sur pied un projet d'envergure provinciale visant des « Stratégies de protection, de conservation et de mise en valeur du Saint-Laurent ». Ce projet de trois ans et comportant un budget important est déjà financé à 60 % et devrait être lancé au début de 1989.

Le projet regroupe, en plus de l'UQCN elle-même, sept autres organismes régionaux ou sectoriels, dont trois membres affiliés. L'objectif de cette collaboration à grande échelle de la part des organismes non gouvernementaux, qui vise principalement des contacts avec les décideurs, est la création d'outils régionaux, coordonnés par l'UQCN sur le plan provincial, capables de maintenir la concertation nécessaire pour aboutir à une stratégie intégrée pour le Saint-Laurent.

Il s'agit donc d'un projet constituant une contribution du secteur non gouvernemental aux efforts actuels de redonner le fleuve aux citoyennes et citoyens.

L'UQCN, comme membre du Groupe directeur du projet de mise en valeur du Saint-Laurent du gouvernement du Québec, collaborera étroitement avec les intervenants participant à ce projet exemplificateur des recommandations de la Commission Brundtland. Le projet « Stratégies » sera adapté pour lui permettre de tenir compte des recommandations qui seront élaborées d'ici quelques semaines par le Groupe directeur du projet provincial, dans le cadre de la préparation d'un plan d'action pour le Saint-Laurent pour la prochaine décennie.

L'UQCN est aussi en contact avec les responsables du ministère de l'Environnement du Canada à Québec qui sont responsables de la mise en application du Plan d'action fédéral portant sur le Saint-Laurent, plan annoncé par le Premier Ministre Mulroney en juin 1988. Les moyens de collaboration restent à préciser, mais encore une fois une concertation est prioritaire. Dès le lancement du projet, les secteurs privé et municipal, ainsi que la communauté en général, seront invités à participer.

Le projet « Stratégies » de l'UQCN constitue un pôle de l'effort du Comité pour une stratégie québécoise de la conservation de l'organisme. D'autres groupes de travail se chargeront d'intervenir dans les domaines du développement des ressources, de l'aménagement du milieu bâti et des parcs et sites protégés.

Par l'intermédiaire de ce dernier groupe de travail, le maintien de pressions pour que le parc marin Saguenay-Saint-Laurent soit créé, ainsi que le suivi du processus d'implantation des infrastructures sociales et matérielles associées au futur parc, feront aussi l'objet d'efforts soutenus de l'UQCN. Ceux-ci prendront la forme d'appuis aux organismes du milieu autant que d'interventions directes.

RECOMMANDATIONS

1. L'UQCN voit dans la création d'un parc marin d'envergure dans l'estuaire l'ajout d'un outil de grande importance en ce qui concerne la survie du béluga et l'amélioration de la qualité du milieu en général. La création de ce parc devrait être accompagnée de l'identification de zones de conservation à plus grande échelle, pour tenir compte de l'habitat du béluga.

Plus généralement, le parc constituera un outil privilégié dans l'effort de faire adopter une stratégie de conservation. La reconnaissance d'un tel site permettra de meilleurs résultats dans la sensibilisation du public et des intervenants industriels et commerciaux. Elle devrait aussi aider à faire avancer les efforts de dépollution et de recherche dans la région et même dans tout le corridor fluvial.

2. L'UQCN recommande que la Fondation pour la sauvegarde des espèces menacées (FOSEM), par l'intermédiaire du comité organisateur du Forum, soit mandaté comme organisme de concertation, à assurer le suivi du Forum.

Fondation pour la sauvegarde des espèces menacées

Gaston Déry

La Fondation pour la sauvegarde des espèces menacées annonce la création d'un FONDS BÉLUGA

Au cours de la tenue du Forum pour l'avenir du béluga, il s'est dégagé une forme de consensus à l'effet que la participation de l'ensemble des intervenants était nécessaire afin d'atteindre les objectifs de protection et de conservation du béluga dans l'estuaire du Saint-Laurent.

La Fondation pour la sauvegarde des espèces menacées (FOSEM) considère que la participation directe du grand public est essentielle dans une action de concertation en vue de la sauvegarde du béluga. La FOSEM a rencontré, au cours du Forum, les bateliers qui offrent des visites guidées aux gens qui veulent admirer les mammifères marins du Saint-Laurent.

Ces échanges ont permis d'en venir à des ententes avec les compagnies qui offrent actuellement ce type d'activité, soit :

— Navimex ;
— Les Croisières du grand fleuve ;
— Les Croisières de l'hôtel Tadoussac ;
— La Société linnéenne.

Ainsi, la participation du public répondra à diverses formes de financement, soit par l'achat de macarons que les compagnies revendront aux touristes, par une invitation aux gens, les incitant à encourager financièrement les recherches sur le béluga ou encore en augmentant de 1 $ les prix pour une visite aux baleines.

Les sommes recueillies par cette participation populaire seront entièrement remises à la FOSEM, qui versera cet argent dans un **Fonds Béluga** utilisé uniquement pour financer des projets de recherche ou de vulgarisation concernant la protection et la conservation du béluga.

La FOSEM considère que cette participation volontaire des bateliers aura comme effet de sensibiliser le public sur la nécessité de protéger le béluga du Saint-Laurent.

LE PROGRAMME

MERCREDI 28 SEPTEMBRE

Après-midi et soirée **Arrivée des participants**
Inscriptions

JEUDI 29 SEPTEMBRE

Avant-midi

8 h 30 **Ouverture du Forum**
— Jacques Prescott
Président de FOSEM et du Forum

8 h 45 **Les baleines menacées, des systèmes de gestion de l'eau et du milieu marin**
— Leone Pippard
Canadian Ecology Advocates
Sainte-Pétronille, Québec

9 h 45 **Les stratégies de conservation des espèces menacées au niveau international**
— Ulysses Seal
Commission sur la survie des espèces menacées de l'UICN
Minneapolis, Minnesota, États-Unis

10 h 45 **Pause**

11 h **Un plan d'action pour la survie des bélugas du Saint-Laurent**
— Mimi Breton
Pêches et Océans Canada
Québec

11 h 30	**Un plan de recherche pour les bélugas du Saint-Laurent** — Jean Boulva Pêches et Océans Canada, Institut Maurice-Lamontagne, Sainte-Flavie, Québec
12 h 30	**Dîner**

Après-midi

14 h	**Un état de la distribution, de l'exploitation et de la conservation des bélugas à travers le monde** — Randall Reeves Okapi Wildlife Associates Hudson, Québec
14 h 30	**Évolution des populations de bélugas dans l'estuaire du Saint-Laurent** — David E. Sergeant Sainte-Anne-de-Bellevue, Québec
15 h	**Revue et analyse des méthodes d'inventaire de populations de cétacés** — Michael Kingsley Pêches et Océans Canada Winnipeg, Manitoba
15 h 30	**Pause**
16 h	**Nouvelles méthodes de recherche applicables aux bélugas du Saint-Laurent** — Tom G. Smith Pêches et Océans Canada Sainte-Anne-de-Bellevue, Québec
16 h 30	**Dynamique de la population de bélugas dans l'estuaire du Saint-Laurent** — Pierre Béland Institut national d'écotoxicologie du Saint-Laurent Rimouski, Québec
17 h	**Reproduction et dynamique de population des bélugas du Nouveau-Québec** — Bill Doidge Consultant Sainte-Anne-de-Bellevue, Québec
17 h 30	**Analyse critique des méthodes d'inventaire du béluga** — John Burns Living Resources Fairbanks, Alaska, États-Unis
18 h	**Cocktail**
19 h	**Souper**
21 h	**Hommage à Vadim-D. Vladykov** (Halte côtière Pointe-Noire) Organisé par la Société linnéenne du Québec

VENDREDI 30 SEPTEMBRE

Avant-midi

8 h — **Mouvements, comportements et zones fréquentées par le béluga du Saint-Laurent**
— Robert Michaud
Groupe de recherche et d'éducation sur les mammifères marins
Tadoussac, Québec

8 h 30 — **Variation annuelle de la composition et des déplacements des groupes de bélugas à l'embouchure du Saguenay**
— Louise Caron
Kétos, Montréal, Québec

9 h — **Impacts de la circulation maritime sur les déplacements des cétacés**
— Kerry Finley
Consultant
Sydney, Colombie Britannique

9 h 30 — **Le statut du béluga en captivité**
— Stefani Hewlett
Aquarium de Vancouver
Vancouver, Colombie-Britannique

10 h — **Pause**

10 h 30 — **L'importance de la recherche sur les cétacés du Saint-Laurent pour le développement économique régional**
— Ned Lynas
Ocean Research Information Society
Pickering, Ontario

11 h — **La contamination du Saint-Laurent**
— Murray Charlton
Centre canadien des eaux intérieures
Burlington, Ontario

11 h 30 — **Pollution et altération de la productivité du Fjord Saguenay**
— Denis Larrivée
Université du Québec à Chicoutimi
Chicoutimi, Québec

12 h 30 — **Dîner sous la présidence de monsieur Clifford Lincoln, ministre de l'Environnement du Québec**

Après-midi

14 h — **Métaux lourds dans les sédiments de surface et les crevettes du Saguenay**
— Émilien Pelletier
Institut national de la recherche scientifique
INRS-Océanologie
Rimouski, Québec

14 h 30	**Contamination des bélugas de l'Arctique** — Derek Muir Fresh Water Institute Winnipeg, Manitoba
15 h	**L'influence des processus de transformations biologiques sur la toxicité des polluants en milieu marin** — Mark E. Hahn Woods Hole Oceanographic Institution Woods Hole, Massachusetts, États-Unis
15 h 30	**Pause**
16 h	**Effets pathologiques des polluants aquatiques sur les bélugas** — Robert Massé Institut national de la recherche scientifique, INRS-Santé Pointe-Claire, Québec
16 h 30	**Aperçu général des HAP au Québec** — Jean-Yves Saucier Environnement Canada Montréal, Québec
17 h	**Problèmes pathologiques décelés chez les bélugas du Saint-Laurent** — Daniel Martineau Institut national d'écotoxicologie du Saint-Laurent Rimouski, Québec
17 h 30	**La présence des contaminants (HAP) chez les bélugas** — Lee Shugart Oak Ridge National Laboratory Oak Ridge, Tennessee, États-Unis
19 h	**Souper**
21h00	**Hommage à Vadim-D. Vladykov** (Halte côtière Pointe-Noire) Organisé par la Société linnéenne du Québec

SAMEDI 1er OCTOBRE

Avant-midi

8 h	**Présentations des organismes environnementaux et socio-économiques** **Préoccupations et actions à prendre**
10 h - 10 h 30	**Pause**
12 h 30	**Dîner**

Après-midi

14 h	**Table ronde sur les actions et suites au Forum**
16 h - 16 h 30	**Pause**

16 h 30	**Clôture**
18 h	**Cocktail**
19 h	**Souper sous la présidence de l'Honorable Thomas E. Siddon, ministre des Pêches et Océans du Canada**

DIMANCHE 2 OCTOBRE

Avant-midi	**Excursion d'observation des baleines, en bateau** **Départ des participants**

AGENDA

WEDNESDAY, SEPTEMBER 28

Afternoon and evening	**Arrival of participants** **Registration**

THURSDAY, SEPTEMBER 29

Morning

8:30	**Opening of Forum** — Jacques Prescott President of FOSEM and Forum
8:45	**Ailing Whales, Water and Marine Management Systems — An Urgency for Fresh, New Approaches** — Leone Pippard Canadian Ecology Advocates Sainte-Pétronille, Québec
9:45	**Survival Plan for Endangered Animal Population** — Ulysses Seal IUCN, Species Survival Commission Minneapolis, Minnesota, U.S.A.
10:45	**Break**
11:00	**Action Plan for the Survival of the St. Lawrence Beluga** — Mimi Breton Fisheries and Oceans Canada Québec
11:30	**Research Plan for the St. Lawrence Beluga** — Jean Boulva Fisheries and Oceans Canada Maurice Lamontagne Institute Sainte-Flavie, Québec
12:30	**Lunch**

Afternoon

2:00	**An Overview of the Distribution, Exploitation and Conservation Status of Belugas, Worldwide** — Randall Reeves Okapi Wildlife Associates Hudson, Québec
2:30	**An Update of the Status of White Whales on the St. Lawrence Estuary, Canada** — David E. Sergeant Sainte-Anne-de-Bellevue, Québec
3:00	**Review and Analysis of Inventory Methods for Cetacean Populations** — Michael Kingsley Fisheries and Oceans Canada Winnipeg, Manitoba
3:30	**Break**
4:00	**New Techniques Applicable to Research on the Belugas of the St. Lawrence** — Tom G. Smith Fisheries and Oceans Canada Sainte-Anne-de-Bellevue, Québec
4:30	**Beluga Population Dynamics in the St. Lawrence Estuary** — Pierre Béland Institut national d'écotoxicologie du Saint-Laurent Rimouski, Québec
5:00	**Beluga Reproduction and Population Dynamics in Nouveau Québec** — Bill Doidge Consultant Sainte-Anne-de-Bellevue, Québec
5:30	**Options for the Management of White Whales** — John Burns Living Resources Fairbanks, Alaska, U.S.A.
6:00	**Cocktail**
7:00	**Dinner**
9:00	**Tribute to Vadim-D. Vladykov** (Halte côtière Pointe-Noire) Organized by Société linnéenne du Québec

FRIDAY, SEPTEMBER 30

Morning

8:00	**Migrations, Behaviour and Zones Frequented by St. Lawrence Belugas** — Robert Michaud Groupe de recherche et d'éducation sur les mammifères marins Tadoussac, Québec.
8:30	**Annual Variation in Composition, Migration and Behaviour of Belugas in the Saguenay** — Louise Caron Kétos Montréal, Québec
9:00	**Impact of Shipping on Cetacean Migration** — Kerry Finley Consultant Sidney, British Columbia
9:30	**The Status of Captive Belugas** — Stefani Hewlett Vancouver Aquarium Vancouver, British Columbia
10:00	**Break**
10:30	**The Importance of Research on St. Lawrence Cetaceans for Regional Economic Development** — Ned Lynas Ocean Research Information Society Pickering, Ontario
11:00	**Pollution in the St. Lawrence** — Murray Charlton Canada Center for Inland Waters Burlington, Ontario
11:30	**Assessment of Water and Sediment Quality in the Saguenay** — Denis Larrivée Université du Québec à Chicoutimi Chicoutimi, Québec
12:30	**Luncheon presided over by Mr. Clifford Lincoln, Québec Minister of the Environment**

Afternoon

2:00	**Shrimp and Heavy Metals in Surface Sediments in the Saguenay** — Emilien Pelletier Institut national de la recherche scientifique INRS-Oceanology Rimouski, Québec

2:30	**Level and possible effects of PCB's and other organochlorine contaminants in Arctic and St. Lawrence Belugas** — Derek Muir Fresh Water Institute Winnipeg, Manitoba
3:00	**The Role of Biotransformation in the Toxicity of Marine Pollutants** — Mark E. Hahn Woods Hole Oceanographic Institution Woods Hole, Massachusetts, U.S.A.
3:30	**Break**
4:00	**Pathological Effects of Aquatic Polluants on Belugas** — Robert Massé Institut national de la recherche scientifique INRS-Health Pointe-Claire, Québec
4:30	**The PAH Situation in the St. Lawrence and the Saguenay** — Jean-Yves Saucier Environment Canada Montréal, Québec
5:00	**Pathological Problems Detected in St. Lawrence Belugas** — Daniel Martineau Institut national d'écotoxicologie du Saint-Laurent Rimouski, Québec
5:30	**Traces of Contaminants (PAH) in Belugas** — Lee Shugart Oak Ridge National Laboratory Oak Ridge, Tennessee, U.S.A.
7:00	**Dinner**
9:00	**Tribute to Vadim-D. Vladykov** (Halte côtière Pointe-Noire) Organized by Société linnéenne du Québec

SATURDAY, OCTOBER 1

Morning

8:00	**Presentations by environmental and socio-economic organizations** **Concerns and action proposals**
10:00 - 10:30	**Break**
12:30	**Lunch**

Afternoon

2:00	**Round-table discussion on proposed action proposals and Forum follow-up**
4:00	**Break**
4:30	**Closing of Forum**
6:00	**Reception**
7:00	**Conference dinner presided over by the Honorable Thomas E. Siddon, Canadian Minister of Fisheries and Oceans**

SUNDAY, OCTOBER 2

Morning	**Whale-watching excursion, by boat** **Departure of participants**

COMPOSÉ AUX ATELIERS
GRAPHITI BARBEAU, TREMBLAY INC.
À SAINTE-MARIE-DE-BEAUCE

Achevé d'imprimer
en avril 1990 sur les presses
des Ateliers Graphiques Marc Veilleux Inc.
Cap-Saint-Ignace, Qué.